lonely

The Italian Lakes

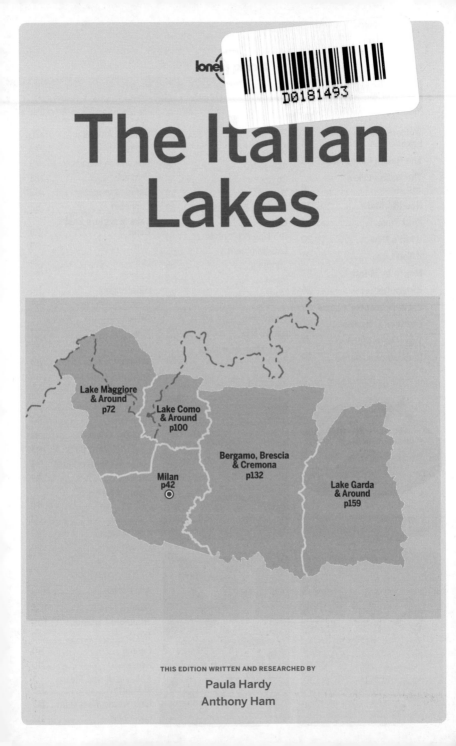

Lake Maggiore
& Around
p72

Lake Como
& Around
p100

Bergamo, Brescia
& Cremona
p132

Milan
p42
◉

Lake Garda
& Around
p159

THIS EDITION WRITTEN AND RESEARCHED BY

Paula Hardy

Anthony Ham

Contents

MUSHROOM RISOTTO P233

LAKE COMO P100

LAKE GARDA P159

BELLAGIO, LAKE COMO
P110

Contents

UNDERSTAND

SURVIVAL GUIDE

SPECIAL FEATURES

Welcome to the Italian Lakes

Formed at the end of the last ice age, and a popular holiday spot since Roman times, the lakes have an enduring, beguiling beauty.

Artful Landscapes

Travellers traversing the Alps wind down from the mountains to be greeted by a Mediterranean burst of colour: gardens filled with rose-red camellias, hot-pink oleanders and luxurious palms surrounding cerulean blue lakes. It's impossible not to be seduced. Fishing boats bob in tiny harbours, palaces float in the Borromean Gulf, rustic churches cling to cliff faces and grand belle époque spas and hotels line the waterfronts. No wonder George Clooney is smitten.

A Modern Legacy

Since Leonardo da Vinci broke all the rules in his stunning *Last Supper,* the indefatigably inventive Lombards seem to have skipped straight from the Renaissance to the 22nd century. Not only is Milan a treasure trove of 20th-century art, but art deco and rationalist architecture abound. Around the lakes, Michelin-starred restaurants push the boundaries of traditionalism, and vintners and oil producers experiment with the latest technologies and techniques. Even now, jackhammers are hard at work on the 420-acre Expo 2015 site, producing new Milanese neighbourhoods and a futuristic skyline modelled by star-chitects Zaha Hadid, Daniel Libeskind, Arata Isozaki and César Pelli.

Living By Design

Though Italian design is distributed globally, seeing it in a home context offers fresh appreciation. From Como's silk weavers to the wool merchants of Maggiore and the violin artisans of Cremona, this region has an outstanding craft heritage. Today Milan is home to all the major design showrooms and an endless round of trade fairs. But it's not just a coterie of insiders who get to have all the fun. Milanese fashion houses have branched out into spas, bars, hotels, galleries and restaurants. So, why not join them for a touch of *la vita moda* (the stylish life).

The Lake Lifestyle

Home to many of Italy's foremost classical musicians, writers and artists, Milan and Verona are on the tour circuit of the best European and North American music acts, dance troupes, opera and theatre. In summer, film, music and art festivals abound in lakeside gardens and historic villas. At weekends, urbanites escape to the mountains and lakes for morning markets, sailing, cycling and walking, and long afternoon lunches. What could be more perfect?

Why I Love the Italian Lakes

By Paula Hardy, Author

From cutting-edge design showcases to hi-tech olive presses and a sidewalk scene that makes Fashion Week seem entirely redundant, Milan and the lakes are both thrilling and fun. Everyone here is fizzing with ideas, ambition and energy, and it's catching. Unlike nonna's Italy further south, Lombards, like New Yorkers, are refreshing modernists and after a few days, you'll begin to see why. The main currency here isn't the euro or amazing design gadgetry. It's inspiration – and that's what I love.

For more about our authors, see page 272

Above: Lezzeno, Lake Como (p199)

The Italian Lakes

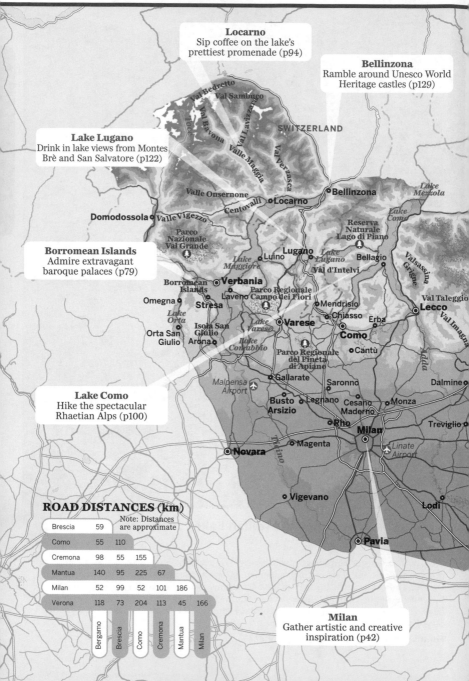

Locarno
Sip coffee on the lake's prettiest promenade (p94)

Bellinzona
Ramble around Unesco World Heritage castles (p129)

Lake Lugano
Drink in lake views from Montes Brè and San Salvatore (p122)

Borromean Islands
Admire extravagant baroque palaces (p79)

Lake Como
Hike the spectacular Rhaetian Alps (p100)

Milan
Gather artistic and creative inspiration (p42)

ROAD DISTANCES (km)

Note: Distances are approximate

	Bergamo	Brescia	Como	Cremona	Mantua	Milan
Brescia	59					
Como	55	110				
Cremona	98	55	155			
Mantua	140	95	225	67		
Milan	52	99	52	101	186	
Verona	118	73	204	113	45	166

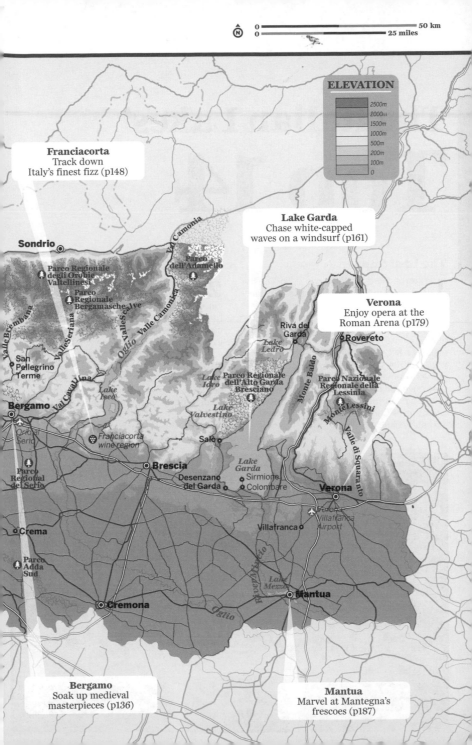

The Italian Lakes'
Top 14

The Last Supper

1 When Leonardo da Vinci was at work on the *Il Cenacolo* (p55; The Last Supper), a star-struck monk noted that he would sometimes arrive in the morning, stare at yesterday's effort, then promptly call it quits for the day. Your visit may be similarly brief (and it's no mean feat nabbing a ticket in the first place), but the baggage of a thousand dodgy reproductions and one very dubious best-selling novel is quickly shed once you're actually face to face with the astonishing beauty and enthralling psychological drama as Christ reveals one of the apostles will betray him.

Milan's Duomo

2 Whether it's your virgin visit to Milan or your fiftieth, your first glimpse of the city's cathedral (p45), with its organic ferment of petrified sky-piercing pinnacles and buttresses, can never fail to elicit a gasp of awe. Under the ever-watchful gaze of the golden Madonnina, you can also wander the rooftop, feeling just a little closer to heaven. It's said that you can see the Matterhorn on a clear day, but given Milan's notorious haze, you'll probably have to ask in favours from Our Lady to guarantee that.

Opera at the Arena

3 Even those normally immune to arias will be swept up in the occasion. On balmy summer nights, when 14,000 music lovers fill Verona's Roman Arena (p181) and light their candles at sunset, expect goosebumps even before the performance starts. The festival (p183), which runs from mid-June to the end of August, was started in 1913 and is now the biggest open-air lyrical music event in the world. It draws performers such as Placido Domingo and the staging is legendary – highlights have included Franco Zeffirelli's lavish productions of *Carmen* and *Aida*.

A Room with a View

4 Book a room with a view and every morning you'll wake up to an unforgettable experience. Watch clouds gather around Monte Baldo at Villa Arcadio (p204) or sip cocktails at sunset at the Grand Hotel des Iles Borromees (p197). Croissant and cloud-naming are breakfast sports at Dimora Bolsone (p203) on Lake Garda; views over Como's gardens are sweet at Albergo Silvio (p111), and Agriturismo San Mattia (p205) offers an almost aerial view of Verona, snug in the embrace of the Adige river.

Above: View of Isola Bella (p79) and Isola Superiore (p81), Lake Maggiore

Mantegna in Mantua

5 Maverick Mantegna (1431–1506) was a carpenter's son who married into the acclaimed Bellini clan in Venice, painted a golden altar in Verona, frescoed the Belvedere chapel in Rome and finally became court painter in Mantua in 1460. His flinty landscapes and radical foreshortening of perspective demonstrate a sculptural approach to painting. *Cristo Morto*, in the Brera gallery (p52) in Milan, and the *Camera degli Sposi* (Bridal Chamber) in the Palazzo Ducale (p188; pictured) in Mantua still have the power to shock and amaze.

Wine Routes

6 Northern Italians have been in the business of wine production since the ancient Greeks introduced their *passito* (dried grape) technique in the 6th century and gave us Valpolicella's blockbuster reds, Amarone and Recioto. From Oltrepò Pavese (p70) in the east to Leonardo da Vinci's favourite Valtellina (p119) vintages in the foothills of the Alps and Italy's finest fizz in Franciacorta (p148), Lombardy offers up miles of vineyards perfect for touring and tastings.

Above: Vineyards, Valpolicella (p185)

Borromean Palaces

7 The Borromean Gulf forms Lake Maggiore's most beautiful corner, and the Borromean Islands harbour its most spectacular sights: the privately owned palaces of the Borromei family. On Isola Bella, the grandiose Palazzo Borromeo (p80; pictured below) presides over 10 tiers of terraced gardens and a shell-encrusted grotto, while on Isola Madre (p80) white peacocks stalk English-style gardens around an older family residence complete with a neoclassical puppet theatre designed by La Scala's set designer.

Italian Masters

8 Founded in the late 18th century, Milan's Pinacoteca di Brera (p52) and Bergamo's Accademia Carrara (p139) housed the teaching aids of the day: a roll call of Italian masters including Titian, Tintoretto, Botticelli, Raphael, Caravaggio and the Bellini brothers. The masterpieces number in their thousands and represent the stunning arc of Italian artistic development between the 15th and 18th centuries. Accademia Carrara will reopen in 2014.

Right: Botticelli's *Portrait of Giuliano de' Medici*, Accademia Carrara (p139), Bergamo

WALTER BIBIKOW/GETTY IMAGES ©

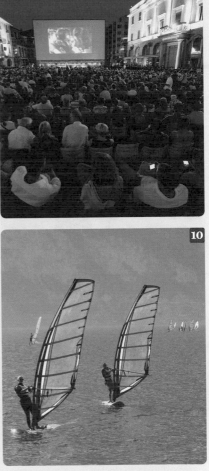

Locarno

9 Once part of the Lombard duchy of Anghera, Locarno (p94) made its name in 1925 with the Treaty of Locarno, a noble attempt at fixing Europe's borders. Since then the town has taken a less serious bent, devoting itself to pleasure: cultivating a waterfront of extravagant beauty, running cable cars up the mountain to frescoed chapels and stunning view points, and hosting a multitude of summer festivals, including the International Film Festival with shows screened nightly beneath the stars in Piazza Grande.

Top right: Festival Internazionale di Film (p95), Locarno

Water Sports on Lake Garda

10 Sailors, windsurfers, kitesurfers and paragliders come to Lake Garda (p161) to test their metal on winds first mentioned by Virgil. The Peler swoops south from the mountains in the morning, catching the sails of speedmeisters until noon, when the gentler Ora puffs north from the southern valleys in the afternoon and early evening. Experts fine tune their experiences on some of the 20 other winds that skim across the lake, winds like the Ander and Fasanella as well as the violent Vinesa from Verona.

KRZYSZTOF DYDYNSKI/GETTY IMAGES ©

PETER HING/GETTY IMAGES ©

Medieval Bergamo

11 There's no shortage of fresh air, breathtaking views and urban appeal in this medieval Lombard town (p136), at the foot of the Orobie Alps. The city's defining feature is its double identity. The ancient hilltop Città Alta (Upper Town) is a tangle of tiny medieval streets, Lombard Romanesque architecture and the most beautiful piazza in the world according to Le Corbusier. Below, connected by funicular, the sprawling Città Bassa (Lower Town) sports boulevards lined with patrician *palazzi* (palaces) and a wealth of wine bars and taverns.

Lakeside Gardens

12 Imagine a landscape caught between fantasy and reality, a green theatre where statues might easily move, fountains and sculpture embody encoded messages and the air is full of strange noises as water trickles down walls and gurgles in shell-encrusted grottoes. No, this isn't Shakespeare's magical isle in *The Tempest*, but the fabulous world of high Renaissance, baroque and neoclassical gardens such as Giardino Giusti (p182), Isola Bella (p79), Isola Madre (p80), Villa Balbianello (p117) and Villa Carlotta (p117; pictured).

Mountain Hikes

13 Ringed with a range of spectacular Alpine peaks reflected gloriously in dozens of glassy glacial lakes, northern Italy is a paradise for hikers and strollers alike. The more populous southern towns of Stresa, Como and Salò sport flower-fringed promenades from where pilgrim paths and mule tracks disappear into the hills. To the north, challenging hiking routes crest mountain ridges, arriving at spectacular viewing points on Monte Baldo, Monte Brè, Monte San Salvatore, Cimetta and Gargnano.

Top right: Hiking, Monte Baldo (p175)

13

Shopping the Quad

14 For anyone interested in the fall of a frock or the cut of a jacket, a stroll around Quadrilatero D'Oro (p49), the world's most famous shopping district, should be on your lifetime to-do list. And even if you don't have the slightest urge to sling a swag of glossy carriers over your arm, the people-watching is priceless. Bespoke-suited silver foxes prowl, gazelle-limbed models lope up and down, and aggressively accessorised matrons crowd the bar at Pasticceria Cova (p63) for short blacks and some obligatory flirting with the baristas.

14

Need to Know

For more information, see Survival Guide (p243)

Currency
Euro (€), Swiss franc (Sfr)

Language
Italian, Swiss, German

Visas
Not needed for residents of Schengen countries or for many visitors staying for less than 90 days. See p250

Money
ATMs widely available. Credit cards accepted in most hotels and restaurants.

Mobile Phones
Local SIM cards can be used in European and Australian phones. Other phones must be set to roaming.

Time
Central European Time (GMT/UTC plus one hour).

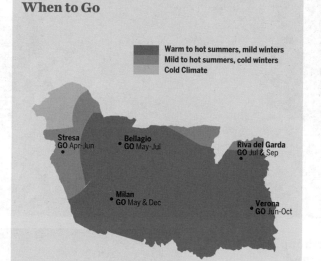

When to Go

Warm to hot summers, mild winters
Mild to hot summers, cold winters
Cold Climate

Stresa
GO Apr-Jun

Bellagio
GO May-Jul

Riva del Garda
GO Jul & Sep

Milan
GO May & Dec

Verona
GO Jun-Oct

High Season
(Mar & Apr, Jul & Aug, Oct)

➡ Accommodation prices rise at least 50%

➡ Cities and lake resorts are hot and crowded in July and August

➡ Trade fairs are held in Milan and Verona March to April and October

Shoulder
(May & Jun, Sep)

➡ Perfect weather and gardens are in bloom

➡ By June lake resorts are buzzing and the water is warming up

➡ September is harvest time and a perfect time to tour wine roads

Low Season
(Nov–Mar)

➡ Accommodation bargains abound, but many lake and mountain hotels close for the season

➡ Some tourist info offices close and many restaurants operate with reduced hours

➡ Christmas fairs are held in Milan and Verona

Useful Websites

RegioneLombardia (www.turismo.regione.lombardia.it) Lombardy tourism site.

Provincia di Verona (www.tourism.verona.it) Covers Verona, Lake Garda and Valpolicella.

Milano e Turismo (www.turismo.milano.it) Downloadable map and city guide.

Lago Maggiore (www.lagomaggioreturismo.it) Covers the southern (Italian) half of the lake.

Lago di Como (www.lakecomo.org) Covers the whole Como area.

Lonely Planet (www.lonelyplanet.com/italy/lombardy-and-the-lakes) Destination information, hotel bookings and traveller forum.

Important Numbers

Italy country code	☏39
International access code	☏00
Ambulance	☏118
Local police	☏113
All emergency services from a mobile phone	☏112

Exchange Rates

Australia	A$1	€0.67
Canada	C$1	€0.71
Japan	¥100	€0.76
New Zealand	NZ$1	€0.58
UK	UK£1	€1.16
USA	US$1	€0.75

For current exchange rates see www.xe.com.

Daily Costs

Budget:
Less than €120

➡ Dorm bed: €25–€30

➡ Sandwich: €2.50–€4

➡ Pizza or pasta: €8–€12

➡ Coffee drunk at bar: €1

Midrange:
€120–220

➡ Midrange double room: €100–€220

➡ Restaurant meal: €20–€45

➡ Aperitivo: €8

➡ Average museum entry: €5–€10

Top End:
More than €220

➡ Top-end hotel double: €220 and over

➡ Fine-dining restaurant meal: €60–€150

➡ Top-end aperitivo: €15–€20

➡ Evening tour of *Il Cenacolo*: €70

➡ Parking: €10–€25 per day

Opening Hours

Opening hours vary throughout the year. We've provided high and low season opening hours. Hours will generally decrease in shoulder and low season. Many city clubs close in summer.

Banks 8.30am–1.30pm and 3.30–4.30pm Monday to Friday

Restaurants noon–3pm and 7.30pm–midnight (kitchens usually close as early as 10pm)

Cafes & Bars 7.30am–8pm

Nightclubs 10pm–4am

Shops 9am–1pm and 3.30–7.30pm (or 4–8pm) Monday to Saturday; some shops only open for half the day on Monday

Arriving in the Italian Lakes

Malpensa Airport (p251) Malpensa Express runs to the Stazione Centrale (adult/child €10/5) every 30 minutes from 5.25am to 11.40pm, after which the night bus offers limited services. Taxis are a €90 set fare (50 minutes).

Linate Airport (p251) Air Bus coaches run between Linate and the Stazione Centrale (adult/child €5/2.50). They depart every 30 minutes between 6am to 11pm; it takes 20 minutes. A taxi costs €15 to €20.

Orio al Serio (p251) Between 3am and midnight, buses run every 30 minutes from Bergamo's airport to Milan. The Orio Shuttle takes one hour (purchased on board/online €5/3.50).

Verona-Villafranca Airport (p251) Regular buses (adult/child €6/3) depart every 20 minutes for Porta Nuova train station between 6.35am and 11.35pm. A taxi costs €25.

Getting Around

Train Reasonably priced, with extensive coverage and frequent departures.

Car Useful for travelling at your own pace around the lakes and in the mountains. Cars can be hired in most towns. Drive on the right.

Boat Often the fastest way to get around the lakes. Each lake has an extensive network of ferry and hi-speed hydrofoil services. Car ferries only service lakeside hubs.

Bus Useful for smaller villages around the lakes and off-line connections such as Mantua–Brescia.

For much more on **getting around**, see p253

First Time the Italian Lakes

For more information, see Survival Guide (p243)

Checklist

➡ Check visa requirements (www.esteri.it, p250)

➡ Check airline baggage restrictions

➡ Inform your debit-/credit-card company that you'll be visiting Italy

➡ Organise appropriate travel insurance, especially for activity holidays

➡ Download the Milan transport app at www.atm-mi.it

What to Pack

➡ Good walking shoes for lakeside walking

➡ A corkscrew for picnicking

➡ Mosquito repellent – a must in summer

➡ Warm clothes for cool evenings in the mountains

➡ Swimming costume and towel

➡ Sunglasses and sunscreen

➡ Travel plug (adaptor)

Top Tips for Your Trip

➡ The best time to be out and about is between 5pm and 9pm, when northern Italians take to the piazze for the *passeggiata*, *spritz* and *aperitivo*. Join the throng and save some money on dining out.

➡ Northern Italians are fairly formal. Make eye contact and say *buongiorno/buonasera* (good morning/evening) and *piacere* (pleased to meet you) when greeting people.

➡ Get off the main roads – not only will you avoid paying tolls, but you'll enjoy the region's best scenery, photo ops and villages.

➡ Bear in mind the mountainous terrain surrounding the lakes. Fast motorways link the lakes at the northern and southern ends, otherwise you're in for a lot of zigzagging north/south.

What to Wear

In northern Italy, especially Milan, maintaining *la bella figura* (ie making a good impression) is extremely important. It's all very well being a nice soul, but northern Italians expect a well-cut suit, shiny shoes and neatly coiffed hair to boot. In general, T-shirts, shorts and flip-flops don't cut it unless you're on the beach, and topless sunbathing is a no-no around the family-friendly lakes. Smart-casual dress should cover most situations; trainers, short-sleeved shirts and light blue jeans are frowned upon for evening wear.

Sleeping

➡ **Hotels** Hotels range from one- to three-star *pensione* (guesthouses) through to grand lakeside villas. At three-stars and above expect good standards and ensuite rooms.

➡ **B&Bs** Often the best value accommodation and a good way to meet the locals. More luxurious versions border on boutique hotels.

➡ **Agriturismi (farmstays)** These are working farms offering accommodation in the farmhouse.

➡ **Rifugi (mountain huts)** Mountain huts in the Alps are open from July to September and offer basic accommodation in dormitories.

➡ **Camping** Campgrounds cluster around the lakes and offer spots for caravans as well as campers.

Money

Credit and debit cards are widely accepted. Visa, MasterCard and Cirrus are the most popular options; American Express is only accepted by international hotel chains, luxury boutiques and major department stores; a few places take Diners Club. Always check if restaurants take cards before you order; most bars and cafes do not. Chip-and-pin is the norm for card transactions – few places accept signatures as an alternative.

Bancomats (ATMs) are everywhere; most offer withdrawal from overseas savings accounts and cash advances on credit cards. Both transactions will incur international transaction fees. You can change cash and travellers cheques at a bank, post office or *cambio* (exchange office). **For more information, see p247.**

Bargaining

Gentle haggling is common in flea markets and antiques markets; in all other instances you're expected to pay the stated price.

Tipping

➡ **Restaurants** Tips of 10% are standard – though check to see that a tip hasn't already been added to your bill or included in the flat *coperto* (cover) charge. Change is often left on the counter at cafes.

➡ **Hotels** €1 per bag is standard for baggage handling; €1 per night for cleaning service is welcome.

➡ **Transport** Round up taxi fares to the nearest euro.

Language

With its business focus, industrial hinterland and extensive program of international trade fairs, English is widely spoken in Lombardy and around the lakes, as is German and, to some degree, French. That said, locals are always pleased when visitors deploy some Italian, and a few choice phrases will enhance your travel experience no e.

Phrases to Learn Before You Go

 What's the local speciality?
Qual'è la specialità di questa regione?
kwa·le la spe·cha·lee·ta dee kwes·ta re·jo·ne

A bit like the rivalry between medieval Italian city-states, these days the country's regions compete in speciality foods and wines.

 Which combined tickets do you have?
Quali biglietti cumulativi avete?
kwa·lee bee·lye·tee koo·moo·la·tee·vee a·ve·te

Make the most of your euro by getting combined tickets to various sights; they are available in all major Italian cities.

 Where can I buy discount designer items?
C'è un outlet in zona? che oon owt·let ln zo·na

Discount fashion outlets are big business in major cities – get bargain-priced seconds, samples and cast-offs for *la bella figura*.

 I'm here with my husband/boyfriend.
Sono qui con il mio marito/ragazzo.
so·no kwee kon eel mee·o ma·ree·to/ra·ga·tso

Solo women travellers may receive unwanted attention in some parts of Italy; if ignoring fails have a polite rejection ready.

 Let's meet at 6pm for pre-dinner drinks.
Ci vediamo alle sei per un aperitivo.
chee ve·dya·mo a·le say per oon a·pe·ree·tee·vo

At dusk, watch the main piazza get crowded with people sipping colourful cocktails and snacking the evening away: join your new friends for this authentic Italian ritual!

Etiquette

➡ **Greetings** The standard form of greeting is a handshake. If you know someone well, air-kissing on both cheeks (starting on the left) is the norm.

➡ **Be polite** Say *mi scusi* to attract attention or 'I'm sorry'; *grazie* (*mille*) to say 'thank you (very much)'; *prego* to say 'you're welcome' or 'please, after you' and *permesso* if you need to get past.

➡ **Cafe culture** Don't linger at an espresso bar; drink your coffee and go. It's called espresso for a reason.

➡ **Paying the bill** Whoever invites usually pays. Splitting the bill between friends is OK, but itemising it is *molto vulgare* (very vulgar).

➡ **Boating** Allow passengers to disembark before boarding boats. For those in need of assistance, the crew are happy to lend a hand.

What's New

Expo 2015

In 1851, the world's first Expo took place in London exhibiting the 'Works of Industry of all Nations.' It featured 25 countries and from the profits emerged the Victoria & Albert Museum, the Science Museum and the Natural History Museum. With 131 countries signed up, Milan is looking forward to hosting one of the biggest Expos (www.expo2015.org) ever, starting on 1 May 2015 and running for six months. The theme is food, of course!

Il Cenacolo, By Night

Get up close and personal with *The Last Supper* in the soft glow of an extended, after-hours Tickitaly tour between 7pm and 9pm. (p56)

Ansaldo Workshops

To see the craft behind La Scala's world-class opera, including a peak at some 60,000 costumes, take a workshops tour at 3pm every Tuesday and Thursday. (p53)

MiArt

Under the direction of Vincenzo de Bellis, Milan's contemporary art fair now features 61 international galleries as well as the city's finest public and private art institutions, including the Prada and Trussardi Foundations. (p59)

IATM

Milan's new city transport app (www.atm-mi.it) features a handy interactive map, detailing your nearest bus and tram stops. It's especially useful if you're staying in the south and west of the city where metro coverage is less extensive.

Bellagio Cooking Classes

Go shopping at the market then learn to cook northern Italian specialities with those who know best, Bellagio's no-nonsense housewives. (p111)

Museo dei Fossili, Meride

Meride's Unesco World Heritage Site–listed fossils have a new museum worthy of their importance, a light-and-airy structure that's the work of star Lugano architect Mario Botta. (p129)

Museo del Violino, Cremona

Cremona's new museum showcases the city's world-class violin-making traditions under one roof. (p154)

Avemaria Boat

Jump aboard this floating hotel for a seven-day odyssey down the Po river all the way to Venice. En route you can enjoy cycle rides to Ferrara and across the Po Delta. (p206)

New Generation Valpolicella

Change is afoot in traditional Valpolicella, with dynamic new vintners such as Camilla Chauvet at Massimago and organic producers Fratelli Vogadori and Valentina Cubi. (p187) (p187) (p187)

For more recommendations and reviews, see lonelyplanet.com/italy

If You Like...

Fabulous Food

Risotto alla milanese Cooked in beef-marrow broth and flavoured with saffron, Milan's signature dish should be *all'onda* (wave-like). (p70)

Designer Dining A bevy of Michelin stars and luxe food emporium **Peck** put Milan at the vanguard of Lombard food. (p61)

Sweet Tooth Instead of a bar-crawl, sample pastries, strudels and *torte* at Milan's august *pasticcerie* (pastry shops). (p63)

Mantua Sample heritage dishes spiced with pumpkin and cinnamon that can trace their origins back to the Renaissance. (p192)

Cheese Italy's biggest cheese-producer, Lombard cheeses like gorgonzola, taleggio, robiola and mascarpone have conquered the world. (p31)

Wine Tasting

Aperitivo Milan's habit of pre-dinner drinks has taken the world by storm; see why at the city's fabulous wine bars. (p64)

Franciacorta If you like a little fizz, head to Franciacorta where monks first perfected the art of sparkling wines. (p148)

VinItaly Sample exceptional, rarely exported producers and blends at Italy's largest wine expo. (p183)

Oltrepò Pavese Oltrepò's wines are influenced by the varietals of Piedmont and are perfect with rustic foods. (p70)

Valpolicella Home to some of Italy's biggest and boldest red wines, including Amarone, otherwise known as 'the big sour one.' (p185)

Art

Brescia Hidden in Brescia's urban sprawl are the ruins of two Roman villas, complete with frescoes and mosaics. (p148)

The Renaissance From Leonardo da Vinci's *Il Cenacolo* to Michelangelo's final sculpture, Milan is no art slouch. (p45)

Museo del Novecento Modernist Milan's first-class museum devoted to 20th-century art. (p45)

House Museums Milan's private collections – **Poldi Pezzoli** and **Bagatti Valsecchi** – are as impressive as any civic museum. (p52) (p53)

The Academies Come to see the Italian masters at Milan's **Pinacoteca di Brera** and Bergamo's **Accademia Carrara**. (p52) (p139)

Mantegna Master of dramatic perspectives, Mantegna executed his biggest commission in Mantua's **Palazzo Ducale**. (p188)

Villa Olmo Como's art nouveau landmark now hosts blockbuster exhibits in its ornate interiors. (p106)

The Great Outdoors

Greenway del Lago di Como An easygoing, 10km walk on the sunny western side of Lake Como. (p114)

Glide & Surf Make the most of the Pelèr and Ora winds to windsurf, kitesurf and sail around Lake Garda. (p159)

Giro d'Italia Follow in the tracks of cycling greats to the

IF YOU LIKE... VIEWS

For extraordinary views over Lake Lugano and onto Monte Rosa and the Matterhorn, head for the high point of Cima Sighignola (p83), known as the Balcone d'Italia (1320m). From here you can see Lake Maggiore, Varese, the Alps and the Lombard plains.

Santuario della Madonna del Ghisallo above Bellagio and leave your memento to the patron saint of cyclists. (p112)

Family Fun Lake Maggiore's **Monte Mottarone** attracts families for mountain biking, bobsledding and lake views, while the **Valtenesi** offers horse riding and beaches. (p76)

Off-the-Beaten-Track Trails Cycle around Lake Iseo's **Monte Isola** (p145) or tour the villages of **Franciacorta** (p148)

Parco Sempione Join the joggers, roller-bladers and picnickers in Milan's grand public park. (p55)

Climbing Made famous by the likes of Maurizio Zanolla, **Arco** hosts the Rockmaster competitions and tops the must-visit list for climbers. (p173)

Villa Gardens

Villa Taranto One of Europe's finest botanic gardens, with over 20,000 different species. (p81)

Isola Bella The Borromeo's outdoor baroque fantasy is adorned with classical statuary and white peacocks. (p79)

Villa Carlotta A 17th-century villa stuffed with sculpture by Antonio Canova and gardens filled with azaleas, rhododendrons and camellias. (p117)

Villa del Balbianello Located at Lenno on Lake Como, these terraced gardens drip down the promontory like ice-cream on a cone. (p117)

Villa Melzi D'Eril Neat neo-classical elegance combines with the studied informality in Lake Como's first English-style garden in Bellagio. (p111)

Grotte di Catullo The lakes' largest Roman ruin sits amid olive trees at the tip of Sirmione's promontory. (p164)

(Above) Villa Carlotta (p117), Tremezzo, Lake Como.
(Below) Palazzo Ducale (p188), Mantua.

Month by Month

February

Bitterly cold mountain winds and many shuttered doors signal the quietest month of the year for lakeside tourism. Cities in the Po valley shrug off the winter blues with Carnevale celebrations.

⚜ Carnevale

In the period leading up to Ash Wednesday, many Italian towns stage pre-Lenten carnivals; the best are in Milan, Lecco, Bellinzona and Verona, the latter led by King Gnoco.

March

The weather in March is capricious. If you get lucky, you could bag some early sunshine at great prices. Towards the end of the month, early-blooming camellias herald the start of spring.

☉ Mostra Nazionale della Camelia

Verbania gets a splash of extra floral colour in late March from a display of more than 200 varieties of camellia (www.cameliein mostra.it)

🛍 Fashion Week

At the end of March, the population of Milan swells with over 100,000 designers, buyers, photographers and models as the city launches the autumn/winter collections. Book everything in advance.

April

Lakeside gardens burst into bloom, although temperatures still retain their chilly edge. Easter sees the tourist season kick off in earnest, and global fairs pack hotels in Milan and Verona.

☉ Salone Internazionale del Mobile

Milan's Furniture Fair (www.cosmit.it) is the design industry's premier global event, even bigger than the fashion shows. Although the main event takes place at the Fiera Milano, satellite events, showcasing the work of emerging talents, are held all over town in the Fiera Fuorisalone (www.fuorisa lone.it).

☉ Settimana del Tulipano

Forty thousand tulips erupt in bloom on the grounds of Villa Taranto; the dahlia path is also in bloom, as is the dogwood. (p81)

🍷 VinItaly

Sandwiched between the Valpolicella and Soave wine regions, Verona hosts Italy's largest wine fair (www.vinitaly.com).

May

The month of roses and new-season produce, May is a perfect time to travel, especially for walkers and cyclists. Prices are also good value, and river cruises launch for the season.

☉ MiArt

Milan's contemporary art fair attracts more than 30,000 art lovers, over 200 exhibitors and increasing amounts of international attention. It's held at the Fiera Milano. (p59)

🎭 Festival di Cremona Claudio Monteverdi

This month-long series of concerts (www.teatro ponchielli.it) celebrating baroque composer Claudio Monteverdi, among others, draws the biggest performers of ancient music and countless madrigal fans.

July

☆ Arena di Verona

Verona's open-air Roman Arena is a spectacular location for opera; the season kicks off in mid-June and runs to the end of August. Book tickets online, in advance. (p183)

☆ Bellagio Festival

From June to early September catch weekly classical music concerts in Bellagio (www.bellagiofestival.com) and some of Lake Como's most spectacular villa venues.

☆ Estival Jazz

Set in Lugano and the nearby town of Mendrisio, this open-air jazz concert (www. estivaljazz.ch) takes over city piazze for three days of world-class jazz in early July.

August

Locals take their annual holidays and life in the cities slows to a snail's pace. Be warned: the weather can be stifling in cities on the plains, and lakeside beaches are crowded.

🎭 Festival Internazionale di Film

This two-week film festival (www.pardo.ch) in Locarno, one of Europe's most important, has been going since 1948. A big, open-air screen is pitched in Piazza Grande so the public can attend for free.

☆ Stresa Festival

Classical concerts and midsummer jazz in lakeside gardens are held from mid-July to early September (www.stresafestival.eu).

☆ Blues to Bop

Lugano's picturesque piazze become an outdoor stage for 50 musicians who perform over 40 blues and jazz concerts (www.bluestobop. ch) over three days at the end of August.

September

Autumn is when *La Vendemmia* (the grape harvest) is celebrated alongside the rice harvest. Mountain forests proffer intensely scented porcini mushrooms and creamy chestnuts.

🔒 Fashion Week

The fashion crowd are back in Milan, this time to launch the spring/summer collections. Unless you're in the business, skip the shows and go to the fashion events instead.

🏎 Italian F1 Grand Prix

Monza's historic autodrome hosts the F1 circuit (www. monzanet.it). See p70 for more.

🤸 Centomiglia

As many as 350 vessels turn out for this prestigious sailing regatta (www.cen tomiglia.it) on Lake Garda.

🍷 Bardolino Grape Festival

Sit down at outdoor tables and drink and dine with local families at the Bardolino wine festival, held on the last weekend in September.

November

Summer resorts have shut for the season and there's a chill in the northern air, but late season produce and truffles from Piedmont fill menus with tasty treats.

🍴 Festa del Torrone

A weekend celebration of the sticky Christmas sweet *torrone* (nougat) in Cremona (www.festadeltor ronecremona.it).

December

December is cold and rainy but cities stave off the grey with Christmas markets, roasted chestnuts and festive illuminations. Alpine resorts open for the ski season.

🎭 Festa di Sant'Ambrogio & Fiera degli Obei Obei

The feast day of Milan's patron saint is celebrated on 7 December with a large Christmas fair at Castello Sforzesco. La Scala's opera season kicks off the same day.

Itineraries

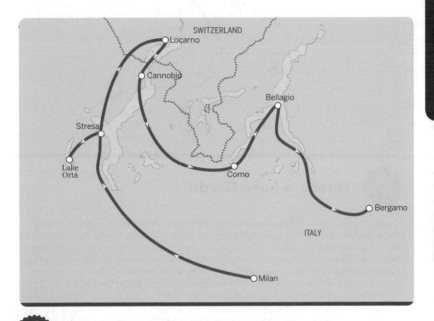

14 DAYS Milan, Lake Maggiore & Lake Como

Modernist **Milan** gets this whirlwind tour off to a spectacular start with big city treats like Leonardo da Vinci's *Il Cenacolo,* a tour of La Scala's costume department and world-class art collections in the Pinacoteca di Brera, the Museo Poldi Pezzoli and Museo del Novecento. Give yourself at least three days to eat, drink, shop and sight-see, and possibly take in a concert or opera. Then head for belle époque **Stresa**. Base yourself here or on Isola Superiore and ferry-hop to the extravagant Borromean palaces, the pleasure playground of Monte Mottarone and the voluptuous gardens of Villa Taranto. On day six, take a day trip to **Lake Orta**, before heading north by ferry or train to **Locarno**, where you should spend another few days soaking up this swanky Swiss town. Make your way back via quiet **Cannobio**. Then skip across the lake to Luino on the eastern shore and onto **Como**, via Varese. Amble the flower-laden lakeside to impressive Villa Olmo before taking a fast boat to **Bellagio**. Return to Milan, via **Bergamo**, and catch the extraordinary Carrara art collection amid some of the finest Lombard Renaissance architecture in the region.

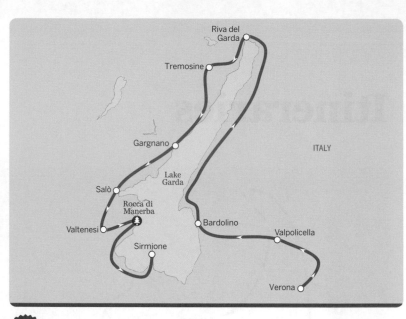

16 DAYS Verona & Lake Garda

Combine culture and the great outdoors by flying into **Verona**, then striking out for the wine country and touring Garda's activity laden shoreline. Spend three or four days in Verona, visiting its museums and frescoed churches, playing tag with Shakespeare's star-crossed lovers, drinking coffee and *spritz* in its magnificent piazze and enjoying theatre and opera in its Roman Arena and hillside amphitheatre. Then pick up a car from the train station and head out for the nearby hills of **Valpolicella**. You could whiz around two or three wineries in a day, but instead take things slow and hunker down in Agriturismo San Mattia and get to know your Amarones from your Reciotos. Then push on through the hills of **Bardolino** at week's end and treat yourself to a day at the plush Aqualux Hotal Spa or at night the romantic Locanda San Vigilio. Then, in the morning, head to **Riva del Garda** for three days of nonstop activity. Plan ahead for sailing, windsurfing or climbing classes, or get down to the waterfront early to hire some gear. Spend at least half a day hiking the old Ponale Road and another half day cycling up the Sarco river to Drò. For families, a trip to the Varone waterfall will be a hit, or ferry-hop to Malcesine and take the funicular up Monte Baldo. Alternatively, its easy to while away the hours playing, swimming or cycling along the landscaped lakefront. On day 12 begin the drive south – a thrilling highlight in itself through mountain-blasted tunnels along a twisting road that overhangs the lake. Take the high road over the **Tremosine plateau**, before spending a night or two in idyllic **Gargnano** and heading on to patrician **Salò**. Base yourself here or just back from the lakeside in the vineyards of the **Valtenesi** and spend a further three days day-tripping to the extraordinary house-museum, Il Vittoriale, the private island of Isola del Garda and cruising vineyards and olive groves for tastings. Make sure you spend a full day hiking in the natural reserve of **Rocca di Manerba** and take a late boat to **Sirmione** to watch the sunset from lakeside thermal pools once the crowds have dispersed.

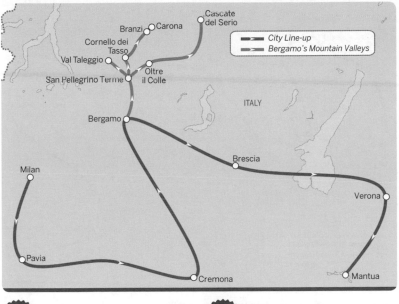

7 DAYS City Line-Up

For an architectural and artistic tour of northern Italy's glittering medieval and Renaissance heyday, look no further than the elegant cities of the Po valley. **Milan**, with its huge crenellated castle and glittering Duomo, was the medieval muscle in the west. Just check out the collection in Castello Sforzesco and the rich legacy of art in its four basilicas. But Milan didn't have the medieval monopoly on culture. A half-day trip to nearby **Pavia** will give you time to enjoy Giangaleazzo's enormous Certosa monastery, and you'll need another day to browse the violin shops in **Cremona**, where Stradivarius started a musical tradition that resonates around the world even today. Then head onto **Bergamo** for Lombardy's finest Renaissance architecture and to **Brescia** and **Verona** for Roman ruins and fine dining. Finally, finish up in lake-bound **Mantua**, with Mantegna's frescoes, a Renaissance pleasure palace and some fine Renaissance-style dining at Il Cigno.

4 DAYS Bergamo's Mountain Valleys

Join the proud and prosperous Bergamaschi in **Bergamo's** Città Alta (Upper Town) for a sedate *passeggiata* around its elegant Renaissance piazze, admiring its medieval towers and the magnificent Lombard Romanesque mausoleum of mercenary commander Bartolomeo Colleoni. Take in Renaissance masters at the Palazzo Ragione, stroll the ramparts of La Rocca and eat in as many of the town's excellent restaurants as you can manage. Then head north through art nouveau **San Pellegrino Terme** to the **Val Taleggio**, where you can stock up on one of Lombardy's signature cheeses from local farmers and cooperatives. Afterwards, return to the SS470 and head north through the medieval hamlet of **Cornello dei Tasso** to the Valle Brembana in the foothills of the Orobie Alps. Hikers will want to push deep into the mountains for trails at **Branzi** and **Carona**, which lead to glassy glacial lakes. But for those touring the country by a car, double-back south through **Oltre il Colle** into the Valle Seriana, for more fabulous forest vistas and Europe's tallest waterfall, the **Cascate del Serio**.

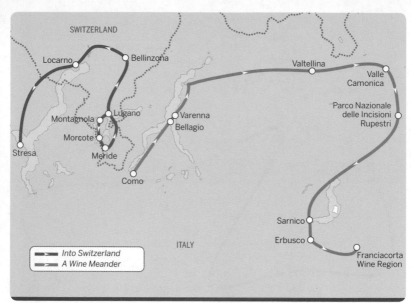

Into Switzerland
A Wine Meander

6 DAYS — Into Switzerland

Start in **Lugano**, an elegant lakeside town on the Swiss side of the border that's worth a busy day of your time. Spend a morning in its old town and museums, and the afternoon whizzing up the funiculars of Monte Brè and Monte San Salvatore. Also use Lugano as a base for visiting lakeside towns, among them charming **Morcote** and museums devoted to Herman Hesse in **Montagnola** and some extraordinary fossils in **Meride**. Then head northwest to **Bellinzona** and tour its three Unesco World Heritage Site–listed castles. As you head further west, detour into wonderfully quiet and pretty Val Verdasca and Valle Maggia en route to **Locarno** with its picturesque waterfront and engaging old town. With just a day or two left, and to make the most of your time, take the Lake Maggiore Express that includes the gorgeous Centovalli train from Locarno to Domodossola and another train down to **Stresa**. Then return to Locarno aboard a ferry that traces the lake shore back with the best of Maggiore lake views along the way.

5 DAYS — A Wine Meander

Kick off this whirlwind wine tour with a day in **Como** before taking the fast boat to Albergo Silvio in **Bellagio**, where you're booked for lunch on the terrace. Then hop across to pretty **Varenna** and tour the botanical gardens of the Villa Monastero before heading north up the east bank to the wine valley of the **Valtellina**. Tour some of the sunny hillside wineries and stock up on rare regional varietals such as the punchy Sforzato. On day three, emerge from the valley at Edolo and turn southwards down the **Valle Camonica**, lined with Bronze Age rock carvings, which you can tour in the 30-hectare **Parco Nazionale della Incisioni Rupestri** near Capo di Ponte. Then head for pretty **Sarnico** at the southern end of Lake Iseo and enjoy a laid-back day wandering its medieval lanes. You'll then want another two days: one to dine in style at Gualtiero Marchesi's extraordinary restaurant at the five-star, rust-red hotel L'Albereta in **Erbusco** and another to cycle off the indulgence with a tailor-made tour of in the vineyards of the **Franciacorta wine region**.

Plan Your Trip
Eat & Drink Like a Local

Let's be honest: you came for the food. Just don't go expecting the stock-standards served at your local Italian. Northern Italian food features a broad spectrum of flavours from delicate freshwater fish to exotic saffron risotto and hearty helpings of goose sausage and spiced pheasant. Whet your appetite with the following food-trip essentials. To dig deeper, see p233.

Food Experiences
Meals of a Lifetime

➡ **Dal Pescatore** (p192) Winner of Veuve Cliquot's Best Female Chef 2013 and the first female Italian chef to hold three Michelin stars, Nadia Santini is a self-taught culinary virtuoso.

➡ **Cracco** (p62) Star chef Carlo Cracco keeps the Milanese in thrall with his off-the-wall inventiveness.

➡ **Il Sole** (p87) Creative, nouvelle cuisine in a near-perfect setting in Ranco on the banks of Lake Maggiore.

➡ **Locanda 4 Cuochi** (p183) The definition of a modern trattoria, manned by four exceptional chefs with a zealous attention to fresh, seasonal ingredients. Fine dining at democratic prices.

➡ **Osteria Numero Uno** (p185) One of those old-fashioned *osteria* that everyone dreams of discovering.

Cheap Treats

➡ **Arancini** Sicilian rice balls are now gaining in popularity as an *aperitivi* snack in Milan.

➡ **Mortadella di Ossola** A Slow Food Movement–protected sausage from Lake Maggiore made with pork and liver flavoured with salt, wine and spices.

The Year in Food
Spring
Markets burst with artichokes, green and pink Mezzago asparagus from Monza, *radicchio* (chicory) and, towards the season's end, cherries and courgette flowers. Early spring cheeses are curdled and VinItaly showcases regional Italian wines.

Summer
Summer treats include strawberries, peppers, figs and citrus fruit as well as an abundance of freshwater fish. Chickpeas and beans are harvested late in the season.

Autumn
Food festivals galore, the olive and grape harvests, and forest gems such as chestnuts, porcini mushrooms and game birds. Oenophiles head to Bardolino in September for the wine fair. By mid-October truffle season starts in nearby Piedmont.

Winter
The rice and corn harvest commences. Winter greens such as cabbage and kale feature heavily, but pumpkins add a warm glow to Mantuan specialities. The year ends with Milan's speciality Christmas cake, *panettone*.

➡ **Polentone** (p140) Italy's first take-away polenta place in Bergamo's old town.

➡ **Sciatt** Deep-fried buckwheat balls filled with cheese, a speciality of the Valtellina.

➡ **Sbrisolona** A cornmeal cake flavoured with almonds, lemon rind and vanilla, found in Mantua and Verona.

Dare to Try

➡ **Anguilla alla gardesana** Eels marinated with Garda lemons, oil, salt and pepper and cooked on an open grill.

➡ **Missoltini** A boldly flavoured Como speciality of sun-dried shad cured in salt and bay leaves.

➡ **Pastissada de caval** Wine-drenched horse-meat stew served with polenta.

➡ **Rane in umido alla Pavese** Frogs sauteed with leeks in a tomato sauce typical of Pavia.

➡ **Zampone** Pork sausage stuffed in a pig's trotter, typical of Cremona.

Local Specialities

The stretch of northern Italy marked by its glittering glacial lakes covers four distinct culinary zones from the western Piedmontese shores of Lake Maggiore and the upper Alpine reaches of Lombardy and the Valtellina valley to the soupy rice paddies of the Po valley and the spice-laden flavours of the Veneto, bounding Lake Garda's eastern shore.

Milan

Milan is Italy's wealthiest city and its cuisine is similarly golden-hued. *Cotoletta*, sliced buttery veal, mellow yellow risotto and Yuletide *panettone* are cases in point. Since the Renaissance, the Milanese have been great meat eaters – pork, veal, beef, offal and game are all popular, as are hefty casseroles and *minestre* (soups) bulked up with rice or pasta. Surrounded by freshwater rivers and home to the largest wholesale fish market in Europe, fish is another staple of the diet.

➡ **Coffee & cake** Meet at Milan's historic *pasticerrie* (p60) for a brioche (sweet bread) or slice of strudel.

➡ **Aperitivo** Milanese often forgo dinner and feast for free on copious buffets fashioned by trendy *aperitivo* bars from 7pm onwards (p64).

➡ **Risotto alla Milanese** Milan's signature dish is a risotto simmered in marrow stock, wine, butter and saffron. Peck Italian Bar (p60) is the place to try it.

➡ **Panettone** The eggy, brioche-like Yuletide bread is now a national Easter and Christmas tradition. Biffi Pasticceria (p63) and Gattullo (p63) are proud keepers of heritage recipes.

➡ **Cotoletta alla Milanese** Inch-thick cutlets from the loin of a milk-fed calf dipped in breadcrumbs and fried. Try the real deal at Trattoria del Nuovo Macello (p60).

Brescia Province

The cuisine of Brescia and Bergamo is Alpine-Venetian, combining strong flavours in simple dishes. In Bergamo, polenta is served 'wet' with almost everything, including sweets. Alpine herds provide an ample supply of meat for braised stews (*brasato*), oven baking (*al forno*) and spit roasts, while their milk is transformed for famous Lombard cheeses such as Grana Padano, Bagoss and Rosa Camuna.

➡ **Bergamo** Famous for *schisöl* (polenta cooked with cheese and mushrooms) and the *polenta e osei* (sweet polenta cake), garnished with chocolate birds (*osei*).

➡ **Brescia** A porcine paradise, the window of Brescia's Salumeria Fratelli Castiglioni overflows with sausages, *cotechino* (a boiled salami), *lardo* (lard), *guanciale* (pig cheek) and *pestöm* (a minced pork salami).

➡ **Casoncelli** (or *casoncèi*) Bergamo's distinctive ravioli stuffed with sausage meat.

Lake Como

Isolated within a steep mountain valley, Larian cuisine is fish-focused. Perch, pike, tench, shad, sardines, local *lavarello* (white fish) and eels are all plentiful. Often fish is served lightly fried (*fritto*), grilled or poached. More elaborate treatments include fish soups, marinades and risotto. The surrounding mountain valleys yield up taleggio, Bitto and Formagella cheeses along with cured meats.

➡ **Bellagio** Renowned for its super rich Toc polenta, blended with butter and cheese. Sample it straight from the fire at Albergo Silvio (p111).

➡ **Lavarello in salsa verde** A local white fish marinated in a green parsley and garlic sauce.

Lake Garda

Influenced by the regions of Lombardy, Trentino and the Veneto, which border its expansive shoreline, Garda's cuisine combines fish and meat with the more Mediterranean flavours of citrus and olives. Mountain meat dishes and Austro-Hungarian influences linger on in the north, while the southern shores of the lake are characterised by fish flavoured with fruity olive oils and citrus, and accompanied by zesty local wines from the vineyards of Bardolino and Lugana.

➡ **Riva del Garda** This is the place to sample Austrian-style *carne salata* (thinly sliced salted beef) at Trattoria Piè di Castello (p174).

➡ **Valpolicella** Young vintners at Massimago (p187) and Fratelli Vogadori (p187) are reviving the region's reputation as a producer of some of Italy's finest red wines.

➡ **Valtenesi** This corner of Lake Garda is famous for its superior olive oils. Comincioli (p167) is an award-winning producer.

Lake Maggiore

Combining the blockbuster cuisines of Piedmont and Lombardy, the area surrounding Lake Maggiore boasts many celebrated products, including Bettelmatt and gorgonzola cheeses, chestnuts and rhododendron-flavoured honeys from Verbano and Varese, herb-flavoured lard from Macugnaga and cured goat's leg from the Vigezzo Valley. To the south, around Novara, farms cultivate innumerable rice varieties including the rare Black Venus rice.

➡ **Ticino** The Swiss tradition of grotto restaurants is the ideal setting for a platter of Ticino mountain cheeses.

➡ **Stresa** In 1857 Princess Margherita of Savoy graced Stresa with a visit. In commemoration they created the lemon, butter biscuit *Margheritine di Stresa*.

➡ **Varese** Exquisite soft-centred, almond-based biscuits, *amaretti di Gallarate,* have impressed internationally recognised chef, Giorgio Locatelli.

➡ **Val d'Ossola** Venture north to Domodossola or into the Val Grande and look out for *Mortadella di Ossola*, a pork salami with liver, wine and spices.

TOP CHEESES

➡ **Stracchino** Made from cow's milk extracted during the seasonal moves to and from Alpine pastures.

➡ **Gorgonzola** A well-known cheese whose two-curd, blue-mould version is strong on the nose.

➡ **Taleggio** A popular soft cheese.

➡ **Mascarpone** Used especially to make desserts.

➡ **Bagoss** Mature and strong flavoured.

➡ **Robiola** Soft-ripened cheese with a thin rind.

Po Valley

Vegetable gardens, orchards, rice and maize fields stretch between the prosperous patrician towns of Pavia, Lodi, Cremona and Mantua. Traditionally a land of peasant farmers, local fruits, vegetables and polenta loom large on the menu as do river fish, frogs, poultry, wild boar, horse, salami and game birds.

➡ **Cremona** Sample typical dishes of *bollito* (boiled meats), *marubini* (meat and cheese stuffed pasta boiled in broth) and *cotechino* (boiled pork sausage). Or attend the nougat festival in November.

➡ **Mantua** Renaissance Mantua remains addicted to spiced pumpkin *tortelli alla zucca.*

➡ **Pavia** The most traditional dish is a soupy *risotto alla certosina* (risotto with frog's legs). Eat it riverside at Antica Osteria del Previ (p70).

➡ **Salami d'oca di Mortara** Originally a Jewish speciality, goose sausage is now a favourite throughout the Po valley

Valtellina

Stretching across the northern reaches of Lombardy, this Alpine valley is famous for its rich, red wines, Bitto cheese, *bresaola* (air-cured beef) and buckwheat pasta. Otherwise, expect to see a menu generously supplied with goat, lamb, beef and plenty of dairy products.

➡ **Sondrio** Sample Austrian-influenced *chisciöl* (buckwheat pancake topped with casera cheese), *pizzocheri alla Valtellinese* (buckwheat pasta with cabbage and grana padano cheese) and *sciatt* (deep-fried buckwheat balls).

Top: Fried fish, Lake Como

Bottom: Marchesi (p63), Milan

→ **Violino di capra della Valchiavenna** A slow-cured goat shank, traditionally served by slicing the meat as a violin player moves his bow.

Verona

Combining both simple rural fare with sophisticated sweets, Veronese cuisine is much influenced by its proximity to Venice. Risotto, polenta and potato gnocchi provide the staples, accompanied by braised horse, pork, beef, donkey, duck and freshwater fish from the Tincio river. Cabbages from Castagnaro, bitter red *radicchio*, apples and Soave cherries are seasonal treats. Those with a sweet tooth will enjoy *pandoro* (the Veronese yeast bread equivalent of *panettone*).

How to Eat & Drink Like a Local

Mealtimes

→ **Colazione (breakfast)** Lombards rarely eat a sit-down breakfast, but instead bolt down a cappuccino with a brioche or other type of pastry (generically known as *pastine*) at a coffee bar before heading to work.

→ **Pranzo (lunch)** Served from noon to 2.30pm; few restaurants take orders for lunch after 2.30pm. Traditionally, lunch is the main meal of the day, though many Lombards now share the main family meal in the evening. Smaller shops and businesses close to accommodate a proper sit-down meal between 1pm and 4pm. The traditional belt-busting, five-course whammy usually only takes place on Sunday.

→ **Aperitivo (aperitif)** At the strike of 6pm Milanese bars swell with crowds of workers indulging in that all-essential post-work, pre-dinner ritual of *aperitivo*, when the price of your cocktail (€6 to €20 in Milan) includes an eat-yourself-silly buffet of finger food, salads, pasta and even sushi.

→ **Cena (dinner)** Served between 7pm and 10pm. Opening hours vary, but many places begin filling up by 7.30pm. In summer and in larger cities like Milan hours may extend to midnight.

Choosing Your Restaurant

→ **Ristorante (restaurant)** Crisp linen, formal service and refined dishes make restaurants the obvious choice for special occasions.

→ **Trattoria** A family-owned version of a restaurant, with cheaper prices, more relaxed service and classic regional specialities. Avoid places offering tourist menus.

→ **Osteria** Intimate and relaxed, the *osteria* has its roots in a traditional tavern serving wine with a little food on the side; these days they are hard to distinguish from *trattorie* although the menu is usually more limited and, sometimes, verbal.

→ **Enoteca (wine bar)** A real trend in cities, wine bars are another affordable and atmospheric place to dine and offer a perfect place to sample regional wines by the glass.

→ **Agriturismo (farmstay)** A working farmhouse offering accommodation as well as food made with farm-grown produce. Some allow guests to participate in farm activities.

→ **Braceria (grill)** A meat-focused menu often with a meat counter displaying different cuts of meat. The selected portion is then cut and cooked to order on an open grill.

The Menu

→ **Menu a la carte** Choose whatever you like from the menu.

→ **Menu di degustazione** Degustation menu; usually consisting of six to eight 'tasting size' courses.

→ **Menu turistico** Good value as it might appear, tourist menus usually feature non-regional standards and mediocre quality – steer clear!

→ **Pane e coperto** 'Bread and cover' charges range from €1 to €6 at most restaurants.

→ **Piatto del giorno** Dish of the day.

→ **Antipasto** A hot or cold appetiser. For a tasting plate of different appetisers, request an *antipasto misto* (mixed antipasto).

→ **Primo** First course; usually a substantial rice, pasta or *zuppa* (soup) dish.

→ **Secondo** Second course; either *carne* (meat) or *pesce* (fish).

→ **Contorno** Side dish; typically *verdure* (vegetables).

→ **Dolce e Frutta** 'Sweet and fruit,' consisting of either *torta* (cake), pudding or fresh fruit.

→ **Nostra produzione (or fatti in casa)** Made in-house; used to describe anything from bread and pasta to *liquori* (liqueurs).

→ **Surgelato** Frozen; usually used to indicate fish or seafood that has not been freshly caught.

Plan Your Trip

Outdoor Activities

Northern Italy's stunning Alpine landscape offers outdoor enthusiasts a plethora of activities, some of which offer the best opportunities for escaping the crowds. Blessed with rolling hills, riverine deltas, glacial lakes and soaring mountains, you can take your pick of hiking, biking, climbing, skiing, horse riding, sailing and surfing, or you can simply sit back and enjoy the view.

Best Outdoors

Best Short Walks

Up the wooded Valle delle Cartiere, around Lake Ledro, between Valle Maggia villages and down from the funicular stations of Monte Brè or Monte San Salvatore and Cimetta.

Best Easy Bike Rides

Around the vineyards of Franciacorta and the Valtenesi, as well as around Lake Orta and beside the lakes in Lugano, Verbania Pallanza and Mantua.

Best for Water Sports

Make the best of the Pelèr and Ora winds to windsurf, kitesurf and sail on Lake Garda.

Best Spa Towns

The Roman's favourite was lakeside Sirmione, but Bardolino's state-of-the-art Aqualux Hotel Spa is now equally as popular.

Best Scenic Drives

Through the Brasa Gorge and up the Val Cannobino; from Como to the peak of Cima Sighignola; and from Cernobbio to Monte Bisbino.

When to Go

Spring and autumn, with their abundance of wildflowers and forest fruits, are the prettiest times to be outdoors. Autumn, when the harvests start in the vineyards and olive groves, has a mellow appeal.

Best Times

➡ **April–June** Pleasantly warm days and valleys drenched in poppies and wildflowers – perfect for cyclists, walkers and climbers.

➡ **July** Water-sports enthusiasts flock to Lake Garda. Hiking in the higher mountains is best this month.

➡ **September–October** Still warm enough for water sports, but cooler days mean mellow hikes and cycle rides through vineyards and mountain forests.

➡ **December–February** The best ski months for atmosphere (Christmas), snow and value.

Where to Go

➡ **Orobie Alps** Rising to the northeast of Lake Como with valleys funnelling down to Bergamo, the Orobie Alps peak at 3000m and are covered in forests and pastures.

➡ **Lake Como** Hit Gravedona for water sports, the western mountains for scenic drives, and the rugged Triangolo Lariano for scenic hikes between Como, Bellagio and Lecco.

➡ **Lake Garda** A veritable outdoor playground with world-class windsurfing and sailing at Riva del Garda, Torbole and Gargnano; championship rock climbing in Arco; paragliding, biking, hiking and skiing on Monte Baldo; horse riding on the Tremonsine plateau and through Bardolino vineyards; and cycling through the olive groves of the Valtenesi.

➡ **Lake Iseo** Bordering the region of Franciacorta, Lake Iseo is a perfect spot for easy cycling, either around Monte Isola or through Franciacorta's vineyards.

➡ **Lake Ledro** Off the mainstream tourist radar, pretty Lake Ledro offers scenic hiking and adrenaline-inducing canyoning.

➡ **Lake Maggiore** Ascend Monte Mottarone for family-friendly biking, hiking and skiing, or escape northwest from Locarno to explore the Ticino valleys on foot.

➡ **Mantua** Family-friendly walking, cycling and river cruising around Mantua's three lakes and beside the Mincio and Po rivers.

➡ **Parco Nazionale Val Grande** Get back to nature in one of Italy's wildest parks with guided walks amid majestic chestnut forests and marble quarries.

Cycling

Northern Italians are cycling fanatics. On weekends you can see whole gangs of cyclists scooting up hill and down dale with frightening alacrity.

More relaxed cycling is possible on the Lombard plains, in Mantua, along the Mincio river and through the Franciacorta and Valtenesi wine territory. Tourist offices in Como, Lecco and Varese can supply maps with suggested cycle routes between Lake Maggiore and the east bank of Lake Como.

For more challenging trails head to Monte Mottarone on Lake Maggiore and Monte Baldo on Lake Garda, where numerous off-road trails snake down the mountainsides. Most famous of all, though, is the challenging climb from Bellagio to the Santuario della Madonna del Ghisallo.

Apart from being a classic Giro d'Italia stage, the chapel is an extraordinary shrine to cycling.

If you're bringing your own bike, check with your airline if there's a fee and how much, if any, disassembling is required. Bikes can be transported by train in Italy, either with you or to arrive within a couple of days. Bike hire or city cycle schemes are available in most towns and resorts.

Top Trails

➡ **Dorsale** Ideal for a day's mountain-bike exploration.

➡ **Monte Mottarone** Rent a mountain bike for the 20km to 30km descent to Stresa.

➡ **Madonna del Ghisallo** Feel like a champion on this classic climb from Bellagio.

➡ **Monte Isola** Cycle round Lake Iseo's island.

➡ **Rocca di Garda** An 11km trail from Garda to Costermano and Albarè.

➡ **The Valtenesi** A 38km circular route takes you from the Castle of Padenghe through the nature reserve of the Rocca di Manerba and the olive groves of Puegnago del Garda.

Horse Riding

Riding is big region-wide, with plenty of *agriturismi* (farmstay accommodation) having horses for guests to ride. Several farms such as La Basia (p167), Agriturismo Scuderia Castello (p170) and Ranch Barlot (p177) around Lake Garda specialise in equestrian holidays and offer treks of one or several days. Combining the intimacy of *agriturismi* and meals around a shared table with the formality of a riding school, these equestrian farms are the most atmospheric way of experiencing the lakes on horseback.

Walking

At first glance one might think there is little in the line of walking to be done around Italy's northern lakes except for the occasional shoreline promenade. Nothing could be further from the truth.

Easy Walking

In many towns along the lakes you can simply head for a stroll along the shoreline. Some of the best include the waterfront promenades in Lugano and Ascona on Lake Maggiore, Sarnico on Lake Iseo, Salò and Riva del Garda on Lake Garda and Como on Lake Como.

On Lake Como, the Greenway del Lago di Como links Cadenabbia and Colonna, while on Lake Orta it is possible to walk right around the lake in three relaxed days, and west of Garda and Bardolino easy, scenic trails snake through the vineyard-clad hills.

In some cases, no more than a couple of hours of walking can bring you to lovely sights and viewpoints. A 3km walk north out of Riva del Garda leads to the Varone waterfall (p172), or take the old Ponale Road (p172) east out of town for panoramic views. North of Lake Iseo, the Val Camonica is dotted with prehistoric rock art.

Heading for the Hills

More seasoned walkers have a choice of hikes rising to 2000m in altitude. On Lake Garda's Monte Baldo, you can hop off at the intermediate station of San Michele and hike back down to Malcesine. More serious hikers can scale Monte Altissimo (2053m). Likewise, you can hike up and/or down Monte Mottarone, Monte Brè, Monte San Salvatore, Cimetta or Cardada on Lake Maggiore.

In Lake Como's Triangolo Lariano, there are more challenging walking options that require some fitness and preparation. They include the two-day Dorsale hike, which takes you from Brunate to Bellagio.

Club Alpino Italiano (CAI; www.cai.it) trails are staked out in a web across northern Italy. You could search out little-known Romanesque churches like the Abbazia di San Pietro al Monte on Lake Como or drive up to Monte Bisbino and embark on some high-level walks. One of the best walks is the Via dei Monti Lariani, a six-day, 130km trail from Cernobbio to Sorico, which is part of the 6000km Sentiero Italia.

More serious hikes can be undertaken in the Valle Brembana, north of Bergamo.

Most of the area is covered by two parks, the Parco delle Orobie Valtellinesi and Parco delle Orobie Bergamasche (www.parks.it), of which the first is easily the most spectacular. The tourist office in Bergamo has details and you can find more information at www.sentierodelle orobie.it. Otherwise, behind Ghiffa on Lake Maggiore, the Via delle Genti is an historic walking path that has connected Switzerland and northern Italy via the St Gotthard pass for centuries.

Top Walks

➡ **Greenway del Lago di Como** (p114) A 10km stroll on the west bank of Lake Como.

➡ **Monte Mottarone** (p76) Opt to hike all or part of the way up or down Monte Mottarone.

➡ **Cimetta** (p95) A gentle walk that leads to 360-degree views above Locarno.

➡ **Via dei Monti Lariani** (p114) A classic 130km trail along high ground above the west flank of Lake Como.

➡ **La Strada del Ponale** (p172) An easy 7km hike along the old Ponale Road from Riva del Garda to hilltop Pregasina.

➡ **Monte Altissimo** A demanding six-hour hike rising from Torbole through 1800m to summit of Monte Altissimo (2053m), the highest peak in the Baldo-Altissimo range.

Water Sports

Sailing, windsurfing and kitesurfing have a cult following around Riva, Torbole, Gargnano, Toscolano-Maderno and Malcesine on Lake Garda (p159), where schools and hire outlets abound along the lakefront. There's a smaller scene at the north end of Lake Como around Gravedona, where waterskiing and wakeboarding are also popular.

Various boat hire outlets on all the lakes will also rent out zodiacs and other small boats for a run-around. And on resort beaches, you can usually rent pedaloes and kayaks.

Plan Your Trip
Travel with Children

The Italian lakes are a fabulous family-friendly destination, packed with outdoor activities, safely landscaped lakefront beaches and promenades, and two of Italy's largest theme parks. Even rides on turn-of-the-century trams, high-speed hydrofoils and cloud-scraping funiculars are bound to delight, while reasonably priced *agriturismi* (farmstay accommodation) and camping grounds abound.

The Italian Lakes for Kids

If you're looking for a family-friendly destination, the Italian lakes certainly fit the bill. The variety of museums, adventure parks, gardens, beaches, activities and shopping (yes, even 16-year-old girls are catered for here) means that there is truly something for everyone. Even in Milan and Verona, large parks and family-friendly attractions and dining keep everyone happy. And when everyone's hot and exhausted, an endless supply of gelato usually gets everyone going again.

Planning

Accommodation

Your most important decisions will be about accommodation. In Milan, where accommodation can be scarce and pricey, book well in advance and opt for centrally located B&Bs or hotels near a convenient metro stop. Around the lakes, you'll also need to book ahead for high season (Easter, July and August) and avoid low season when many places close. Here, we

Best Regions for Kids

Milan
Home to Italy's best science museum, a castle and grand park, and turn-of-the-century trams and canal cruises, Milan is more child-friendly than most imagine.

Lake Maggiore & Around
Whiz up funiculars with bikes and binoculars, traverse the 'Hundred Valleys' by rail, picnic in flower-filled gardens, bobsled high in the mountains and wander with while peacocks on the Borromean Islands.

Lake Como & Around
Head for the hills for walking and cycling trails or to Lenno and Villa Olmo near Como for lido-style lakeside swimming. To the north, in Gravedona, waterski or zip around in a zodiac.

Lake Garda & Around
Ringed with camp sites, furnished with two theme parks and blessed with an endless number of exciting activities, Garda is the most family-friendly lake. Windsurf, hike, cycle and horse ride with specialist operators who provide classes and tours for all age groups.

highly recommend staying in *agriturismi*, villa B&Bs or well-serviced camp sites (many of which also feature bungalows), as these often offer kid-friendly activities such as swimming, horse riding and biking and many have in-house restaurants.

Driving

Most visitors to the lakes tend to drive. Fortunately, distances between destinations aren't particularly long. Children under 12 are not allowed to sit in the passenger seat, and child restraints and seatbelts are mandatory. You'll need to book car seats in advance from your rental provider.

If you're travelling on public transport, note that a seat on a bus costs the same whether you're an adult or child. You don't need to pay for toddlers and babies who sit on your lap, though. On trains, discounts can apply if you're travelling in a family group – check the 'Offers and Deals' pages of the Trenitalia (www.trenitalia.com) website.

Discounts

If your kids are EU citizens, they will almost always be eligible for discounted or free entry to museums and other attractions. These discounts don't always apply to non-EU citizens. There's usually three tiers of discount: free entry for kids under four years of age, another tier for kids under 12 and a third for young adults up to the age of 18 and students up to the age of 26 (with ID).

Children's Highlights

Theme Parks

➡ **Gardaland** (p179) One of Italy's top theme parks, with dinosaurs, pirate ships and roller coasters.

➡ **CanevaWorld** (p179) Medieval shows, an aqua park and Movieland Studios.

➡ **Swissminiatur** (p128) Countless Swiss monuments presented as kid-size replicas.

➡ **Parco della Villa Pallavicino** (p77) Animals and exotic birds roam free.

➡ **Alpyland** (p77) A 1.2km bobseld run with panoramic views.

Outdoor Activities

➡ **Windsurfing & Sailing** The lakefront at Riva del Garda and Torbole are lined with schools.

➡ **Canyoning** Jump, slide and abseil into crystal clear waters with expert guides on Lake Ledro.

➡ **Horse Riding** Take classes and trek Tremosine mountain trails.

➡ **Ferry Rides** Hop on any ferry on any lake and enjoy the views.

Beaches & Swimming

➡ **Piscina Solari** (p58) A covered pool with windows on Parco Solari in Milan.

➡ **Lido di Villa Olmo** (p107) Lakeside lido backed by Como's landmark Villa Olmo.

➡ **Riva del Garda** (p172) Three kilometres of landscaped waterfront join Riva del Garda with Torbole.

➡ **Rocca di Manerba** (p166) A Unesco-protected nature reserve of evergreen woods and picturesque beaches.

Cool Stuff

➡ **Museo Nazionale della Scienza e della Tecnologia** (p56) Let little Leonardos loose in Italy's best science museum in Milan.

➡ **Centovalli Train** (p76) Cross the vertiginous 'Hundred Valleys' on this historic train ride into Switzerland.

➡ **Museo Europeo dei Trasporti** (p86) A museum stacked with trains, horse-drawn carriages and a 1912 Fiat.

➡ **Laveno Funivia** (p85) Lake Maggiore's funkiest funicular with open-air capsules.

Gardens to Explore

➡ **Parco Sempion**e (p55) Rollerblade around Parco Sempione then take the lift up the Torre Branca.

➡ **Il Vittoriale degli Italiani** (p169) Tour the wildly eccentric house then find the full-sized battleship in the garden.

➡ **Villa Taranto** (p81) Picnic and play amid rolling hillsides of rhododendrons and camellias.

➡ **Parco Scherrer** (p128) Subtropical vegetation and world architectural landmarks in Morcote.

Regions at a Glance

Milan

Museums
Shopping
Nightlife

Modern Italians

From Leonardo da Vinci's groundbreaking *Il Cenacolo* to the 20th-century greats in the Museo del Novecento, Milan has always had a penchant for the avant-garde.

Fashion City

Paris, New York and London may have equally influential designers but they can't compete with an industry town that lives and breathes fashion and takes retail as seriously as it does biotech or engineering.

Cocktails & Culture

Home to Italy's major music producers, Milan is also on the international tour circuit of the best European and North American music acts, theatre and dance troupes; and during the furniture and fashion trade fairs, the city hosts an endless round of stylish cocktail parties.

p42

Lake Maggiore & Around

Villas & Gardens
Scenery
Islands

Lakeside Luxury

Lake Maggiore's reputation for elegance is well earned, with an A-list portfolio of villas (many of them upmarket hotels) around Stresa and Verbania, and expansive gardens where white peacocks wander around Renaissance palaces.

Panoramic Perches

For unforgettable views whiz up Monte Mottarone in the cable car from Stresa or the funiculars that travel high above Locarno.

Water Palaces

Isola Madre and Isola Bella are home to extravagant palaces, while Isola Superiore feels like the island time forgot. Put them together and you've a memorable day out. Away to the west, don't miss Isola San Giulio on Lake Orta.

p72

Lake Como & Around

Towns
Scenery
Villas & Gardens

Urban Style

With its lakeside promenade, medieval lanes and fine, frescoed churches, Como is as beautiful as its chic inhabitants. Away to the northwest, Lugano is a Swiss version of the same, although its old town wraps further around the lake.

Extraordinary Views

Lake Como and the surrounding area has countless spectacular lookouts. Above the lake itself, there's Brunate, Castello di Vezio, Monte Bisbino and Peglio, while further afield consider Cima Sighignola, Monte Brè and Monte San Salvatore.

Lakeside Living

Como's lakeside villas have attracted everyone from Pliny to George Clooney and even James Bond. The best examples are to be found at Como, Cernobbio, Bellagio and Varenna, although the most fabulous are Villa Balbianello and Villa Carlotta.

p100

Bergamo, Brescia & Cremona

Architecture
Scenery
Food & Wine

Medieval Marvels

Bergamo's Città Alta wonderfully evokes a medieval hilltop Italian city, but Cremona, with its grand piazza, and Brescia, with its extant Roman ruins, equally deserve your time.

Alpine Foothills

The valleys north of Bergamo serve as pathways into the Orobie Alps that rise like ramparts along Italy's northern border. Val Taleggio is the most scenic, closely followed by Valle Seriana, but on no account miss Cornello dei Tasso.

Culinary Excellence

The good burghers of Brescia, Bergamo and Cremona know a thing or two about hearty mountain cuisine and heritage Renaissance recipes. Join them for a blow-out meal or get on your bike and track down Italy's finest fizz in Franciacorta.

p132

Lake Garda & Around

Water Sports
Food & Wine
History

All Aboard!

Lake Garda has an unusual meteorological quirk – the winds that blow over its surface are almost as regular as clockwork. Their predictability has ensured Riva, Torbole, Gargnano and Malcesine are magnets for windsurfers and sailors.

Gourmet Garda

A fleet of ferries enables mini voyages of discovery in a landscape rich in food and wine. To the south, Valtenesi olive groves produce some of Italy's finest oils, while the vineyards of Valpolicella, Bardolino and Soave wow the palates with unusual regional wines.

Arty Itineraries

Trace a trail from Roman Verona to medieval Mantua for an eyeful of Renaissance art and architecture, and a marathon tour of Mantegna's masterly frescoes.

p159

On the Road

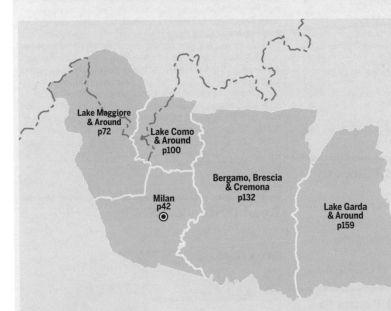

Milan

POP 1.3 MILLION

Best Places to Eat

➡ Cracco (p62)

➡ Latteria di San Marco (p59)

➡ Ristorante Da Giacomo (p61)

➡ Al Bacco (p60)

Best Places to Stay

➡ Tara Verde (p196)

➡ Brera Apartments (p195)

➡ Antica Locanda dei Mercanti (p196)

➡ Bulgari Hotel (p196)

Why Go?

Home of Italy's stock exchange, an industrial powerhouse and the internationally accepted arbiter of taste in fashion and design, Milan is a seething metropolis. At times it can seem brash and soulless but beneath the veneer is a serious sense of history and place. The grand Gothic cathedral, the Duomo, lies at the geographical heart of this one-time Imperial Roman capital, and expresses the love of beauty and power that still drives the city today. Art collections old and new, unparalleled shopping, one of Europe's biggest trade-fair complexes, sparkling nightlife, the prestige of opera at La Scala, the mark of Leonardo da Vinci's genius, a religious addiction to *calcio* (football), and endless opportunities to eat the best of Lombard and Italian food make Milan much more than the puritanically work-obsessed city it is often portrayed as. The city's next big date with destiny is Expo 2015, a world exhibition.

Road Distances (KM)

	Milan	Legnano	Monza	Pavia
Legnano	39			
Monza	23	50		
Pavia	41	93	67	
Vigevano	35	78	55	38

Where to Stay

Finding a room in Milan (let alone a cheap one) isn't easy, particularly during trade fairs and fashion weeks, when rates skyrocket. Services you'd take for granted elsewhere, such as breakfast, sometimes command an extra fee. There may not be a public area such as a bar or lounge, and wi-fi and bar fridges are never a given. Also, don't forget to consider location. The city's sprawl means what constitutes 'the centre' can be highly subjective.

3 PERFECT DAYS

Day 1: The Highlights
Head to the Duomo for a stroll around the gargoyled parapets, then immerse yourself in one of Milan's blockbuster museums: modernists at Museo del Novecento, international exhibits at Palazzo Reale and Italian masters at the Pinacoteca di Brera. Lunch at Peck Italian Bar and, in the afternoon, mix culture with pleasure at Castello Sforzesco and Parco Sempione. Finish your day in front of Leonardo da Vinci's *Il Cenacolo*.

Day 2: Fashion & Design
Breakfast at Princi, then take a quick course in Milanese interior design in the Renaissance apartments of Gian Giacomo Poldi-Pezzoli or the modernist villa of the Necchi-Campiglio sisters. Afterwards lunch with models in Il Salumaio di Montenapoleone and spend the afternoon browsing the Quadrilatero d'Oro. In the evening jump on the tram and head for buzzing Navigli for dinner canal-side.

Day 3: Science & Saints
Rise early to visit Milan's outstanding Science Museum, the mosaics in the Basilica di Sant'Ambrogio and Leonardo da Vinci's drawings in the Unesco World Heritage Site of Basilica di Sant Maria delle Grazie. Then hotfoot it to Monza for lunch and an adrenalin-pumping drive around Monza's race track.

Getting Away From It All

➡ **Artistic alone-time** Seek out the amazing Boschi-di Stefano (p53) apartment for an art fix all to yourself.

➡ **Aperitivo** Shed your cares with a cocktail in the tranquil garden of the Bulgari Hotel (p61).

➡ **Get some green** Picnic and sunbathe in Parco Sempione (p55).

➡ **A trip to the country** Take a short train ride to the rolling vineyards of Oltrepò Pavese (p70).

DON'T MISS

Fashion alert: reserve ahead for fascinating behind-the-scenes tours (p53) of La Scala's costume and craft workshops.

Best Tours

➡ Tickitaly (p56)
➡ Enrico Toti (p56)
➡ Bike & the City (p58)
➡ Tours of Milan (p59)

Advance Planning

➡ **Three months** Book accommodation if travelling during trade fairs.

➡ **Two months** Buy tickets for *Il Cenacolo* and Serie A football matches.

➡ **One month** Reserve seats at La Scala and Michelin-starred restaurants.

➡ **One week** Checkout *aperitivi* hotspots and events at *Corriere della Sera*.

Resources

➡ **Cenacolo Vinciano** (www.cenacolovinciano. org) Booking for *The Last Supper*.

➡ **Milan Is Tourism** (www. turismo.milano.it) Milan's city website.

➡ **Milano da Bere** (www. milanodabere.it) Events, dining and drinking.

➡ **Angloinfo Milan** (http:// milan.angloinfo.com) A global expat network.

Milan Highlights

1 Climbing to the roof terraces of Milan's marble **cathedral** (p45) for views of spires and flying buttresses.

2 Admiring centuries of invention in da Vinci's masterful mural, **Il Cenacolo** (p55), and Italy's finest **Science Museum** (p56).

3 Getting passionate about form at the **Triennale Design Museum** (p55).

4 Glimpsing Renaissance art in Poldi Pezzoli's **house-museum** (p52) and the **Pinacoteca di Brera** (p52).

5 Discovering the modernists at the **Museo del Novecento** (p45).

6 Mingling with old and new money during an evening of opera at **Teatro alla Scala** (p64).

7 Strutting your stuff on Planet Fashion's finest block, the **Quadrilatero d'Oro** (p49).

8 Racing or rollerblading around Monza's world-famous **autodrome** (p70).

History

From its founding as a Celtic settlement, Milan (or Mediolanum – Middle of the Plain) was always an important crossroads. It was here that Christianity was declared the official religion of the Roman Empire in AD 313. As a powerful medieval city-state, Milan expanded its influence by conquest under a series of colourful (and often bloody) dynasties – the Torrianis, the Viscontis and finally the Sforzas. However, under Spanish rule from 1525 and then the Austrians from 1713, Milan lost some of its *brio*. In 1860, it joined the nascent, united Kingdom of Italy.

Benito Mussolini founded the Fascist Party in Milan in 1919 and his lifeless body was strung up in the same city, in Piazzale Loreto, by the partisans who had summarily executed him towards the end of WWII in 1945. Allied bombings during WWII destroyed much of central Milan. Treasures that survived include the Duomo, Leonardo da Vinci's *Il Cenacolo* (just), the Castello Sforzesco and the Teatro alla Scala opera house. Milan was quick to get back on its feet after the war and what still sets it apart today is its creative streak and can-do attitude.

Armani, Versace, Prada, Dolce & Gabbana, Gucci and many more took off on Milan's runways. Fashionistas make a pilgrimage here to shop at the designers' flagship stores in the Quadrilatero d'Oro (Golden Quad).

Inevitably, not all that glistens is squeaky clean gold. In 1992 the Tangentopoli scandal broke, implicating thousands of Italian (and among them many Milanese) politicians, officials and businesspeople. Tax evasion on a huge scale and pay-offs to financial police were at the heart of the investigations – fashion designer Giorgio Armani accepted a plea bargain following bribery charges.

One of those investigated but never convicted is Milan's self-made media mogul Silvio Berlusconi. He moved into politics in the 1990s and has since been elected prime minister three times, most recently in 2008, although he was forced to resign his post in 2011 after losing his majority amid the growing European debt crisis. The city's centre-left mayor, Giuliano Pisapia (the city's first mayor from a left-wing party), elected in 2011, runs a coalition government with various centrist and left-wing parties.

◉ Sights

◉ Duomo & San Babila

Milan's centre is conveniently compact. The splendid cathedral sits in a vast piazza which throngs with tourists and touts. Further west, the city's interior design showrooms cluster around Piazza San Babila amid grand Novecento and Liberty buildings.

★**Duomo** CATHEDRAL
(Map p50; www.duomomilano.it; Piazza del Duomo; adult/reduced Battistero di San Giovanni €4/2, terraces stairs €7/3.50, terraces lift €12/6, treasury €2; ⊙ 7am-6.45pm, roof terraces 9am-6pm, baptistry 9.30am-5pm, treasury 9.30am-5pm Mon-Sat; [♿]; [M] Duomo) A vision in pink Candoglia marble, Milan's cathedral aptly reflects the city's creativity and ambition. Its pearly white facade, adorned with 135 spires and 3200 statues, rises like the filigree of a fairy tale tiara, wowing the crowds with extravagant detail. The vast interior is no less impressive, with the largest stained glass windows in Christendom, while below is the early Christian baptistry and crypt, where the remains of the saintly Carlo Borromeo are on display in a rock crystal casket.

Begun by Giangaleazzo Visconti in 1387, the cathedral's design was originally considered unfeasible. Canals had to be dug to transport the vast quantities of marble to the centre of the city and new technologies were invented to cater for the never-before-attempted scale. There was also that small matter of style. The Gothic lines went out of fashion and were considered 'too French,' so it took on several looks as the years, then centuries, dragged on. Its slow construction became the byword for an impossible task (*fabrica del Dom* in the Milanese dialect). Indeed, much of its ornament is 19th-century neo-Gothic, with the final touches only applied in the 1960s. Crowning it all is a gilded copper statue of the Madonnina (Little Madonna), the city's traditional protector.

The most spectacular view is through the innumerable marble spires and pinnacles that adorn the rooftop. On a clear day you can see the Alps.

★**Museo del Novecento** ART GALLERY
(Map p50; [✆] 02 88 44 4072; www.museodelnove cento.org; Piazza del Duomo 12; adult/reduced €5/3; ⊙ 9.30am-7.30pm Tue-Sun, 2.30-7.30pm Mon; [M] Duomo) Overlooking the Piazza del

Greater Milan

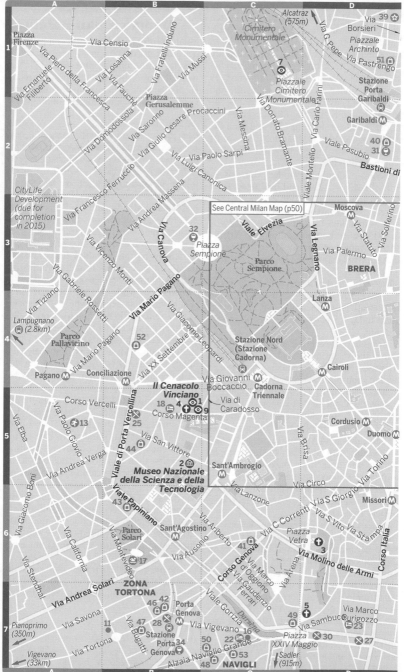

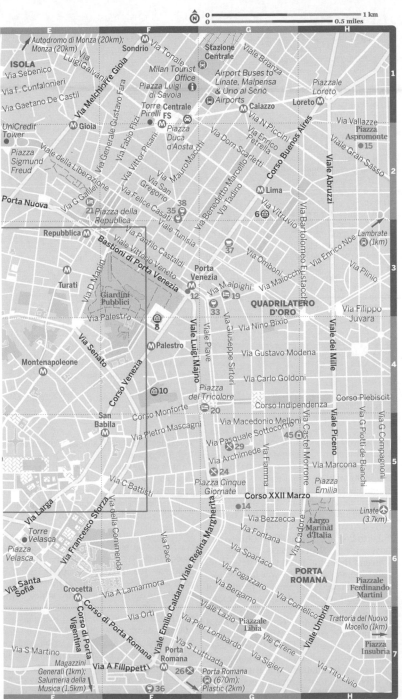

N

0 — 1 km
0 — 0.5 miles

Greater Milan

Duomo, with fabulous views of the cathedral, is Mussolini's Arengario, from where he would harangue huge crowds in the glory days of his regime. Now it houses Milan's museum of 20th-century art. Built around a futuristic spiral ramp (an ode to the Guggenheim), the lower floors are cramped, but the heady collection, which includes the likes of Umberto Boccioni, Campigli, de Chirico and Marinetti, more than distracts.

Ascend the spiral ramp through chronological rooms, which take you from Volpedo's powerful neo-impressionist painting of striking workers, *Il Quarto Stato*, through the dynamic work of Futurist greats such as Boccioni, Carlo Carra, Gino Severini and Giacomo Balla, and on to Abstractism, Surrealism, Spatialism and Arte Povera. Aside from the unique coherence of the collection, it provides a fascinating social commentary on Italy's trajectory through Fascism, two world wars and into the new dawn of the technological era.

Afterwards dine in Giacomo Arengario (Map p50; ☑02 720 9 3814; www.giacomoaren gario.com; Via Guglielmo Marconi 1; meals €30-40; ☉noon-midnight; ❀; Ⓜ Duomo), the third-floor *bistrot* overlooking the Duomo.

Teatro alla Scala   OPERA HOUSE
(La Scala; Map p50; www.teatroallascala.org; Via Filodrammatici 2) Giuseppe Piermarini's grand 2800-seat theatre was inaugurated in 1778 with Antonio Salieri's *Europa Riconosciuta*. It replaced the previous theatre, which burnt down in a fire after a carnival gala. Costs were covered by the sale of *palchi* (private boxes), of which there are six gilt-and-crimson tiers. When rehearsals are not in session you can stand in boxes 13, 15 and 18 for a glimpse of the jewel-like interior.

Above the private boxes, two *loggione* (galleries) allow you to peek over the heads of Milanese plutocrats at one of the largest stages in Italy. Occupants of these seats, the *loggionisti*, are the opera's fiercest critics, famously booing tenor Roberto Alagna off stage in 2006, to be hurriedly replaced by his understudy Palombi who, lacking the time to change into full costume, appeared in his T-shirt and jeans.

In the theatre's **museum** (La Scala Museum; Map p50; ☑ 02 433 53 521; Largo Ghiringhelli 1; admission €6; ☺ 9am-12.30pm & 1.30-5.30pm), harlequin costumes and a spinet inscribed with the command 'Inexpert hand, touch me not!' hint at centuries of Milanese musical drama, on and off stage.

Palazzo Reale   MUSEUM, PALACE
(Map p50; www.comune.milano.it/palazzoreale; Piazza del Duomo 12; exhibitions €5-12, Museo della Reggia free; ☺ exhibitions 2.30-7.30pm Mon, 9.30am-7.30pm Tue, Wed, Fri & Sun, 9.30am-10.30pm Thu & Sat, museo 9.30am-5.30pm Tue-Sun; Ⓜ Duomo) Empress Maria Theresia's favourite architect Giuseppe Piermarini gave this town hall and Visconti palace a neoclassical overhaul in the late 18th century. The supremely elegant interiors were all but destroyed by WWII bombs; the **Sala delle Cariatidi** remains unrenovated as a reminder of war's indiscriminate destruction. Now blockbuster shows wow the crowds with artists as diverse as Titian, Bacon and Dario Fo.

Chiesa di Santa Maria Presso di San Satiro   CHURCH
(Map p50; Via Speronari 3; ☺ 7.30am-11.30am Mon-Fri, 3.30-6.30pm Sat; Ⓜ Duomo) **FREE** Here's an escape from the Zara/Benneton/H&M maelstrom. Ludovico Sforza saw potential in this little church, built on top of the 9th-century mausoleum of martyr San Satiro, and asked architect Donato Bramante to refurbish it in 1482. His ambition wasn't dampened by the project's scale: a trompe l'œil coffered niche on the shallow apse makes the backdrop to the altar mimic the Pantheon in Rome.

Biblioteca e Pinacoteca Ambrosiana   GALLERY, LIBRARY
(Map p50; ☑ 02 80 69 21; www.ambrosiana.it; Piazza Pio XI 2; adult/conc €8/5; ☺ 10am-5.30pm Tue-Sun; Ⓜ Cordusio) Europe's first public library, built in 1609, the **Biblioteca Ambrosiana** was more a symbol of intellectual ferment than quiet scholarship. It houses over 75,000 volumes and 35,000 manuscripts including Leonardo da Vinci's priceless collection of drawings, the *Atlantic Codex*. Later an art gallery, the **Pinacoteca**, was added exhibiting Italian paintings from the 14th to the 20th century, most famously Caravaggio's *Canestra di Frutta* (Basket of Fruit), which launched his career and Italy's ultrarealist traditions.

Galleria Vittorio Emanuele II SHOPPING ARCADE
(Map p50; Piazza del Duomo; Ⓜ Duomo) So much more than a shopping arcade, the neoclassical Galleria Vittorio Emanuele is a soaring iron-and-glass structure known locally as *il salotto bueno*, the city's fine drawing room. Shaped like a crucifix, it also marks the *passeggiata* (evening stroll) route from Piazza di Duomo to Piazza di Marino and the doors of La Scala.

◉ Brera & the Quadrilatero d'Oro

North of the Duomo, Brera's ancient buildings and cobbled streets are a reminder that Milan wasn't always a modern metropolis,

---

ADOPT A SPIRE

The building of Milan's cathedral was such an epic feat that it necessitated the creation of a 'factory' responsible for all operational activities and construction. That factory is the Fabbrica del Duomo, Italy's oldest company. It has overseen the work of the Duomo's construction from 1387 until the last gate was inaugurated in January 1965.

Today it continues the enormous task of maintaining the cathedral. This is no mean feat when five million people (and 40% of all the visitors to Milan) pass through the bronze doors each year and new austerity measures slashed 30% off Italy's culture budget.

But now you, too, can chip in with the Fabbrica's latest inspired idea, **Adopt a Spire** (www.getyourspire.com). This crowd-sourced campaign aims to raise some €25 million in order to restore 134 of the cathedral's fabulous spires. Major donors (contributing €100,000) will even have their names engraved on the spires, but you can donate as little as €10.

Central Milan

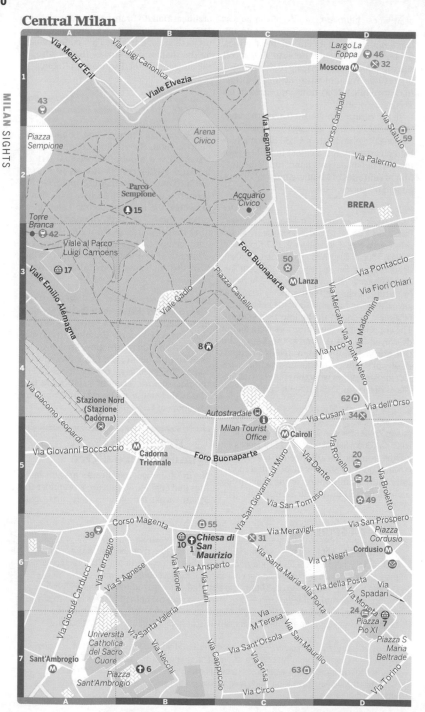

A **B** **C** **D**

Via Melzi d'Eril
Via Luigi Canonica
Largo La Foppa 46
Moscova 32

Viale Elvezia

43

Piazza Sempione

Arena Civico

Via Legnano

Corso Garibaldi

Via Statuto 59

Via Palermo

Parco Sempione 15

Acquario Civico

BRERA

Torre Branca 42

Viale al Parco Luigi Camoens

17

Viale Emilio Alemagna

Viale Gadio

Piazza Castello

Foro Buonaparte

50

Lanza

Via Pontaccio

Via Fiori Chiari

Via Mercato Via Ponte Vetero Via Madonnina

Via Arco

8

Via Giacomo Leopardi

Stazione Nord (Stazione Cadorna)

Autostradale
Milan Tourist Office

Cairoli

62

Via dell'Orso

Via Cusani 34

Via Rovello

20

21

Via Broletto

Via Giovanni Boccaccio

Cadorna Triennale

Foro Buonaparte

Via San Giovanni sul Muro

Via Dante

Via San Tomaso

49

Corso Magenta

39

55

10 Chiesa di San Maurizio 1

31

Via Meravigli

Via San Prospero
Piazza Cordusio

Cordusio

Via Terraggio

Via S Agnese

Via Nirone

Via Ansperto

Via Luini

Via Santa Maria alla Porta

Via G Negri

Via della Posta

Via Spadari

Via Moneta

24

Piazza Pio XI 7

Via Giosuè Carducci

Università Cattolica del Sacro Cuore

Via Santa Valeria

Via Necchi

Via M Teresa

Via Sant'Orsola

Via San Maurilio

Via Brisa

Piazza S Maria Beltrade

Sant'Ambrogio

6

Piazza Sant'Ambrogio

Via Cappuccio

63

Via Circo

Via Torino

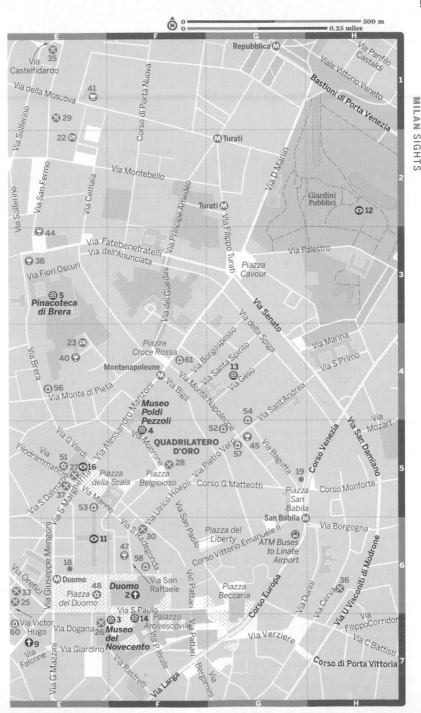

Central Milan

while northeast the Quadrilatero d'Oro (Golden Quad) sings a siren song to luxury label lovers the world over. It also goes by the diminutive Monte Nap after Via Monte Napoleone, which is one of its defining four streets along with Via della Spiga, Via Sant'Andrea and Via Borgospesso.

★ **Pinacoteca di Brera**   GALLERY
(Map p50; ☎02 722 63 264; www.brera.benicul turali.it; Via Brera 28; adult/reduced child €6/3; ⊙8.30am-7.15pm Tue-Sun; ⓜLanza) Located upstairs from the centuries-old Accademia di Belle Arti (still one of Italy's most prestigious art schools), this gallery houses Milan's most impressive collection of old masters, much of the bounty 'lifted' from Venice by

Napoleon. Rembrandt, Goya and van Dyck all have a place in the collection, but you're here to see the Italians: Titian, Tintoretto, glorious Veronese, groundbreaking Mantegna, the Bellini brothers and a Caravaggio.

★ **Museo Poldi Pezzoli**   HOUSE MUSEUM
(Map p50; ☎02 79 48 89; www.museopoldipezzoli. it; Via Alessandro Manzoni 12; adult/reduced €9/6; ⊙10am-6pm Wed-Mon; ⓜMontenapoleone) Inheriting his vast fortune at the age of 24, Gian Giacomo Poldi Pezzoli also inherited his mother's love of art and during extensive European travels he was inspired by the 'house museum' that was later to become London's V&A. As his collection grew, Pezzoli had the idea of transforming his apart-

ments into a series of historically themed rooms based on the great art periods of the past (the Middle Ages, Early Renaissance, Baroque and Rococo). Although crammed with a collection of big ticket artworks, including Botticelli, Bellini and the beautiful *Portrait of a Woman* by Pollaiolo, these Sala d'Artista are exquisite works of art in their own right.

Museo Bagatti Valsecchi   HOUSE MUSEUM
(Map p50; ✆02 7600 6132; www.museobagattivalsecchi.org; Via Gesù 5; adult/reduced €8/4, Wed €4; ◷1-5.45pm Tue-Sun; Ⓜ Montenapoleone) Though born a few centuries too late, the Bagatti Valsecchi brothers, Fausto and Giuseppe, were determined to be Renaissance men, and from 1878 to 1887 they built their home as a living museum of the Quattrocento. Decorated after the style of the ducal palaces in Mantua, the apartments are full of Renaissance furnishings, ceiling friezes, tapestries and paintings. Even the period stone bath was discreetly retrofitted for running water, a modernisation of their own era.

Villa Necchi Campiglio   HOUSE MUSEUM
(Map p46; ✆02 763 40 121; www.casemuseo.it; Via Mozart 14; adult/child €8/4; ◷10am-6pm Wed-Sun; Ⓜ San Babila) Set in a beautiful garden with tall magnolia trees, this villa is a symbol of Milan's modernist imaginings in the early 1930s. Designed by Rationalist architect Piero Portaluppi for Pavian heiresses Nedda and Gigina Necchi, the house blends art deco and rationalist styles symbolising an outlook that was astoundingly modern while at the same time anchored in a world that was fast slipping away.

Quotidian details – Bauhaus-influenced monograms on hair brushes, silk evening frocks hanging at the ready – are as enthralling as the sleek architectural lines and big ticket artworks by Morandi and de Chirico.

Giardini Pubblici   GARDEN
(Map p50; ◷6.30am-sunset; Ⓜ Palestro) A life story unfolds as you follow pebble paths past bumper cars and a carousel, onward past a game of kick to kick, kissing teens, a beer kiosk, baby prams, jogging paths and shady benches. Jump in, or just stop and smell the roses. For grey days the charming Museo Civico di Storia Naturale (Natural History Museum; Map p46; ✆02 8846 3337; Corso Venezia 55; adult/conc €3/1.50; ◷9am-5.30pm Tue-Sun; Ⓜ Palestro) beckons families; the grand neo-Romanesque building houses di-

BEHIND THE SCENES AT LA SCALA

To glimpse the inner workings of La Scala visit the **Ansaldo Workshops** (Map p46; ✆390 243353521; www.teatroalascala.org; Via Bergognone 34; admission €5; ◷individuals 3pm, groups 9am-noon & 2-4pm Tue & Thu; Ⓜ Porto Genova) where the stage sets are crafted and painted, and where some 800 to 1000 new costumes are handmade each season. Tours on Tuesday and Thursday must be booked in advance and are guided by the heads of each creative department.

MILAN SIGHTS

nosaurs, fossils and the largest geology collection in Europe.

Casa Museo Boschi-di Stefano   HOUSE MUSEUM
(Map p46; ✆02 2024 0568; www.fondazioneboschidistefano.it; Via Giorgio Jan 15; ◷2-6pm Tue-Sun Sep-Jul, daily Aug; Ⓜ Lima) **FREE** Milan's most eccentric museum of 20th-century Italian painting is crowded salon-style in a purpose-built, 1930s apartment that still has the appearance of the haute-bourgeois home it once was. It's a heady art hit with Boccioni's dynamic brushstrokes propelling painting towards Futurism, the nostalgically metaphysical Campigli and de Chirico, and the restless, expressionist Informels all crowding the small salons decked with suitably avant-garde furnishings.

◉ Parco Sempione & Corso Garibaldi

Walk beneath the imposing battlements of Castello Sforzesco en route to one of its museums or Parco Sempione, and modern Milan slips away. On the southwestern edge of the park is the imposing Design Triennale, to the northeast the emerging skyscrapers of the Porta Nuova and buzzing Corso Como and Corso Garibaldi, which have a cruisey, southern Californian feel in summer.

Castello Sforzesco   CASTLE, MUSEUM
(Map p50; ✆02 884 63 700; www.milanocastello.it; Piazza Castello; ◷7am-7pm summer, to 6pm winter; Ⓜ Cairoli) Originally a Visconti fortress, this iconic red-brick castle was later home to the mighty Sforza dynasty who ruled Renaissance Milan. The castle's defences were

PINACOTECA DI BRERA

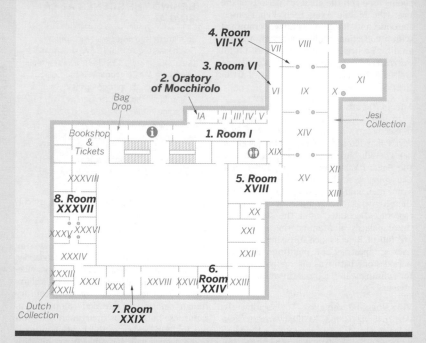

4. **Room VII–IX**

3. **Room VI**

2. **Oratory of Mocchirolo**

Bag Drop

Bookshop & Tickets

1. **Room I**

Jesi Collection

5. **Room XVIII**

8. **Room XXXVII**

6. **Room XXIV**

Dutch Collection

7. **Room XXIX**

🏃 Museum Tour
Pinacoteca di Brera

LENGTH 2.5 HOURS

Start with a blast of Renaissance brilliance in ❶ **Room I**, lined with Donato Bramante's superhero *Men at Arms* and Bernardino Luini's charming frescoes. To your left is a reconstruction of the ❷ **Oratory of Mocchi-rolo**, thought to be the work of Giotto.

Whiz through rooms II–V and emerge in ❸ **Room VI** in front of Mantegna's shocking *Lamento sul Cristo morto* (Lamentation Over the Dead Christ), where the use of rigorous perspective on the foreshortened corpse gives you an eerie sense of standing at the foot of Christ's death bed. To the right is Bellini's sad-eyed *Madonna col Bambino*.

From here you're vaulted into the High Renaissance in ❹ **Rooms VII–IX**, where you'll find canvases by Venetian heavy-weights Titian, Veronese and Tintoretto. Room IX brings together some of their great-est works including Titian's *St Jerome* and

Veronese's *Cena in Casa di Simone* (Supper in the House of Simon).

Continue to ❺ **Room XVIII**, where you'll find museum restorers at work in a temperature-controlled room. From here the collection journeys south to artists of the Emilia-Romagna school. Piero della Franc-esca's monumental Montefeltro altarpiece (1472–74) is the prize of ❻ **Room XXIV** along with Raphael's *Wedding of the Virgin* (1504).

From their glimmering colours you're barely prepared for the emotional thump that ❼ **Room XXIX** delivers. It's home to the academy's only Caravaggio, *Cena in Emmaus* (Supper at Emmaus).

Breeze through Canaletto's views of Venice to ❽ **Room XXXVII**, where you'll find Franc-esco Hayez. Director of the academy, Hayez was *the* portrait painter for the Lombard no-bility; his sitters included Teresa Manzoni and the Conte Giovanni Battisti, both of whom are represented here. Hayez's luminous *Il Bacio* (The Kiss; 1859) is one of the most repro-duced artworks in the gallery.

designed by the multitalented da Vinci; Napoleon later drained the moat and removed the drawbridges. Today, it shelters seven specialised museums, which gather together intriguing fragments of Milan's cultural and civic history, including Michelangelo's final work, the *Rondanini Pietà*.

➡ *Civiche Raccolta d'Arte Antica*

Housed in the ducal apartments, the **Museum of Ancient Art** is a stellar collection. From paleo-Christian frescoes to the fine equestrian tomb of Bernarbò Visconti and sculpted reliefs depicting Milan's triumph over Barbarossa, the artworks tell the turbulent story of the birth of Italy's first city *comune*, murderous dynastic and regional ambitions and lavish artistic patronage, which made this one of Europe's finest courts.

➡ *Pinacoteca e Raccolte d'Arte*

On the first floor the **Furniture Museum** and castle **Art Gallery** blend seamlessly, leading you from Ducal wardrobes and writing desks through to a collection of Lombard Gothic art. Among the masterpieces are Andrea Mantegna's *Trivulzio Madonna*, Vincenzo Foppa's St Sebastian and Bramantino's *Noli me tangere* (Touch me not).

Parco Sempione   PARK
(Map p50; ⊙6.30am-nightfall; MCadorna, Cairoli) FREE Situated behind the Castello Sforzesco, Parco Sempione was a resounding success, and even today Milanese of all ages come to enjoy its winding paths, copses and ornamental ponds. Giò Ponti's spindly, 1933 steel tower (built in two months for a Triennale exhibition) provides a fantastic 108m-high viewing platform over the park. Take the lift up at sunset, or at night to watch city lights twinkle, and lord it over the **Just Cavalli Café** (Map p50; ⊘02 311817; www.justcavallimilano.com; Torre Branca; ⊙8pm-2am Mon-Sun; underground rail Cadorna) crowd below.

Triennale di Milano   DESIGN MUSEUM
(Map p50; ⊘02 72 43 41; www.triennaledesignmuseum.it; Viale Emilio Alemanga 6; adult/reduced €8/6.50; ⊙10.30am-8.30pm Tue, Wed, Sat & Sun, to 11pm Thu & Fri; P; MCadorna) Italy's first Triennale took place in 1923 in Monza. It aimed to promote interest in Italian design and applied arts, from 'the spoon to the city', and its success led to the creation of Giovanni Muzio's **Palazzo d'Arte** in Milan in 1933. Since then it has championed design in all its forms, although the triennale formula has since been replaced by long annual events, with international exhibits as part of the program.

Planet Expo 2015: Learn, Enjoy, Have Fun is the latest multisensory exhibition that focuses on the 2015 Expo.

Cimitero Monumentale   CEMETERY
(Map p46; ⊘02 8846 5600; www.monumentale.net; Piazzale Cimitero Monumentale; ⊙8am-6pm Tue-Sun; MGaribaldi) FREE Behind striking Renaissance-revival black-and-white walls, Milan's wealthy have kept their dynastic ambitions alive long after death with grand sculptural gestures since 1866. Nineteenth-century death-the-maiden eroticism gives way to some fabulous abstract forms from midcentury masters. Studio BBPR's geometric steel-and-marble memorial to Milan's WWII concentration camp dead is stark and moving. Grab a map inside the forecourt.

⊙ Corso Magenta & Sant'Ambrogio

It's usually Leonardo da Vinci's *Il Cenacolo* or the Basilica di Sant'Ambrogio that draw visitors here, but there's an equal mix of the sacred and the secular in these leafy streets. Piazza Cordusio is the home of high finance, hence the bars full of young bankers, while to the south Bramante's cloisters ring with the chatter of students at the sprawling Università Cattolica del Sacro Cuore.

★ **Il Cenacolo Vinciano**   MURAL
(Map p46; ⊘02 8942 1146; www.architettonicimilano.lombardia.beniculturali.it; adult/reduced €6.50/3.25, plus booking fee €1.50; MCadorna Triennale) Milan's most famous mural, Leonardo da Vinci's *Il Cenacolo* (Last Supper), is hidden away on a wall of the refectory adjoining the Basilica di Santa Maria delle Grazie. Depicting Christ and his disciples at the dramatic moment when Christ reveals he is aware of the betrayal afoot, it is a masterful

---

ⓘ CASEMUSEOCARD

The House Museum Card (€15; www.casemuseomilano.it) gives discounted access to Milan's four historic houses: the Ba gatti Valsecchi palazzo, the Piero Portaluppi–designed Villa Necchi Campiglio and Boschi-di Stefano apartment, and the 19th-century Poldi Pezzoli. Valid for six months, it also entitles the bearer to 10% off in the museum bookshops. You can purchase the card at any of the houses.

FIERA

Milan's two *fiera* (fairgrounds) play host to an endless round of trade fairs as well as the biannual fashion blockbusters. Massimiliano Fuksas' brilliantly engineered **Fiera Milano** (www.fierami lano.it) exhibition space was built on the Agip oil refinery in Rho-Pero, around 40 minutes out of town by metro. In action since 2006, its billowing glass-and-steel sail floats over 1.4km of halls, capable of holding up to half a million visitors. The city's historic fairgrounds just northwest of Parco Sempione are the site of the CityLife redevelopment but smaller fairs are still held at the remaining pavilions, known as Fiera Milano City.

psychological study and one of the world's most iconic images.

Restoration of *Il Cenacolo* was completed in 1999 after more than 22 years' work. The mural was in a lamentable state after centuries of damage. Da Vinci himself is partly to blame: his experimental mix of oil and tempera was applied between 1495 and 1498, rather than over a week as is typical of fresco techniques. The Dominicans didn't help matters in 1652 by raising the refectory floor, hacking off a lower section of the scene, including Jesus' feet. The most damage was caused by restorers in the 19th century, whose alcohol and cotton-wool technique removed an entire layer. But its condition does nothing to lessen its astonishing beauty. Stare at the ethereal, lucent windows beyond the narrative action and you'll wonder if da Vinci's uncharacteristic short-sightedness wasn't divinely inspired.

When Leonardo was at work on the masterpiece a star-struck monk noted that he would sometimes arrive in the morning, stare at yesterday's effort, then promptly call it quits for the day. Your visit too will be a similarly brief (15 minutes) unless you invest in a **Tickitaly** (www.tickitaly.com; guided tour €69; ☉ 7.15pm & 8pm) guided, after-hours tour, which allows an extended 30 minute visit.

Basilica di Santa Maria
delle Grazie BASILICA
(Map p46; Corso Magenta; ☉ 8.30am-7pm Tue-Sun; Ⓜ Conciliazione, Cadorna) **FREE** Any visit to *Il Cenacolo* must be accompanied by a tour of

Santa Maria delle Grazie, a Unesco World Heritage Site. Built by Guiniforte Solari with later additions by Bramante, it encapsulates the magnificence of the Milanese court of Ludovico 'il Moro' Sforza and Beatrice d'Este. Articulated in fine brickwork and terracotta, the building is robust but fanciful; its apse is topped by Bramante's masterful cupola and its interior lined with frescoes.

In the **sacristy** (Map p46; Via Caradosso 1; admission €10, combination ticket with Biblioteca Ambrosiana €20; ☉ 8.30am-7pm Tue-Sun), Sagrestia Monumentale del Bramante, more treasures await. Illuminated pages from the *Codex Atlanticus,* the largest collection of da Vinci's drawings in the world. Over 1119 of them were gathered together by sculptor Pompeo Leoni, enough to make up 12 immense volumes. Every page will be displayed in a rotating exhibit here and at the Biblioteca Ambrosiana until the start of Expo 2015.

★ Chiesa di San Maurizio CHAPEL, CONVENT
(Map p50; Corso Magenta 15; ☉ 9am-noon & 2-5.30pm Tue-Sun; Ⓜ Cadorna) The 16th-century royal chapel and convent of San Maurizio is Milan's hidden crown jewel, every inch of it covered in Bernardino Luini's breathtaking frescoes. Many of them immortalise Ippolita Sforza, the star of Milan's literary scene at the time, and her family. Duck through a small doorway on the left to enter the secluded convent hall where blissful martyred women saints bear their tribulations serenely – note Santa Lucia calmly holding her lost eyes, and Santa Agata casually carrying her breasts on a platter.

Civico Museo Archeologico MUSEUM
(Map p50; ☏ 02 8844 5208; Corso Magenta 15; adult/child €2/1; ☉ 9am-5.30pm Tue-Sun; Ⓜ Cadorna) Adjoining the church of San Maurizio is the 9th century Monastero Maggiore, once the most important Benedictine convent in the city and now the backdrop for the archaeological museum. Accessed via a cloister where fragments of the city's Roman walls can be seen, and through 3rd-century frescoed **Ansperto Tower**, it provides great insight into old Mediolanum with well-curated collections of Etruscan, Greek, Roman, Gothic and Lombard artefacts.

★ Museo Nazionale della
Scienza e della Tecnologia MUSEUM
(Map p46; ☏ 02 48 55 51; www.museoscienza.org; Via San Vittore 21; adult/child €10/7, submarine tour €8; ☉ 9.30am-5pm Tue-Fri, to 6.30pm Sat, Sun

& holidays; Ⓜ Sant'Ambrogio) Kids, would-be inventors and geeks will go goggle-eyed at Milan's impressive museum of science and technology, the largest of its kind in Italy. It is a fitting tribute in a city where arch-inventor Leonardo da Vinci did much of his finest work. The 16th-century monastery, where it is housed, features a collection of over 10,000 items, including models based on da Vinci's engineering sketches, halls devoted to sciences of physics, astronomy and horology, and outdoor hangars housing steam trains, planes, full-sized galleons and Italy's first submarine, Enrico Toti.

Basilica di Sant'Ambrogio   BASILICA

(Map p50; ☑ 02 8645 0895; Piazza Sant'Ambrogio 15; ⊗ 8.30am-7pm; Ⓜ Sant'Ambrogio) **FREE** St Ambrose, Milan's patron saint and one-time superstar bishop, is buried in the crypt of the Basilica di Sant'Ambrogio, which he founded in AD 379. It's a fitting legacy, built and rebuilt with a purposeful simplicity that is truly uplifting; the seminal Lombard Romanesque basilica. Shimmering altar mosaics and a biographical 835 AD gilt altarpiece light up the shadowy vaulted interior.

The second chapel on the right contains frescoes by Tiepolo. While along the south aisle, there's some precious 5th-century sparkle: mosaics adorn the Sacello San Vittore in Ciel d'Oro, its 'golden sky' dome supported by winged monkeys and griffins.

◉ Navigli & Porta Romana

The Navigli neighbourhood is named after its most identifiable feature – canals. Designed as the motorways of medieval Milan,

they powered the city's fortunes until the railroads, WWII bombs and neglect brought about their demise in the 1970s. These days they provide a scenic backdrop to the bookshops, boutiques and bars, which make this Milan's most kicking bohemian 'burb.

Basilica di San Lorenzo   BASILICA

(Map p46; Parco delle Basiliche; Ⓜ Missori) Virtually ignored by everyone, yet, when you stumble across it, it is difficult not to be bowled over by this hotchpotch jumble of towers, lodges, apses and domes. In spite of appearances, it really is one basilica. At its heart is an early-Christian circular structure with three attached, octagonal chapels, dating to about the 4th century. What's left of a Romanesque atrium leads to the heart of the church and before it stand 16 Roman columns, now a primary hangout for kissing teens.

Basilica di Sant'Eustorgio   BASILICA

(Map p46; Piazza Sant'Eustorgio; ⊗ 7.45am-6.30pm; ☒ 2, 3) Built in the 4th century to house the bones of the Three Kings, Sant'Eustorgio is one of Milan's oldest churches. Its harmonious exterior belies its rabble-rousing past as Milan's Inquisition HQ, but the real draw is Pigello Portinari's private chapel. Representative of the Medici bank in Milan, Portinari had the cash to splash on Milan's finest Renaissance chapel, built in Gothic style and frescoed with masterpieces by Vicenzo Foppa.

In the centre, borne aloft on life-size statues of the Cardinal Virtues, is the white marble Ark of St Peter Martyr, Prior of Como. It's sculptural detail and fancy gothic *aedicule* (canopy supported by columns) sheltering

---

NAVIGLI MARKETS

Overlooking the Darsèna, once the city's main port where the confluence of two canals, linking the city with the Ticino and Po rivers, converged, is the Mercato Comunale (Food Market; Map p46; Piazza XXIV Maggio; ⊗ 8.30am-1pm Mon, 8.30am-1pm & 4-7.30pm Tue-Fri, 8.30am-1.30pm & 3.30-6.30pm Sat; Ⓜ Porta Genova, ☒ 3). Open Monday to Saturday, it is the city's main covered market, selling fresh fruit, vegetables and fish. Northwest, Viale Gabriele d'Annunzio merges into Viale Papiniano, where the city's main flea market (Map p46; Viale Papiniano; ⊗ 8am-2pm Tue, to 5pm Sat) operates. It's at its best on Saturday morning.

On the last Sunday of the month the city's most scenic market, the Mercatore Antiquario di Navigli (Map p46; www.naviglilive.it; ⊗ 9am-6pm last Sun of month; Ⓜ Porta Genova), sets-up along a 2km stretch of the Navigli Grande. With over 400 well-vetted antique and secondhand traders, it provides hours of treasure-hunting pleasure.

DON'T MISS

ZONA TORTONA

When Italian *Vogue* art director Flavio Lucchini opened a photo studio on scruffy Via Tortona in 1983 everyone thought he was mad. But now the 'zone' is a home to the head offices of Diesel and Armani, and is a magnet for designers, artists and artisans. Find cult eyewear at Mafalda 86 (Map p46; ✆ 333 854 9929; www.mafalda86.it; Via Tortona 19; Ⓜ Porta Genova), methacrylate costume jewellery at iStudio (Map p46; ✆ 02 8942 2722; Via Tortona 12; Ⓜ Porta Genova) and funky footwear at Federea Milano (Map p46; ✆ 02 8339 0446; www.federeamilano.it; Via Tortona 12; Ⓜ Porta Genova).

During the Salone del Mobile, the area hosts satellite shows, launches and parties, and is a destination in itself.

the Virgin and Christ make it one of the finest sarcophagi in Italy.

🏃 Activities

Habits Culti Spa
SPA

(Map p46; ✆ 02 4851 7588; Via Angelo Mauri 5; baths per couple €110, hammam €90-150; ⊙ 11am-10pm Mon-Sat, 10am-8pm Sun; Ⓜ Conciliazione) Culti's ethno-sacred aesthetic lives large at this seriously sensual spa. The touted total well-being, radiance and renewed internal resources don't come cheap (prices start at €80 for a basic manicure) but this is no corner nail bar.

Navigli Lombardi
BOAT TOUR

(Map p46; ✆ 02 9227 3118; www.naviglilombardi.it; Alzaia Naviglio Grande 4; adult/concession €12/10; Ⓜ Porta Genova, 🚋 3) Canals were the autostrade of medieval Milan, transporting timber, marble, salt, oil and wine into town. The largest of them, the Navigli Grande, grew from an irrigation ditch to one of the city's busiest thoroughfares by the 13th century. From April to mid-October you can take a boat tour along it for views of the churches, farms and villas that line its banks.

Piscina Solari
SWIMMING

(Map p46; ✆ 02 469 5278; www.milanosport.it; Via Montevideo 20; admission €4 Mon-Fri, €5 Sat & Sun; ⊙ 7am-2.30pm Mon-Fri, 7.30-11pm Tue & Fri, 9.30-11pm Wed, 7am-9am & 1-7pm Sat, 7am-

6.30pm Sun Sep-Jul; Ⓜ Sant'Agostino) Missoni hosted their first Milan show at the covered Piscina Solari in 1968, complete with inflatable, floating furniture. It was a stunning success. Today the pool, designed by architect Arrigo Arrighetti and located in leafy Parco Solari, plays a central role in Milan's summer scene.

🎓 Courses

La Cucina Italiana
COOKING

(Map p46; ✆ 02 7064 2242; www.scuolacucinaitaliana.com; Piazza Aspromonte 15) Cucina Italiana is not just a gourmet magazine, but also a cookery school. Courses include kitchen adventures for children. Lessons from €80.

Istituto Europeo di Design
DESIGN

(Map p46; ✆ 02 579 69 51; www.ied.edu; Via Sciesa 4; Ⓜ San Babila) You can embark on anything from amateur-oriented evening courses in design, the visual arts and fashion, through to year-long and three-year full-time courses.

Istituto di Moda Burgo
FASHION

(Map p50; ✆ 02 78 37 53; www.imb.it; Piazza San Babila 5; Ⓜ San Babila) A broad range of fashion-related courses, from pattern creation to dressmaking, is available at this central Milan fashion school.

👉 Tours

Autostradale
BUS TOUR

(Map p50; ✆ 02 720 01 304; www.autostradale.it; ticket €60; ⊙ 9.30am Tue-Sun Sep-Jul) The tourist office on Piazza Castello sells tickets (good for the whole day) for Autostradale's three-hour city bus tours including admission to *The Last Supper*, Castello Sforzesco and La Scala's museum. Tours depart from the taxi rank on the western side of Piazza del Duomo.

Bike & the City
BIKE TOUR

(Map p46; ✆ reservations 346 9498623; www.bikeandthecity.it; day/sunset tour €35/30; ⊙ morning/afternoon/sunset tour 9.30am/3.30pm/6.30pm) Make friends while you get the inside scoop on city sights on these leisurely, four-hour cycle tours. Tours depart from Piazza G Oberdan at the corner of Corso Buenos Aires.

Madeininterior
DESIGN TOUR

(✆ 02 9170 90 15; www.madeininterior.it; per person in a 6-person group €130-180) Get an insider's view of the Furniture Fair with Madeininterior's tours led by design and interiors experts who have exclusive access to the coolest exhibits, showrooms and after-hours parties. Book at least two weeks in advance.

Tours of Milan GUIDED TOUR
(www.toursofmilan.com) Discover Milan's deep historical roots, unusual art galleries, avant-garde architecture and profound culture of creativity with knowledgeable tours in Italian, English, French and Spanish.

Tram ATMosfera TRAM TOUR
(✆800 808 181; www.atm-mi.it; Piazza Castello; dinner & tour €65; ⊘8pm Tue-Sun; 🖬) One of Milan's historic trams has been renovated to incorporate a restaurant where you can eat your way through a five-course menu as you tour the city. The food isn't stunning but the varnished teak walls, glass lanterns and upholstered benches are a treat. Tours depart from Piazza Castello.

⭐ Festivals & Events

Corteo dei Re Magi RELIGIOUS
Legend says the remains of the three wise men are buried in Milan. Be that as it may, each year on 6 January they parade in costume from the Duomo to the Porta Ticinese.

Carnevale Ambrosian RELIGIOUS
Lent comes late to the Milanese Ambrosian church, with Carnevale sensibly held on the Saturday that falls after everyone else's frantic Fat Tuesday.

Cortili Aperti CULTURE
For one May Sunday, the gates to some of the city's most beautiful private courtyards are flung open. Print a map and make your own itinerary.

MiArt FAIR
(www.miart.it) Milan's annual modern and contemporary art fair held in April may not be Basel but it attracts more than 30,000 art lovers, more than 200 exhibitors and increasing amounts of international attention.

Salone Internazionale del Mobile FAIR
(www.cosmit.it) The world's most prestigious (and profit-driven) furniture fair is held annually at Fieramilano (Rho), with satellite exhibitions in Zona Tortona. Alongside the Salone, runs the **Fuorisalone** (http://fuorisalone.it; literally, the outdoor lounge), which incorporates the dozens of spontaneous design-related events, parties, exhibits and shows that animate the entire city.

Festa del Naviglio CULTURAL
Parades, music and performances; held the first 10 days of June.

Milano Film Festival FILM
(www.milanofilmfestival.it/eng) September sees 10 days of international features, shorts and retrospectives at the Teatro Piccolo, as well as open-air screenings, music and parties at Parco Sempione.

La Nivola e il Santo Chiodo RELIGIOUS
In September, the Archbishop of Milan ascends to the Duomo's chancel roof in a cloud-adorned papier mâché basket; he's up there to retrieve what is supposedly one of the nails from Christ's cross (fashioned, bizarrely, by Constantine into a horse's bridle).

**Festa di Sant'Ambrogio &
Fiera degli Obei Obei** RELIGIOUS
The feast day of Milan's patron saint is celebrated on 7 December with a large Christmas fair. It goes by the name Obej! Obej! (pronounced o-bay, o-bay). Stalls sell regional foods, especially sweets, and seasonal handicrafts in the grounds of Castello Sforzesco.

🍴 Eating

Milan's generations of internal Italian immigrants have injected the cuisine of virtually every region into the lifeblood of the city, where you'll also find plenty of Lombard classics alongside a rich international selection of anything from Ethiopian to sushi. Milan's clutch of Michelin-starred chefs cook up some of Italy's most sophisticated food. Smart spots gather around the streets near Piazza del Duomo and plenty of options dot the Navigli area. Reservations are a good idea and essential for top-end establishments.

Luini PASTRIES & CAKES €
(Map p50; www.luini.it; Via Santa Radegonda 16; panzerotti €2.50; ⊘10am-3pm Mon, to 8pm Tue-Sun; 🖬; Ⓜ Duomo) *Panzerotti* is Milanese for yummy at this historic purveyor of pizza-dough pastries stuffed with cheeses, spinach, tomato, pesto and prosciutto.

Latteria di San Marco TRATTORIA €
(Map p50; ✆02 659 76 53; Via San Marco 24; meals €18-25; ⊘7-11pm Mon-Fri; 🖬; Ⓜ Moscova) If you can snare a seat in this tiny and ever-popular restaurant, you'll find old favourites like *spaghetti alla carbonara* mixed in with chef Arturo's own creations, such as *polpettine al limone* (little meatballs with lemon)

WORTH A TRIP

TRATTORIA DEL NUOVO MACELLO

A real Milanese will tell you that those thin, battered 'elephant ears' that currently masquerade as *cotoletta alla Milanese* (cutlets Milanese-style) are a poor immitation of the real deal. For authentic Milanese *cotoletta* take a taxi ride to the old meat district to **Nuovo Macello** (☑ 02 5990 2122; www.trattoriadelnuovomacello.it; Via Cesare Lombroso 20; meals €28-50; ☉ noon-2.15pm & 8-10.30pm Mon-Fri, 8-10.30pm Sat) where you'll be presented with a thick, juicy slab of veal on the bone cooked slowly to perfection in butter.

Other traditional dishes to sample here are the perfectly *al dente* risotto, *farro* (spelt) with scampi, fried foccacia with chicory and ricotta, and sweet rice with wild strawberries. To compliment the traditional menu the restaurant has an understated industrial vibe.

or *riso al salto* (risotto fritters) on the ever-changing, mostly organic menu.

Osteria del Binari   ITALIAN €€
(Map p46; ☑ 894 06753; www.osteriadelbinari.com; Via Tortona 1; ☉ 7-11pm Mon-Sat; Ⓜ Porta Genova) Crashing an Italian wedding is the only other way you'd come by such heaping platters of handmade pasta, select cuts of meat and home-baked pastries. With Tuscan wine and loved ones gathered around, someone's bound to feel a toast coming on.

Trattoria da Pino   MILANESE €€
(Map p50; ☑ 02 7600 0532; Via Cerva 14; meals €20-25; ☉ noon-3pm Mon-Sat; Ⓜ San Babila) In a city full of models in Michelin-starred restaurants, working-class da Pino offers the perfect antidote. Sit elbow-to-elbow at long cafeteria-style tables and order up bowls of *bollito misto* (mixed boiled meats), handmade pasta and curried veal nuggets.

Sushi Koboo   JAPANESE €€
(Map p46; ☑ 02 837 26 08; www.sushi-koboo.com; Viale Col di Lana 1; meals €20-35; ☉ noon-2.30pm & 7.30-11.30pm Tue-Sun; ✿; 🚊 3, 9) Elegant Sushi Koboo serves delectable sushi, sashimi and tempura at a traditional *kaiten* (conveyor belt) and tables in several stylish restaurant rooms. The atmosphere is warm and welcoming, with tables aglow beneath large, moonlike light fittings. If you're a group order the mixed sushi boat, which actually comes in a handcrafted vessel.

Maxelâ   STEAKHOUSE €€
(Map p50; ☑ 02 2906 2926; www.maxela.it; Via della Moscova 50; meals €18-30; ✿; Ⓜ Moscova) Come with a hearty appetite and order Maxelâ's 1kg *bistecca Fiorentina* and a bottle of house red. When it arrives, don't be intimidated by the size, the first bite of that velvety soft, grilled-to-perfection Fassone beef

sprinkled lightly with salt crystals will make you want to weep with joy.

Al Bacco   MILANESE €€
(Map p46; ☑ 02 5412 1637; Via Marcona 1; meals €25-30; ☉ dinner Mon-Sat) One-time pupil to the famous chef Claudio Sadler, Andrea now has his own Slow Food–recommended restaurant where he prepares Milanese classics with love. Try the homemade pasta with fava beans, pancetta and pecorino or the rabbit with Taggiasche olives.

Dongiò   CALABRESE €€
(Map p46; ☑ 02 551 13 72; Via Bernardino Corio 3; meals €30-40; ☉ noon-2.30pm & 7.30-11.30pm Mon-Fri, 7.30-11.30pm Sat; 🖼; Ⓜ Porta Romana) One of the best value-for-money restaurants in Milan, this big-hearted Calabrese trattoria serves the spicy flavours of the south on delicious homemade pasta. Starters include bountiful platters of southern salami and piquant cheeses. Reservations recommended.

Café Trussardi   ITALIAN €€
(Map p50; ☑ 02 806 88 295; www.trussardiallas cala.it; Piazza della Scala 5; ☉ 7.30am-11pm Mon-Fri, 9am-11pm Sat; Ⓜ Duomo) Whether it's for a glass of wine and root vegetable crisps at the bar, or a leisurely meal from a small, changing menu beneath Patrick Blanc's beautiful vertical garden in the courtyard, this is one of Milan's most stylish and low-key dining options.

Peck Italian Bar   ITALIAN €€
(Map p50; ☑ 02 869 30 17; www.peck.it; Via Cesare Cantù 3; mains from €16.50; ☉ 7.30am-8.30pm Mon-Fri, 9am-8.30pm Sat; ✿; Ⓜ Duomo) Peck's dining room lets quality produce shine with staples like *cotoletto* (cutlets), risotto and roasts done with fabulously fresh, well-sourced ingredients, if not a smidgen of contemporary flair.

Pescheria da Claudio — SEAFOOD €€

(Map p50; ☎02 805 68 57; www.pescheriada claudio.it; Via Cusani 1; meals €35-55; ⏰8.30am-2.30pm & 4-9pm Tue-Sat; ❋; Ⓜ Cairoli, 🚋3, 4) Join the savvy suits for a power lunch or early dinner of *pesce crudo* (raw fish). Plates loaded with marinated tuna, mixed salmon, tuna and white fish with pistachios or lightly blanched octopus carpaccio are consumed with a glass of light fizz.

L'Antico Ristorante Boeucc — MILANESE €€€

(Map p50; ☎02 7602 0224; www.boeucc.com; Piazza Belgioioso 2; meals €60-80; ⏰lunch & dinner Mon-Fri, lunch Sun; Ⓜ Duomo) Set in the basement of the grand-looking neoclassical Palazzo Belgioioso, Milan's oldest restaurant has been regaling diners since 1696. Vaulted dining rooms and service reminiscent of more regal times lend your evening meal a sense of theatre. From *crespelle al prosciutto* (a kind of cross between pasta and crêpe with ham) you might move on to a *trancio di salmone al pepe verde* (slice of salmon with green pepper).

Ristorante Solferino — MILANESE €€€

(Map p50; ☎02 290 05748; www.ilsolferino.com; Via Castelfidardo 2; meals €45-60; ❋🖋; Ⓜ Moscova) Salivary glands have worked overtime here for a century, thanks to hearty classics like osso buco swathed in risotto, unexpected delights like fish tortelloni, and an extensive vegetarian menu. Join Italian film stars risking their figures with the in-house pastry chef's creations, and journalists steadily losing their objectivity over a superior wine selection.

Ristorante Da Giacomo — SEAFOOD €€€

(Map p46; ☎02 7602 3313; www.giacomomilano. com; Via Pasquale Sottocorno 6; meals €30-40; 🚋9, 23) This sunny Tuscan restaurant with its custard-coloured walls and mint-green panelling serves an unpretentious menu featuring mainly fish and shellfish. Start with a slice of sardine and caper pizza and follow with the fresh linguine with scampi and zucchini flowers.

🍸 Drinking & Nightlife

Milanese bars are generally open until 2am or 3am, and virtually all serve *aperitivi* (p64). The Navigli canal district, the cobbled backstreets of Brera, and swish Corso Como and its surrounds are all great areas for a drink.

Princi — BAKERY

(Map p50; www.princi.it; Largo Foppa 2; pastries from €2.50; ⏰7am-2am; Ⓜ Moscova, Garibaldi) Not all Princi branches are created equal. This one is blessed with the same beautiful Claudio Silvestrin design as its Via Speronari sister, and is open similarly long hours, giving you lots of opportunities to sample their artisan range.

Torrefazione Il Caffè Ambrosiano — CAFE

(Map p46; http://torrefazioneambrosiano.it; Corso Buenos Aires 20; ⏰7am-8pm; Ⓜ Porta Venezia) No seating, just the best coffee in Milan. There's also a branch on Corso XXII Marzo 18.

Caffeteria degli Atellani — CAFE, BAR

(Map p50; www.atellani.it; Via della Moscova 28; ⏰8.30am-9.30pm Mon-Fri, 9.30am-7.30pm Sat & Sun; 🔊; Ⓜ Moscova, Turarti) Next to the Santa Teresa Mediateca digital library, Cafe Atellani's glasshouse design is modelled on a tropical greenhouse and overlooks a tranquil garden. Inside, the long sleek bar is lined with an extensive selection of Italian wines, which you can enjoy after a browse in the cinema bookshop.

Bulgari Hotel — BAR

(Map p50; www.bulgarihotel.com; Via Privata Fratelli Gabba 7b; ⏰7.30am-1am; Ⓜ Montenapoleone) Whether it's inside beneath the giant botanical sculptures at the earth-toned bar or outside on the terrace overlooking the brilliantly green garden, the *aperitivo* scene here is an intense slice of Milan life. The second-cheapest wine on the list may weigh in

---

FEELING PECKISH

Forget *The Last Supper*: gourmets head to the food and wine emporium **Peck** (Map p50; www.peck.it; Via Spadari 7-9; ⏰3-7.30pm Mon, 8.45am-7.30pm Tue-Sat). This Milanese institution opened its doors as a deli in 1883. The Aladdin's cave-like food hall is smaller than its reputation suggests, but what it lacks in space it makes up for in variety, with some 3200 variations of *parmigiano reggiano* (Parmesan) at its cheese counter, for just starters. Other treasures include an exquisite array of chocolates, pralines and pastries; freshly made gelato; seafood; caviar; pâtés; a butcher, and fruit and vegetable sellers; truffle products; olive oils and balsamic vinegar.

at €20 but it's cheap for the theatre, darling. The restaurant serves a light Med menu.

Pandenus   BAR

(Map p46; www.pandenus.it; Via Alessandro Tadino 15; cocktails €8, brunch €20; ⊙7am-10pm; 🔊; Ⓜ Porta Venezia) Originally a bakery, Pandenus was named after the walnut bread that used to emerge from its still active oven. Now the focaccia, pizzetta and bruschetta on its burgeoning *aperitivo* bar are some of the best in town. Given its proximity to the Marconi Foundation (which is dedicated to contemporary art) expect a good-looking, arty crowd.

Vinile   BAR

(Map p46; www.vinilemilano.com; Via Alessandro Tadino 17; ⊙11am-midnight; Ⓜ Porta Venezia) Calling all comic connoisseurs and geeks, Vinile serves a limited-production wine list and artisanal cold cuts in the midst of an impressive collection of Star Wars and Marvel memorabilia. Check out its Facebook page for community art and music events.

Straf Bar   BAR

(Map p50; www.straf.it; Via San Raffaele 3; ⊙8am-midnight; Ⓜ Duomo) This place is the pick of the centre's hotel bars with a busy nightly *aperitivo* scene that kicks on until pumpkin hour. The decor is along the now familiar mod-exotic lines: wood/metal/stone played up against minimalist concrete.

10 Corso Como   BAR

(Map p46; www.10corsocomo.com; Corso Como 10; ⊙12.30pm-midnight Mon-Fri, 11.30am-1.30am Sat & Sun; Ⓜ Garibaldi) A picture-perfect courtyard, world-class people-watching and an elegant *aperitivo* scene lit at night by a twinkling canopy of fairy lights make Corso Como the best lifestyle concept bar in Milan.

HClub   BAR

(Diana Garden; Map p46; www.hclub-diana.com; Viale Piave 42; cocktails €10, brunch €33; ⊙10am-1am; Ⓜ Porta Venezia) Secreted behind a vast leather curtain at the back of the Sheraton, the *aperitivo* at the Diana is one of Milan's most varied. Grab a freshly crushed peach Bellini and lounge around the low-lit garden.

N'Ombra de Vin   WINE BAR

(Map p50; www.nombradevin.it; Via San Marco 2; ⊙9am-midnight Mon-Sat; Ⓜ Montenapoleone) This *enoteca* (wine bar) is set in a one-time Augustine refectory. Tastings can be had all day and you can also indulge in food such as *carpaccio di pesce spade agli agrumi* (swordfish carpaccio prepared with citrus) from a limited menu.

La Vineria   WINE BAR

(Map p46; www.la-vineria.it; Via Casale 4; ⊙3.30-8pm Mon, 10am-1pm & 3.30-8pm Tue-Sat Nov-Mar to 1am Apr-May & Oct, 3.30pm-1am daily Jun-Sep; Ⓜ Porta Genova) La Vineria strips away all the *aperitivo* hoopla and serves up glasses, carafes and bottles of wine (and olive oil) straight from the barrel. A glass of wine will set you back just €1.50 instead of the usual €8, but if you do fancy a bite to eat they'll happily put together a hearty cheese and meat board.

MILAN'S BRIGHTEST MICHELIN STARS

Milan's most important contemporary Italian restaurants are equally fashion- and food-oriented:

Cracco (Map p50; ☎02 87 67 74; www.ristorantecracco.it; Via Victor Hugo 4; meals €130-160; ⊙Tue-Fri, dinner Mon, lunch Sat; Ⓜ Duomo) Star chef Carlo Cracco conjures up exemplary deconstructed *alta cucina* in a formal contemporary environment.

Il Marchesino (Map p50; ☎02 7209 4338; www.ilmarchesino.it; Via Filodrammatici 2; meals €50-80, tasting menu €110; ⊙8am-1am Mon-Sat, kitchen closes 10.30pm; Ⓜ Duomo) Gualtiero Marchesi, Italy's most revered chef, presides over an elegant modern dining room at La Scala.

Sadler (☎02 87 67 30; www.sadler.it; Via Ascanio Sforza 77; meals €120; ⊙7.30-11pm Mon-Sat; Ⓜ Romolo, 🚋3) On the Milanese scene since 1995, Claudio Sadler's culinary wisdom remains undisputed.

Trussardi alla Scala (Map p50; ☎02 8068 8201; www.trussardiallascala.com; Piazza della Scala 5; meals €120; ⊙7.30am-11pm Mon-Fri, dinner Sat; ❋; Ⓜ Duomo) Gualtiero Marchesi alumnus, Andrea Berton, runs the kitchen of this subdued, sexy dining room overlooking La Scala.

HISTORIC CAFES

Few cafes have seen or heard as much as these fabulous old Milanese beauties.

Pasticceria Cova (Map p50; www.pasticceriacova.com; Via Monte Napoleone; ⊙8.30am-8pm Mon-Sat; MMontenapoleone) Milan's oldest cafe, opened in 1817 by Antonio Cova, a soldier of Napoleon.

Marchesi (Map p50; www.pasticceriamarchesi.it; Via Santa Maria alla Porta 11a; ⊙8am-8pm Tue-Sat, to 1pm Sun; MCairoli, Cordusio) Baking since 1824, Marchesi's window displays have the wonky logic of a Hitchcock dream.

Biffi Pasticceria (Map p46; www.biffipasticceria.it; Corso Magenta 87; pastries €2.50; ⊙7am-8.30pm; ❋ ❖; MConciliazione) Proud keepers of a *panetùn* (panettone) recipe that once pleased Pope Pius X, Biffi has changed little since its 1847 opening.

Gattullo (Map p46; www.gattullo.it; Piazzale di Porta Lodovico 2; pastries from €1.50; ⊙7am-9pm Sep-Jul; ❋❖; ⊒3, 9) Hailing from that great southern baking town Ruvo di Puglia, Joseph Gattullo's retro bakery serves artisanal pastries.

Bar Magenta BAR
(Map p50; Via Giosué Carducci 13; ⊙8am-2am; MCadorna) Grab a seat in this historic bar and let Milan come to you. Drift in during the day for espresso, sandwiches and beer, or join the students during early evening for wine from a tap and a pavement position under the Liberty signage.

Bar Jamaica BAR
(Map p50; www.jamaicabar.it; Via Brera 32; ⊙8am-2am Mon-Sat, to 8.30pm Sun; MLanza) Bar Jamaica may no longer be the bohemian dive that gave Milan a fleeting reputation for brains as well as style, but it's still an unpretentious watering hole. Students from nearby Accademia di Brera nurse drinks for days on coveted sidewalk seats.

Living BAR
(Map p50; www.livingmilano.com; Piazza Sempione 2; ⊙8am-2am Mon-Fri, 9am-2am Sat & Sun; MMoscova) Living has one of the city's prettiest settings, with a corner position and floor-to-ceiling windows overlooking the Arco della Pace. The bounteous *aperitivo* spread and expertly mixed cocktails draw crowds of smart-casual 20- and 30-somethings. Its sister bar, **Refeel** (Map p46; www.refeel.it; Viale Sabotino 20; ⊙7am-2am Mon-Sat, noon-4pm Sun; MPorta Romana), in Porta Romana is also worth a trip.

Bhangra Bar BAR
(Map p46; www.bhangrabar.it; Corso Sempione 1; admission free-€6; ⊙7pm-midnight Wed & Thu, 7pm-2am Fri, 10pm-2am Sat, 7pm-10pm Sun; MMoscova) Bhangra Bar is famous for its cushions and couscous and curry *aperitivo*, served with a side of African percussion on Friday.

Indeed, music and other cultural happenings constitute a fairly steady diet – expect anything from jazz nights to chilled trip-hop with the option of a shiatsu massage between cocktails.

Plastic NIGHTCLUB
(Via Gargano 15; ⊙11pm-4am Fri-Sun mid-Sep–Jun; MLodi) Friday's London Loves takes no prisoners with an edgy, transgressive indie mix and Milan's coolest kids. If you're looking fab, club art director Nicola Guiducci's private Match à Paris on Sunday mashes French pop, indie and avant-garde sounds. You'll find it just south of the Lodi metro stop just off Viale Brenta.

Magazzini Generali NIGHTCLUB
(www.magazzinigenerali.it; Via Pietrasanta 14; ⊙11pm-4am Wed-Sat Oct-May; MLodi, ⊒24) When this former warehouse is full of people working up a sweat to an international indie act, there's no better place to be in Milan. Most gigs are under €20, and there's free entry on other nights when DJs get the party started.

☆ Entertainment

The tourist office stocks several entertainment guides in English: Milano Mese, *Hello Milano* (www.hellomilano.it) and *Easy Milano* (www.easymilano.it). For club listings, check out ViviMilano (http://vivimilano.corriere.it), which comes out with the *Corriere della Sera* newspaper on Wednesday; *La Repubblica* (www.repubblica.it) is also good on Thursday. Another source of inspiration is Milano-2night (http://2night.it).

APERITIVO

Happy hour elsewhere in the world might mean downing cut-price pints and stale crisps, but not in oh-so-stylish Milan. Its nightly *aperitivo* is a two- or three-hour ritual, starting around 6pm, where for €8 to €20, a cocktail, glass of wine, or beer comes with an unlimited buffet of bruschetta, foccacia, cured meats, salads, and even seafood and pasta. (Occasionally you'll pay a cover charge up front that includes a drink and buffet fare, which generally works out the same.) Take a plate and help yourself; snacks are also sometimes brought to your table. Most of the city's bars offer *aperitivi*, in some form or other.

Teatro alla Scala   OPERA

(Map p50; ☑02 8 87 91; www.teatroallascala.org; Piazza della Scala; Ⓜ Duomo) You'll need perseverance and luck to secure opera tickets at La Scala (€13 to €210, up to €2000 for opening night). About two months before the first performance, tickets can be bought by telephone and online. One month before the first performance, remaining tickets are sold at the **box office** (Map p50; Galleria del Sagrato, Piazza del Duomo; ☺noon-6pm; Ⓜ Duomo). On performance days, 140 tickets for the gallery are sold two hours before the show (one ticket per customer) – queue early.

San Siro Stadium   FOOTBALL

(Stadio Giuseppe Meazza; ☑02 404 24 32; www.sansiro.net; Via dei Piccolomini 5, museum & tours Gate 14; museum admission €7, plus guided tour €13/10; ☺nonmatch days 10am-6pm; Ⓜ Lotto) Unlike the Duomo, San Siro Stadium wasn't designed to hold the entire population of Milan. On a Sunday afternoon amid 85,000 football-mad citizens, however, it can certainly feel like it. The city's two clubs, AC Milan and FC Internazionale Milano (aka Inter), play on alternate weeks from October to May.

Guided tours of the 1920s-built stadium take you behind the scenes to the players' locker rooms and include a visit to the **Museo Inter e Milan**, a shrine of memorabilia and film footage. The accompanying stadium tour covers the locker room, where you can gingerly rest your bum on the same bench as countless naked football legends.

You can buy tickets for games on the day at kiosks around the site. To purchase them you need to take some form of ID. To purchase tickets in advance see www.livefootballtickets.com.

Take tram 24, bus 95, 49 or 72, or the metro to the Lotto stop, from where a free bus shuttles to the stadium.

La Salumeria della Musica   CLUB

(☑02 5680 7350; www.lasalumeriadellamusica.com; Via Pasinetti 4; ☺9pm-2am Mon-Sat Sep-Jun; ☐24) The 'delicatessen of music' is a firm favourite with Milan's alternative scene. Come here for new acts, literary salons, cultural events and jazz. Shows start around 10.30pm and if you get the munchies grab a plate of cheese and cold cuts. You'll find it south of the city centre, just off Via Giuseppe Ripamonti.

Blue Note   JAZZ

(Map p46; ☑02 690 16 888; www.bluenotemilano.com; Via Borsieri 37; tickets €20-35; ☺Tue-Sun Sep-Jul; Ⓜ Zara, Garibaldi) Top-class jazz acts perform here from around the world; get tickets by phone, online or at the door from 7.30pm. It also does a popular easy-listening Sunday brunch (€35 or €55 for two adults and two children).

Piccolo Teatro   THEATRE

(Map p50; ☑02 4241 1889; www.piccoloteatro.org; Via Rovello 2; ☺box office 10am-6.45pm Mon-Sat, to 5pm Sun; Ⓜ Cordusio) This risk-taking little repertory theatre was opened in 1947 by Paolo Grassi and none other than the late, great theatre director Giorgio Strehler, and then embarked on a nationwide movement of avant-garde productions and Commedia dell'Arte revivals. Additional programming, including ballet, goes on at the larger, second sibling space over at the **Teatro Strehler** (Map p50; ☑02 4241 1889; Largo Greppi; ☺box office 10am-6.45pm Mon-Sat, 1pm-6.30pm Sun; Ⓜ Lanza).

Alcatraz   CLUB

(☑02 6901 6352; www.alcatrazmilano.com; Via Valtellina 25; ☺11pm-4am Fri & Sat Sep-Jun; ☐70, ☐3, 4, 7, 11) Founded by Italian rockstar Vasco Rossi, Alcatraz is now a multifunctional venue for live concerts, DJ sets, fashion shows and a weekly dance club. The 1800 sq metre, former garage space rocks to the sound of Latino, house and revival on Friday and classic rock 'n' roll on Saturday.

Shopping

Milan's interior and industrial designers have showrooms throughout the city, with a number of them in the streets surrounding Piazza San Babila. Younger labels and a hip new breed of multibrand retailers can be found in Brera, Corso Como, Corso Magenta, Porta Ticenese and Navigli, while midrange labels and chains line bustling Via Torino, Corso Vercelli and Corso Buenos Aires.

Aspesi   FASHION
(Map p50; www.aspesi.com; Via Monte Napoleone 13; ⊙10am-7pm Mon-Sat; Ⓜ San Babila, Montenapoleone) The size of this Antonio Citterio–designed shop is a clue to just how much Italians love this label – Aspesi outerwear is *de rigueur* for mountain and lake weekends. The arty industrial sprawl is ironically at odds with an essentially practical marque: sportswear at its most understated.

10 Corso Como   FASHION
(Map p46; www.10corsocomo.com; Corso Como 10; ⊙10.30am-7.30pm Tue & Fri-Sun, to 9pm Wed & Thu, 3.30-7.30pm Mon; Ⓜ Garibaldi) It might be the world's most hyped 'concept shop,' but Carla Sozzani's selection of desirable things (Lanvin ballet flats, Alexander Girard wooden dolls, a demi-couture frock by a designer you've not read about *yet*) makes 10 Corso Como a tempting shopping experience. Next to the gallery upstairs is a bookshop with art and design titles.

Biffi   FASHION
(Map p46; www.biffi.com; Corso Genova 5 & 6; ⊙3-7.30pm Mon, 9.30am-1.30pm & 3-7.30pm Tue-Sat; 🚊2) Retailer Rosy Biffi spotted potential in the young Gio and Gianni long before Armani and Versace became household names (more recently, she got Milanese women hooked onto US cult-brand jeans). She has a knack for interpreting edgier trends and making them work for conformist Milan; check out her selection of international fashion heavyweights for both men and women.

Borsalino   ACCESSORIES
(Map p50; www.borsalino.com; Galleria Vittorio Emanuele II 92; ⊙3-7pm Mon, 10am-7pm Tue-Sat; Ⓜ Duomo) The iconic Alessandrian milliner has worked with design greats like Achille Castiglioni, who once designed a pudding-bowl bowler hat. This outlet in the galleria stocks seasonal favourites. The main showroom is at **Via Sant'Andrea 5** (Map p50; ✆02 87 89 10; Ⓜ Montenapoleone).

Calé Fragranza d'Autore   PERFUMERIE
(Map p50; www.cale.it; Corso Magenta 22; ⊙3-7pm Mon, 10am-7pm Tue-Sat; Ⓜ Cairoli) Since 1955 artistic perfumery Calé has been a creator and purveyor of artisan fragrances, featuring cult names such as Parfums d'Orsay, Rigaud and Truefitt & Hill. It's own-brand range embodies the sophisticated, minimalist Milanese style with poetic names such as *Brezza di Seta* (silk breeze) and *Dolce Riso* (sweet rice).

G Lorenzi   HOMEWARES, DESIGN
(Map p50; www.lorenzi.it; Via Monte Napoleone 9; ⊙3-7.30pm Mon, 9am-12.30pm & 3-7.30pm Tue-Sat; Ⓜ San Babila) One of Milan's extant early-20th-century gems, G Lorenzi specialises in the finest-quality grooming and kitchen paraphernalia. There are things here – handcrafted pocket knives set into stag antlers, say – so fine and functional they stand as classic examples of utilitarian design.

Galleria Rossana Orlandi   FASHION
(Map p46; www.galleriarossanaorlandi.com; Via Matteo Bandello 16; ⊙10am-7pm Tue-Sat; Ⓜ Conciliazione) Super stylist Rossana Orlandi's fashion choices are no less inspired than her interiors. Clothes here depart from the OTT Milanese norm with some pieces paired back, smart and pretty, others totally left of field. Dare we say it feels a little French?

La Rinascente   DEPARTMENT STORE
(Map p50; www.rinascente.it; Piazza del Duomo; ⊙10am-midnight; Ⓜ Duomo) Italy's most prestigious department store doesn't let the fashion capital down – come for Italian diffusion lines, French lovelies and LA upstarts. The basement also hides an amazing homewares department. Take away edible souvenirs from the 7th-floor food market (and peer across to the Duomo while you're at it).

La Vetrina Di Beryl   SHOES
(Map p50; Via Statuto 4; Ⓜ Moscova) Barbara Beryl's name was known to cultists around the world way before 'Manolo' became a byword for female desire. Stumbling upon this deceptively nondescript shop is like chancing upon the shoe racks at a *Vogue Italia* photo shoot.

Monica Castiglioni   JEWELLERY
(Map p46; www.monicacastiglioni.com; Via Pastrengo 4; ⊙11am-8pm Thu-Sat; Ⓜ Garibaldi) Located in the up-and-coming neighbourhood of Isola, Monica's studio turns out organic and industrial-style jewellery in bronze, silver

and gold. Deeply rooted in Milan's modernist traditions, these are statement pieces and well priced for the workmanship.

Pianoprimo
DESIGN, HOMEWARES

(www.pianoprimo.it; Via Tolstoi 5; ⊘10am-8pm; ⊠14) Midway between a gallery and a design store, Pianoprimo (so-called because it's located on the first floor) is the brainchild of design trio Fabio Cocchi, Luigi Rotta and Alessandra Mauri. As well as their own exclusive home-design collection, the store carries brands such as Fog Linen from Japan and Pappelina from Sweden.

Pellini
JEWELLERY, ACCESSORIES

(Map p50; www.pellini.it; Via Alessandro Manzoni 20; ⊘3.30-7.30pm Mon, 9.30am-7.30pm Tue-Sat Sep-Jul; MMontenapoleone) For unique, one-off costume jewellery pieces, bags and hair pieces look no further than Donatella Pellini's boutique. Granddaughter of famous costume designer Emma Pellini, the Pellini women have been making jewellery for three generations, and their fanciful, handmade creations are surprisingly affordable.

Pupi Solari
CHILDREN'S CLOTHING

(Map p46; www.pupisolari.it; Piazza Tommaseo 2; ⊘10am-7.30pm Tue-Sat; MConciliazione, ⊠29, 30) Many Milanese from a certain kind of family will recall regular Pupi Solari visits for shoe fittings and picking out exquisitely decorated party dresses or tweed jackets just like daddy's. There's now a women's department and in the same square, a men's-wear branch Host.

Wait and See
FASHION

(Map p50; www.waitandsee.it; Via Santa Marta 14; ⊘3.30-7.30pm Mon, 10.30am-7.30pm Tue-Sat;

MMissori) With collaborations with Missoni, Etro and Molinari under her belt, Uberta Zambeletti launched her own collection in 2010. Quirky Wait and See indulges her eclectic tastes showcasing, unfamiliar brands alongside items exclusively designed for the store, such as gorgeous Raptus & Rose dresses.

ⓘ Information

EMERGENCY
Police Station (Questura; ☑02 6 22 61; Via Fatebenefratelli 11; ⊘8am-2pm & 3-8pm Mon-Fri, 8am-2pm Sat; MTurati)
Tourist Police (☑02 863 701) offers an English-speaking service for tourist complaints.

MEDICAL SERVICES
Pronto Farmacia (☑800 801 185; ⊘24hrs) Freephone helpline with details of open pharmacies in Lombardy. It also assists those in need of urgent prescriptions and general information.
24-Hour Pharmacy (☑02 669 09 35; Galleria delle Partenze, Stazione Centrale; MCentrale FS) Located on 1st floor of the central station.
Hospital (Ospedale Maggiore Policlinico; ☑02 5503 3137; www.policlinico.mi.it; Via Francesco Sforza 35) Milan's main hospital offering an outpatient service.

TOURIST INFORMATION
Milan Tourist Office (www.turismo.milano.it) Main tourist office (Map p50; ☑02 7740 4343; www.turismo.milano.it; Piazza Castello 1; ⊘9am-6pm Mon-Fri, 9am-1.30pm & 2-6pm Sat, to 5pm Sun; MDuomo); Linate airport (☑02 7020 0443; Ground Fl, Arrivals; ⊘7.30am-11.30pm); Malpensa airport (☑02 5858 0080; Ground Fl, Terminal B; ⊘8am-8pm); Stazione Centrale (Map p46; ☑02 7740 4318; ⊘9am-6pm Mon-Sat, 9am-1pm & 2-5pm Sun; MCentrale FS)

VINTAGE FINDS

Il Salvagente (Map p46; www.salvagentemilano.it; Via Fratelli Bronzetti 16; ⊘10am-7pm Tue-Sat, 3-7pm Mon; ⊠60, 62 & 92) A basement room crammed with heavily discounted big brand names.

Cavalli e Nastri (Map p50; www.cavallienastri.com; Via Brera 2; ⊘10am-7pm; MPonte Vetero) Mythical early and mid-20th-century Italian fashion house names.

Vintage Delirium (Map p50; www.vintagedeliriumfj.com; Via Sacchi 3; ⊘10am-1pm & 2-7pm Mon-Fri Sep-Jul; MCairoli) Pristine woollens, 1930s eveningwear from Chanel, and Neapolitan silk ties from the 1960s.

Superfly (Map p46; www.superflyvintage.com; Ripa di Porta Ticinese 27; ⊘11am-8pm Tue-Sat, 3-7pm Sun; MPorta Genovese; ⊠2, 3) Disco diva vintage finds from the 1970s.

Mauro Bolognesi (Map p46; www.maurobolognesi.com; Ripa di Porta Ticinese 47; ⊘9.30am-12.30pm & 3-7pm Tue-Sat; MPorta Genova) Midcentury modern collectibles and furniture.

❶ Getting There & Away

AIR

Malpensa Airport (☏02 232323; www.sea
aeroportimilano.it) Located 54km northwest
of the city; northern Italy's main international
airport.

Linate Airport (☏02 7485 2200; www.milano-
linate.eu) Located 7km east of the city century;
domestic and a handful of European flights.

BUS

National and international buses depart from
Lampugnano bus terminal (Via Giulia Natta)
(next to the Lampugnano metro stop), 5km west
of central Milan. The main national operator is
Autostradale (www.autostradale.it). Tickets
can be purchased at the main tourist office.

CAR & MOTORCYCLE

The A1, A4, A7 and A8 converge on Milan from
all directions.

TRAIN

International, high-speed trains from France,
Switzerland and Germany arrive in Milan's vast
Stazione Centrale (Piazza Duca d'Aosta). The
ticketing office and left luggage are located on
the ground floor; the **tourist information booth**
is opposite platform 13. For domestic tickets,
skip the queue and buy your tickets from the
multilingual, touch-screen vending machines,
which accept both cash and credit card. High-
speed Freccia trains have their own information
lounge. Daily international destinations include:
Florence (€19-50; 1½-3½ hours; hourly)
Geneva (€78; 4 hours; 3 daily)
Munich (€99-130; 7½-8½ hours; 7 daily) via
Verona, Bologna or Venice
Napoli (€40-95; 4½-9 hours; hourly)
Paris (from €80; 7½-9 hours; 3 daily) via
Geneva, Lausanne, Basel or Dijon
Rome (€55-86; 3 hours; half hourly)
Venice (€18.50-37; 2½-3½ hours; half hourly)
Vienna (from €80; 11-14 hours; 2 daily) over-
night
Zurich (€71; 3¾ hours; 5 daily)

❶ Getting Around

TO/FROM THE AIRPORT

Bus Malpensa Shuttle (☏02 585 83 185;
www.malpensashuttle.it; ticket €10) coaches
depart from Piazza Luigi di Savoia, next to
Stazione Centrale, every 20 minutes from
3.45am to 12.30am, taking 50 minutes to the
airport. **Air Bus** (www.atm-mi.it) coaches,
run by ATM, depart from the same location
for Linate Airport (adult/child €5/2.50, 25
minutes) every 30 minutes from 6am to 11pm.

Autostradale (Map p50; ☏02 720 01 304;
www.autostradale.it) runs buses every 30 minutes between 2.45am and 11.30pm from Piazza
Luigi di Savoia to Orio al Serio Airport, near
Bergamo (adult/child €5/3.50, one hour). **Orio
Shuttle** (☏035 33 07 06; www.orioshuttle.
com; adult/child €5/3.50, one hour) is similar,
running every 30 to 60 minutes between 3am
and midnight.

Taxi There is a flat fee of €90 to and from
Malpensa to central Milan. The drive should
take 50 minutes outside peak traffic times.
For travellers to Terminal 2, this might prove
the quickest option. The taxi fare to Linate is
between €10 and €20.

Train The **Malpensa Express** (☏02 7249
4494; www.malpensaexpress.it) departs
every 30 minutes from Terminal 1 to Stazione
Centrale (adult/child €10/5; 50 minutes) and
Cadorna Nord (adult/child €11/5; 30 minutes)
between 5.25am and 11.40pm. Passengers
arriving or departing from Terminal 2 will need
to catch the free shuttle bus to Terminal 1 train
station.

BICYCLE

BikeMi (www.bikemi.it) is a public bicycle system with stops all over town. Get passes online
or by dropping into the **ATM Info Point** (☏800
80 81 81; www.atm.it; ⏰7.45am-7.15pm Mon-
Sat) at the Duomo, Cadorna or Centrale metro
stops.

CAR & MOTORCYCLE

It simply isn't worth having a car in Milan. Many
streets have restricted access and parking is a
nightmare. In the centre, street parking costs
€1.50 per hour in the city centre. To pay, buy a
SostaMilano card from a tobacconist, scratch off
the date and hour, and display it on your dash-
board. Underground car parks charge between
€25 and €40 for 24 hours.

PUBLIC TRANSPORT

Milan's public transport is run by **ATM** (☏800
80 81 81; www.atm.it). The metro operates be-
tween 6am and 12.30am and consists of three
major lines: M1 (red) connects Duomo with Porta
Venezia, the castle, Corsa Magenta and the
Fiera; M2 (green) connects Porta Garibaldi with
Brera and Navigli; and M3 (yellow) connects the
Quad with Porta Romana.

A ticket costs €1.50 and is valid for one metro
ride or up to 90 minutes on ATM buses and
trams. Tickets are sold at electronic ticket machines in the station. For trams and buses, tickets must be pre-purchased and validated when
boarding. Route maps are available from ATM
Info points, or download the IATM app. Night
services run between 12.30am and 2.30am.
There is no service between 2.30am and 6am.

ℹ️ TICKETS & PASSES

There are several good money-saving passes available for public transport:

One-day ticket Valid for 24 hours; €4.50

Three-day ticket Valid for 72 hours; €8.25

Carnet of 10 tickets Valid for 90 minutes each; €13.80

TAXI

Taxis cannot be hailed, but must be picked up at designated ranks, usually outside train stations, large hotels and in major piazze. Alternatively, you can call ✆ 02 40 40, ✆ 02 69 69 or ✆ 02 85 85. English is spoken. Be aware that when you call for a cab, the meter runs from receipt of call, not pick up. The average short city ride costs €10.

AROUND MILAN

Pavia

POP 68,350

Founded by the Romans as a military garrison, Pavia has long been a strategic city both geographically and politically. It sits at the centre of an agricultural plain (hence its ugly periphery), it is an important provincial political player with strong Lega Nord leanings, and its university is considered one of the best in Italy, with previous alumni including explorer Christopher Columbus, physicist Alessandro Volta and poet and revolutionary Ugo Foscolo.

Aside from its vibrant atmosphere (Instituto Universitario di Studi Superiori, IUSS, is a partner in over 300 international exchange programs), Pavia's historic centre preserves a clutch of worthwhile sights including, to the north of the city, the fabulous Carthusian monastery Certosa di Pavia.

◉ Sights

The best way to explore the cobble streets and piazze of the old town is on foot – the easy grid layout is a legacy of the original Roman roads, with Corso Cavour and Corso Mazzini running east–west and the Strada Nuova running north–south. In the centre, **Piazza della Vittoria** is the city's outdoor drawing room surrounded by cafes and bars. A little further north around **Piazza Leonardo da Vinci,** you'll find three of the city's original 100 medieval watchtowers. The southern edge of town is bounded by the Ticino river, which is straddled by a covered bridge, a 1940s replica of the medieval original which was bombed during WWII. On the other side, the **Borgo Ticino** is the neighbourhood of the city's fishermen and *raniere* (frog catchers) and the location of some good restaurants.

★**Certosa di Pavia**   MONASTERY
(Pavia Charterhouse; ✆ 0382 92 56 13; www.certosadipavia.com; Viale Monumento; donations appreciated; ⊗ 9-11.30am & 2.30-5.30pm Tue-Sun) **FREE**
One of the Italian Renaissance's most notable buildings is the splendid Certosa di Pavia. Giangaleazzo Visconti of Milan founded the monastery, 10km north of Pavia, in 1396 as a private chapel and mausoleum for the Visconti family. Originally intended as an architectural companion piece to Milan's Duomo, the same architects worked on its design although the final result, completed over a century later, was a unique hybrid between late-Gothic and new Renaissance styles.

While the airy interior is indeed predominantly Gothic, the exterior is almost entirely a creature of the Renaissance. The church is fronted by a spacious courtyard and flanked by a small cloister, which itself leads onto a much grander, second cloister, under whose arches are 24 cells, each a self-contained living area for one monk. Several cells are open to the public, but you need to join one of the guided tours (Italian only) to access these. In the former sacristy is a giant sculpture, dating from 1409 and made from hippopotamus teeth, including 66 small bas-reliefs and 94 statuettes. In the chapels you'll find frescoes by, among others, Bernardino Luini and the Umbrian master, Il Perugino.

Sila bus 175 (Pavia–Binasco–Milano) links Pavia bus station and Certosa di Pavia (15 minutes, at least seven daily).

Castello Visconteo   CASTLE
(Viale XI Febbraio 35) **FREE** Looming over the old town is the red-brick Castello Visconteo, built in 1360 for Galeazzo II Visconti. Inside the forbidding ramparts is an enormous walled garden, where art exhibits and wine tastings are held in spring and summer. The castle is also home to **Musei Civici** (✆ 0382 30 48 16; www.museicivici.pavia.it; Viale XI Febbraio 35; adult/reduced €6/free; ⊗ 9am-1.30pm Tue-Sun Jul-Aug & Dec-Feb, 10am-6pm Tue-Sun Mar-Jun &

Around Milan

Sep-Nov), which houses interesting, if poorly curated, archaeological, ethnographic and art collections.

Basilica di San Michele BASILICA
(Piazzetta Azzani 1; ☉7.30am-noon & 3-7pm) FREE
Pavia's most important church isn't the Duomo, but the beautiful Romanesque San Michele, where medieval Lombard kings came to receive their iron crown and where Barbarossa was crowned Holy Roman Emperor in 1155.

Duomo CATHEDRAL
(Piazza del Duomo; ☉7am-noon & 3-7pm) FREE
Dominating the town centre is the immense dome of Pavia's red-brick Duomo, which is Italy's third-largest cathedral. Leonardo da Vinci and Donato Bramante contributed to the design, which was begun in 1488 but was not completed until the 19th century. In 1989, its bell tower collapsed, killing four people.

Università degli Studi di Pavia UNIVERSITY
(University of Pavia; ☎0382 98 11; www.unipv.it; Corso Strada Nuova 65) FREE The University of Pavia was formally established in 1361 by Holy Roman Emperor Charles V, although there had been a school of divinity here as early as 825. The oldest colleges, dating from the 16th century are the Collegio Borromeo and the Collegio Ghislieri. Another three have since been added and they are now all linked via the Pavia University System, Instituto Universitario di Studi Superiori (IUSS).

You can wander around the grounds, the historic **botanical garden** (Via Sant'Epifanio 14; ☉9am-12.30pm & 2.30-5pm Mon-Thu, 9am-12.30pm Fri) FREE and courtyards when the university is open. The stately campus houses the small **Museo per la Storia dell'Università di Pavia** (☎0382 98 47 09; www.unipv.it; Corso Strada Nuova 65; ☉2-5pm Wed, 9am-noon Thu-Tue) FREE.

WORTH A TRIP

OLTREPÒ PAVESE

To really escape the urban bustle of Milan and its peripheral cities, consider hiring a car for the day and heading for the rolling hills of Oltrepò Pavese, just south of Pavia. Oltrepò is the Tuscany of the north and riots broke out in the Middle Ages when Milanese markets were cut off from the regions wineries. These days the area is a picture of tranquility; medieval villages perch on hilltops amid zigzagging vineyards, fine *osterie* (casual taverns or eateries presided over by a host) serve five-course Sunday lunches and there's nary a tourist in sight anywhere. So take a tour of these highlights:

➡ **Cigognola**, **Oramala**, **Montesegale** and **Zavattarello** For medieval castles and unchanging views.

➡ **Fortunago** For a perfectly preserved *borgo* (medieval town) and traditional Sunday lunch at **Agriturismo Cascina Casareggio** (🗷 0383 87 52 28; www.cascinacasareggio.it; Loc. Casereggio 1; meals €45; ⊘ noon-2.30pm & 7-10pm Wed-Sun, noon-2.30pm Mon; 🅿 ✱ 🖕).

➡ **Ponte Nizza** For views of the Val di Nizza and medieval frescoes in the **Eremo di Sant'Alberto di Butrio** (🗷 0383 54 21 79; www.eremosantalbertodibutrio.it; Frazione Sant'Alberto di Butrio 59) FREE.

➡ **Salice Terme** For a thermal **spa** (🗷 0383 930 46; www.termedisalice.it; Via delle Terme 22) in art deco decadence.

➡ **Santa Maria della Versa** For wine, grappa and lunch at **Mama Angela** (🗷 0385 27 82 81; www.osteriamammaangela.com; Frazione Valdamonte 3; meals €20-25; ⊘ 10am-3pm Thu-Tue, 7.30-10pm Thu-Tue by reservation only).

✗ Eating

★ La Torre degli Aquila   ITALIAN €€

(🗷 0382 263 35; www.latorredegliaquila.it; Strada Nuova 20; meals €30-40; ⊘ noon-2.30pm & 8-10.30pm Mon-Sat) It is almost worth a trip to Pavia just to eat in Dimo and Maria's medieval tower. Although rooted in tradition, the sensational cooking is highly creative. Homemade pistachio bread is followed by tender black bean and potato gnocchi with prawns and sliced sirloin with prunes and *lardo di Colonnata* (lard from Colonnata).

Antica Osteria del Previ   PAVESE €€

(🗷 0382 262 03; www.anticaosteriadelprevi.com; Via Milazzo 65; meals €25-30; ⊘ 12.30-2.30pm & 7.30-10pm Mon-Sat, 12.30-2.30pm Sun; 🅿) Located in the Borgo Ticino, the menu at this rustic *osteria* (think gauze curtains, a terracotta tiled floor and pink silky napkins) is well-rooted in the territory. Expect superlative risotto with seasonal asparagus, trout or scallops, soused trout, goose salami and Pavian-style salt cod. Local wines from Oltrepò Pavese and the Valtellina are also well represented.

Bardelli Ristorante   PAVESE €€

(🗷 0382 2 74 41; www.bardellipv.it; Viale Lungo Ticino Visconti 2; meals €35-45; ⊘ noon-2.30pm & 7-10pm Mon-Sat) This frescoed riverside mansion has a glassed-in winter garden and courteous, old-school service. It serves up traditional dishes such as *risotto mantecato la serre* (creamed risotto with asparagus and saffron) accompanied by regional wines from Oltrepò Pavese.

ℹ Information

Tourist Office (🗷 0382 07 99 43; http:// turismo.provincia.pv.it; Via del Comune 16; ⊘ 9am-1pm & 2-5pm Mon-Fri, to 6pm Sat & Sun)

ℹ Getting There & Away

Pavia is on the Milan–Genoa line with regular services out of Milan's Centrale Station (€3.80, 25 to 40 minutes).

Monza

POP 120,000

Known to many as the home of a classic European Formula One track (where high-speed races have been held annually in September since 1950), Monza (population 120,000) is sadly overlooked by visitors to Milan. Aside from the **racetrack** (🗷 039 2 48 21; www.monzanet.it; Via Vedano 5, Parco di Monza; race tickets adult/reduced €10-20/€8-14, use of circuit €45; ⊘ 8am-1pm & 2.30-6.30pm Mar-Sep, 8am-1pm & 2-6pm Oct-Feb), which you can actually drive on most days in winter, history and architecture buffs are also rewarded.

The Gothic **Duomo** (☎039 38 94 20; www.duomomonza.it; Piazza Duomo; corona ferrea adult/reduced €4/3; ☺9am-noon & 2-6pm) **FREE**, with its white-and-green banded facade (largely the result of a 19th-century restoration), contains a key early-medieval treasure, the **Corona Ferrea** (Iron Crown), fashioned according to legend with one of the nails from the Crucifixion. Emblazoned with precious jewels and gold leaf, the crown is said to date to the 5th century AD and may have belonged to Rome's Ostrogoth rulers and later the Lombards. King of the Franks and the first Holy Roman Emperor, Charlemagne, saw it as a symbol of empire and he was not alone. Various Holy Roman Emperors, including Frederick I (Barbarossa) and Napoleon, had themselves crowned with it. The crown is on show in the **chapel** (☺Tues-Sun only), dedicated to the Lombard queen Theodolinda.

The **Museo e Tesoro del Duomo** (☎039 32 63 83; www.museoduomomonza.it; Piazza del Duomo; adult/reduced €6/4, with Corono Ferrea €8/6; ☺9am-1pm & 2-6pm Tue-Sun) next door contains one of the greatest collections of religious art in Europe. Recently extended, the collection is split in two parts: the first incorporating the treasures from the original Palatine Chapel founded by Queen Theodolinda, and the second filled with masterpieces intended for the new cathedral. Among the highlights are Queen The-

odolinda's crown, a unique collection of Barbarian and Carolingian art (from the 4th to the 9th century), Palestinian ampullae, a priceless collection of Lombard gold and the stunning,15th-century rose window.

A stroll in the **Giardini Reale** (www.reggiadimonza.it; Viale Regina Margherita; ☺7am-8pm Apr-Oct, to 6.30pm Nov-Mar) **FREE**, at the southern end of Parco di Monza, will bring you to the **Villa Reale**. Built between 1777 and 1780 as a viceregal residence for the Archduke Ferdinand of Austria, it is modelled on Vienna's Schönbrunn Palace. It was abandoned in 1900, after the murder of Umberto I, and has only recently been restored in preparation for a key role in Expo 2015.

The larger **park** (Porta Monza, Viale Cavriga; ☺7am-7pm) **FREE** is the green lung of the city and one of the largest enclosed parks in Europe with some 295 hectares of *bello bosco* (charming woodland). It sits on the Lambro river and incorporates not only the Autodromo but a horse racing track, a golf course, tennis court, a 50m Olympic **swimming pool** (Porta Santa Maria delle Selve, Via Vedano; adult/reduced €8/3; ☺10am-7pm Jun-Aug), horse-riding tracks and cycle paths. You can hire bikes at the **Porta di Monza entrance** (per hour €3; ☺9am-1pm & 2-7pm Tue-Fri, 9am-7.30pm Sat & Sun Apr-Oct, 2-6pm Mon-Fri, 9am-7.30pm Sat & Sun Nov-Mar).

Frequent trains connect Milan's Porta Garibaldi station with Monza (€2.10, 15 to 20 minutes), 23km to the north, making this an easy half-day trip.

Lake Maggiore & Around

Why Go?

Italy's second-largest lake, Maggiore is one of Europe's more graceful corners. Arrayed around the lakeshore is a series of pretty towns (Stresa, Verbania, Cannobio and, on the Swiss side of the border, Locarno) and these serve as gateways to gorgeous Maggiore islands. Behind the towns, wooded hillsides rise, strewn with decadent villas, lush botanical gardens and even the occasional castle. Further still from the lakeshore but not as far as you might think, the snow-capped peaks of Switzerland provide the perfect backdrop, and idyllic vantage points over the lake are many – from the breakfast terrace of your lakeside hotel to the eyries reached by cable car from Locarno, Laveno and Stresa. And fabulous detours await, whether into the high valleys from the northern end of the lake or to Orta San Giulio to the southwest, one of the region's most beguiling villages.

Best Places to Eat

➡ Casabella (p81)

➡ Il Sole (p87)

➡ Ristorante Milano (p82)

➡ Ristorante Locanda Locarnese (p95)

➡ La Botte (p78)

Best Places to Stay

➡ Grand Hotel des Iles Borromees (p197)

➡ Locanda di Orta (p198)

➡ Caffe dell Arte (p198)

➡ Hotel Pironi (p197)

➡ Albergo Verbano (p197)

Road Distances (KM)

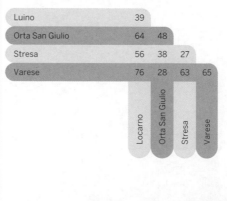

	Locarno	Orta San Giulio	Stresa	Varese
Luino	39			
Orta San Giulio	64	48		
Stresa	56	38	27	
Varese	76	28	63	65

Getting Around

Lake Maggiore is well served by ferries that cover most towns along the lakeshore and connect them with the lake's islands. There are also buses and trains, although services are infrequent and don't serve all towns – the most picturesque train services are between Locarno and Domodossola. The prettiest drives hug the lake's west bank, and climb up through the Val Cannobina and then down to Locarno.

3 PERFECT DAYS

Day 1: Maggiore Islands

It's worth catching a ferry (with an all-day ticket) from Stresa or Baveno to Isola Bella in order to marvel at the baroque wealth of the Borromeo family's island pleasure palace and gardens. Once saturated by all this richness, it's possible to transfer to Isola Superiore for lunch at one of this Fishermen's Island's restaurants. The perfect way to complete this experience of the Borromean Islands is to enjoy an afternoon on Isola Madre. For an extra treat, sleep on Isola Superiore.

Day 2: Lake Orta

Splendid views of the lakes and the Alps can be seen by driving, hiking or taking the funicular from the belle époque lakeside town of Stresa to Monte Mottarone. Then it's worth heading down the other side to enchanting little Lake Orta and its star village, Orta San Giulio, a quintessential romantic spot and the perfect base for local exploration, in particular of Isola San Giulio and the *sacro monte* (holy mountain).

Day 3: Northern Mountains

It's possible to enjoy a string of mountain valley villages by catching a train in Stresa bound for Domodossola, which is the starting point for the scenic Centovalli railway trip through mountain valley villages to Locarno in Switzerland. You can then explore this elegant film-festival town and its pretty lakeside neighbour, Ascona, for the rest of the day. From there you can head south, back over the Italian border, to reach captivating Cannobio, one of the most enticing villages on Lake Maggiore.

Where to Stay

Accommodation is especially abundant in Stresa and Verbania, both of them launch pads for the Borromean Islands and the latter home to the sumptuous Villa Taranto. There is also a fair choice in Locarno. The most romantic hotel locations are Isola Superiore, Orta San Giulio and Cannobio.

DON'T MISS

An early morning start to beat the crowds on the decadent Borromean Islands.

LAKE MAGGIORE & AROUND

Best Gardens

➡ Isola Bella (p79)
➡ Isola Madre (p80)
➡ Villa Taranto (p81)
➡ Villa della Porta Bozzolo (p86)
➡ Giardino Botanico Alpinia (p76)

Best Viewpoints

➡ Cardada (p95), Locarno
➡ Cimetta (p95), Locarno
➡ Monte Mottarone (p76), Stresa
➡ Funivia (p85), Laveno

Resources

➡ **Borromeo** (www.borromeoturismo.it) All you need to know about the Borromean Islands.

➡ **Lago Maggiore** (www.lagomaggioreturismo.it) General information on Lake Maggiore.

➡ **Lago d'Orta** (www.lagodortaturismo.it) General information on Lake Orta.

➡ **Varese Land of Tourism** (www.vareselandoftourism.it) Varese province resource, including Lake Maggiore's east bank.

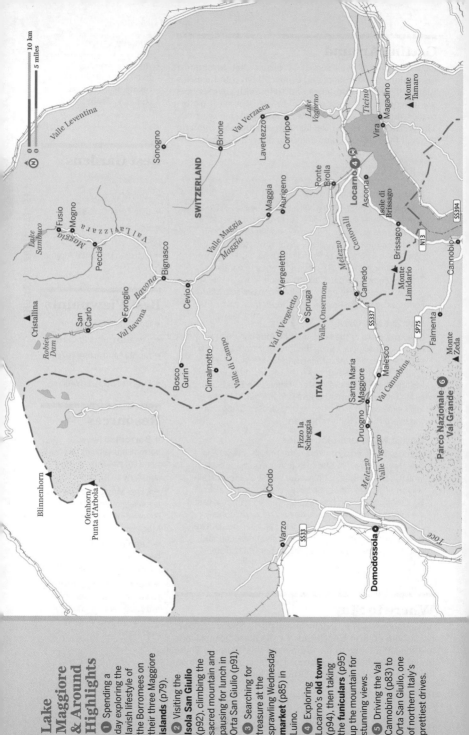

Lake Maggiore & Around Highlights

1 Spending a day exploring the lavish lifestyle of the Borromees on their three Maggiore **islands** (p79).

2 Visiting the **Isola San Giulio** (p92), climbing the sacred mountain and pausing for lunch in Orta San Giulio (p91).

3 Searching for treasure at the sprawling Wednesday **market** (p85) in Luino.

4 Exploring Locarno's **old town** (p94), then taking the **funiculars** (p95) up the mountain for stunning views.

5 Driving the Val Cannobina (p83) to Orta San Giulio, one of northern Italy's prettiest drives.

6 Parco Nazionale Val Grande

⑥ Leaving the crowds behind by hiking deep into the **Parco Nazionale Val Grande** (p84).

⑦ Marvelling at the frescoes in the improbably sited **Santa Caterina del Sasso** (p86).

⑧ Wandering amid the rich variety of plants in Verbania's **Villa Taranto** (p81).

⑨ Eating well at **Casabella** (p81) then sleeping in utter tranquillity on Isola Superiore.

LAKE MAGGIORE WEST BANK

Lake Maggiore's west bank is a series of pretty vistas and towns, some of which serve as launchpads for the undoubted highlight: a visit to the Borromean Islands.

ℹ Getting Around

Ferries and hydrofoils around the lake are operated by **Navigazione Lago Maggiore** (☏ 800 551801; www.navigazionelaghi.it), which has ticket offices at most boat landings around the lake and a main office in Arona. Services are drastically reduced in autumn and winter.

The only car ferry connecting the western and eastern shores for motorists crosses between Verbania-Intra and Laveno. Ferries run every 20 minutes; one-way transport costs from €7.80 for a car and driver, €5 for a bicycle and cyclist, or €6 for a motorcycle and its rider.

One-day return tickets from key points at the Italian end of the lake to the towns (including Locarno) on the Swiss side are available from March to October. Adults/children pay around €17/8.50 for a typical day's travel, but it could be more or less depending on your departure port – check the website for details. Day passes per adult/child cost Sfr36/18 on the Swiss side.

Lake Maggiore Express (www.lagomaggioreexpress.com; adult/child €30/15) is a picturesque day trip under your own steam (no guide) that is an excellent way to get an overview of Lake Maggiore and its hinterland, particularly if you have limited time. It includes train travel from Arona or Stresa to Domodossola, from where you get the charming little **Centovalli Train** (www.centovalli.ch) to Locarno (Switzerland) and a ferry back from Locarno to Stresa. The two-day version is perhaps better value if you have the time. Tickets are available from any ticket office of Navigazione Lago Maggiore on the boat landings.

Stresa & Around

POP 5226

Perhaps more than any other Lake Maggiore town, Stresa, with a ringside view of sunrise over the lake, captures the lake's prevailing air of elegance and bygone decadence. This is most evident in the string of belle époque confections along the waterfront, a legacy of the town's easy access from Milan, which has made it a favourite for artists and writers since the late 19th century. Hemingway was one of many who visited; he arrived in Stresa in 1918 to convalesce from a war wound. A couple of pivotal scenes towards the end of his novel *A Farewell to Arms* are set at the Grand Hotel des Iles Borromees, the most palatial of the historic hotels (others include the Grand Hotel Bristol and the Regina Palace) garlanding the lake.

People still stream into Stresa to meander along its promenade and explore the little hive of cobbled streets in its old centre (especially pleasant for a coffee break is shady Piazza Cadorna).

◎ Sights & Activities

Monte Mottarone   MOUNTAIN
The cable-car trip up Monte Mottarone (1491m) from the northwestern end of Stresa offers pretty views over Lake Maggiore, including Isola Bella and Isola Superiore. From the summit on a clear day you can see Lake Orta, several other smaller lakes and Monte Rosa, on the Alpine border with Switzerland.

The 20-minute cable-car journey on the **Funivia Stresa–Mottarone** (☏ 0323 3 02 95; www.stresa-mottarone.it; Piazzale della Funivia, Mottarone; return adult/child €18/12, Alpino station €12.50/8.50; ☒ 9.30am-5.30pm Apr-Oct, 8.10am-5.30pm Nov-Mar; ☒ Stresa) takes you to the Mottarone station at 1385m, from where it's a 15-minute walk or free chairlift (when it's working) up to the summit. At the Alpino midstation (803m) more than 1000 Alpine and sub-Alpine species flourish in the **Giardino Botanico Alpinia** (☏ 0323 3 02 95; www.giardinoalpinia.it/info.htm; adult/child €3/2.50; ☒ 9.30am-6pm Apr-Oct), a botanic garden dating from 1934. On a clear day, the views from here over Maggiore are truly special.

For the more active, there are plenty of good mountain-biking and hiking trails on the mountain. **Bicicò** (☏ 0340 357 21 89; www.bicico.it; half-/full-day rental €23/28, half-/full-day guide €80/150; ☒ 9.30am-12.30pm & 1.30-5.30pm) rents out mountain bikes at the lower Stresa cable-car station. Rates include a helmet and road book detailing a number of 20km to 30km panoramic descents (about three hours, of which only about 30 minutes require slight ascents) from the top of Mottarone back to Stresa. A one-way trip with a bike on the cable car to Alpino/Mottarone costs €9/12.

Walkers can ask at the cable-car station or the tourist office for a free copy of *Trekking on the Slopes of Mount Mottarone*, which outlines a two-hour walk from Stresa to the Giardino Botanico Alpinia and a four-hour walk to the top of Mottarone.

Stresa

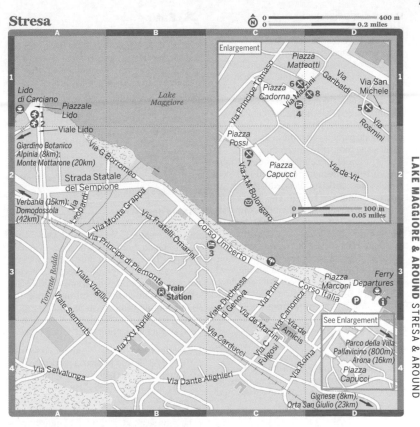

Skiing Mottarone's gentle slopes (www. mottaroneski.it) is limited to five green and two blue runs, making it good for beginners. The ski pass includes the cost of the cable car and you can hire gear from the station at the top of Mottarone. It is possible to ski in summer, too: on a green synthetic-grass piste unrolled from June to September. The ski pass costs €16 per adult per day while equipment costs extra.

Also possible from the summit is **Alpyland** (☑ 0323 3 02 95; www.alpyland.com; Mottarone; adult/child €5/3.50; ☺ 10am-5pm Mon-Fri, to 6pm Sat & Sun Apr-Oct, weekends only Dec-Mar, closed Nov), a 1200m-long bobsled descent with adjustable speeds that makes it ideal for families.

Parco della Villa Pallavicino   ZOO
(☑ 0323 3 15 33; www.parcozoopallavicino.it; adult/ child €9.50/6.50; ☺ 9am-6pm Mar-Oct; ⏷) Barely 1km southeast of central Stresa along the SS33 main road, exotic birds and animals

Stresa

✦ Activities, Courses & Tours

roam relatively freely at the child-friendly Parco della Villa Pallavicino. Some 40 species of animals, including llamas, Sardinian donkeys, flamingos and toucans, keep everyone amused.

Museo dell'Ombrello e del Parasole
MUSEUM

(Umbrella & Parasol Museum; ☑0323 8 96 22; www.gignese.it/museo; Via Panorama Golf 2; adult/child €2.50/1.50; ⊙10am-noon & 3-6pm Tue-Sun) Those driving to Mottarone or Orta San Giulio (for Lake Orta) from Stresa could stop in Gignese (8km from Stresa) for the intriguing Museo dell'Ombrello e del Parasole. Regional artisans once made a living from handmade parasols and umbrellas, and later small-scale industrial production.

The parasol became an indispensable part of ladies' fashion in the mid-19th century, as Romanticism dictated that my fair lady had indeed to be fair. This passion for pallor wore off only from the 1920s onwards. The museum has more than 1000 items, of which only a part is on show. Starting with tiny parasols from the 1850s, the gamut runs to more modern umbrellas up until about the time of WWII. It is startling what work once went into these items, with carved ivory handles, printed silk covers and intricate lace decoration for fancier ones.

🎉 Festivals & Events

Stresa Festival
MUSIC

(www.stresafestival.eu) A prestigious festival that dates back more than half a century, with classical concerts, as well as midsummer jazz performances. It runs from mid-July to early September.

BEST HIKING AROUND LAKE MAGGIORE

Parco Nazionale Val Grande (p84) Extensive wilderness trails northwest of Lake Maggiore.

Monte Mottarone (p76) Take the cable car up and walk back down with fine Lake Maggiore views.

Cimetta (p95) High-altitude trekking from the top chairlift station above Locarno.

Cardada (p95) Take the cable car up high above Locarno, with forest trails leading back down.

Via delle Genti (p82) Historic path that links Switzerland to Ghiffa on Lake Maggiore's west bank.

Valle Maggia (p99) Remote mountain trails in one of Swiss Ticino's loveliest valleys.

🍴 Eating

La Botte
PIEDMONTESE €€

(☑0323 3 04 62; Via Mazzini 6; meals €25-30; ⊙noon-2pm & 6.30-9pm Fri-Wed) Polenta is at the heart of this Piedmontese trattoria's business where they serve up all sorts of regional dishes that will warm the cockles of your heart. The location is an unchanged traditional *osteria* (casual tavern or eatery presided over by a host) just in from the lakefront, with simple, dark timber furniture and decades of accumulated baubles hanging on the walls. The grilled polenta or risotto with blue cheese and pears are fine ways to get things going.

Osteria degli Amici
ITALIAN €€

(☑0323 3 04 53; Via Anna Maria Bolongaro 33; pizzas €5-10, meals €30-35; ⊙noon-2.30pm & 7-11pm Thu-Tue, closed Jan) You may need to queue here, but it's worth it to dine under vines on one of Stresa's prettiest terraces in the centre of town, just off pedestrianised Via Mazzini. If it's a little cool for sitting outside, the indoor dining room, with its canary-yellow paint job and round tables, is an equally good setting for getting stuck into a pizza.

Il Clandestino
ITALIAN €€

(☑0323 3 03 99; www.ristoranteilclandestino.com; Via Rosmini 5; meals €35-40, tasting menu €40-60; ⊙12.30-1.45pm & 7.30-10pm Wed-Mon) An elegant, corner dining room with parquet floors, creamy white linen, soft music and a largely seafood menu, Il Clandestino is worth searching out. Some dishes have a Sicilian touch, with Sicilian prawns a recurring theme. It does some excellent lake-fish dishes, too, but acknowledges the existence of red meat only occasionally.

Piemontese
ITALIAN €€

(☑0323 3 02 35; www.ristorantepiemontese.com; Via Mazzini 25; set menu from €28, meals €35-45; ⊙12.30-2pm & 6.30-9.30pm) Refined surrounds and high-quality cooking dominate this well-regarded place. Try the polenta with cheese fondue and air-dried beef, or the *menu di mezzogiorno* (lunchtime set menu).

ℹ Information

Stresa Tourist Office (☑0323 3 13 08; www.visitstresa.com; Piazza Marconi 16; ⊙10am-12.30pm & 3-6.30pm mid-Mar–mid-Oct, 10am-12.30pm & 3-6.30pm Mon-Fri, 10am-12.30pm Sat mid-Oct–mid-Mar).

ⓘ Getting There & Around

BOAT

Boats depart from the ferry dock on Piazza Marconi and connect Stresa with Arona (one way adult/child €6.50/3.10, 40 minutes), Angera (€6.50/3.10, 35 minutes), Baveno (€3.90/2, 20 minutes) and Verbania Pallanza (€5/2.50, 35 minutes).

BUS

Buses leave from Piazza Marconi on the waterfront at Stresa for destinations around the lake and elsewhere, including Milan, Novara and Lake Orta. The daily Verbania–Milan intercity bus service operated by **SAF** (☑ 0323 55 21 72; www.safduemila.com) links Stresa with Arona (€2.25, 20 minutes), Verbania Pallanza (€2.25, 20 minutes) and Verbania-Intra (€2.25, 25 minutes) and Milan (€9, 1½ hours).

CAR

Coming from Milan, take the A8/A26 motorway, following signs for Gravellona. To follow the lake road, exit the autostrada at Castelletto del Ticino. From there, the SS33 hugs the shore to Arona, Stresa and Baveno. From Feriolo, the SS34 continues the lakeside run to the Swiss border (where it becomes route 13 to Locarno and beyond).

Parking in Stresa can require patience and is mostly metered.

TRAIN

Stresa is 1¼ hours from Milan (from €8) on the Domodossola–Milan train line. Domodossola (€3.35 to €9), 30 minutes northwest, is on the Swiss border, from where the train line leads to Brig and on to Geneva.

Arona

POP 14,547

It was in Arona, 20km south of Stresa, that the son of the Count of Arona and Margherita de' Medici, who would go on to be canonised San Carlo Borromeo (1538–84), was born. In 1610 he was declared a saint and his cousin, Federico, ordered the creation of a *sacro monte* (holy mountain), with 15 chapels lining a path uphill to a church dedicated to the saint. The church and three of the chapels were built, along with a special extra atop the **Sacro Monte di San Carlo** (☑ 0322 24 96 69; Piazza San Carlo; admission €4; ☺ 9am-12.30pm & 2.30-6pm Mar-Oct, to 4.30pm Sat & Sun Nov-Feb; ⓟ; ⓠ Arona): a hollow, 35m bronze-and-copper statue of San Carlo. Commonly known as the Sancarlone (Big St Charles) or the Colosso di San Carlo (St Charles Colos-

sus) and erected between 1614 and 1698, it can be climbed, affording a spectacular view from the top. You climb spiral stairs to a platform surrounding the giant's feet. There you will be handed a miner's-type helmet and wait in a queue to head up. It's a bit of a vertiginous ascent and children under six years old are not allowed up.

To reach this hill, with nice views over the south end of Lake Maggiore and across to the Rocca di Angera, walk or drive about 2km west from Piazza del Popolo, Arona's most charming piazza. The broad square, with its little marina, sits pretty on the lake and offers several restaurants and cafes for a post-Sancarlone break.

ⓘ Information

Arona Tourist Office (☑ 0322 24 36 01; Piazzale Duca d'Aosta; ☺ 9.30am-12.30pm Mon-Wed, 9.30am-12.30pm & 3-6pm Thu-Sat)

ⓘ Getting There & Away

Boats connect Arona with both Stresa and Verbania Pallanza (each one way adult/child €6.50/3.10, 40 minutes) from where there are connections to elsewhere on the lake.

Borromean Islands

Forming Lake Maggiore's most beautiful corner, the Borromean Islands (Isole Borromee) can be reached from various points around the lake, but Stresa and Verbania offer the best access. Three of the four islands – Bella, Madre and Superiore (aka dei Pescatori) – can all be visited, but tiny San Giovanni is off limits. The Borromeo family, a noble family from Milan, has owned these islands (they own six of the lake's nine islands) since the 17th century.

Isola Bella

The grandest and busiest of the islands – the crowds can get a little overwhelming on weekends – Isola Bella is the centrepiece of the Borromeo Lake Maggiore empire. The island took the name of Carlo III's wife, the bella Isabella, in the 17th century, when its centrepiece, Palazzo Borromeo, was built for the Borromeo family.

It's difficult to imagine that prior to its construction the island was little more than a chunk of rock inhabited by a handful of hardy fishing families. To this day, only 16 people live year-round on the island, but in

> ### ℹ️ VISITING THE ISLANDS
>
> Ferries chug to the Borromean Islands from Stresa (the main dock), Lido di Carciano (by the Stresa–Mottarone cable car) and Verbania Pallanza. Services connect them all but more regular half-hourly runs connect Stresa, Isola Bella, Isola Superiore and Baveno. If you plan to visit all three islands from either Verbania or Stresa, you're better off buying a day ticket for €16.50 – it's a round-trip ticket that includes stops in Verbania, Stresa, Baveno and the three islands. More expensive one-day passes include admission to the various villas.

summer the place looks like a scene from the Normandy landings of 1944, with countless vessels ferrying battalions of visitors to and fro. Construction of the villa and gardens was thought out in such a way that the island would have the vague appearance of a vessel, with the villa at the prow and the gardens at the rear.

⊙ Sights

Palazzo Borromeo PALACE
(☏0323 3 05 56; www.isoleborromee.it; adult/child €13/5.50, combined ticket with Isola Madre €18/8, Galleria dei Quadri €3; ⊙9am-5.30pm Apr–mid-Oct) Presiding over 10 tiers of terraced gardens, the baroque palace is arguably the finest structure anywhere around Lake Maggiore. In summer, the family who owns it moves in and occupies the 2nd and 3rd floors (which are off limits to visitors), totalling a mere 50-odd rooms. Visitors can see the ground and 1st floors, the latter also known as the 'noble' floor.

As was typical in such mansions, the noble floor was largely one of representation, including guestrooms, ballrooms, studies and reception halls. Beneath a 23m-high ceiling in the Salone Grande (part of the ballroom) is a 200-year-old wooden model of the palace and island.

A separate ticket gains access to the Galleria dei Quadri (Picture Gallery), a hall in which the walls are covered from top to bottom with 130 paintings of the Borromeo collection. It includes pieces by several Old Masters, including Rubens, Titian, Paolo Veronese, Andrea Mantegna, Van Dyck and José Ribera (Spagnoletto). Works of art are also scattered elsewhere in the building, as well as Flemish tapestries and sculptures by Antonio Canova.

In the grotto below the ground floor, a 3000-year-old fossilised boat is displayed behind glass. The grottoes are studded with pink marble, lava stone, and pebbles from the lakebed. White peacocks, whose fanned feathers resemble bridal gowns, strut about the gardens, which is considered one of the finest examples of a baroque Italian garden design.

🍴 Eating

Elvezia ITALIAN €€
(☏0323 3 00 43; Isola Bella; meals €30-35; ⊙noon-2pm & 6.30-9pm Tue-Sun Mar-Oct, Fri-Sun Nov-Feb) With its rambling rooms, fish-themed portico and upstairs pergola and balcony dining area, this is the best spot on the island for home cooking. It serves pastas including ricotta-stuffed ravioli, various risottos and a hearty lasagne, as well as lake fish such as *coregone alle mandorle* (lake whitefish in almonds). Booking ahead is essential for winter dinners.

Isola Madre

The closest of the three islands to Verbania, Isola Madre is entirely taken up by the Palazzo Madre and the lovely gardens that surround it.

⊙ Sights

Palazzo Madre PALACE
(☏0323 3 05 56; adult/child incl gardens €11/5.50, combined ticket with Isola Bella €18/8; ⊙9am-6pm Mar-Oct) The 16th- to 18th-century Palazzo Madre is a wonderfully decadent structure crammed full of all manner of antique furnishings and adornments. Highlights include Countess Borromeo's doll collection, a neoclassical puppet theatre designed by a scenographer from Milan's La Scala, and a 'horror' theatre with a cast of devilish marionettes.

Isola Madre Gardens GARDEN
(⊙9am-6.15pm) The Isola Madre gardens are even more lavish than those of Palazzo Borromeo on Isola Bella, although in June 2006 a freak tornado struck the island, uprooting many of the island's prized plants. Nevertheless, this English-style botanic garden remains full of interest, with azaleas, rhododendrons, camellias, eucalypts, banana trees, hibiscus, fruit orchards, an olive grove and much more.

Exotic birdlife, including white peacocks and golden pheasants, roam the grounds.

Isola Superiore (Pescatori)

Tiny 'Fishermen's Island,' with a permanent population of around 50, retains much of its original fishing-village atmosphere. Apart from an 11th-century apse and a 16th-century fresco in the charming Chiesa di San Vittore, there are no real sights. Many visitors make it their port of call for lunch, but stay overnight and you'll fall in love with the place. Restaurants cluster around the boat landing, all serving grilled fish fresh from the lake (from around €15). On some days in spring and autumn, abundant rainfalls can lift the lake's level a fraction, causing minor flooding on the island. The houses are built with this in mind, with entrance stairs facing internal streets and built high enough to prevent water entering the houses.

✖ Eating

La Pescheria　　　　　ITALIAN €€
(☏ 0323 93 38 08; www.la-pescheria.it; Via Lungolago 6; meals €30-40; ⊗ noon-2pm & 6-9pm Feb-Nov) Choose between a vine-covered terrace overlooking the lake and the terracotta-hued interior dining rooms at this friendly restaurant. Start things off with *misto di filetti di lago* (a combination of lake fish) and follow it up with *ravioli di pesce di lago con zafferano e pistacchi* (lake fish ravioli with saffron and pistachio nuts).

Casabella　　　　　ITALIAN €€€
(☏ 0323 3 34 71; www.isola-pescatori.it; Via del Marinaio 1; meals €40-50, 5-course tasting menu €55; ⊗ noon-2pm & 6-8.30pm Feb-Nov) This spot is warmly recommended by locals. Lots of timber panelling, well spread out tables and fine white linen abound, and some sort of lake view is inevitable from almost wherever you sit. The menu is rich in variety, with lake whitefish and perch among the highlights. For those who don't want to leave, it has two rooms.

🛍 Shopping

Concreta　　　　　CERAMICS
(Via di Mezzo; ⊗ 9am-5.30pm) Souvenir stalls have arrived on Isola Superiore but this charming little ceramics shop is a cut above them all. Think perfectly executed pieces in a range of muted colours, and the potter, Wanda Patrucco, is happy to let you browse without pressure.

Verbania

POP 31,243

Verbania, the biggest town on the lake, makes a good base for exploring the west bank. The town is strung out along the lakeshore and consists of three districts. Verbania Pallanza, the middle chunk, is the most interesting of the three, with a pretty waterfront and a ferry stop.

Running north from Pallanza, the waterfront road, Via Vittorio Veneto, has a jogging and cycling path that follows the lakefront, which is especially pretty around the little port and the nearby Isolino San Giovanni, a wooded islet moored just off the shore. It connects Pallanza with Villa Taranto and Verbania-Intra, which has handy car ferries to Laveno on the lake's east bank.

◎ Sights

Villa Taranto　　　　　GARDEN
(☏ 0323 40 45 55; www.villataranto.it; Via Vittorio Veneto 111, Verbania Pallanza; adult/child €10/5.50; ⊗ 8.30am-6.30pm; ℙ; 🚢 Villa Taranto) Pallanza's highlight is the grounds of the late-19th-century Villa Taranto. In 1931 royal archer and Scottish captain Neil McEacharn bought the Normandy-style villa from the Savoy family after spotting an ad in the *Times*. He planted some 20,000 species over 30 years, and today it is considered one of Europe's finest botanic gardens.

The main entrance path is a grand affair, bordered by a strip of lawn and a cornucopia of colourful flowers. Depending on when you visit, the experience will differ. The winding dahlia path, for instance, shows off blooms from more than 300 species from June to October. In April and May, the dogwood and related flowers run riot. In the hothouses you can admire extraordinary equatorial water lilies. The villa itself is not open to the public as it houses the offices of the local prefecture. Boats stop at the landing stage in front of the villa.

Museo del Paesaggio　　　　　MUSEUM
(☏ 0323 55 66 21; www.museodelpaesaggio.it; Via Ruga 44, Verbania Pallanza; admission €5; ⊗ 10am-noon & 3.30-6.30pm Tue-Sun) Up the hill from the waterfront in Verbania Pallanza's old town, this engaging museum is worth an hour of your time, with regional archaeology, sculptures and paintings dominated by Lake Maggiore landscapes.

LAKE MAGGIORE & AROUND VERBANIA

✴ Festivals & Events

Mostra Nazionale della Camelia　FLOWERS
(www.camelieinmostra.it) Twice a year, in spring and autumn, a splash of extra floral colour comes to Verbania Pallanza with a display of more than 200 varieties of camellia in the gardens of **Villa Giulia** (☑0323 55 62 81; Corso Zanitello 8) or **Villa Rusconi-Clerici** (www.villarusconiclerici.it; Via Vittorio Veneto) or both. Dates vary, but you are looking at a weekend in late March or late November.

Settimana del Tulipano　FLOWERS
In the last week of April, tens of thousands of tulips erupt in magnificent multicoloured bloom in Verbania's Villa Taranto.

✖ Eating

Bolongaro　ITALIAN €
(☑0323 50 32 54; Piazza Garibaldi 9, Verbania Pallanza; meals €20-25; ⊘noon-2.30pm & 6-9.30pm) Large pizzas, a wide range of pastas and other mains and a choice between indoor and outdoor dining have made this is an unremarkable but perenially popular choice along the Verbania Pallanza waterfront.

Il Burchiello　ITALIAN €€
(☑0323 50 45 03; Corso Zanitello 3, Verbania Pallanza; meals €25-30; ⊘noon-2pm & 6-9pm Thu-Tue) A modern eatery close to the Verbania Pallanza waterfront, Il Burchiello does good Italian staples without ever becoming too adventurous. The *spaghetti di frutti di mare* is brimful of mussels and other shellfish, and the pasta is perfectly *al dente*.

★Ristorante Milano　MODERN ITALIAN €€€
(☑0323 55 68 16; www.ristorantemilanolagomaggiore.it; Corso Zanitello 2, Verbania Pallanza; meals €60-70; ⊘noon-2pm & 7-9pm Wed-Sun, noon-2pm Mon; ❀) It is difficult to imagine a prettier setting for a meal. Antique-filled Ristorante Milano sits off its own shady gravel-and-lawn garden where a handful of tables are set up and birdsong provides the background music. It overlooks Verbania Pallanza's cute port and Isolino San Giovanni. The cuisine is broadly Italian, with some interesting variations on the theme, such as *risotto ai petali di rosa* (risotto with rose petals).

❶ Information

Verbania Tourist Office (☑0323 50 32 49; www.verbania-turismo.it; Corso Zanitello 6-8; ⊘9am-1pm Mon-Fri) Located on the Verbania Pallanza waterfront, this office has accommodation details and a range of brochures. Opening hours were in a state of flux at the time of writing.

❶ Getting There & Away

BOAT
Ask at the boat landing for various deals on ferry and hydrofoil tickets for market days in the lakeside towns. Otherwise, a hop-on-hop-off round trip taking in Isola Madre, Isola Superiore, Isola Bella and Stresa costs €16.50. Further afield, one way/return tickets to Cannobio cost €6.50/12.50.

CAR
Verbania Pallanza is on the S34 that runs along Lake Maggiore's western shore.

Ghiffa

The main (some would say only) reason for stopping in Ghiffa, a blip of a village 4km northeast of Verbania, is to make a pilgrimage 3km inland and uphill (by road – a stone-paved walking trail is a little shorter and steeper) to the **Sacro Monte della Santissima Trinità**. This holy mount was laid out in the mid-17th century but apparently was not completed. The lovely tree-filled sanctuary, including its church and a couple of chapels (not to mention the handy restaurant), is sited within a small nature reserve and provides a balcony view over Lake Maggiore below (albeit partly obscured by the thick foliage). One chapel on the walking path (about 100m away) was completed but, presumably, a series of them, running all the way downhill, was originally planned.

Hikers have plenty of paths to choose from around here. The Via delle Genti, an historic walking path that has connected Switzerland and northern Italy via the St Gotthard pass for centuries, passes by here (it's almost a 1½-hour walk to Verbania). Other signed walking paths abound – for more information, ask at the Verbania tourist office (p82).

Cannobio

POP 5225

Just 5km south of the Swiss border, Cannobio's toy-town, cobblestone streets are delightfully quaint. Nicely set apart from the busier towns to the north and south, it's a dreamy place that makes for a charming lake base.

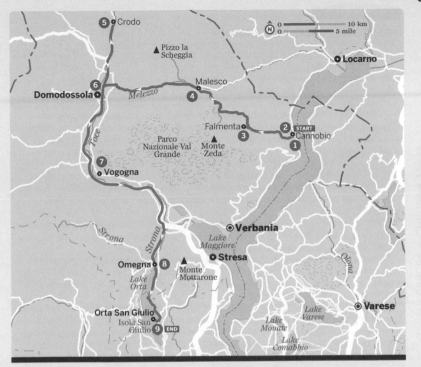

Driving Tour
Lakes & Mountains

START CANNOBIO
FINISH ORTA SAN GIULIO
LENGTH 110KM; HALF A DAY

This picturesque drive combines some of the best lake and mountain scenery anywhere in Italy's north. While half a day is ample, this drive could easily fill a most pleasurable day of your life.

Begin in the charming lake-shore village of **1 Cannobio**, before taking the scenic P75 which leads high into the heavily wooded hills of the Val Cannobina. Just 2.5km along the valley from Cannobio, in Sant'Anna, the Torrente Cannobio forces its way powerfully through a narrow gorge known as the **2 Orrido di Sant'Anna**, crossed at its narrowest part by a cute Romanesque bridge. If you've started the journey just before lunch, consider pausing for a meal at **Grotto Sant'Anna**, a Ticino-style grotto that overlooks the thundering gorge. About 7km further up the valley, a

steep 3km side road consisting of hairpin bends leads up to the central valley's main town, **3 Falmenta** (666m – they say the town's priest would like to have 1m added to or subtracted from the official figure). It's pleasant to wander around and worth a lunch stop at Circolo Falmenta. At the top of the valley in **4 Malesco**, turn left (west) towards Domodossola. If you haven't eaten by the time you arrive, take the 33km round trip detour to the village of **5 Crodo** which hides **Ristorante Marconi** in a simple but welcoming stone house, where you'll be regaled with fine food from the kitchen of chef Denis Croce.

Forsake the autostrada and follow the S33 past **6 Domodossola** to **7 Vogogna** where a 14th-century castle keeps watch over the town. With the forested hillsides of the wilderness Parco Nazionale Val Grande visible away to the north, continue east then southeast, following the signs for **8 Omegna** at the head of Lake Orta. From here it's just 10.5km into charming **9 Orta San Giulio**.

WORTH A TRIP

PARCO NAZIONALE VAL GRANDE

A wooded wilderness set amid a little-visited stretch of the Italian Alps, the **Parco Nazionale Val Grande** (☑ 0324 8 75 40; www.parcovalgrande.it) is far removed from the more domesticated beauty of the lakes only a short distance away (Verbania is 10km from its southeastern edge). Declared a park in 1992, it covers 150 sq km and styles itself as Italy's largest wilderness area.

Never more than sparsely inhabited by farmers in search of summer pastures for cattle and loggers, the area has been largely free of human inhabitants since the 1940s. The last of them were partisans who fought the Germans in the latter half of WWII. (In June to October 1944, 5000 German troops moved against 500 partisans holed up in the Val Grande, killing 300 of them and destroying farms across the area.)

The lower Val Grande is dominated by chestnut trees, which give way to beech trees further up. Milan's Duomo had a special licence to log here from the 14th century. Wood was needed in the Candoglia marble quarries, to float the marble on canals to Milan and for use in scaffolding.

The absence of humans in the park today has seen wildlife proliferate. Most numerous is the chamois, and Peregrine falcons and golden eagles can be spotted. Wolves are also believed to be present, although seeing one is near impossible.

Information centres are located in five villages surrounding the park. The handiest for those staying around Lake Maggiore are Intragna and Cicogna (both near Verbania), the latter actually inside the park boundary. They tend to open only in spring and summer – call the main park number for opening hours.

Walks into the park will bring you to some majestic locations but as a rule should be done with local guides. Extremely basic, unstaffed refuges where you can sleep (if you have your own sleeping bag) dot the park. They come with a stove and wood for heating, and little else. Otherwise, some much easier *sentieri natura* (nature paths) have been staked out. Routes are available at the information centres and on the website.

◉ Sights

Most beguiling of all is Cannobio's east-facing waterfront promenade. Its central stretch, the elongated **Piazza di Vittorio Emanuele III** (closed off at its north end by the Bramante-style Santuario della Pietà church), has pastel-hued houses that overlook the pedestrian-only flagstone square across to the hills of the east shore. A series of restaurants and cafes occupy the houses' ground floors and spill on to the square. Otherwise, meandering the small web of lanes that makes up the old town is a pleasant way to while away your time, although specific sights are few and far between.

🏃 Activities

Tomaso Surf & Sail   WATER SPORTS
(☑ 0323 7 22 14; www.tomaso.com; Via Nazionale 7) Cannobio has an active sailing and windsurfing school, Tomaso Surf & Sail, next to a patch of gritty beach at the village's northern end. You can also hire small sailing boats here (from €120 a day).

🍴 Eating

Lo Scalo   MODERN ITALIAN €€
(☑ 0323 7 14 80; www.loscalo.com; Piazza Vittorio Emanuele III 32; meals €35-45; ⊙ 6-9pm Tue, 11.30am-2.30pm & 6-9pm Wed-Sun; ✱; 🚌 Cannobio) The pick of the restaurants along the main promenade, Lo Scalo has a fine setting. The cooking is sophisticated and clean, featuring dishes such as *tagliolini* (ribbon-thin pasta) with black truffles and mountain butter.

ℹ Information

Cannobio Tourist Office (☑ 0323 7 12 12; www.procannobio.it; Via Giovanola 25; ⊙ 9am-noon & 4-7pm Mon-Sat, 9am-noon Sun & holidays)

ℹ Getting There & Away

A parking area (per hour €1) is signposted off the main road through town; from here it's a short walk down through the old town.

Boat services connect Cannobio with most other Lake Maggiore towns.

LAKE MAGGIORE EAST BANK

The lake's eastern shore has less to detain you than does the west, but there are still enough worthwhile sights for at least a half-day's detour, although you'll need your own vehicle. If you can, make it a Wednesday to coincide with Luino's weekly market.

ℹ Getting Around

BOAT

Ferries call in at all the lakeside stops mentioned. This can be slow-going but some runs are handy, like the Stresa ferry to Santa Caterina del Sasso, and the car ferry linking Laveno with Verbania-Intra (on the western shore).

BUS

Local buses shuttle up and down the east bank of the lake. For Santa Caterina del Sasso, jump on one of the buses running between Laveno and Ispra.

CAR

The A26 tollway from Milan arrives at the south end of Lake Maggiore at Sesto Calende. From there you exit and follow the S north (it becomes the SS394 at Luino).

TRAIN

Trains from Milan serve the east shore of Lake Maggiore. FNM trains from Milan (Cadorna station) arrive in Laveno via Varese.

Vira

POP 680

In the hills above Vira, about 8km on the Swiss side of the border and 16.5km southeast of Locarno spread the gardens of the **Parco Botanico del Gambarogno** (☑091 795 18 66; www.parcobotanico.ch; admission Sfr5; ⊙8am-6pm). Hundreds of types of azalea, camellia, magnolia, rhododendron and other spring and summer flowers fill the air with their vivid colours and heady perfumes. Simply wander in at any time (there seems to be no real closing time) and pop a Sfr5 coin into the box at the entrance (it works on a trust system), then wander around. The gardens are located at the north end of the village of Piazzogna. From Locarno, you need to take a ferry to Magadino and pick up a local bus to Piazzogna, from where it is a short walk. The trip takes 45 minutes. By car, head for Piazzogna from either Vira or San Nazzaro (about 2.5km either way).

Luino

POP 14,471

The otherwise sleepy town of Luino hosts Lake Maggiore's biggest **market** (⊙8.30am-4.30pm Wed) on Wednesday year-round. This is no ordinary local flea market; rather it's an enormous bazaar that snakes off into the surrounding streets with all manner of trash and treasure, not to mention some good street food. The records show that an important weekly market was first held here in 1535. Today more than 350 stands are set up in the old town centre, with everything from local cheese to secondhand fashion on sale. Bargain-hunters come from as far away as the Netherlands.

It's madness if you try to get in here with a vehicle (unless you arrive very early). There are parking areas south of the town centre for €6 per day, but they fill up fast. Extra ferry services from the other side of the lake run on market day.

Laveno

POP 9053

Laveno is a pleasant enough lakeside town but the main reason for coming is to take the **Laveno Funivia** (☑0332 66 80 12; www.funiviedellagomaggiore.it; one-way/return adult €7/10, child €5/7; ⊙11am-5pm Mon Fri, 11am-6pm Sat, 10am-6pm Sun Apr-Oct, shorter hrs rest of year), a cute little capsulelike funicular which whisks you up to a panoramic beauty spot 949m above sea level, in the shadow of the **Sasso del Ferro** (1062m) peak. The views over the lake and beyond to the Alps are breathtaking.

If that all seems a bit bland, extreme-sports enthusiasts can approach **Icaro 2000** (☑0332 64 83 35; www.icaro2000.com; basic hang-gliding course €900) about doing a hang-gliding course here, as the terminus of the Funivia is a popular launch spot for hang-gliders.

DON'T MISS

MARKET DAYS

⇒ **Wednesday** Luino

⇒ **Friday** Verbania Pallanza & Stresa

⇒ **Saturday** Verbania-Intra

⇒ **Sunday** Cannobio

DON'T MISS

TOP FRESCOES

Among the best-kept secrets of the Lake Maggiore area are the fabulous frescoes – artistic remnants with centuries of history, in some cases remarkably well preserved. The cream range from pre-Romanesque to wonderful Florentine Renaissance. Our favourites:

Basilica di San Giulio (p92) The 12th-century church on Lake Orta's island is jammed with vibrant frescoes depicting saints.

Collegiata (p90) Florentine master Masolino da Panicale carried out a series on the life of St John the Baptist in 1435.

Chiesa di Santa Maria Foris Portas (p90) A modest Lombard church contains extraordinary pre-Romanesque frescoes that may date back to the 7th century.

Santa Caterina del Sasso (p86) The church in this former monastery is filled with well-preserved frescoes.

Walkers should stop by the **Laveno tourist office** (☑ 0332 66 87 85; Piazza Italia 6; ⊙ 9.30am-1pm & 2.30-5pm Tue-Sun) for the free Via Verde Varesina map (1:35,000), which has various hiking trails marked.

Casalzuigno

POP 1360

In the unassuming town of Casalzuigno, about 9km east of Laveno, generations of nobles have swanned about the magnificent gardens of **Villa della Porta Bozzolo** (☑ 0332 62 41 36; www.fondoambiente.it; adult/child €6/3; ⊙ 10am-6pm Wed-Sun Mar-Sep, to 5pm Wed-Sun Oct & Nov, Sat & Sun only Feb, closed Dec & Jan), completed in 1690. The grand, two-storey building, surrounded by various outbuildings, has a calm, self-assured feel. Inside, the ballroom and upstairs gallery are richly decorated with frescoes. The cool, dark library, with its 18th-century walnut book cabinets, is only open on Sunday. Outside, fine Italianate gardens create a pleasing world of natural harmony.

Santa Caterina del Sasso

The monastery of **Santa Caterina del Sasso** (www.santacaterinadelsasso.com; ⊙ 8.30am-noon & 2.30-6pm Apr-Sep, to 5pm Mar, closed Mon-Fri Nov-Feb) **FREE** is one of the most spectacularly located such places in northern Italy. Clinging to the high rocky face of the southeast shore of Lake Maggiore, it is reached by a spiralling stairway (there's also a lift for €0.50 each way) from 60m above. A word of warning, however: the fabulous photos you'll have seen were taken from the air and there is no comparable land-based vantage point.

First news of this convent came in the 13th century, when Dominican friars founded it; bits were tacked on subsequently down the centuries. It was abandoned in the course of the 20th century.

You enter by a portico overlooking the lake, and pass through the south monastery and a small courtyard (with an 18th-century winepress), which leads into another Gothic portico. A 16th-century fresco series depicting the *Danza macabra* (Dance of Death) can still be made out on its upper level. Finally you reach the church, fronted by a four-arch portico. The church is a curious affair; it's actually the cobbling together of a series of 13th- and 14th-century chapels that form an oddly shaped whole. Inside, you behold a carnival of frescoes, among them the Christ Pantocrator in the Cappella di San Nicola, the first chapel on the right upon entering.

Ferries from Stresa (return €7) call here irregularly. Otherwise, by car or bus it's 6.5km south of Laveno (watch for the signs for Leggiuno and then a sign for the convent, 1km in off the main road).

Ranco

POP 1371

Just outside the tranquil lake town of Ranco is the eccentric **Museo Europeo dei Trasporti** (European Transport Museum; ☑ 0331 97 51 98; www.museodeitrasportiogliari.it; Via Alberto 99; ⊙ 10am-noon & 3-6pm Tue-Sun) **FREE**, fun for anyone who likes machines and potentially a great distraction for kids. Collection items stretching from the 1800s include a tricycle, various horse-drawn carriages from around Europe and beyond, a double-decker horse-drawn tram from Milan and a strange wind-powered tram with sail (which generally had to be dragged along by horses or oxen). Among the various steam-train locomotives and cars, there is one that was put at the personal disposal of composer Giuseppe Verdi. Among the buses is a wonderful 1912 Fiat. Also on show are cable cars, hot-air balloons and a recreation of a Milan metro stop.

Aside from the transport museum, the main thing to do in Ranco is call by the fantastic restaurant **Il Sole** (☑ 0331 97 65 07; www.ilsolediranco.it; Piazza Venezia 5; meals €80-100, tasting menu €100; ⊗ noon-2.30pm & 7-10pm Wed-Sun), with lake views, beautiful garden and even better cooking. Some local critics consider it among the best in Italy. It's difficult to choose: a risotto with Parmesan froth? Lobster salad perfumed with orange, *Mozzarella di bufala* (buffalo mozarella)? Or perhaps the heavenly light *fritto misto* (mixed fried fish and seafood)? Leave the thinking up to staff and opt for one of the tasting menus. Oh, and it has rooms too.

Angera

POP 5694

The Borromeo clan bought the chunky medieval **Rocca di Angera** (www.borromeoturismo.it; Via Rocca Castello 2; adult/child €8.50/5, combined ticket incl Isola Bella & Isola Madre €21/10.50; ⊗ 9am-6pm) from Milan's Visconti family in 1449 and the fortress lords over the town of Angera. Inside is the 12-room **Museo della Bambola**, displaying the Borromeo family's priceless collection of dolls. What better place for them than this towering, fairy-tale castle with its high, crenellated walls atop a rocky outcrop? Modest vineyards cling to the slopes on the west side. Various rooms and halls open on to the courtyard, among them the awe-inspiring Sala della Giustizia (Hall of Justice), with its overarching vault and lively 13th-century frescoes. From the tower, when it's open, you have breathtaking views. The doll collection counts more than 1000 items, while a separate collection of French and German mechanical dolls and figurines (dating from 1870 to 1920) becomes highly amusing when they are set in sometimes noisy motion. The easiest way up is by car (signposted from the centre of An-

gera). By foot, follow the signs from Piazza Parrocchiale. The rest of Angera repays a stroll, too. The shady waterfront is speckled with villas and old fishing families' houses and there are good views across the water to Arona.

If you like fresh lake fish then **Hotel Lido Angera** (☑ 0331 93 02 32; www.hotellido.it; Viale Libertà 11; meals €35-45; ⊗ lunch & dinner Tue-Sun, dinner Mon) is the place to go. Set right on the lake and surrounded by greenery, this hotel restaurant serves up a mix of classical local dishes with a contemporary spin, especially in the pleasing presentation. The wine list is broad, including products from all over the country, and they'll ensure you choose the best wines to go with each dish. Grab a table by the large windows, gaze over the lake and enjoy. It's signposted along the road into town from Ranco.

VARESE

POP 81,579

Spread out to the south of the Campo dei Fiori hills, between Lake Maggiore and Como province, Varese is a prosperous provincial capital with a pretty old town and some grand villas worth exploring.

◉ Sights

Palazzo Estense   ARCHITECTURE
(off Via Montebello) From the 17th century, nobles and the rich, many from Milan, began to build second residences around Varese's historic centre. Of these, the most sumptuous is the Palazzo Estense, completed in 1771 for Francesco III d'Este, the Austrian-appointed governor of the Duchy of Milan.

From Via Sacco, the main entrance is surprisingly understated as the main graceful facade actually looks south onto the Italianate **Giardini Estensi** (admission free; ⊗ 8am-dusk). The building now belongs to the town hall and cannot be visited, but anyone may swan through the entrance into the gardens, punctuated by ponds, an, hidden on a rise behind Villa Mirabello is a giant cedar of Lebanon.

From Palazzo Estense, villa fans could round off by walking half a kilometre from Via Sacco to the 17th-century **Villa Recalcati**, now seat of the provincial government. You can wander around the outside of the building.

Varese

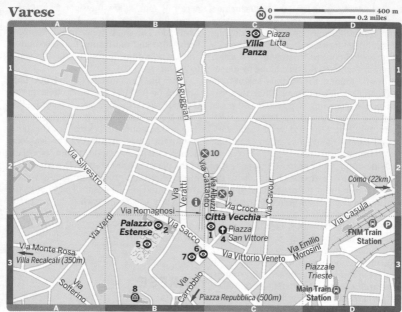

Varese

◎ Top Sights
1 Città Vecchia C3
2 Palazzo Estense B3
3 Villa Panza C1

◎ Sights
4 Basilica di San Vittore C3
5 Giardini Estensi B3
6 Piazza Monte Grappa B3
7 Torre Civica B3
8 Villa Mirabello Museum B3

✖ Eating
9 Ristorante Teatro C2
10 Vecchia Trattoria della Pesa C2

Villa Mirabello Museum MUSEUM
(off Viale Sant'Antonio; adult/child €4/2; ⊙10am-12.30pm & 2-6pm Tue-Sun Jun-Oct, 9.30am-12.30pm & 2-5.30pm Nov-May) Villa Mirabello houses the city's main museum, of which only a modest section with Roman remnants is open. The villa is accessible through the Giardini Estensi, which was once a separate property.

Villa Panza ARCHITECTURE, MUSEUM
(📞0332 28 39 60; www.fondoambiente.it; Piazza Litta 1; adult/child €8/3, park only €2/free; ⊙10am-6pm Tue-Sun) On a rise north of Varese's centre, where the high walls of private residences enclose narrow, winding lanes, Villa Panza enjoys beautiful views of the Alps from its extensive gardens. The villa was donated to the nation in 1996 and part of that donation was an intriguing art collection, mostly monochrome canvases by American post-WWII artists, scattered about the opulent rooms and halls of the villa.

One of the finest rooms is the 1830 Salone Impero (Empire Hall), with heavy chandeliers and four canvases by American David Simpson (born 1928). More can be seen in the outbuildings, which are also used for temporary art exhibitions. The gardens, a combination of 18th-century Italianate and early-19th-century English style make for a lovely meander before or after the art.

Città Vecchia HISTORIC QUARTER
(Old Town) North off Piazza Monte Grappa, the delightful pedestrianised **Corso Matteotti** signals the western boundary of the tiny old centre, at whose heart rises the baroque **Basilica di San Vittore** (Piazza San Vittore). The interior is a lavish affair, while the exterior is watched over by the muscular, freestanding **Torre Campanaria** (Bell Tower) which dates from the 17th and 18th centuries.

The surrounding tangle of lanes makes for a pleasant meander, dotted with several eateries and cafes.

Piazza Monte Grappa   PIAZZA

Piazza Monte Grappa, on the cusp of the old town, is fascinating for history and architecture buffs. The square was completely remade in grand fascist fashion in 1935. Most extraordinary is the **Torre Civica**, an enormous and somehow menacing clock tower; at the base flowers an *arengario* (a balcony, from which Mussolini and co could harangue the populace). It has an almost sci-fi quality about it.

✖ Eating

Vecchia Trattoria
della Pesa   MODERN ITALIAN €€

(Da Annetta; ☑0332 28 70 70; www.daannetta.it; Via Cattaneo 14; meals €35-40; ⊙noon-2.30pm & 6.30-10pm) New York–style decor meets Italian trattoria at this attractive place in the old town. The owners have a number of well-regarded restaurants around the Varese area, including **Da Annetta** (☑0332 49 02 30; www.daannetta.it; Via Fé 25, Capodilago; meals €60-70; ⊙noon-2.30pm & 7-10pm Thu-Mon, noon-2.30pm Tue Sep-Jul) where it all began in 1928, and this in-town option is a bit like the decor – a mix of the traditional staples with contemporary riffs on the theme in a menu that changes regularly.

Ristorante Teatro   ITALIAN €€€

(☑0332 24 11 24; www.ristoranteteatro.it; Via Croce 3; meals €50-60; ⊙noon-2pm & 6.30-9pm Wed-Mon) A Varese stalwart for fine cooking, Ristorante Teatro serves up fresh local specialities with an emphasis on the best ingredients rather than frilly elaborations – think local truffles, mushrooms and fresh fish.

❶ Information

Varese Tourist Office (☑0332 28 19 13; www. vareseturismo.it; Via Romagnosi 9; ⊙9.30am-1pm & 2-6.30pm Mon & Wed-Sat, 9.30am-1pm & 3-5pm Tue, 9.30am-1pm Sun Apr-Oct, 9.30am-5.30pm Mon-Sat Nov-Mar)

❶ Getting There & Around

BUS

Local buses depart from outside the train station and fan out from Varese to most towns around the province. Local city bus C runs from various stops around central Varese to the *sacro monte*.

CAR

The fastest way to Varese is via the A8 motorway from Milan. If you're driving into central Varese, follow the signs to the parking station at Piazza Repubblica.

TRAIN

Regular but sluggish trains leave from Milan's Porta Venezia and Porta Garibaldi stations for Varese (€60, 55 to 80 minutes). Some of these continue to Laveno on Lake Maggiore. For around the same price and taking around the same duration, FNM trains (www.ferrovienord. it) run from Milan's Stazione Nord to Varese (and one to Laveno) via Voltorre and Gemonio.

AROUND VARESE

Santa Maria del Monte

The medieval hamlet of Santa Maria del Monte (880m), 8km north of Varese and with a sanctuary devoted to Our Lady, was long a site of pilgrimage for the faithful. Then, at the beginning of the 17th century, the Church and Lombardy's Spanish rulers came up with the idea of creating a sacred way to lead up to this sacred mount, **Sacro Monte del Rosario** (☑0332 28 46 24; www. sacromonte.it), one of a dozen or so built in the 16th and 17th centuries in Lombardy and Piedmont. The result is a cobbled, 2km climb (the starting point is at 585m). Fourteen chapels dotted along the way are representative of the mysteries of the Rosary (hence the name). At the end of the climb you can drink in the magnificent views with a well-deserved beer on the terrace of **Ristorante Monforte** (☑0332 22 70 27; Via del Santuario 74; ⊙noon-3pm & 6.30-9pm Wed-Mon). The *sacro monte* is inside the Parco Regional Campo dei Fiori, a patch of thickly wooded hills.

After taking in the views, the hamlet is worth exploring too. Its tight lanes will lead you to a funicular to get back down, but this operates only on weekends, holidays and daily in sweltering August. It's also possible to drive up to the back side of the *sacro monte* this way (but that might be considered cheating). Many folks make the sacrifice of climbing up in the evening for a romantic evening meal at the *stile liberty* (Italian art nouveau) **Al Borducan** (☑0332 22 29 16; www.borducan.com; meals €45; ⊙12.30-2pm & 7.30-9.30pm Thu-Tue). Inside is a fine dining room of elegant simplicity, with timber furniture, cream linen and artistic tile floor. The terrace is great for sipping a wine. Mains tend to be meaty; the homemade tagliatelle in rabbit stew might tempt you.

Castiglione Olona

The nondescript modern town of Castiglione Olona, 8km south of Varese off the S road, contains a quite extraordinary gem. The old centre was largely rebuilt under the auspices of its most favoured son, Cardinal Branda Castiglioni (1350–1443), in Florentine Renaissance style. Via Branda leads from the central square up to the **Collegiata** (www.museocollegiata.it; Via Cardinal Branda 1; admission €6.50; ☺10am-1pm & 3-6pm Tue-Sun Apr-Oct, 9.30am-12.30pm & 2.30-5.30pm Tue-Sat & 10am-1pm & 3-6pm Sun Nov-Mar, 10am-6pm 1st Sun of every month), a church that contains the town's masterpiece. Inside its baptistery, Florentine master Masolino da Panicale carried out a series of frescoes on the life of St John the Baptist in 1435.

Castelseprio & Torba

Spread out in peaceful woods about 1.5km outside the village of Castelseprio, around 20km south of Varese, is the ancient archaeological site of **Sibrium**, a Lombard castrum (fortified settlement) with remains of fortress walls, various churches and towers. As long ago as the 5th or 6th century AD, the Lombards began erecting a fort on this site. By the 7th century it was a small town, with its Basilica di San Giovanni, houses and watchtowers.

Four kilometres away by road, but a short walk from the **Parco Archeologico di Castelseprio** (☑0331 82 04 38; Via Castelvecchio 1513; ☺8.30am-7.20pm Tue-Sat, 9.30am-6.20pm Sun & holidays Feb-Nov, shorter hrs Nov-Jan) FREE is the **Monastero di Torba** (☑0331 82 03 01; www.fondoambiente.it; adult/child €5/2.50; ☺10am-6pm Wed-Sun Mar-Sep, to 5pm Wed-Sun Oct, Nov & 2nd half of Feb, closed Dec & Jan), which started life as a forward watchtower for the castrum (it was the only one to remain intact). It was then turned into the centrepiece of a Benedictine convent and adorned with rare frescoes. A short walk west from the Monastero di Torba is the **Antiquarium** (☺2.45-5.15pm Sun & holidays) FREE, a small repository of objects and documents on the site.

To get to the archaeological park take a leafy 1.5km drive from Castelseprio village. The church is 200m from the parking area and information office. Torba is about a 1.5km drive northeast from the village.

Outside the village walls is the small pre-Romanesque **Chiesa di Santa Maria Foris Portas** (Holy Mary Outside the Gates; Castelseprio; ☺8.30am-2.30pm & 5.30-7pm Sat, 9.45am-2.30pm & 5.30-6pm Sun & holidays) FREE, which was built around the 7th century. Inside in the apse are some remarkable frescoes depicting scenes from the infancy of Jesus Christ and dominated by an image of Christ Pantocrator. Art historians tend to think these were painted in Lombard times but some believe they are from the Carolingian period (8th or 9th century). Either way, they are a rare and vivid example of pre-Romanesque artistic beauty. The realism, life and colour of the human figures seem to owe something to classical art of ancient times, not at all like the stiff and, to some eyes, childlike religious art of the Romanesque period, still several centuries away.

LAKE ORTA

Enveloped by thick, dark-green woodlands, tranquil Lake Orta (aka Lake Cusio) could make a perfect elopers' getaway. Measuring 13.4km long by 2.5km wide, it's separated from its bigger and better-known eastern neighbour, Lake Maggiore, by Monte Mottarone. The focal point of the lake is the captivating medieval village of Orta San Giulio, often referred to simply as Orta.

If it's romance you want, come during the week and you'll have the place largely to yourself. On spring and summer weekends, good-natured groups of day trippers from Milan and beyond descend on the place, creating plenty of atmosphere, but crowding the town. You can't blame them: it's perfect for a day out and a long Sunday lunch.

You could drive right around the lake in a day. Outside Orta, specific sights are few and far between. The ride along the largely flat, east bank of the lake is the best for lake views, while on the west bank, the main road runs mostly high up in the hills and out of sight of the lake. Some out-of-the-way villages on the west bank are fun to explore, however. Roads stretch away from the lake on either side to the mountains. To the east is Monte Mottarone. To the north-west stretches the beautifully wild and little-visited Valstrona.

Orta San Giulio

POP 1167

There's a very northern Italian magic about Orta San Giulio, one of the prettiest old lakeside towns you'll find anywhere. Aside from its lovely architecture and tangle of narrow lanes – it's the kind of place that rewards aimless wandering – it also serves as the gateway to the lovely Isola San Giulio and is watched over by a forested hillside strewn with chapels. As you can imagine, it's a great place to spend a few days, particularly during the week when it's likely to be just you and the locals.

◉ Sights

Piazza Mario Motta   PIAZZA

Here's a picture of how life really should be lived: rise early and head for a coffee on Piazza Mario Motta, gazing across at

LAKE MAGGIORE & AROUND ORTA SAN GIULIO

Orta San Giulio

the sun-struck Isola San Giulio in the early morning quiet. From your vantage point, contemplate the Palazotto, a squat, fresco-enlivened structure sitting atop pillars like giant stilts at the north end of the square.

Once the seat of a local council, the Palazotto now occasionally opens for temporary exhibitions but climb the stairs anyway for good views. The square burbles with local life on market day (Wednesday).

Sacro Monte di San Francesco   CHAPEL, PARK

Beyond the lush gardens and residences that mark the hill rising behind Orta is a kind of parallel 'town', the *sacro monte*. The views down the lake are captivating, and meandering from chapel to chapel is a wonderfully tranquil way to pass a few hours.

From Piazza Mario Motta, Salita della Motta leads up a cobbled hill between centuries-old houses to the baroque-fronted Chiesa dell'Assunta and then bends right (south) to the cemetery and back right up the sacred mountain, with its 20 chapels scattered about, each dedicated to recounting a part of the biography of St Francis of Assisi. Some boast wonderful frescoes while others are more modest affairs. A road also leads up from near the tourist office if you're driving.

Isola San Giulio   ISLAND

Anchored barely 500m in front of Piazza Mario Motta is Isola San Giulio. The island is dominated by the 12th-century **Basilica di San Giulio** (Isola San Giulio; ☉9.30am-6.45pm Tue-Sun, 2-5pm Mon Apr-Sep, 9.30am-noon & 2-5pm Tue-Sun & 2-5pm Mon Oct-Mar) [FREE], full of vibrant frescoes that alone make a trip to the island worthwhile. The frescoes mostly depict saints (and sometimes their moment of martyrdom – St Laurence seems supremely indifferent to his roasting on a grate). Step inside after mass, when the air is thick with incense and the frescoes seem to take on a whole new power.

The church, island and mainland town are named after a Greek evangelist, Giulio, who's said to have rid the island of snakes, dragons and assorted monsters in the late 4th century. His remains lie in the crypt of the Basilica di San Giulio.

The footpath encircling the island makes for a peaceful stroll, hence its popular name of **Via del Silenzio**. Indeed, a series of aphorisms on the wonders of silence (all very fine when screaming school groups have the run of the place) have been placed along the way.

If you walk it clockwise, they now call it the Via della Meditazione, with a whole load of other multilingual signs to inspire you on your search for inner peace.

Regular ferries (one way/return €2/2.85) run from Orta San Giulio's waterfront. More expensive private launches (one way/return €4/8) also run, departing when there are sufficient passengers to warrant the five-minute crossing.

✖ Eating

Enoteca Al Boeuc   PIEDMONTESE €

(☎339 584 00 39; http://alboeuc.beepworld.it; Via Bersani 28; meals €15-20; ☉11.30am-3pm & 6.30pm-midnight Wed-Mon) This candlelit stone cavern has been around since the 16th century, and in its present incarnation you'll be served light meals to be savoured with fine wines by the glass (eg a velvety Barolo for €8). It's a classy alternative to the clamour of the waterfront.

Choose between a lovely mixed bruschetta with truffles and mushrooms, sausage, platters of cheese and cold meats or a Piedmontese favourite, *bagna caùda* (a hot dip made with butter, olive oil, garlic and anchovies in which you bathe vegetables).

Agriturismo Cucchiaio di Legno   AGRITURISMO €€

(☎0322 90 52 80; www.ilcucchiaiodilegno.com; Via Prisciola 10, Località Legro; set menu €24; ☉6-9pm Thu & Fri, noon-2.30pm Sat & Sun) This honest-to-goodness *agriturismo* (farmstay) restaurant cooks up delicious local dishes including risotto, fish straight out of the lake, and salami and cheese from the surrounding valleys. Dine alfresco on the vine-draped patio overlooking the herb-planted garden. It really is like being at someone's house. It's about 800m from the Orta Miasino train station.

Ristorante Sant'Antonio   ITALIAN €€

(☎0322 91 19 63; Tortirogno; meals €25-30; ☉noon-2pm & 7-9.30pm Wed-Sun) About 1.5km north of Orta on the main road, this family-run place has a winning combination of lakeside tables and simple, no-nonsense cooking. Not surprisingly, it's deservedly popular. While the occasional meat dish appears, fish is the name of the game.

Venus Ristorante   ITALIAN €€

(☎0322 9 03 62; www.venusorta.it; Piazza Mario Motta 50; meals €30-35; ☉noon-2.30pm & 6-9.30pm Tue-Sun) Every now and then a place surprises. We sat down here for lunch, drawn more by the views over the water than any expectation of good cooking – it's rare to get both in Orta. But despite a large weekend crowd, service was fast and friendly, and by the time we'd finished eating – raw Parma ham, sliced wafer-thin, with green apple sauce and sesame-seed foccacia, followed by gnocchi with vanilla, bourbon and red prawns – we were hooked.

Ristoro Olina   NORTHERN ITALIAN €€
(☑ 0322 90 56 56; Via Olina 40; meals €35-40; ☺ noon-2.30pm & 6.30-9pm Thu-Tue) A modern alternative to your typical low-lit trattoria, this place offers a range of imaginative dishes combining creativity with fine products. Dishes push the boundaries a little, such as the risotto creamed with beetroots and pure chocolate. Service is thoughtful.

🛈 Orientation

If you're arriving by car, park at one of the two parking stations on the road into town and walk the rest of the way. The main street is shop- and eatery-lined Via Olina (later Via Bossi and Via Gippini), which straggles north from the square. A series of uneven lanes branches off it to the lake, while others wiggle their way inland. Via Gippini finally changes name to Via Ettore Motta on its way past the lakeside Villa Motta – a pleasant waterside wander.

🛈 Information

Main Tourist Office (☑ 0322 90 51 63; Via Panoramica; ☺ 10am-1pm & 2.30-5.30pm Mon-Thu, 11am-1pm & 2.30-6.30pm Fri-Sun) Has information on the whole lake area.
Pro Loco (☑ 0322 9 01 55; Via Bossi 11; ☺ 11am-1pm & 2-4pm Mon, Tue & Thu, 10am-1pm & 2-4pm Fri-Sun) In the Comune (town hall) Building, for town information. There's a nice garden out the back.

🛈 Getting There & Around

BOAT
Navigazione Lago d'Orta (☑ 0322 84 48 62; www.navigazionelagodorta.it) runs boats to numerous lakeside spots from its landing stage at Piazza Mario Motta, including Isola San Giulio (one way/return €2/2.85), Omegna (€4.50/7), Pella (€2.50/4.60) and Ronco (€3/4.60). A day ticket for unlimited travel on the whole lake costs €8.50.

BUS
Only intermittent bus services serve the west bank towns. From June to September, three buses a day run between Stresa and Orta (€4).

CAR
The most direct way to reach Orta from Milan or other distant location is to follow the A26 tollway and exit at Meina for the south end of the lake or Gravellona Toca for the north end.

There are two parking areas where the road dips down into town, one outdoor with parking meters, the other under cover. At both you pay €2/10 per hour/day.

TRAIN
Orta Miasino train station is a 3km walk from the centre of Orta San Giulio. It is on the line from Novara to Domodossola and trains stop at all the towns on the east shore of the lake. From Milan, there are trains from Stazione Centrale (change at Novara) every two hours or so (€6.50, two hours). Between March and October, a little **tourist train** (www.treninodiorta.it/ita; one way/return €2.50/4; ☺ 9am-7pm May-Sep, 9am-5.30pm Mar, Apr & Oct, 9.30am-5.30pm rest of year) shuttles between the town centre, *sacro monte* and the train station approximately every half-hour.

Lake Orta West Bank

Heading out of Omegna – the large town at the northern end of the lake (Thursday is market day) – follow the signs for Varallo and the road quickly takes you up high and out of view of the lake. At **Nonio**, you can then follow a steep, minor road down to the lake at **Oira**, a tiny hamlet with a church, boat landing and lakeside pizzeria. A few kilometers further south, at Cesara, turn east for Egro. The 4km country road leads you past the half-abandoned stone hamlet of **Grassona** before reaching **Egro**. From this quiet, stone village a wooded walking trail leads down to the lakeside town of **Pella** (about 45 minutes). As you descend, you have views across Isola San Giulio and the lake. High above Pella you may detect a small chapel built in a seemingly impossible outcrop of rock. More interesting is the narrow road that leads 3km north of Pella to **Ronco**, a little gem of a village, all dark-stone houses huddled around a grid of teensy lanes and facing the lake.

It is also possible to circle the lake on foot. Known locally as the **Anello Azzurro** (Blue Ring), the circuit walk of the entire lake can take about three days at a leisurely pace. Starting at Orta and heading south, you are looking at about 14km to Pella, about 13km the following day to Omegna and another 14km back from Omegna to Orta. The recommended kick-off point is *sacro monte*

WORTH A TRIP

VALSTRONA

West out of Omegna, 14km of winding valley road follows a deep river gorge (some locals bring their own equipment for a little white-water fun on weekends), the Torrente Strona, on a verdant, meandering course northwest to the settlement of Forno (850m). The object of the trip is essentially to dive into the splendid scenery, which becomes more dramatic the higher you climb. Keep your eyes open for majestic spring waterfalls and snowcapped mountains (most of the year) in the background.

From Forno, a 3km track leads west to the Campello Monti, mountain pasture land that was inhabited in the 13th century by the Walser community. The Walsers, speakers of a German dialect from the Upper Valais area of southern Switzerland, migrated to various parts of southern Switzerland, Austria and northern Italy during the Middle Ages. In the 13th century they arrived here. To this day, they maintain their dialect and a scattering of their traditional timber farmhouses.

in Orta. Readers of Italian can get a closer route description at www.lagodorta.net, which offers all sorts of ideas on other walks in the area.

LOCARNO (SWITZERLAND)

POP 15,303

With its palm trees and much vaunted 2300 hours of sunshine a year, Locarno has attracted northern tourists to its Mediterranean-style setting since the late 19th century. The lowest town in Switzerland and the most striking one on Lake Maggiore, it has a pretty and compact old town, a castle, good restaurants and shopping, and an august history: the 1925 Locarno Conference was where treaties were signed to bring peace to Europe after WWI.

◉ Sights & Activities

Santuario della
Madonna del Sasso   SANCTUARY

(◷6.30am-6.30pm) Up on the hill, with panoramic views of the lake and town, this sanctuary was built after the Virgin Mary allegedly appeared in a vision to a monk in 1480. There's a small museum, a church and several, rather rough, near-life-sized statue groups (including one of the Last Supper) in niches on the stairway. The best-known painting in the church is *La Fuga in Egitto* (Flight to Egypt), painted in 1522 by Bramantino. Contrasting in style are the naive votive paintings by the church entrance where the Madonna and Child appear as ghostly apparitions in life and death situations.

A **funicular** (adult one way/return Sfr4.80/7.50, child Sfr2.20/3.60; ◷7am-8pm) runs every 15 to 30 minutes from the town centre, but the 20-minute climb is not demanding (take Via al Sasso off Via Cappuccini) and you pass some shrines on the way.

Old Town   HISTORIC QUARTER

Stride out and about the Italianate piazzas and arcades, and admire the Lombard houses. There are some interesting churches. Built in the 17th century, the **Chiesa Nuova** (New Church; Via Cittadella) has a dizzyingly ornate baroque ceiling. Outside, left of the entrance, stands a giant statue of St Christopher with disproportionately small feet. The 16th-century **Chiesa di San Francesco** (Piazza San Francesco) has frescoes by Baldassare Orelli, while the Chiesa di Sant'Antonio is best known for its altar to the *Cristo morto* (Dead Christ).

A fortified castle, **Castello Visconteo** (☑091 756 31 80; Piazza Castello; adult/reduced Sfr7/5; ◷10am-noon & 2-5pm Tue-Sun Apr–mid-Nov) is named after the Visconti clan who long ruled Milan. The castle changed hands various times and was occupied by the Milanese under Luchino Visconti in 1342. Taken by French forces in 1499, the castle and town of Locarno eventually fell to the Swiss confederation in 1516. Today it houses a museum with Roman and Bronze Age exhibits. Locarno is believed to have been a glass-manufacturing town in Roman times, which accounts for the strong showing of glass artefacts in the museum. This labyrinth of a castle, whose nucleus was raised around the 10th century, also hosts a small display (in Italian) on the 1925 Locarno Treaty.

Isole di Brissago
ISLAND

([☎]091 791 43 61; www.isolebrissago.ch; adult/child Sfr8/2.50; [⊙]9am-6pm Apr-late Oct) The Ticino authorities could not have chosen a more enchanting spot to locate their botanical garden. On Isole di Brissago you can visit San Pancrazio, one of the two specks of green. Renowned for its spring-blooming rhododendrons, camellias and azaleas, the garden (which contains some 1500 flora species) is rich in sub-tropical plants from as far off as Southeast Asia and South America. The mild climate here makes this possible. Ferries run from Locarno (35 minutes), Ascona (15 minutes) and other points at the Swiss end of Lake Maggiore. The last one back to Ascona and Locano leaves at 6.10pm.

Cimetta
CABLE CAR

(www.cardada.ch; one way/return from Orselina adult Sfr30/36, child Sfr15/18; [⊙]9.15am-12.30pm & 1.30-4.50pm Mar-Nov) A series of funiculars, cable cars and chairlifts whisks you high above Locarno. Take the funicular (p94) to the Orselina funicular stop, from where a cable car goes to **Cardada** (one way/return adult Sfr24/28, child Sfr12/14; [⊙]8am-8pm Jun-Sep, 9am-6pm Mon-Thu, 8am-8pm Fri-Sun Mar-May, Oct & Nov), and then a chairlift soars to Cimetta at 1672m. You can engage in some gentle hikes at Cardada and Cimetta. At the former, make for the promenade suspended above the trees, at the end of which is a lookout point with 180-degree views over the city, Lake Maggiore and the valleys beyond. The geological observation point at Cimetta goes one better, with 360-degree views. The mountain is sliced up by walking trails (paths are marked) that can have you stomping along from 1½ to four or so hours, depending on the trails you choose. Longer routes lead into the Valle Maggia and Val Verzasca.

Cimetta is a popular launch spot for paragliders. If you want to have a go with an instructor in a tandem flight, contact **Volo Libero Ticino** (www.cvlt.ch). On the web page is a list of qualified instructors and details for contacting them; click on 'voli passeggeri' on the home page. Locals get in a little ski practice up here in winter.

★ Festivals & Events

Festival Internazionale di Film
FILM

(International Film Festival; www.pardo.ch; Via Ciseri 23) Locarno has hosted this prestigious two-week film festival in August since 1948. Cinemas are used during the day but at night films are screened on a giant screen in Piazza Grande.

✗ Eating

Caffe dell Arte
CAFE €

(www.caffedellarte.ch; Via Cittadella 9; meals Sfr15-20; [⊙]8.30am-6pm Tue-Sat; [📶]) This classy, light-filled cafe is right at home on one of the prettiest corners of Locarno's old town. There's a quiet courtyard and some outdoor tables on the lane, free wi-fi and a small but light menu that includes plates of local mountain cheeses.

Manora Ristorante
CAFETERIA €

([☎]091 743 76 76; Via Stazione 1; meals Sfr15-25; [⊙]7.30am-9pm Mon-Sat, 8am-9pm Sun) It's not often we recommend cafeteria-style places, but step inside this appealing place and you'll soon see that it's different. Laid out like an upmarket produce store, it has everything from salads and hot meals to snacks. It's particularly good for families or if you're hungry outside of normal lunch or dinner hours. Getting a table is the only problem.

Svizzero Ristorante
ITALIAN €€

([☎]091 751 28 74; Largo Zorzi 18; meals Sfr25-30; [⊙]11.30am-11.30pm) With bow-tied waiters serving up decent pizzas, pasta and soups, Svizzero could be anywhere in Italy. Try the local Ticino speciality, *conoglio con polenta* (rabbit with polenta). It's one of the better midrange place clustered close to Piazza Grande.

Osteria Chiara
ITALIAN €€€

([☎]091 743 32 96; www.osteriachiara.ch; Vicolo della Chiara 1; meals Sfr70-80; [⊙]9am-2pm & 7pm-midnight Tue-Sat; [♿]; [🚌]Cannobio) Tucked away on a cobbled lane, this place has all the cosy feel of a grotto. Sit at granite tables beneath the pergola or at timber tables by the fireplace for chunky pasta and mostly meat dishes. From the lake follow the signs up Vicolo dei Nessi.

Ristorante Locanda Locarnese
MODERN ITALIAN €€€

([☎]091 756 87 56; www.locandalocarnese.ch; Via Bossi 1; meals Sfr70-80; [⊙]11.30am-2.30pm & 6.30-11.30pm Mon-Sat) One of Locarno's best, Locanda Locarnese's catch-cry is 'creative cooking with local products.' A small but carefully chosen set of fish and meat mains changes with the seasons, but whatever you order leave room for the tiramisu with Grand Marnier and orange sorbet. They

Locarno (Switzerland)

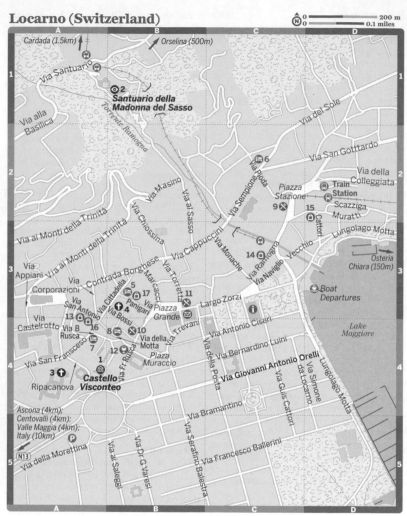

have a range of lunch set menus (Sfr27.50 to Sfr 50.50) or set tasting menus (from Sfr74).

Drinking & Nightlife

Pardo Bar
BAR

(www.pardobar.com; Via della Motta 3; 11am-midnight Mon-Thu, to 1am Fri & Sat) With its background music, scattered timber tables (a couple of computers on one) and wine and cocktails on offer, Pardo Bar attracts a relaxed and mixed crowd.

Shopping

Locarno's old town has a number of lovely little boutiques, from upmarket ladies' fashion to antiques.

Renzo Ugas Art & Design Gallery
ACCESSORIES

(Via San Antonio 3; 9am-noon & 2-6.30pm Tue-Fri, 9am-5pm Sat) Leather wallets, Porsche (and other brand) pens, and bags made from recycled bags by Vargu or Aunts & Uncles make this a place to savour the good things in life. It's only small, but that's part of its charm.

Locarno (Switzerland)

Bellerio Antichità   ANTIQUES
(www.bellerio-antichita.ch; Via San Antonio 11; ⊙9am-noon & 2-6.30pm Mon-Fri, to 5pm Sat) A wonderful collection of antiques, including jewellery, makes this place a haven for collectors and the curious alike.

Merkur Chocolaterie   CHOCOLATE
(Via Ramogna 10; ⊙9am-6.30pm Mon-Fri, to 6pm Sat) If you love chocolate, just try leaving this shop without buying a slab of Läderach or a perfectly conceived box of hand-crafted little chocolates. Then again, we'd err on the side of indulgence.

Negozio Prima Eta   CHILDREN'S CLOTHING
(☑091 743 38 47; Piazza Stazione 6; ⊙10am-noon & 2-6pm Mon-Fri, to 5pm Sat) Children's clothing lines from the classic to the contemporary crowd this friendly little store between the train station and the waterfront. It also has a thoughtfully chosen collection of children's toys.

Verde Oliva   FOOD
(☑091 751 51 40; Via Panigari 8; ⊙10am-noon & 2-6.30pm Fri, 10am-5pm Sat) It may not open often, but it's worth being here when it does. Its stock-in-trade is olive oils and fine foods from Liguria and a small but classy selection of homewares.

ℹ Information

Lago Maggiore Tourist Office (☑091 791 00 91; www.maggiore.ch; Largo Zorzi 1; ⊙9am-6pm Mon-Fri, 10am-6pm Sat & holidays, 10am-1.30pm & 2.30-5pm Sun mid-Mar–Oct, 9.30am-noon & 1.30-5pm Mon-Fri, 10am-noon & 1.30-5pm Sat Nov–mid-Mar) Ask about the Lago Maggiore Welcome Card and its dis-

counts. If you're keen to hike, pick up the *Walking in Ticino* brochure which covers a number of day walks.

ℹ Getting There & Around

BOAT
Lake Maggiore boats call in at the wharf equidistant from Piazza Grande and Piazza Stazione in Locarno and at Ascona.

BUS
Postal buses to the western valleys leave from outside Locarno train station. Bus 31 from Locarno's train station and Piazza Grande stops at Ascona's post office, with departures every 15 minutes (Sfr3).

CAR
The SS34 road from Verbania follows Lake Maggiore north to Locarno. From Lugano, follow the A2 motorway north and take the Locarno turnoff. There is cheap street parking (Sfr4 for 10 hours) along Via della Morettina.

TRAIN
Trains run every one to two hours from Brig (Sfr53, 2½ hours), passing through Italy (bring your passport). Change trains at Domodossola. Various trains reach Locarno from Zürich (Sfr60, three hours) and other locations in central and northern Switzerland, mostly via Bellinzona (Sfr8.50, 30 to 60 minutes).

ASCONA

POP 5453

A phalanx of pretty pastel-hued houses sidles up to the placid lakefront in Ascona, Locarno's smaller twin across the Maggia river delta. Behind them, a tangle of little streets makes for pleasant wandering, with plenty of eateries and bars to distract you. Walking paths file up into the green hills around the town from the southern end of the waterfront.

◎ Sights

Museo Casa Anatta MUSEUM
(🖉 091 785 40 40; www.monteverita.org; Via Collina 78) The late 19th century saw the arrival of 'back to nature' utopians, anarchists and sexual libertarians from northern Europe in Ascona. Their aspirations and eccentricities are the subject of the Museo Casa Anatta on Monte Verità (take the small bus to Buxi from the post office; Sfr1.20). All sorts of characters, including Herman Hesse, dropped by to look at the goings on. The museum was closed for renovations when we visited – ask at the Locarno tourist office (p97) to see if it has reopened.

Museo Comunale d'Arte Moderna MUSEUM
(🖉 091 759 81 40; www.museoascona.ch; Via Borgo 34; adult/reduced Sfr7/5; ☉ 10am-noon & 3-6pm Tue-Sat, 10.30am-12.30pm Sun Mar-Dec) The Museo Comunale d'Arte Moderna, in Palazzo Pancaldi, includes paintings by artists connected with the town, among them Paul Klee, Ben Nicholson, Alexej Jawlensky and Hans Arp.

Collegio Papio HISTORIC BUILDING
(Via Cappelle) The Collegio Papio, now a high school, boasts a fine Lombard courtyard and includes the 15th-century **Chiesa Santa Maria della Misericordia**, with medieval frescoes. You can wander into the grounds on weekends.

✕ Eating

Antica Osteria Vacchini TICINESE €€
(🖉 091 791 13 96; www.osteriavacchini.ch; Contrada Maggiore 23; meals Sfr30-35; ☉ noon-2.30pm & 6.30-10pm Mon-Sat) Diners find no shortage of pasta, meat and fish options in this old-time eatery (with outdoor section across the lane), but the house special is *piodadella della Vallamaggia* (a set of three kinds of cold meats with three matching sauces, salad and fries) – a filling and tasty summer option.

✦ Festivals & Events

Jazz Ascona MUSIC
(www.jazzascona.ch) With the weather warming up in the second half of June, Ascona grooves into summer with local and international jazz acts.

Settimane Musicali MUSIC
(www.settimane-musicali.ch) International classical music festival held annually in Ascona since 1946 from the end of August to mid-October.

❶ Getting There & Away

A ferry runs from Locarno to Ascona (20 minutes, Sfr10.50 one way).

TICINO'S WESTERN VALLEYS

The valleys ranging to the north and west of Locarno teem with grey-stone villages, gushing mountain streams, cosy retreats, traditional *grotti* (cellars carved out of great blocks of granite) and endless walking opportunities.

For canyoning, rafting or climbing, contact **Indepth Outthere Adventures** (🖉 078 614 98 77; www.indepthoutthere.com).

❶ Getting There & Around

BUS
Postal buses to the western valleys leave from outside Locarno train station. For instance, buses operate to Sonogno from Locarno as often as once hourly (Sfr10.50, 1¼ hours). Regular buses run from Locarno to Cevio and Bignasco (Sfr10.50, 50 minutes), from where you make less regular connections into the side valleys. In Valle Maggiore, a bus runs four times a day from Bignasco to San Carlo (Sfr8.50, 30 minutes) from April to October.

CAR
Your own transport is by far the most flexible way to get around the valleys.

Centovalli

The 'hundred valleys' is the westward valley route from southern Ticino to Domodossola in Italy, known on the Italian side as Valle Vigezzo (which is an access route to the Parco Nazionale Val Grande; see p84).

A picturesque **train** (www.centovalli.ch; one way adult/child under 6yr Sfr35/free) clatters along the valley, trundling across numerous precarious-looking viaducts, from Locarno to Domodossola (or vice versa). There are around a dozen departures a day; the journey is one hour and 50 minutes. Take your passport.

By car, the route is slightly less exhilarating but you have greater flexibility to stop and explore on the way. The road winds west of Ponte Brolla (4km from Locarno) in a string of tight curves, high on the north flank of the Melezzo stream. The quiet towns with their stone houses and heavy slate roofs, mostly high above the road and railway line on either side of the valley, make tranquil bases for mountain hikes. Among the best stops are **Verdasio, Rasa** and **Bordei**. Rasa is only accessible by cable car from Verdasio.

At **Re**, on the Italian side, there is a procession of pilgrims on 30 April each year, based on a tradition that originated when a painting of the Madonna was reported to have started bleeding when struck by a ball in 1480. More startling than the legend is the bulbous basilica built in the name of the **Madonna del Sangue** (Madonna of the Blood) from 1922 to 1950.

From Re, the route passes through a series of picturesque villages. **Valle Vigezzo** is also locally known as the Valley of the Painters. An art school was established in Santa Maria Maggiore in the 19th century, and many houses and chapels are gaily adorned with frescoes. The road and train line end in **Domodossola**, a frontier town on the train line that links Milan with Geneva.

Valle Maggia

The broad Valle Maggia follows the Maggia river from Ponte Brolla (4km northwest of Locarno); the valley's **tourist office** (☑ 091 753 18 85; www.vallemaggia.ch) is in Maggia. Visit **Aurigeno**, a village known for its colourful frescoes. At **Cevio**, where the valley splits, 12km northwest of Maggia, admire the colourful facade of the 16th-century Pretorio, covered with local ruling families' coats of arms, and old-town mansions. A short, signposted walk away are *grotti*. At **Cerentino**, the road forks – the right fork leads 5.5km

along hairpin bends to **Bosco Gurin**, a minor ski centre and high pasture village, where the main language is German. The left fork from Cerentino leads up the 8km-long **Valle di Campo** along a winding forest road to another upland valley. The prettiest of its towns is **Campo**, with its Romanesque bell tower.

Back in Cevio, the Valle Maggia road continues 3km to Bignasco. Turn west for the **Val Bavona**, the valley's prettiest area. A road follows a mountain stream through narrow meadows set between rocky walls to a series of irresistible hamlets. **Foreloin** is dominated by a waterfall (a 10-minute walk away), and is home to **Ristorante La Freda** (☑ 091 754 11 81; Foroglio; meals Sfr45-50; ☺ lunch & dinner Apr-Oct). Sit by a crackling fire for the *stinko di mailer* (pork shank), served with the best polenta you're likely to taste. Just after San Carlo, at the northwestern end of Val Bavona in the inner reaches of Valle Maggia, a **cable car** (www.robiei.ch; adult/child return Sfr24/12; ☺ mid-Jun–early Oct) rides up to the Robiei dam and nearby lakes – a great spot for hiking.

Val Verdasca

Located about 4km northeast of Locarno, this rugged 26km valley snakes north past the impressive Vogorno dam, fed by the gushing Verzasca (Waters) river. Just beyond Lake Vogorno, look to the left and you will see the picture-postcard hamlet of **Corripo** seemingly pasted on to the thickly wooded mountain flank. To reach it you cross the **Gola Verzasca**, a scintillating gorge. About 5km upstream, **Lavertezzo** is known for its narrow, double-humped, Romanesque bridge (rebuilt from scratch after the 1951 floods destroyed it) and natural pools in the icy stream. Be careful, as storms upstream can turn the river into a raging torrent in no time. Another 12km takes you to **Sonogno**, a once abandoned hamlet at the head of the valley that has been resuscitated largely due to tourism.

Lake Como & Around

Includes ➡

Best Places to Eat

➡ Albergo Silvio (p111)
➡ Gatto Nero (p114)
➡ Ristorante La Vista (p121)
➡ Locanda dell'Isola (p115)
➡ Osteria del Gallo (p108)
➡ Sale e Tabacchi (p122)

Best Places to Stay

➡ Avenue Hotel (p199)
➡ Hotel Silvio (p200)
➡ Hotel La Perla (p200)
➡ Hotel Gabbani (p201)
➡ Albergo Milano (p201)

Why Go?

In the shadow of the snow-covered Rhaetian Alps and hemmed in on both sides by steep, verdant hillsides, Lake Como (aka Lake Lario) is perhaps the most spectacular of the three major lakes. Shaped like an upside-down Y, measuring around 160km in squiggly shoreline, it's littered with villages, including exquisite Bellagio and Varenna. Where the southern and western shores converge is the lake's main town, Como, an elegant, prosperous Italian city.

Among the area's siren calls are some extraordinarily sumptuous villas, often graced with paradisiacal gardens. The mountainous terrain means that opportunities for taking bird's-eye views of the lake and its towns are numerous. And with a fraction of the visitors drawn here compared to Lake Maggiore or Lake Garda, Lake Como and its surrounding area offer the traveller the chance to enjoy a real sense of discovery.

Road Distances (KM)

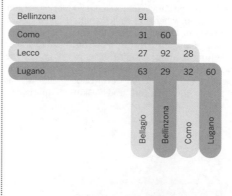

	Bellagio	Bellinzona	Como	Lugano
Bellinzona	91			
Como	31	60		
Lecco	27	92	28	
Lugano	63	29	32	60

Getting Around

The SS340 more or less shadows the western and eastern shores of Lake Como, bypassing many of the smaller lakeside villages which are served by smaller roads. Narrow mountain roads climb up from Varenna, Gravedona, Cernobbio, Argegno, Bellagio and elsewhere. Buses run from Como to most of the lake's towns, passing through smaller villages en route, while public ferries connect most lakeside towns (except those south of Varenna along the East Bank) with regular departures.

3 PERFECT DAYS

Day 1: Como & Above

Take an early funicular up to Brunate to catch views of Como and the lake under the rising sun's rays. Back in Como, explore the old centre, making time for the Duomo and to see the remarkable frescoes in the Basilica di Sant'Abbondio. It's then time for lunch at Osteria del Gallo, after which you can head 7km around the lake to Cernobbio, to admire the pretty lakeside villas, followed by a drive up to Monte Bisbino, arriving in time for sunset views over the lake. You could finish with a splendid meal at Gatto Nero.

Day 2: Bellagio & Villa Carlotta

Catch a ferry from Como to Bellagio, where you could take a room and spend the morning discovering the gardens of two fine villas and the topsy-turvy beauty of the town itself. Lunch at Albergo Silvio before taking a car ferry to Cadenabbia for an afternoon visit to nearby Tremezzo's Villa Carlotta. Car ferries returning to Bellagio run late into the evening.

Day 3: Varenna & the East Bank

From Bellagio, jump on another car ferry to Varenna, a rival in beauty to Bellagio. You could spend the bulk of a day here, especially if you include a walk up to the Castello di Vezio to gaze back down on Varenna. Those with wheels can easily head north for the medieval hamlet of Corenno Plinio and, just further on, the lovely Abbazia di Piona, where you can stay if you don't want to turn back.

Where to Stay

Finding vacant rooms around Lakes Como and Lugano can be problematic in key places (including Como, Bellagio, around Tremezzo and Varenna especially) in July and August and, to a lesser extent, at Easter. Not surprisingly, these also happen to be the most desirable places to stay along the lakeshore, although Lugano is also lovely. Bookings should be made at least a month (and sometimes even further) in advance.

DON'T MISS

The view down to Varenna and across the lake from Castello di Vezio.

Best Lake Views

➡ Castello di Vezio (p122)
➡ Monte Bisbino (p114)
➡ Cima Sighignola (p116)
➡ Monte Brè (p125)
➡ Monte San Salvatore (p125)
➡ Sacro Monte di Ossuccio (p115)
➡ Brunate (p107)
➡ Peglio (p118)

Best Escapes

➡ Val d'Intelvi & Erbonne (p116)
➡ Corenno Plinio (p120)
➡ Valtellina (p119)
➡ Valsassina (p123)
➡ Dorsale (p110)
➡ Rifugio Menaggio (p118)

Resources

➡ **Bellagio** (www.bellagiolakecomo.com) Everything you need to know about lovely Bellagio.

➡ **Lago di Como** (www.lakecomo.org) One-stop portal for Lake Como's attractions and services.

➡ **Lugano** (www.luganotourism.ch) Comprehensive tourist office site on Lugano and its immediate surrounds.

➡ **Ticino** (www.ticino.ch) Region-wide information on Switzerland's corner of the lakes region.

LAKE COMO & AROUND

Lake Como & Around Highlights

1 Wandering the back lanes and waterfront of **Varenna** (p121), then climbing to **Castello di Vezio** (p122) for superlative views.

2 Imagining how 19th-century royalty lived in the opulent rooms and gorgeous garden of **Villa Carlotta** (p117).

3 Staying on after the crowds have left and having timeless **Bellagio** (p110) all to yourself.

4 Exploring the tangle of lanes in **Como's old town** (p105), then rising above it all to **Brunate** (p107).

5 Riding the funiculars and ambling along the waterfront in lakeside **Lugano** (p123).

6 Stepping back into medieval times by visiting the three Unesco World Heritage–listed castles of **Bellinzona** (p129).

7 **Hiking** the length of Lake Como in one of the most beautiful weeks you'll ever spend.

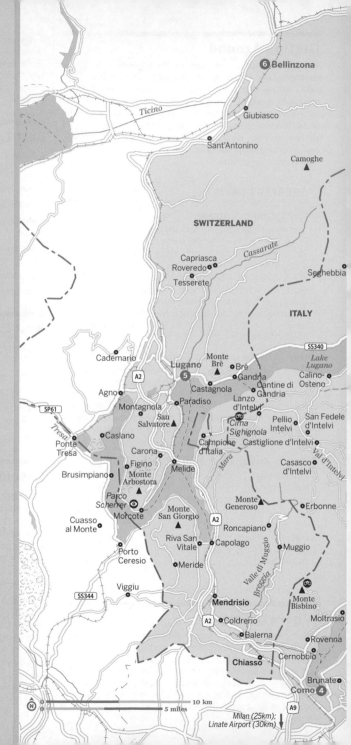

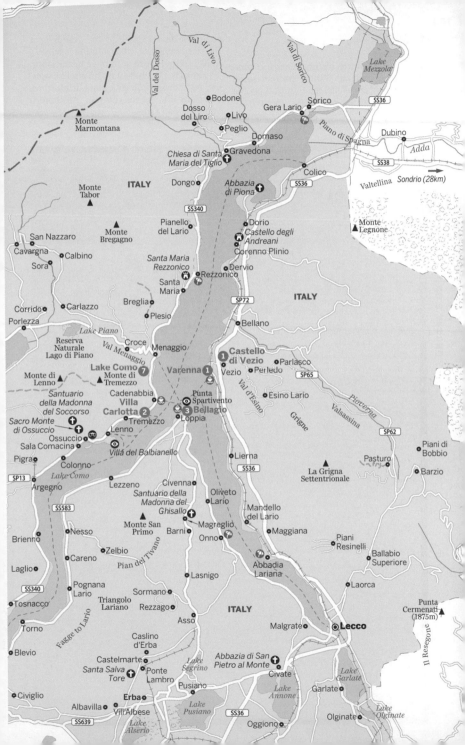

COMO

POP 85,263

With its charming historic centre, Como sparkles year round. Within its remaining 12th-century city walls, the beautiful people of this prosperous city whisk about from shop to cafe, sweeping by the grandeur of the city's cathedral, villas and the loveliness of its lakeshore with admirable insouciance. The town is a lovely spot for an aimless wander, punctuated with coffee and drink stops, especially in Piazzas Cavour, Alessandro Volta and San Fedele.

Como

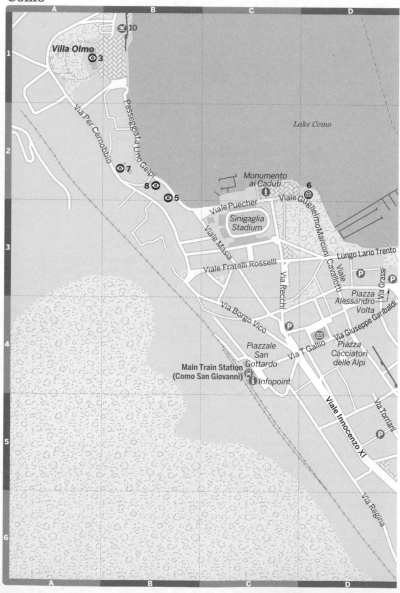

In 1127, the Milanese conquered Como's forces and ordered the destruction of all walls and buildings, save its churches. Centuries later, Como built its wealth on the silk industry and it remains Europe's most important producer of silk products. You can buy silk scarves and ties for a fraction of what is charged at boutiques internationally.

◉ Sights

While the churches and piazzas will be the focal point of your wandering through the

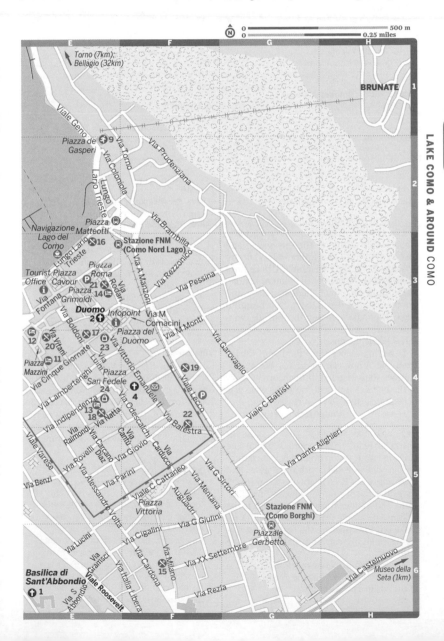

Como

◉ Top Sights
1 Basilica di Sant'Abbondio E6
2 Duomo E3
3 Villa Olmo A1

◉ Sights
4 Basilica di San Fedele F4
  Broletto ....(see 2)
5 Passeggiata Lino Gelpi B2
6 Tempio Voltiano D2
7 Villa Gallia B2
8 Villa Saporiti B2

◉ Activities, Courses & Tours
9 Funicolare Como-Brunate E2
10 Lido di Villa Olmo B1

◉ Sleeping
11 Albergo del Duca E4

12 Albergo Firenze E4
13 Avenue Hotel E4
14 Le Stanze del Lago E3

◉ Eating
15 Enoteca 84 ....F6
16 Gelateria Ceccato E3
17 Loft E4
18 Natta Café E4
19 Osteria Angolo del Silenzio F4
20 Osteria del Gallo E4
21 Ristorante Sociale E3
22 Trattoria dei Combattenti F4

◉ Shopping
23 A Picci E4
24 Craft & Antiques Market E4

old town, don't miss Via Vitani, the loveliest of the pedestrian thoroughfares.

Basilica di Sant'Abbondio
BASILICA
(Via Regina; ☉ 8am-6pm Apr-Sep, to 4pm Oct-Mar) About 500m south of the city walls, and just beyond busy and rather ugly Viale Innocenzo XI, is the remarkable 11th-century Romanesque Basilica di Sant'Abbondio. Aside from its proud, high structure and impressive apse decorated with a beautiful geometric relief around the outside windows, the highlight is the remarkable fresco series inside the apse.

Depicting scenes from the life of Christ, from the Annunciation to his burial, the frescoes were restored to their former glory in the 1990s. A university occupies what was once the cloister. To get a closer glimpse of the apse exterior, amble into its grounds.

Basilica di San Fedele
BASILICA
(Piazza San Fedele; ☉ 8am-noon & 3.30-7pm) The circular layout of the originally 6th-century Basilica di San Fedele, with three naves and three apses, has been likened to a clover leaf. Its 16th-century rose window and precious 16th- and 17th-century frescoes add to its charm. The facade is the result of a 1914 remake but the apses are the real McCoy, featuring some eye-catching sculpture on the right side.

A craft and antiques **market** (Piazza San Fedele; ☉ 9am-7pm Sat) fills the piazza in front of the basilica on Saturday.

Duomo
CATHEDRAL
(Piazza del Duomo; ☉ 8am-noon & 3-7pm) Although largely Gothic, elements of Romanesque, Renaissance and baroque styles can also be seen in Como's imposing, marble-clad Duomo. The cathedral was built between the 14th and 18th centuries, and is crowned by a high octagonal dome.

Next door, the polychromatic **Broletto** (medieval town hall) is unusual in that it butts right up against the church and is rather overwhelmed by it – a singular defeat for lay power.

Villa Olmo
VILLA, MUSEUM
(☎ 031 57 61 69; www.grandimostrecomo.it; Via Cantoni 1; adult/reduced €10/8; ☉ villa during exhibitions 9am-12.30pm & 2-5pm Mon-Sat, gardens 7.30am-7pm Sep-May, 7.30am-11pm Jun-Aug) Set grandly facing the lake, the creamy facade of neoclassical Villa Olmo is one of Como's landmarks. The extravagant structure was

---

ART TALKS

If you speak Italian, a handy service for those wanting to know more about certain central city sights is **Speak Art**. Call ☎ 031 25 22 25 from your mobile phone and then key in the code posted on the information panel at the sight (eg 14, Piazza San Fedele) for an extended description. These calls can be a trifle expensive from non-Italian mobile phones.

built in 1728 by the Odescalchi family, related to Pope Innocent XI. If there's an art exhibition inside, you'll get to admire the sumptuous Liberty-style interiors. Otherwise, you can enjoy the Italianate and English gardens, which are open all day.

During summer the **Lido di Villa Olmo** (www.lidovillaolmo.it; Via Cernobbio 2; adult/reduced full day €6/4, half-day €4.50/2.50; ⊙ 9am-7pm mid-May–Sep), an open-air swimming pool and lakeside bar, is open to the public.

Passeggiata Lino Gelpi   WATERFRONT

Almost as nice as the Villa Olmo gardens is the lakeside stroll from Piazza Cavour. Follow Passeggiata Lino Gelpi along the water, passing the **Monumento ai Caduti** (War Memorial; Viale Puecher 9), a memorial to Italy's war dead from WWI and a classic example of Fascist-era architecture; it dates back to 1931. You'll also pass a series of mansions and villas, including **Villa Saporiti** and the adjacent **Villa Gallia**, both now owned by the provincial government.

Museo della Seta   MUSEUM

(Silk Museum; ☑ 031 30 31 80; www.museoseta como.com; Via Castelnuovo 9; adult/child €10/4; ⊙ 9am-noon & 3-6pm Tue-Fri) Housed in the bowels of the predictably ugly 1970s buildings of the Istituto Tecnico Industriale di Setificio textile technical school (where tomorrow's silk-makers and designers learn their trade), the Museo della Seta unravels the town's silk history, with early dyeing and printing equipment on display.

A wander around takes you through the entire process of producing silk. Explanations start with the humble silkworm and how it is raised (no longer the case in Italy, which imports raw silk mainly from China) through to the creation of bundles and reels of silk, and on to the dyeing and production of finished products.

Brunate   NEIGHBOURHOOD

Como is flanked to the east and west by steep and thickly wooded hills (scarred in part by the spread of residential housing). Northeast along the waterfront from central Como, the **Funicolare Como–Brunate** (☑ 031 30 36 08; www.funicolarecomo.it; Piazza de Gasperi 4, Como; one way/return adult €2.90/5.50, child €1.90/3.50; ⊙ half-hourly departures 8am-midnight mid-Apr–mid-Sep, to 10.30pm mid-Sep–mid-Apr; ⓣ Como) takes just seven minutes to reach Brunate, a quiet residential village which seems to float above Lake Como – it sits at 720m above sea level.

SWITCHED ON

The lakeside **Tempio Voltiano** (☑ 031 57 47 05; Viale Guglielmo Marconi; adult/child €3/free; ⊙ 10am-noon & 3-6pm Tue-Sun Apr-Oct, 10am-noon & 2-4pm Nov-Mar) was built in 1927 in memory of Como-born inventor of the battery, Alessandro Volta (1745–1827). The singular, circular landmark is more significant for what it represents than for its slim contents. In 1800 Volta invented the Voltaic battery, which preceded the electric battery, an invention that would later be refined and revolutionise people's daily life.

The views are pretty but partial – this is not the place for a sweeping panorama unless you walk further into the hills. Brunate's baroque **Chiesa di San Andrea**, with its faded pink exterior and giant bell peeking out of the bell tower, is hard to miss. In **San Maurizio**, a steep 40-minute walk (the first stage of the Dorsale hike) from Brunate's funicular stop, scale 143 steps to the top of the lighthouse, built in 1927 to mark the centenary of Alessandro Volta's death. The Como tourist office (p109) can provide a map with various suggested walks around Brunate.

✖ Eating

★ Natta Café   CAFE €

(☑ 031 26 91 23; Via Natta 16; meals €10-15; ⊙ 9.30am-3.30pm Mon, 9.30am-midnight Tue-Thu, 9.30am-2am Fri, 11.30am-2pm Sat; 🔊) This funky space in the old town, but ever-so-slightly removed from the busier thoroughfares, is Como's antidote to traditional trattorias and *osterias* (casual taverns). A funky cafe with free wi-fi, it serves up light meals that change regularly, baguettes, salads, wine by the glass and well-priced cocktails (€5 to €8). It's a lovely, laid-back little spot.

Gelateria Ceccato   GELATO €

(☑ 031 2 33 91; Palace Hotel, Lungo Lario Trieste 16; gelato €1.50-4; ⊙ noon-midnight) For generations, Comaschi have turned to Ceccato for their Sunday afternoon gelato and then embarked on a ritual *passeggiata* (evening stroll) with the dripping cones along the lakeshore. You can do no better than imitate them: order a creamy *stracciatella* (chocolate chip) or perhaps a mix of fresh fruit flavours and head off for a relaxed promenade along the lakefront.

LAKE COMO & AROUND COMO

ⓘ GETTING AROUND LAKE COMO

Ferries and hydrofoils operated by Como-based **Navigazione Lago del Como** (☑ 800 55 18 01, 031 57 92 11; www.navigazionelaghi.it; Piazza Cavour) criss-cross the lake, departing year-round from the jetty at the north end of Piazza Cavour. Single fares range from €2.50 (Como–Cernobbio) to €13 (Como–Lecco or Como–Gravedona). Return fares are double. Hydrofoil fast services entail a supplement of €1.40 to €5, depending on the trip.

Car ferries connect Bellagio with Varenna and Cadenabbia. A whole host of other tickets is available, including those for day cruises with lunch and those that include admission to lakeside villas.

★ Osteria del Gallo ITALIAN €€
(☑ 031 27 25 91; www.osteriadelgallo-como.it; Via Vitani 16; meals €25-30; ⊙ 12.30-3pm Mon, to 9pm Tue-Sat) This ageless *osteria* is a must. Cheerful green and white gingham is draped over the little timber tables and all around are shelves of wine and other goodies. The menu is recited by staff (in French, if you wish) and might include a first of giant ravioli, followed by lightly fried lake fish. Otherwise, pop by for a glass of wine.

Enoteca 84 ITALIAN €€
(☑ 031 27 04 82; Via Milano 84; meals €20-25; ⊙ noon-2.30pm & 7-10pm Fri & Sat, noon-2.30pm Mon-Thu) Down one side of this minuscule locale are lined-up tables; down the other are shelves of fine wine. The menu changes often, and ranges from platters of cold meats and cheeses to Lombard classics such as *pizzoccheri artigianali* (handmade buckwheat *tagliatelle*).

Ristorante Sociale ITALIAN €€
(☑ 031 26 40 42; www.ristorantesociale.it; Via Rodari 6; meals €20-25; ⊙ noon-2.30pm & 7-10.30pm Wed-Mon) Once attached to a nearby theatre, the Sociale is a local institution. The present location has a pleasant downstairs dining area with reasonably packed tables and an upstairs dining room sporting an outsized baroque fireplace and walls enlivened by frescoes. In addition to the menu, the waiter will announce a constantly changing series of dishes of the day. Cooking is hearty and no-nonsense.

Trattoria dei Combattenti TRATTORIA €€
(☑ 031 27 05 74; www.trattoriadeicombattenti.com; Via Balestra 5/9; meals €30-35; ⊙ 12.15-2.30pm & 7.30-10.15pm Tue-Sat, 12.15-2.30pm Sun & Mon; ▥) Set off a lovely cobblestone lane just inside the old city walls, this popular trattoria has inside timber tables with muted decor, an inner courtyard and a sunny gravel yard at the front. Opt for an *insalatone* (€9) if you want a 'big salad', or the two-course €14 set lunch. Grilled meats take a prominent place.

Loft ITALIAN €€
(☑ 031 26 78 46; 5th fl, Via Pietro Boldoni 3; meals €30-35; ⊙ 9.30am-7.30pm Mon, to 2am Tue-Sat, 10.30am-2am Sun) On the 5th floor of the Coin supermarket building, this trendy eatery offers a little of everything. While enjoying good Duomo views across the nearby rooftops, indulge in snacks and drinks at any time during the day. The menu covers many Italian staples, reasonable salads and mains like Como lake fish with butter and sage. It's all good but the setting makes it even better.

Osteria Angolo del Silenzio ITALIAN €€
(☑ 031 337 21 57; www.osterialangolodelsilenzio-como.com; Viale Lecco 25; meals €35-40; ⊙ noon-3pm & 7-10pm Tue-Sun) The 'Corner of Silence' manages to live up to its name inside with a succession of dining rooms and a fine rear garden. Locals mix with the occasional celeb hoping to pass off unobserved while digging into the succulent and fancily presented *petto d'anatra al pepe rosa* (duck breast cooked with pink pepper). The set lunch menu for €16 is a good choice.

Ristorante Bellavista ITALIAN €€
(☑ 031 22 10 31; Piazza di Bonacossa 2, Brunate; meals €30-35; ⊙ noon-2.30pm & 6.30-9.30pm Wed-Mon) Ride the funicular up to Brunate to dine in this peaceful historic villa a few steps up from the top station and with great views over the lake. The place is essentially one dining room with an adjoining terrace for summertime al fresco dining. As in many restaurants in Brunate, the menu reflects local traditions, with plenty of game meat in autumn and mains accompanied by polenta.

🛍 Shopping

A Picci SILK
(☑ 031 26 13 69; Via Vittorio Emanuele II 54, Como; ⊙ 3-7.30pm Mon, 9am-12.30pm & 3-7.30pm Tue-

Sat; 🚋Como) Open since 1919, this is the last remaining silk shop in town dedicated to selling Como-designed-and-made silk products such as ties, scarves, throws and sarongs. Products are grouped in price category (starting at €15 for a tie) reflecting the skill and workmanship involved in each piece. Sales assistants are happy to advise on colours and styles. If it's a gift, they'll also wrap it for you.

❶ Information

Tourist Office (☑031 26 97 12; www.lake como.org; Piazza Cavour 17; ⊙9am-1pm & 2-5pm Mon-Sat) There is an information kiosk (⊙10am-1pm & 2-5pm) next to the Duomo, and another at the train station (10am-1pm & 2-5pm).

❶ Getting There & Around

BUS

ASF Autolinee (SPT; ☑031 24 72 47; www. sptlinea.it) operates buses around the lake. Key routes include Como–Colico (€6, 1½ hours, three to five daily) via the west shore; Como–Bellagio (€3.20, 70 minutes, roughly hourly); and Como–Erba–Lecco (€3.20, one hour, almost hourly). Further afield, buses link Como with Bergamo (€6, 2¼ hours, up to six daily).

CAR

Traffic in and around Como tends to be intense. From Milan, take the A9 motorway and turn off at Monte Olimpino. The S leads east to Lecco and west to Varese. The roads around the lake are narrow and, on weekends especially, can be hair-raising.

Most parking is metered in Como and there are several covered car parks.

TRAIN

Como's main train station (Como San Giovanni) is served from Milan's Stazione Centrale or Porta Garibaldi (€4.55 to €13 depending on type of train, 30 to 60 minutes, at least hourly) that continue into Switzerland. If travelling between Como and Lugano or Bellinzona, take the regional trains (on the Ticino side, look for the S10 train), as the long-distance trains between Milan and Zürich cost more. Trains from Milan's Stazione Nord (€4.10, one hour, hourly) use Como's lakeside Stazione FNM (aka Como Nord Lago).

TRIANGOLO LARIANO

They call the stretch of territory between Como and Lecco in the south and Bellagio in the north the Triangolo Lariano (Lake Lario

Triangle), a mountainous and crumpled territory jammed with a surprising variety of landscapes. From the high and exhilarating 32km coast road between Como and Bellagio to quiet inland villages, there's plenty to discover.

The pearl is Bellagio, suspended like a pendant on the promontory where the lake's western and eastern arms split and head south. Hidden from view along the Como–Bellagio road are enchanting lakeside villages, like Torno and Careno (which get no direct sunlight in winter). The sunnier 22km eastern branch, between Bellagio and Lecco, is also a pretty drive.

Torno

POP 1214

Spread around a point in the jagged shore, Torno is a lovely stop just 7km from Como – it's easy to understand why Hermann Hesse fell in love with it when he visited in 1913. The lakeside Piazza Casartelli, fronted by three restaurants and the **Chiesa di Santa Tecla** (a baroque remake of the Romanesque original), the tiny port and shady trees complete the picture of this front-row seat on the lake.

About a 10-minute walk northeast around the point is the Romanesque-Gothic **Chiesa di San Giovanni**. It holds what is purported to be a holy nail from the cross of Jesus Christ, left behind by a German crusading bishop in the 11th century.

About 1.5km further east along the lake, **Villa Pliniana** was built in the 16th century (and therefore did not belong to the Plinys) and is one of the oldest ones located on the lake (Lord Byron stayed here and Percy Shelley thought about buying it). There are long-standing plans to open the villa to the public, but it's yet to happen and still seems a while off. An intermittently flowing fountain occasionally gushes from under the building into the lake. The phenomenon was observed by the Plinys and, much later, by Leonardo da Vinci.

At the south end of Torno's lakeside square, the **Albergo Belvedere** (☑031 41 91 00; Piazza Casartelli 3; meals €20-30; ⊙noon-2.30pm & 6.30-9pm Wed-Mon Mar-Dec), an old-time hotel-restaurant, has a bucolic touch, with timber tables and walls dripping with black-and-white photos. In the warmer months, it opens out to a series of terrace tables, shaded by the twisting branches of a linden tree that, since 1987, has been patiently cultivated sideways to form a pergola. Lake fish and meat options feature prominently.

Careno

About 1.5km south of the town of Nesso, Careno is signposted, but if you blink, you'll miss it. This tiny, lakeside hamlet looks like an inverted triangle from the opposite shore, with its church, the Romanesque **Chiesa di San Martino**, at the bottom. Satisfaction with discovery and a shady, lakeside stroll should be followed by a meal at the charming **Trattoria al Porto** (☑ 031 91 01 95; Via al Pontile 26; meals €20-25; ☺ noon-2.30pm & 6.30-9.30pm Tue-Sun). With its oddly shaped balcony-pergola just above the ferry landing, this place is a hit with Como folks in the know and specialises in lake fish.

The bus stop for Careno is between Km15 and Km16. Head down the steep, stone stairs from the road.

Bellagio

POP 3078

It's impossible not to be smitten by Bellagio's waterfront of bobbing boats, its maze of steep stone staircases, red-roofed and green-shuttered buildings, dark cypress groves and rhododendron-filled gardens. Like the prow of a beautiful vessel, it sits at the crux of the inverted Y that is Lake Como; the Como and Lecco arms of the lake wash off to port and starboard. Wander out of the old town centre to Punta Spartivento and gaze north up the third arm towards the Alps. In Roman times, Pliny had one of his favourite villas here.

Bellagio is hardly a secret. On summer weekends, foreign tourists are overwhelmed by hordes of day trippers up from Milan. Try to come midweek if you want a modicum of peace. It makes a nice base for ferry trips to other locations on the lake, in particular Varenna, on Lake Como's east shore.

◉ Sights

Before setting out to explore the town, pick up the three self-guided walking tour brochures from the tourist office. They range from one-hour *(Historical Tour & Itinerary of the Central Part of Town)* to three-hour walks that take in neighbouring villages, including **Pescallo**, a small one-time fishing port about 1km from the centre, and **Loppia** with the 11th-century **Chiesa di Santa Maria**, which is only visible from the outside.

Basilica di San Giacomo   CHURCH
(Piazza della Chiesa) Bellagio's most interesting Romanesque church is the Basilica di San Giacomo in central Bellagio, built in the 12th century by master builders from Como.

Villa Serbelloni   VILLA, GARDEN
(☑ 031 95 15 55; Via Garibaldi 8; adult/child €9/5; ☺ tours 11.30am & 3.30pm Tue-Sun Apr-Oct) The lavish gardens of Villa Serbelloni cover

---

HIKING THE TRIANGOLO LARIANO

Hiking options abound in the Triangolo Lariano. The classic trail is known as the **Dorsale** (Ridge) and zigzags for 31km across the interior of this mountainous country from the Brunate funicular station to Bellagio. The standard trail takes about 12 hours and is usually done in two stages, stopping in mountain huts along the way. The standard route follows mule trails, presents no particular difficulties to moderately fit ramblers and is also ideal for mountain biking.

The more adventurous can follow the Dorsale Creste trail, which follows a series of mountain crests. Several *rifugi* (mountain huts) are dotted along the way, and you'll find a couple of accommodation options at **Pian del Tivano**, roughly halfway along the trail. You can do a little *sci di fondo* (cross-country skiing) here in winter. From the 17th century until the early 1900s, when the coast road from Como to Bellagio was completed, travellers used the 32km **Strada Regia** (Royal Way), a partly stone-paved path that links various villages on the west coast of the Triangolo Lariano from Torno to Lezzeno. The easiest stretch connects Torno and Pognana Lario (about five hours), while the stage from Pognana to Lezzeno via Nesso (or Careno) branches into mountainous back country between villages. Other walking trails abound.

Ask at the main Como tourist office (p109) for the fine *Carta dei Sentieri* (Trail Map; 1:25,000) produced by the Comunità Montana Triangolo Lariano.

much of the promontory on which Bellagio sits. The villa has seen plenty of the great and the good swing by: Austria's Emperor Maximilian I, Ludovico il Moro and Queen Victoria, to name a few. You'll have to be content with the villa's exterior (the interior is closed to the public) and the gardens.

Visits are by guided tour only and numbers are limited; tickets are sold at the small PromoBellagio information office, in the 15th-century Torre di Defensa Medievale near the church.

Villa Melzi D'Eril
VILLA, GARDEN

(📞339 457 38 38; www.giardinidivillamelzi.it; Lungo Lario Manzoni; adult/child €6.50/4; ☉9.30am-6.30pm late Mar-Oct) Garden-lovers can stroll the grounds of neoclassical Villa Melzi d'Eril, built in 1808 for one of Napoleon's associates and coloured by flowering azaleas and rhododendrons in spring. The garden, adorned with scattered statues, was the first English-style park on Lake Como. Other villas, closed to the public, are in this vicinity as well.

🏃 Activities

Bellagio Water Sports
KAYAKING

(📞3403 94 93 75; www.bellagiowatersports.com) Kayak tours (including to Villa Balbianello) and rental are possible from this experienced outfit in Pescallo.

Barindelli's
BOAT TOUR

(📞338 211 03 37; www.barindellitaxiboats.com; Piazza Mazzini; 1hr tour €140) For a touch of George Clooney glamour, consider taking a tour in one of Barindelli's slick, mahogany cigarette boats. They offer hour-long sunset tours around the Bellagio headland, which are well worth the cost for groups up to 12 people. They can also tailor-make outings around the lake, or you could consider making a night of it and using it as a taxi service for a top-class dinner.

🍴 Courses

Bellagio Cooking Classes
COOKING COURSE

(📞333 786 00 90; www.gustoitalianobellagio.com; Salita Plinio 5; per person €60-75) A wonderful way to really get to know Bellagio, these cooking classes have a personal touch – they take you to the local shops to buy the food and then local housewives lead the classes. Classes are small (a minimum of two, maximum of five).

🍴 Eating

There are loads of restaurants along the waterfront, but the best meals are to be had up in the lanes climbing inland and further afield. Opening days of some places may be reduced in the depths of winter.

Albergo Silvio
ITALIAN €€

(📞031 95 03 22; www.bellagiosilvio.com; Via Carcano 12, Bellagio; meals €25-30; ☉noon-3pm & 6.30-10pm Mar–mid-Nov & Christmas) Operating since 1919, this place must be getting something right to achieve the seemingly unanimous acclaim. Simple food offerings at reasonable prices combine with lovely views west over the lake. From the pergola garden outside, you also espy the Romanesque Chiesa di Santa Maria of Loppia in among the cypresses. It's 1km south of the centre of Bellagio above Loppia, which you can walk down to from here along an overgrown stairway.

You might start with a *riso e filetto di pesce* (rice with lemon juice and Parmesan, topped by fillets of the day's lake catch), followed by a *frittura leggera di luccio* (light fry-up of pike chunks).

Ristorante Antica Pozzo
ITALIAN €€

(📞339 873 61 88; www.bellagioanticopozzo.eu; Salita Mella 26; meals €35-40; ☉noon-10pm) They do the simple things well here – think pizza, pasta and other Italian staples served on an agreeable open courtyard.

Terrazza Barchetta
ITALIAN €€

(📞031 95 13 89; www.ristorantebarchetta.com; Salita Mella 13; meals €40-45; ☉noon-2.30pm & 7-10.30pm) The intimate terrace just above a crossroads of laneways in Bellagio's old town is a fine place for a meal. The restaurant has been around since 1887, which is plenty of time to perfect dishes such as deboned white lake fish in a pistachio crust or guinea fowl with whisky and mushroom sauce.

🛍 Shopping

Bellagio's popularity has spawned a disproportionate number of boutiques for a small town. As a general rule, it's antique or souvenir shops along the waterfront, and clothing and craft boutiques climbing the hillside.

Il Cortiletto
FOOD & DRINK

(📞333 7 86 00 90; Salita Plinio 5; ☉10.30am-1pm & 2-7.30pm Thu-Tue) This tiny shop is filled with carefully chosen, high-quality food products from around Italy, from the local

LAKE COMO & AROUND BELLAGIO

WORTH A TRIP

MADONNA DEL GHISALLO

In the high-country village of **Magreglio** (497m), 7km south of Bellagio, stands a simple 17th-century church known as the **Santuario della Madonna del Ghisallo**. But this is not just any old high-mountain chapel.

The road up has frequently been included as a classic stage of the Giro d'Italia cycle race, and is known to professional and amateur cyclists alike. The sanctuary long ago became a symbolic finishing line for cyclists, who began leaving mementoes there. The place's importance for two-wheeled enthusiasts was such that Pope Pius XII declared the Madonna del Ghisallo the patron of cyclists.

The gifts and tokens left at the sanctuary down the years became so numerous that it was decided to open the nearby **Museo del Ciclismo** (☑031 96 58 85; www. museodelghisallo.it; Via Gino Bartali 4; adult/child €6/3; ☺9.30am-5.30pm Tue-Sun Apr-Oct, 9.30am-5.30pm Sat & Sun Nov-Mar) to contain the overflow. The museum is devoted to all aspects of the business of cycling, with 100 film clips of great moments in Italian cycling, memorabilia (including many bicycles) and temporary exhibitions – ample reward for the punishing climb.

(honey and olive oil from Bellagio, wines from Valtellina) to those from further afield (products from Tuscany and Puglia). This is also the place to arrange cooking classes (p111).

atelier ART
(☑031 95 13 96; www.atelierbellagio.it; Salita Mella 27; ☺10am-1pm & 2-5pm) Lili Barone and Gabriel Kantor turn out exquisite etchings, engravings and other design products from their studio high in the old town. Opening hours can be a bit hit or miss.

Magda Guaitamacchi CERAMICS
(☑031 95 14 62; www.bellagio.co.nz/magdaguaita macchi; Salita Serbelloni 27; ☺10am-12.45pm & 2.30-6.45pm) Magda Guaitamacchi turns out gorgeous ceramic and porcelain pieces that have gone on show around the world.

Carmen Como Silk CLOTHING
(☑031 95 01 01; Salita Serbelloni 8; ☺10.30am-6.30pm) Como's renowned silk manufacturing industry sends ties, scarves and other accessories up the road to this small Bellagio shop.

ℹ Information

Bellagio Tourist Office (☑031 95 02 04; Piazza Mazzini; ☺9am-12.30pm & 1-6pm Mon-Sat, 10am-2pm Sun)
PromoBellagio (☑031 95 15 55; www.bel lagiolakecomo.com; Piazza della Chiesa 14; ☺9.30am-1pm Mon, 9.30-11am & 2-4pm Tue, Thu & Fri, 9.30-11am & 2-3.30pm Wed, 10-11am & 2-3.30pm Sat & Sun)

ℹ Getting There & Away

Regular ferries connect Bellagio with Como (€10.40, two hours), Lenno (€4.60, 20 minutes), Villa Carlotta (€4.60, 15 minutes) and Varenna (€4.60, 20 to 30 minutes).

Small buses rattle more or less hourly from Como to Bellagio (€3.25, 70 minutes).

ABBAZIA DI SAN PIETRO AL MONTE

Birdsong and the rush of a mountain stream accompany you as you make the pilgrimage to the Romanesque Abbazia di San Pietro al Monte (St Peter on the Mount). Medieval monks seemed to have had both a thing about punishing themselves and a love of good views. From the upper streets (park at Via del Pozzo) of sprawling hillside **Civate** (330m), 5km southwest of Lecco, it's a beautiful but uphill 30- to 40- minute walk (for the moderately unfit) on waymarked stone trail No 10. The trail finally reaches a clearing where this abbey has stood (at 663m) since the 11th century.

The curious two-part Benedictine abbey (which you may only get to admire from outside) is in an idyllic setting that affords views south over **Lake Annone**, one of a string of peaceful lakes along the Como–Lecco road. The first building is an enchanting chapel dedicated to St Benedict, a squat affair with apses protruding from three sides. The main building rises behind. If you're lucky and it's open, you'll find medieval frescoes depicting mostly Old Testament scenes inside.

LAKE COMO WEST BANK

By not having the mountains block the light, the western shore gets the most sunshine on the lake. For this reason, it's lined with the most lavish villas, where high-fliers from football players to film stars reside. The shore stretches 75km from Como north to Sorico at the lake's tip; from here you can continue north along an Alpine valley to Chiavenna and, 40km further, cross into Switzerland.

In May and June, watch out for musical concerts at some of Lake Como's lakeside villas as part of the **Lake Como Festival** (www.lakecomofestival.com).

❶ Getting Around

BOAT

In addition to the regular ferries linking most Lake Como lake ports (check out Navigazione Lago del Como (p108) for a full timetable), regular car ferries cross from Cadenabbia to Bellagio (€9 per small car and driver) every half-hour through most of the day.

BUS

Buses run the length of the lake from Como to Colico: Como to Menaggio takes about an hour and 10 minutes and from there you change for Colico (another hour). Buses stop in most towns en route.

CAR

Traffic along the west shore of Lake Como can be intense at the best of times and choked on summer weekends. The SS340 road runs some way inland and is characterised largely by tunnels. This is for moving around quickly. More picturesque at the southern end (between Cernobbio and Brienno) is the old Via Regina shore road.

Cernobbio

POP 7059

The shoreline of Cernobbio, a graceful town 5km north of Como (and now melded to it with residential districts), is laced with a series of fine villas fronting the water. It's probably true that half of Cernobbio's visitors come by in the hope of spotting George Clooney at one of its central cafes (he lives about 10km up the road in Laglio), especially since scenes from *Ocean's 12* were shot here.

◉ Sights

Several villas are scattered around the lakeshore, but most are closed to the public. One you may find open occasionally is **Villa**

Pizzo (☑ 031 51 12 62; Via Regina 46) – ask at the tourist office.

Villa d'Este   VILLA

(☑ 031 34 81; www.villadeste.it; Via Regina 40; ⊙ 10.30-11.30am & 3.30-4.30pm Mar-Nov) Villa d'Este, a 16th-century palace that now houses a luxury hotel, has the loveliest gardens of all Cernobbio's villas. They burst with spring colour – rhododendrons, camellias, hydrangeas, oleanders, azaleas and jasmine bushes. Among the many grand trees is a venerable plane tree more than 500 years old. You can visit only in groups of no fewer than 10 people by prior booking.

Villa Erba   VILLA

(☑ 031 34 91; www.villaerba.it; Largo Luchino Visconti 4) **FREE** The 19th-century Villa Erba has been turned into a congress centre, sporting a somewhat incongruous modern glass structure plonked down near the villa. That said, business generated has allowed the creation of a museum inside the villa. It is open only for organised visits that are booked ahead.

Villa Bernasconi   VILLA

(Via Regina 7) One of the most outstanding *stile liberty* (Italian art nouveau) villas in the lakes area, Villa Bernasconi was built by successful textile merchant Davide Bernasconi in 1906. It bears all the classic elements, with use of ceramics, stained class, wrought iron and, a comparative novelty, cement.

The floral relief decoration on the exterior displays silkworms, moths and mulberry leaves – a direct advertisement of where Bernasconi's wealth came from. The local town hall has restored much of the long-abandoned interior of the building, which may open for exhibitions one day.

> ### ROMANESQUE
>
> Architecture buffs might want to search out the sprinkling of fine Lombard Romanesque churches scattered about the Triangolo Lariano. Among the lakeside villages, Careno (Chiesa di San Martino), Bellagio (Basilica di San Giacomo; p110) and Torno (Chiesa di San Giovanni) stand out for their well-preserved churches. Inland, among the most important are those in Lasnigo (Chiesa di San Alessandro), Barni (Chiesa di San Pietro) and Rezzago (Chiesa di SS Cosmo e Damiano).

✖ Eating

Trattoria La Vignetta   TRATTORIA €€
(☑0344 344 70 55; www.lavignetta.it; Via Monte Grappa 32; meals €30-35; ☺noon-3pm & 7-10pm Wed-Mon) A five-minute uphill walk along a jasmine-perfumed residential lane, this hotel restaurant sits atop a little rise. Inside, the timber-panelled dining room with its antique wooden tables is a lovely setting for perfectly oven-cooked fish, perhaps preceded by a creamy risotto. On a balmy evening, take a table in the gravel garden outside and admire the surrounding greenery.

Gatto Nero   ITALIAN €€€
(☑031 51 20 42; www.gattonerocernobbio.com; Via Monte Santo 69, Rovenna; meals €60-70; ☺noon-2pm & 7.30-10pm Wed-Sun, 7.30-10pm Tue) Try to book a front-row table for the unobstructed view of the lake far below this locally renowned eatery above central Cernobbio. The dining rooms, with dark-tile floors, plenty of timber and low lighting, are pure romanticism. If it's on the menu, the risotto with fresh lake perch, a local classic, is particularly delicate in flavour.

The huge scales by the entrance are, mercifully, not used for weighing guests on the way out.

LAKE COMO WALKS

The west bank of Lake Como offers widely diverse walking possibilities. For one suggested strolling route of 10km between Cadenabbia and Colonno, to the south, have a look at **Greenway del Lago di Como** (www.greenwaydellago.it).

For something altogether more challenging, you could head inland and get onto the **Via dei Monti Lariani**, a 130km trail from Cernobbio in the south to Sorico in the north. Keeping largely to high ground well above the lake, the journey is punctuated by *rifugi* (mountain huts) and the occasional village where you can find accommodation. Reckon on six days to do the walk comfortably. The trail is part of the 6000km Sentiero Italia marked out by Club Alpino Italiano, and it's one of the most popular among hikers in Lombardy.

ℹ Getting There & Away

Ferries shuttle between Como's Pier 4 and Cernobbio (one way adult/child €2.50/1.80) around every 15 minutes during daylight hours.

Monte Bisbino

Following signs out of central Cernobbio, take the scenic drive that winds 17km up through the residential villages behind Cernobbio to Monte Bisbino (1325m), a fabulous lookout spot. You won't need to wait to reach the mountain for great views – at every turn on the way up, you look back down on the lake from a different angle. After a seemingly endless series of switchbacks on an increasingly narrow road that, in its latter stages, is enclosed by a canopy of thick woods, you emerge at the top. Climb the stairs to where the TV antennas are and then take in views of the Como end of the lake, the Lombard plain to Milan and as far off as the Swiss Alps (including the Jungfrau) on a clear day.

Moltrasio & Laglio

The lower lakeside road skirts the lakeshore out of Cernobbio and past a fabulous row of 19th-century villas (all private property) around Moltrasio. Winston Churchill holidayed in one (Villa Le Rose) just after WWII and another is owned by the Versace fashion dynasty. Gianni Versace, who was murdered in Miami Beach, Florida, in 1997, is buried in the village cemetery. Near **Villa Passalacqua** (www.thevillapassalacqua.com), which is sometimes used for events, is a lovely, little 11th-century Romanesque church, the **Chiesa di Sant'Agata**, which houses some intriguing frescoes (if you get lucky and find it open). A few kilometres north, the villa-lined hamlet of Laglio is home to *Ocean's* star George Clooney (he lives in Villa Oleandra). In both villages, stop anywhere, clatter down the cobblestone lanes and stairs to the lake, gawp at the villas as best you can and dream about how making it big in Hollywood could transform your life.

✖ Eating

Trattoria del Fagiano   TRATTORIA €€
(☑031 29 00 00; www.trattoriadelfagiano.it; Via Roma 54, Tosnacco; meals €25-30; ☺12.30-2.30pm & 6.30-9.30pm Wed-Sun, 12.30-2.30pm Mon) A short

climb above the SS340 road and Moltrasio, you'll stumble across this easygoing, family affair. The Pheasant serves no-nonsense local food (fish features highly, but several meat dishes are on offer too) in a good-natured, rambunctious atmosphere. Booking is strongly advised for Friday, Saturday and Sunday nights. On weekdays, it has a sensational set menu (excluding drinks) for just €8.

Argegno & Pigra

693 (ARGEGNO), POP 270 (PIGRA)

Argegno is the departure point into the mountains on the **Funivia Argegno-Pigra** (☑ 031 81 08 44; one way/return adult €2.90/3.90, child €1.70/2.40; ☺ 8.30am-noon & 2.30-6pm, shorter hrs in winter). The cable car (about 300m north of Piazza Roma) makes the five-minute climb to the 860m-high village of tiny Pigra every 30 minutes. From the square where the cable car arrives and from the grounds of the tiny Chiesa di Santa Margherita, the views back down over the lake are beautiful. Pigra itself warrants some wandering along its centuries-old lanes and stairways.

In Argegno, **Barchetta** (☑ 031 82 11 05; www.ristorantebarchetta.it; Piazza Roma 2, Argegno; meals €25-30; ☺ noon-2.30pm & 7-9.30pm Tue-Sun), the 'Little Boat', appropriately enough, specialises in lake fish and, come autumn, dishes using mushrooms and truffles. A few tables are scattered along the footpath, but dining inside is a more refined experience. The food is fabulous. Whichever pasta you start with, leave room for the abundant *misto pesce di lago* (a mixed grill of lake fish).

Sala & Isola Comacina

Once the site of a Roman fort and medieval settlement, Lake Como's only island forms its own little bay with the mainland, just offshore from Sala Comacina. When the Lombards invaded northern Italy, the island held out as a Byzantine redoubt, and slowly filled with houses and churches, the whole known as Cristopolis. They even say the Holy Grail was deposited here for a time. The medieval settlement was razed by Como in 1169 as punishment for its loyalty to Milan. Today, as silent witness to this terrible event, lies the scant ruins of the **Romanesque Chiesa di Sant'Eufemia** and, next to it, the more solid remnants of the triple apse of a pre-Romanesque church at the north end of the

island, about a five-minute stroll from the boat landing.

✕ Eating

Taverna Bleu   ITALIAN €€
(☑ 0344 5 51 07; www.tavernableu.it; Via Puricelli 4, Sala Comicina; meals €25-30; ☺ noon-2.30pm & 7-9.30pm Wed Mon) Known all over the lake for its fine fish dishes, the Blue Tavern is in a lovely spot down from the main road at lake level in Sala Comacina. Sit in the shady gravel-and-grass garden by the canary-yellow building that hosts indoor dining and a charming hotel. Eat à la carte or opt for the four-course set menu (€42), which includes a tasty mixed vegetable dish, risotto and a melt-in-the-mouth fillet of lake perch.

Locanda dell'Isola   ITALIAN €€€
(☑ 0344 5 50 83; www.comacina.it; set menu €67; ☺ noon-2.30pm & 7-9.30pm Wed-Mon, closed Dec & Jan) Since 1947 Locanda dell'Isola has been serving the same abundant set menu on the south side of the island, characterised by a round of nine vegetables, cold meats, trout, chicken, cheese and dessert. To finish off, brandy is burned in a huge pot to ward off the excommunication of the island declared by the Bishop of Como back in the 12th century. No credit cards.

❶ Getting There & Away

Six public ferries a day stop on the island, but they're only good for afternoon visits with the last ferries stopping at 4.50pm (northbound) and 5.59pm (southbound). Otherwise, there's a boat service (€7 to €9, 10 to 15 minutes) that shuttles from a landing on Piazza Matteotti in Sala Comacina between 9am and 10pm, with a final return service leaving at midnight.

Sacro Monte di Ossuccio

High above the hamlets that make up the village of Ossuccio, a series of 14 chapels (built from 1635 to 1714) dedicated to the Mysteries of the Rosary lead to the Sacro Monte di Ossuccio. It's one of several such devotional paths created in the 17th century in Lombardy and Piedmont (the only one on Lake Como) and included in a World Heritage Site listing. The 20-minute climb along the cobblestone lane is worth it more than anything else for the matchless views that it offers over olive groves, the Isola Comacina and the lake beyond. At the top, you reach **Santuario della Madonna del Soccorso**,

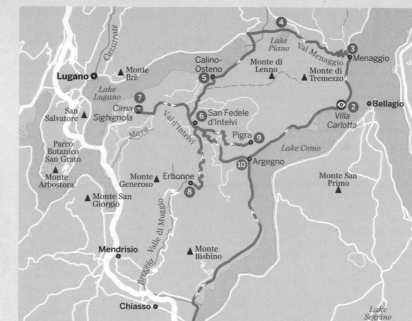

Driving Tour
High into the Hills

START COMO
FINISH COMO
LENGTH 145KM; HALF A DAY

Leave ❶**Como** and drive along the lake's west bank, as far as gorgeous ❷**Villa Carlotta** in the town of Cadenabbia 33km north of Como. Continue on for another 3km to ❸**Menaggio**, which has a cute cobblestone old centre, a useful **tourist office** and a ferry stop. The central square overlooking the lake has a couple of cafes that are perfect for lake-gazing and people-watching.

From Menaggio, follow the signs inland towards Lugano, but instead of heading for Switzerland, pass ❹**Lake Piano** and then take the south (left) turn after 12km and follow the shore of Lake Lugano for ❺**Claino-Osteno**, a pretty lakeside village with a photogenic stone church. The road climbs steeply for 11km to ❻**San Fedele d'Intelvi**, which stands at the crossroads of some intriguing roads. For the first of these, follow the signs for Lanzo d'Intelvi (6km), from where there

are signs to glorious ❼**Cima Sighignola**, also known as the Balcone d'Italia (1320m), a further 6km on. Below lies all of Lugano, its lake and mountain peaks and, beyond, you can make out part of Lake Maggiore, Varese, the Alps and the Lombard plains.

Return to San Fedele d'Intelvi, but only to follow the signs for the lovely, quiet country road to ❽**Erbonne** (963m), a frontier hamlet that was a key crossing point for smugglers until the 1970s. The former barracks of the Guardia di Finanza (customs police) house possibly the smallest museum in Italy (the Museo della Guardia di Finanza e del Contrabbando) – you simply peer in through the glass door. Consider lunching at the **Osteria del Valico**.

Return to San Fedele d'Intelvi (9km), and follow the signs to ❾**Pigra** (7km) for more stunning views, this time of Lake Como's southern end. Back in San Fedele d'Intelvi drive for 9km down to ❿**Argegno**, from where it's a 21km lakeshore drive back to ⓫**Como**.

which houses a 14th-century sculpture of Our Lady to which miraculous powers were long attributed.

From Ossuccio, drive up to Piazza Papa Giovanni XXIII, where the pilgrim path begins. You'll find the **Trattoria del Santuario** (☑ 0344 5 63 11; meals €25-30; ☺ 11.30am-2.30pm & 6-9pm Wed-Mon) at the top.

Keen walkers could proceed uphill (about two hours for the moderately fit) to reach the splendid Romanesque **Chiesa di San Benedetto**, at the heart of a picture-postcard setting.

Down in Ossuccio itself, the main road runs past the tiny 11th-century **Chiesa dei SS Giacomo e Filippo**, whose unique, lollipop-shaped Romanesque bell tower is something of a symbol of Lake Como.

Lenno

POP 1859

It may not look like much from the main road, but it's well worth dropping down into this lakeside village. Aside from a pretty main square, Lenno is home to one of Lake Como's most celebrated villas and has a lovely lakeshore promenade.

◎ Sights

Villa Balbianello   VILLA
(☑ 0344 5 61 10; www.fondoambiente.it; Via Comoedia 5, Località Balbianello; villa & gardens adult/child €13/7, with prior reservation €10/5, gardens only €7/3; ☺ gardens 10am-6pm Tue & Thu-Sun mid-Mar–mid-Nov) A 1km walk along the lakeshore from Lenno's main square, Villa Balbianello has cinematic pedigree: this was where scenes from the 2006 James Bond remake *Casino Royale*, and *Star Wars Episode II*, were shot. The reason? It is one of the most dramatic locations anywhere on Lake Como.

Built by Cardinal Angelo Durini in 1787, Villa Balbianello was used for a while by Allied commanders at the tail end of WWII. The sculpted gardens, which seem to drip off the high promontory like sauce off a melting gelato cone, are the perfect place for hopelessly romantic elopers to spend a day. Visitors are only allowed to walk the 1km path (amid vegetation so florid as to seem Southeast Asian) from the Lenno landing stage to the estate on Tuesday and at weekends. On other days, you have to take a **taxi boat** (☑ 0349 2 29 09 53; www.taxiboatlecco.com; return €7) from Lenno. If you want to see the

villa, you must join a guided tour (generally conducted in Italian) by 4.15pm.

Lido di Lenno   BEACH
(☑ 0344 5 70 93; www.lidodilenno.com; Via Comoedia 1; beach access €5; ☺ 10am-3.30am daily May-Sep) Summer evenings in Lenno take on a hedonistic hue at the Lido di Lenno. People from near and far converge on this artificial sandy beach, located virtually next to the path and boat pier for Villa Balbianello, to enjoy food from the grill, cocktails (€6 to €9) and a (brief) dip in the chilly, clear waters of the lake.

❶ Getting There & Away

Boat services to Lenno arrive from Como (€8.30, one hour 40 minutes), Bellagio (€4.60, 30 minutes) and Varenna (€4.60, one hour) among other Lake Como ports of call.

Tremezzo

POP 1260

Tremezzo is high on everyone's list for a visit to the 17th-century, waterfront **Villa Carlotta** (☑ 0344 4 04 05; www.villacarlotta.it; Via Regina 2; adult/reduced €9/5; ☺ 9am-5pm Easter-Sep, 10am-4pm mid-Mar–Easter & Oct–mid-Nov; ⊛ Cadenabbia), whose botanic gardens are filled with colour in spring from orange trees knitted into pergolas and some of Europe's finest rhododendrons, azaleas and camellias. The villa, strung with paintings, sculptures (some by Antonio Canova) and tapestries, takes its name from the Prussian princess who was given the place in 1847 as a wedding present from her mother. Upstairs, rooms with period furniture provide an insight into the life of the princessly. You too can swan from the Salotto Impero (Empire Room) to Carlotta's bedroom and wonder what it must have been like to hit the hay after a hard day at the villa. Villa Carlotta is a short walk southwest of the Cadenabbia car ferry stop.

Plenty of restaurants line the waterfront, but our favourite restaurant is **La Cucina di Marianna** (☑ 0344 4 31 11; www.lamarianna.com; Cadenabbia; set menus €33-50, light menu €21; ☺ noon-3pm & 6.30-9pm Tue-Sun) in Cadenabbia. With its shady terrace jutting out over the water, this is about the most romantic spot you could choose to eat around the Cadenabbia area. Marianna cooks by theme, so if Tuesday is Venice day (with salted cod pâté and stewed cuttlefish), Thursday is Garden day, with lots of veggies. Food servings are

WORTH A TRIP

MENAGGIO'S HINTERLAND

Menaggio makes a good base for a couple of off-the-beaten-track excursions.

If you have your hiking boots with you, take a minor road out of Menaggio for Plesio and then follow a walking trail (park in the hamlet of Breglia) for about two hours to the **Rifugio Menaggio** (☎ 0344 3 72 82; www.rifugiomenaggio.eu; dm €15, with breakfast/half-board €20/40; ⊘ Sat, Sun & holidays mid-Jun–mid-Sep), where you can sleep and get hot meals. At 1383m, the views down over the lake are ample reward for the climb. Plenty of other walking routes wind off from the refuge.

Menaggio is also the jumping-off point for **Lake Piano** in Val Menaggio, a remote valley connecting Lake Como with Lake Lugano, which straddles the Italy–Switzerland border to the west. Placid Lake Piano is protected by the **Riserva Naturale Lago di Piano**. Three marked nature trails, 4km to 5.3km long, encircle the lake, and the visitors centre, on the lake's northern shore, rents out mountain bikes (€3 per hour) and row boats (€8 per hour), and arranges guided visits on foot (€6 per person per half-day or €9 per person per full day).

copious and of good quality, and there's no pretence at going beyond a down-home feel.

ℹ Information

Tremezzo Tourist Office (☎ 0344 4 04 93; Via Statale Regina; ⊘ 9am-noon & 3.30-6.30pm Wed-Mon Apr-Oct)

ℹ Getting There & Away

Villa Carlotta is well signposted along the lakeside SS340, just north of Tremezzo.

This is one of the more popular boat destinations on Lake Como, with regular ferries arriving from Como (€8.50, 1½ to two hours), Bellagio (€4.60, 15 minutes) and Varenna (€4.60, 30 minutes).

Rezzonico

POP 1078

Beyond Menaggio, the northern stretch of the lake is known as the Alto Lario (Upper Lario). It's far less touristed than other more famous points along the lake but holds some enticing secrets.

At Rezzonico, an extension of Santa Maria, some 6km north of Menaggio, is a quiet pebble **beach** with wooden fisherfolk's seats lined up along it. To find it (when travelling north from Menaggio), follow the signs to Santa Maria and then, just before a tunnel on the SS340, a side road to Rezzonico. This brings you to a 13th-century stone **castle**, built by the Della Torre clan and largely intact (closed to the public). Around it, stone stair paths lead downhill to porticoed houses right to the lake's edge. To the castle's left, a path marked Via al Lago winds past grey-

stone houses and lush green gardens to the beach.

For a fine view of Rezzonico with the Alps as a backdrop, head around 1km south of town along the SS340 – a car park opposite the Cappella Degli Alpini is the place.

Gravedona & Around

Gravedona spreads out behind a gently curved bay on the lake. Towards the southern end stands a unique and beautiful Romanesque church, the late-12th-century **Chiesa di Santa Maria del Tiglio**. Square-based and with apses protruding on three sides, the structure has an unusual bell tower (probably added later), which is octagonal at the top and rises from the centre of the facade. Inside, high arched galleries allow in sunlight at the top of the church. Colourful remnants of frescoes dating back to the 14th and 15th centuries depict, among other things, the Last Judgement. The heavy wooden crucifix is a fine example of Romanesque carving.

A 6km road winds out of Gravedona up to the plateau town of **Peglio** (650m), whose 15th-century stone **Chiesa di Sant'Eusebio** offers wonderful views of the lake and plains around Gravedona. The church boasts 17th-century frescoes, but it's often closed.

Although possible at various points around the lake, boat hire is popular at the north end of the lake, with several outlets at Dongo, Gravedona and Domaso, which is 3km northeast of Gravedona. At **Como Lake Boats** (☎ 333 401 49 95; www.comolakeboats.it; Via Antica Regina 26) you can hire your own

Zodiac (expect to pay €65 for two hours) as well as organise to do waterskiing (€55 for 30 minutes) and wakeboarding (€50 for 30 minutes). It can also provide instructors.

LAKE COMO EAST BANK

Lake Como's eastern shore has a wilder feel to it than the more illustrious west. Less touristed, it hides numerous gems that alone justify the effort. Back-country drives take you still further off the beaten track.

Our coverage of the East Bank below runs from north to south.

ℹ️ Getting Around

BUS
Regular buses connect Lecco with Como. Others run up the shoreline to Colico, but it is often just as easy to take the train.

CAR
The SS36 fast highway, mostly a series of inland tunnels, is for those in a hurry between Lecco and Colico. If you want to *see* the lake, follow the S road. The main inland road along the Valsassina mountain valley is the S between Lecco and Bellano. The SS36 and then S roads lead west 29km from Lecco to Como.

TRAIN
Trains from Milan run to Lecco (€4.55, 40 minutes) and call in at all towns on the east shore of the lake before swinging east at Colico into the Valtellina (heading as far east as Tirano, where Swiss trains connect on a scenic line north to St Moritz). Note that Piona station is in Colico, not at the Abbazia Piona. Trains link Lecco with Bergamo (€3.45, 45 minutes).

Valtellina

From the north end of Lake Como, the Valtellina cuts a broad swathe of a valley (at whose centre runs the Adda river) eastward between the Swiss mountain frontier to the north and the Orobie Alps to the south. Much of its steep, northern flank is carpeted by the vineyards (mostly the *nebbiolo* grape variety) that produce such coveted drops as Sforzato (Sfurzat). You can largely skip the valley towns, but a detour to the hillside wine villages is worthwhile. Two points of reference are **Ponte**, 8km east of Sondrio, and **Teglio** (with a cute Romanesque church), 8km further east. The brisk climb up among the vineyards affords sweeping views across the valley. And what better way to taste Valtellina reds than by calling into any local trattoria?

The prettiest town along the valley floor is **Tirano**, terminus for trains arriving from Milan via Lake Como and others arriving from Switzerland. At its east end is the quiet old town, with winding lanes next to the gushing Adda. About 1.5km west of the centre stands the proud Renaissance **Santuario della Madonna** church.

The Valtellina cuts a broad swathe down the Adda valley, where villages and vineyards hang precariously on the slopes of the Orobie Alps. The steep northern flank is carpeted by nebbiolo grapes, which yield a light red wine. Both body and alcohol content improve with altitude so generations of Valtenesi built upwards, carrying the soil in woven baskets to high mountain terraces. Their reward: a DOC classification for Valtellina Superiore since 1968. In Sondrio, it's possible to visit the cellars of **Pellizzatti Perego** (www.arpepe.com; Via Buon Consiglio, Sondrio), and, in Chiuri, **Nino Negri** (www.ninonegri.it; Via Ghibellini 3).

🍴 Eating

Altavilla   CHALET RESTAURANT €€
(📞 0342 72 03 55; www.altavilla.info; Via ai Monti 46, Bianzone; meals €30; ⏱ noon-2.30pm & 7-10pm Tue-Sun, daily Aug; 🅿🛜📶) Located in the heart of the Valtellina's finest vineyards in Bianzone, just north of Teglio, is Altavilla, Anna Bertola's charming Alpine chalet and restaurant, one of the gastronomic treats of the region. Expect expert wine

---

LAKE BEACHES

With the exception of an unkempt stretch at the lake's northern end around Gera Lario, beaches around Lake Como tend to be of the grey pebble variety. That doesn't stop locals getting out for a bracing dip and sunbathe, though. At some of the more popular ones, sun lounges are set out and you'll find summertime bars. Restaurants and pizzerias are never far off. Among the nicer stretches are the beach at **Rezzonico** on the west bank, a series of strands at **Onno** (about halfway down the road between Bellagio and Lecco) and the strip at **Abbadia Lariana** on the east shore, north of Lecco.

WORTH A TRIP

VAL MASINO

A lovely 17km road, the SP9, leads north up Val Masino from a point 7km east of Morbegno in the Valtellina valley. Almost as soon as you leave the traffic, car dealerships and megamarkets of the valley floor behind, you enter a world of thickly wooded hills, the surging Masino river and snowcapped Alps. From **Valmasino**, 9km north of the valley floor, the scenery takes on an Alpine hue. From **San Martino**, 2km on, take the left fork. A series of switchbacks (watch for some staggering waterfalls) brings you to **Bagni di Masino**, the end of the road, with an old-time spa hotel. Surrounded by fir trees and granite mountains you feel you could touch, the spot has a bracing wilderness feel. Properly equipped hikers can set off into the Alps from here along marked trails.

recommendations to accompany traditional mountain dishes such as *sciàtt* (buckwheat pancakes stuffed with Bitto cheese) and *pizzocheri* buckwheat pasta. The artisanal salami, mountain venison and aged Bitto cheese are particular highlights, as is the 500-label wine list.

Reserve a room (singles €25 to €42, doubles €42 to €68) for the night so you can sleep it off afterwards.

Osteria del Crotto　　　　　OSTERIA €€
(☑0342 61 48 00; www.osteriadelcrotto.it; Via Pedemontana 22; meals €25-35) Osteria del Crotto serves a whole slew of Slow Food Movement–authenticated products such as *violino di capra della Valchiavenna* (literally 'violin goat of the Valchiavenna'), a traditional salami made from the shank, which is sliced by resting it on the shoulder and shaving it as a violin player moves his bow.

❶ Information

Valtellina Tourist Office (☑0342 45 11 50; www.valtellina.it; Piazzale Bertacchi 77, Sondrio; ❂9am-12.30pm & 3.30-6.30pm Mon-Fri, 9am-noon Sat)

Abbazia di Piona

About 3km short of Colico, a side road (half of it cobblestone) leads 2km from the S road to the **Abbazia di Piona** (☑0341 94 03 31; www.cistercensi.info/piona; ❂7am-7.30pm), a Cistercian abbey that has a marvellous setting on a promontory stretching out into the lake. There is evidence that a small chapel was built here in the 7th century. The present church is a Romanesque gem that the Cluniac order raised. The church and its 13th-century frescoes are attractive, but the star (aside from the setting) is the 13th-century, irregularly shaped cloister, a rich example of transitional style from Roman-

esque to Gothic; it's an oasis of peace. The monks who live here today enjoy incomparable views west over the lake to Gravedona and the snowcapped peaks beyond.

Corenno Plinio

Located about 6km north of Bellano, this spot is a bite-sized taste of another era. Even the main square, Piazza Garibaldi, is roughly cobblestoned and it's plain from its time-warped nature that nothing much has changed here down the centuries. Many of the deep-grey, stone houses are still occupied, their inhabitants carefully tending garden plots that give the huddled hamlet flashes of bright colour. On the square, the 14th-century **Chiesa di Tommaso Beckett** competes for attention with the neighbouring **Castello degli Andreani**, built around the same time. Frescoes inside the church were uncovered during restoration work in 1966. Two stout, crenellated towers stand guard over the castle, which is closed to visitors. A series of uneven stone stairways tumbles between the tightly packed houses to the shoreline, one ending up at a tiny port (with space for nine motorboats and a family of ducks).

Bellano

POP 3305

Once an industrial centre, Bellano (5km north of Varenna) is a sleepy lakeside town with a singular sight: the **Orrido** (☑0341 82 11 24; adult/child €3/2; ❂9am-7pm Jul & Aug, shorter hrs rest of year), a powerful waterfall where the river Pioverna thunders down between tight, rock walls before flowing out through the town into the lake. The power of the falls has hammered out weird shapes in the rock walls, topped by thick vegetation. If you suffer from vertigo, you might want to give this a miss.

Varenna

POP 812

Varenna, a beguiling village bursting with florid plantlife, exotic flowery perfumes and birdsong, is a short ferry ride away from its rival in postcard beauty, Bellagio. Its pastel-coloured houses defy the standard laws of physics, seeming to grip for all they're worth to the steep slopes that rise from the lake.

◉ Sights

Varenna is home to two lovely lakeside villas: **Villa Cipressi** (☑0341 83 01 13; www.hotelvillacipressi.it; Via IV Novembre 22; adult/child €4/2; ☺9am-7pm Mar-Oct), now a luxury hotel, and, 100m further south, **Villa Monastero** (☑0341 29 54 50; www.villamonastero.eu; Via IV Novembrea; villa & gardens adult/reduced €8/4, gardens only €5/2; ☺gardens 9am-7pm, villa 2-7pm Fri, 9am-7pm Sat & Sun Mar-Oct, closed Nov-Feb; ☝Varenna), a former convent turned into a vast residence by the Mornico family from the 17th to the 19th centuries. In both cases, a stroll through the magnificent gardens, which reach down to the lake, is a balm for the senses. A wander through Villa Monastero is a lesson in how well the other half can live – in the room that fronts the bathroom, the walls are covered in finely engraved Spanish leather to protect the walls from humidity! Magnolias (including one specimen in front of the villa said to be up to 400 years old), camellias and yucca trees are among the villas' floral highlights.

Much overlooked in all the excitement about Varenna's villas are the lovely 14th-century frescoes, somewhat damaged but nevertheless full of colour, tucked inside the tiny Romanesque **Chiesa di San Giovanni Battista** (Piazza San Giovanni). Unfortunately, finding it open is a bit hit and miss; ask at the tourist office (p122).

✕ Eating

⭐ **Ristorante La Vista** ITALIAN €€
(☑0341 83 02 98; www.varenna.net/eng/ristorante-lavista.php; Via XX Settembre 35; 3-/4-course set menu €38/45, meals €35-40; ☺7-10pm Wed-Sat & Mon mid-Mar–late Oct) Fabulous views from the terrace high in Varenna's old town are only half the story here. The food is fresh and inventive from a menu that changes with the seasons, and service rarely misses a beat.

Osteria Quatro Pass ITALIAN €€
(☑0341 81 50 91; www.quattropass.com; Via XX Settembre 20; meals €35-40; ☺noon-3pm & 6.30-9.30pm Jun-Aug, Thu-Sun only Sep-May) Places that don't have a lake view in Varenna are at a distinct disadvantage, which is why this place works just that extra bit harder with the food and service. Cured meats, lake fish and other local specialities are perfectly prepared and presented.

Vecchia Varenna ITALIAN €€
(☑0341 83 07 93; www.vecchiavarenna.it; Contrada Scoscesa 10; meals €35-45; ☺12.30-2pm & 7.30-9.30pm Tue-Sun Feb-Dec) Of the handful of lakeside dining options in Varenna, this is the best. Dine on homemade little gnocchi cooked in goat-cheese cream and truffle oil, or choose from mains of lake fish or duck breast. A dozen tables are set up in an enclosed terrace suspended over the water.

ⓘ Orientation

High above the lake, the road through Varenna passes two luxurious villas and the town's main square, Piazza San Giorgio, before continuing north and rejoining the main lakeside S road. A series of lanes-cum-stairways slithers down the hill past bunched-up houses to the lake.

Those arriving by ferry land at Piazzale Martiri della Libertà. From there, a 15- to 20-minute stroll follows the shore south and cuts up to Piazza San Giovanni and the town's main attractions.

HIKING

Waymarked walking paths criss-cross the Parco della Grigna Settentrionale; look for the red-and-white signs with path numbers or similarly coloured paint splotches. Some trails include challenging vie ferate (where iron railings or other aids have been installed for climbing) and others require mountaineering experience. The tourist offices in Varenna (p122) and **Lecco** (☑0341 29 57 20; www.turismo.provincia.lecco.it; Via Nazario Sauro 6; ☺9am-1pm & 2.30-6pm) can provide brochures, but you should seek proper hiking maps scaled at 1:25,000 in local bookshops before undertaking the more challenging walks.

WORTH A TRIP

A HIDDEN EATING GEM

Tucked away in the hamlet of Maggiana, signposted 3km uphill from lakeside Mandello del Lario (home to the legendary Moto Guzzi motorcycle manufacturer), **Sale e Tabacchi** (☑ 0341 73 37 15; www.osteriasalietabacchi.it; Piazza San Rocco 3, Maggiana; meals €25-30; ☺ noon-2.30pm & 6.30-10pm Wed-Sun, noon-2.30pm Mon) is an eatery that has appeared in countless Italian good-food guides but could hardly be better disguised. The post office, bar and tobacco store also has a modest dining room situated off to one side, filled with dark timber tables. In the summer months, lake fish dominates the menu – try the perch risotto. Just behind the restaurant is a medieval watchtower, where they say Holy Roman Emperor Frederick Barbarossa stayed in 1158 – too soon for him to try the risotto.

ⓘ Information

Varenna Tourist Office (☑ 0341 83 03 67; www.varennaitaly.com; Via del IV Novembre 7; ☺ 9.30am-12.30pm & 2-6.30pm Tue-Sat, 9.30am-12.30pm Sun Jul, shorter hrs rest of year)

ⓘ Getting There & Away

If driving, take the slip road just before the tunnel coming from either north or south. Metered street parking is almost impossible on weekends, but there's an underground car park (€2 per hour) opposite the entrance to Villa Monastero.

Regular ferries connect Varenna with Como (€12, 2¼ hours), Bellagio (€4.60, 15 to 20 minutes) and further afield. A car ferry runs to Bellagio and on to Cadenabbia.

Vezio

From close to the Varenna ferry landing, an S mountain road winds for 3km high above Varenna into the hills to the hamlet of Vezio, which is thought by some to have Etruscan origins. This tiny village is dominated by the ruins of the 13th-century **Castello di Vezio** (www.castellodivezio.it; adult/child €4/2; ☺ 10am-6pm Mar-Oct), a one-time fortified watchtower (part of a chain of such towers erected along the lake in the Middle Ages and, in this case, the successor to older forts since Roman times). From here, the views down upon Varenna and over the lake are some of the best in Lake Como. A demonstration of falconry is thrown in at about 4.30pm – otherwise you can see the raptors sitting in the shade before the castle walls.

An old mule path from the Olivedo (north end) part of Varenna also leads up here – it's a very steep 30-minute puff uphill.

The S road beyond makes for a pretty drive into the Val d'Esino, through the villages of **Perledo**, **Esino Lario** and **Parlasco** (which has tarted itself up with more than a dozen frescoes on the walls of its stone houses), where it runs into Valsassina.

LAKE LUGANO

Shared by Italy and the Swiss canton of Ticino, Lake Lugano (often known as Lake Ceresio on the Italian side) has in common with its bigger neighbour, Lake Como, a dramatic mountain scenery, especially at its northern end, around Lugano. The city of Lugano itself is a busy banking centre and set prettily between soaring hills on either side. Accessed by a short train ride north, the three castles of Bellinzona are an extraordinary sight, and are justifiably Unesco World Heritage Sites.

ⓘ Getting There & Around

Ticino Discovery Card (www.ticino.ch/en/cartaturistica; adult/child Sfr87/47) gives free travel around the Ticino region (including Lugano, Locarno and Bellinzona), covering local trains, buses, ferries, cable cars and funicular railways for three days over a seven-day period. Available from mid-March to October, it can be purchased from tourist offices, railway stations and local travel agencies.

Società Navigazione del Lago di Lugano (☑ 091 971 52 23; www.lakelugano.ch) Destinations from Lugano include Melide (one way/return Sfr16/26.50), Morcote (Sfr22/36.50) and Ponte Tresa (Sfr27/44). If you want to visit several places, buy a pass: Sfr48/61/76 for one/three/seven days (reduced fares for children).

Lugano (Switzerland)

POP 60,815

The largest city in Switzerland's Ticino canton (but not its capital), Lugano squeezes itself around the heights that close in Lake Lugano at its northern end. Switzerland's third-biggest banking centre (after Geneva and Zürich), Lugano is an elegant, prosperous city chosen by a not insignificant number of Milanese as their main residence. Lugano offers a pretty, if small, old centre and a handful of churches and museums to visit but, above all, it has a splendid natural setting to explore, starting with funicular rides up to steep hills to enjoy marvellous views. Somewhat somnolent in winter, it sparkles to life in summer, when its piazzas, cafes, bars and restaurants fill to bursting with a Mediterranean-style *joie de vivre*.

🞂 Sights & Activities

From the train station, take the stairs or the funicular (Sfr1.40, open 5.20am to 11.50pm) down to the centre, a patchwork of interlocking piazzas. Wander through the porticoed lanes, especially along graceful Via Nassa, and linger around the busy main square, Piazza della Riforma, with a cappuccino and paper. The piazza is presided over by the 1844 neoclassical Municipio (town hall) and becomes even more lively when the Tuesday and Friday morning markets are held.

The city is planning the opening of a major arts centre, the **Centro Culturale della Città di Lugano** (Riva Vela), in 2014.

A good way to get around town is the **Lugano City Tour** (🖉 079 685 70 70; adult/child Sfr9/5; 🕘 10am-10pm mid-Jun-Aug, shorter hrs rest of year) toy train, which starts along the waterfront just outside the tourist office and ranges across the city, including stopping at the two funicular stations.

Chiesa di Santa Maria degli Angioli CHURCH
(St Mary of the Angel; Piazza Luini; 🕘 7am-6pm) The simple Romanesque Chiesa di Santa Maria degli Angioli contains two remarkable frescoes by Bernardino Luini dating from 1529. Covering the entire wall that divides the church in two is a grand didactic illustration of the Crucifixion. The closer you look, the more scenes of Christ's Passion are revealed, along with others of him being taken down from the cross and his resurrection. Note also Luini's depiction of the Last Supper on the left wall.

Cattedrale di San Lorenzo CATHEDRAL
(St Lawrence Cathedral; Via San Lorenzo; 🕘 6.30am-6pm) The early 16th-century Cattedrale di San Lorenzo boasts a Renaissance facade and contains some fine frescoes and ornately decorated baroque statues. The interior was undergoing massive restoration works when we visited, with just one of the chapels open to the public.

LAKE COMO & AROUND LUGANO (SWITZERLAND)

WORTH A TRIP

VALSASSINA

It doesn't occur to too many people to follow this 33km back-valley route between Lecco and Bellano. If you've driven up or down the coast one way, this drive along the Valsassina is an alternative for the return trip. From Lecco, the S road switches back and forth, affording priceless views of the Lecco end of Lake Como over your shoulder. These views are finally cut off by the Grigne mountain range, whose highest peak is **La Grigna Settentrionale** (2408m). The core of this area constitutes the **Parco della Grigna Settentrionale** (www.parks.it/parco.grigna.settentrionale). From Lecco, you cannot fail to notice the jagged crest of **Il Resegone**, a broad-spined mountain with what look like dangerously pointy teeth (the highest of which is Punta Cermenati, at 1875m). About 9km northeast of Lecco, at Ballabio Superiore, a turn-off west sees you ascend about 8km of switchbacks through wooded country to **Piani Resinelli**. Again, you do this mainly for the views. The arrival point is made up of a small settlement, highland fields and woods, backed by bare rockfaces. It is a starting point for several hiking trails.

Some 15km northeast of Lecco, the village of **Barzio** is important above all as the birthplace of Alessandro Manzoni. Nearby, **Pasturo** retains something of its medieval feel and is a starting point of a hiking trail to the Grigna Settentrionale summit. The first part, from Via Cantellone, sidles along a bubbling brook and makes for an effortless stroll in its initial stages. Locals enjoy some modest downhill and cross-country skiing in winter at **Piani di Bobbio**, just outside Barzio.

Lugano (Switzerland)

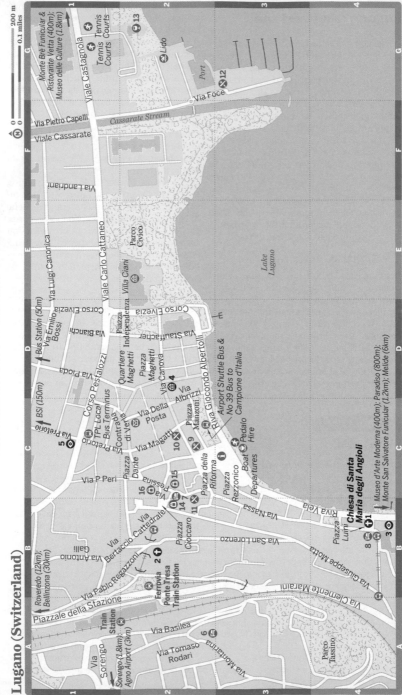

Lugano (Switzerland)

Museo Cantonale d'Arte   GALLERY
(☑ 091 910 47 80; www.museo-cantonale-arte.ch; Via Canova 10; adult/student Sfr12/10, free 1st Sun of every month; ⊙ 2-5pm Tue, 10am-5pm Wed-Sun) The Museo Cantonale d'Arte is the city's premier fine arts museum and celebrates the work of modern artists (mostly 19th and 20th century masters) from around the region.

Museo d'Arte Moderna   GALLERY
(☑058 866 72 14; www.mda.lugano.ch; Riva Antonio Caccia 5; adult/reduced Sfr12/8, free 1st Sun of month; ⊙10am-6pm Tue-Sun, to 9pm Fri) There's creativity from the cutting edge at the Museo d'Arte Moderna. Housed in Villa Malpensata, it is one of the city's main art spaces.

Museo delle Culture   MUSEUM
(Museum of Non-European Cultures; ☑ 058 866 69 09; www.lugano.ch/museoculture; Via Cortivo 24-28; adult/reduced Sfr12/8; ⊙10am-6pm Tue-Sun) About 1.7km from central Lugano, in Villa Heleneum, the Museo delle Culture contains a brew of tribal relics from far-off countries, including a collection of masks and statues. Most of the material comes from Papua New Guinea, Indonesia and Polynesia. They all come from expeditions carried out by the Nodari family, which has lent its collections to the museum. Take bus 1.

Monte Brè Funicular   FUNICULAR
(☑091 971 31 71; www.montebre.ch; adult one way/return Sfr15/23, child Sfr7.50/11.50; ⊙Mar-Dec) For a bird's-eye view of Lugano and the lake, head for the hills. The funicular from Cassarate (walk or take bus No 1 from central Lugano) scales Monte Brè (925m). From Cassarate, a first funicular takes you to Su-vigliana (free up, Sfr1.80 down) to connect with the main funicular. Or take bus No 12 from the main post office to Brè village and walk about 20 minutes.

At the top station, two restaurants have snaffled the best viewpoints; wander down to the Ristorante Vetta for the best views. Although it's a good place to eat, they don't seem to mind people wandering onto the terrace for photos as long as you don't disturb the paying customers. Check the website for funicular timetables, which vary with the months. Ask at the tourist office for a map showing the possible hikes down the hill to Gandria, Lugano and beyond.

Monte San Salvatore Funicular   FUNICULAR
(☑091 985 28 28; www.montesansalvatore.ch; adult one way/return Sfr18/24, child Sfr9/12; ⊙mid-Mar-Oct) From Paradiso, a pleasant 15-minute, sculpture-lined walk around the lake from the town centre, the funicular rises to Monte San Salvatore. Don't miss the views from the church roof. In addition to the fine views, the walk down to Paradiso or Melide is an hour well spent. The funicular operates mid-March through to October.

★ Festivals & Events

Lugano Festival   MUSIC
(www.luganofestival.ch) Lugano takes in some classical tunes during this festival from March to early July in the Palazzo dei Congressi.

Estival Jazz   MUSIC
(www.estivaljazz.ch) Free open-air concert that occurs in early July, plus two days in Mendrisio at the end of June.

ALESSANDRO MANZONI

A slow learner at school, Alessandro Manzoni (1785–1873) became an Italian icon as the country's greatest 19th-century novelist. Born into a family from Barzio, outside Lecco in Valsassina, Manzoni led a life of relative ease, with revenue from farmlands in Lombardy. Thus freed up, he devoted considerable time to writing his magnum opus, *I promessi sposi* (*The Betrothed*), an epic novel set in fictional plague times and at the same time a thinly veiled expression of Italian nationalism at a time when the country was largely under foreign control. He wrote in what he hoped to express as a standard national Italian language, based largely on Tuscan, abandoning his own Milanese dialect. He died three years after Italy achieved his dream of unity and independence.

National Day   LIGHT SHOW
The lake explodes in a display of pyrotechnical wizardry around midnight on 1 August, to celebrate Switzerland's national day.

Blues to Bop Festival   MUSIC
(www.bluestobop.ch) Free open-air music festivals including this one run for three days over the last three days of August.

✗ Eating

A local tradition is to eat at one of the grottoes that dot the mountainside above Montagnola and serve up well-priced local cooking. Visit www.collinadoro.com and click on 'Ristorazione e alloggio' for a full list of options.

★ Bottegone del Vino   ITALIAN €€
(☎ 091 922 76 89; Via Magatti 3; meals Sfr40-45; ⊙ 11am-11pm Mon-Sat) Favoured by the local banking brigade at lunchtime, this is a great place to taste fine local wines over a well-prepared meal. The menu changes daily and might include a *filetto di rombo al vapore* (steamed turbot fillet) or ravioli stuffed with fine Tuscan Chianina beef. Knowledgeable waiters fuss around the tables and are only too happy to suggest the perfect Ticino tipple.

Bar Argentino   ITALIAN €€
(☎ 091 922 90 49; Piazza della Riforma; meals Sfr35-40; ⊙ 8am-midnight) This place is all about people-watching, Lugano's best cappuchinos and decent Italian food that you don't pay over the odds for, despite its location on the main square.

Ristorante Vetta   ITALIAN €€
(☎ 091 971 20 45; www.vetta.ch; Monte Brè; meals Sfr45-50; ⊙ 11.30am-3pm Sun-Thu, 11.30am-3pm & 6.30-11pm Fri & Sat) The food here may be nothing to write home about, but at least you'll have the perfect vantage point from which to do so – come here primarily for the views. A short walk down from the top funicular station atop Monte Brè, Vetta has a perfect terrace where it serves up reasonable pasta dishes.

L'Antica Osteria del Porto   SWISS €€
(☎ 091 971 42 00; www.osteriadelporto.ch; Via Foce 9; meals Sfr50-60; ⊙ 8am-midnight) Set back from Lugano's sailing club, this is the place for savouring local fish and Ticinese dishes. It's hard to resist the *grigliata mista di pesci di mare e crostacei* (mixed fish and shellfish grill) or the perfect polenta dishes. The terrace overlooking the Cassarate stream is pleasant, and you also have lake views.

Grand Café Al Porto   INTERNATIONAL €€€
(☎ 091 910 51 30; www.grand-cafe-lugano.ch; Via Pessina 3; meals Sfr70-80; ⊙ 8am-6.30pm Mon-Sat) This cafe, which began life way back in 1803, has several fine rooms for dining. Be sure to take a look at the frescoed Cenacolo Fiorentino, once a monastery dining hall, upstairs. It's used for private functions. In the cafe the food is mostly snacks and sweets to accompany the coffee, but the à la carte menu does include pasta, risotto and fish and meat mains such as fried rabbit or grilled swordfish.

♗ Drinking

Al Lido Beach Bar & Chiringuito   LOUNGE
(www.allidobar.com; Viale Castagnola; ⊙ 11am-1am) Lugano's lakeside beach bar is popular for its Sunday buffet brunch (Sfr42) and it's a good place to kick back when the weather's warm.

🔒 Shopping

One of the main shopping strips is Via Nassa, lined with purveyors of Swiss watches (what else?!), high-end Italian and international fashion, cigar shops and jewellery stores.

Macelleria Gabbani FOOD & DRINK
(☑ 091 911 30 90; www.gabbani.com; Via Pessina 12; ☺ 8.15am-6.30pm Mon-Fri, to 5pm Sat) You'll find it hard to miss the giant sausages hanging out the front of this irresistible delicatessen. The same people operate a tempting cheese shop, the **Bottega del Formaggio** (☺ 7am-6.30pm Mon-Fri, to 5pm Sat), across the road.

Merkur Chocolaterie CHOCOLATE
(www.merkur.ch; Via Pessina 17; ☺ 9am-6.30pm Mon-Fri, to 6pm Sat) Divine chocolates divinely wrapped or sold in slabs (in the case of Läderach) make this a must for lovers of chocolate.

🛈 Information

Tourist Office (☑ 058 866 66 00; www.lugano-tourism.ch; Municipio Bldg, Riva Giocondo Albertolli; ☺ 9am-7pm Mon-Fri, to 6pm Sat, 10am-6pm Sun & holidays Apr-Oct, shorter hrs rest of year) There are also tourist information booths at the main train station and airport.

🛈 Getting There & Around

AIR
Agno Airport (☑ 091 612 11 11; www.lugano-airport.ch) From Agno airport, Darwin Airline (www.darwinairline.com) flies to Geneva from where there are connecting flights elsewhere in the region. Swiss (www.swiss.com) flies regularly to Zürich.

The FLP (www.flpsa.ch/en.htm; Sfr2.10; ☺ every 15min, 6.25am-8.10pm) train service runs from opposite the main train station in Lugano to Agno, from where it's a 10-minute walk to the terminal.

BUS
Lugano is on the same road and rail route as Bellinzona. All postal buses leave from the main bus station at Via Serafino Balestra. One goes to Menaggio, on Lake Como, via Porlezza. Local bus 1 runs from Castagnola in the east through the centre to Paradiso, while bus 2 runs from central Lugano to Paradiso via the train station. A single trip costs Sfr1.50 to Sfr2.20 (ticket dispensers indicate the appropriate rate) or it's Sfr6 for a one-day pass. The main local bus terminus is on Corso Pestalozzi. For Morcote, get bus 431 at Piazza Rezzonico (30 to 35 minutes).

CAR
From Milan, the A9 autostrada via Como becomes the A2 after the border at Chiasso and proceeds through Lugano to Bellinzona and central Switzerland.

Parking is mostly metered in central Lugano.

TRAIN
There are rail links to most major cities in Switzerland. More locally, trains run to Melide (Sfr4, six minutes). Trains connect Lugano with Como (Sfr12, 35 to 55 minutes) on the Italian side of the border, with onward connections to Milan and elsewhere.

The main train station is likely to be the only one you need – the Ferrovia Ponte Tresa station serves the local 12.3km-long railway line between Lugano and Ponte Tresa on the Italian border.

Around Lake Lugano

The Lugano tourist office has guides to some of the best lakeside walks.

Gandria

Gandria is a compact village almost dipping into the water. They say the glacier that

---

MARIO BOTTA IN THE PINK

Lugano's star architect, Mario Botta (born 1943 in nearby Mendrisio) may be best known for his work abroad (such as San Francisco's Museum of Modern Art, the Kyobo Tower in Seoul and restoration of the La Scala opera theatre in Milan), but he has left an indelible mark on and around Lugano. The 12-storey **casino** across the water in Campione d'Italia is one example. Another is the Museo dei Fossili (p129) in Meride. Botta seems to have a thing about right angles and the colour pink. Located in the centre of Lugano, his landmarks include the **BSí** (Via San Franscini), a series of interconnected monoliths formerly known as the Banca del Gottardo; the pink brick office block at **Via Pretorio 9** (Via Pretorio 9), known to locals as the Cherry Building because of the cherry tree planted on the roof; and the roof of the **TPL local bus terminus**. At night the bus terminus is illuminated... in light pink.

Further afield, he designed the Cardada (p95) cable car and lookout above Locarno.

formed this part of the lake dug so deep that the lake waters here actually reach below sea level! A popular trip is to take the boat from Lugano and walk back along the shore to Castagnola (around 40 minutes) – ask at Lugano's tourist office for its *The Olive Tree Path* brochure.

Across the lake from Gandria is the **Museo delle Dogane Svizzere** (Swiss Customs Museum; ☑ 091 923 98 43; admission free; ⊙ 1.30-5.30pm Apr–mid-Oct), at Cantine di Gandria, and accessible by boat. It tells the history of customs (and, more interestingly, smuggling) in this border area. On display are confiscated smugglers' boats that once operated on the lake.

There's a small **information booth** (☑ 079 331 30 65; Gandria; ⊙ 10am-8pm Mar-Nov) in town.

Monte Generosa

The fine panorama provided by this summit (1704m) includes lakes, the Alps and the Apennines – the clearer the conditions, the further you can see. It's possible to make out Milan and key points in the Swiss Alps, such as Monte Rosa, the Matterhorn and the Jungfrau. Indeed, it is a 360-degree sweeping view and it is easily the most spectacular viewpoint in all of the Canton of Ticino.

To get here, take a boat (except in winter), train (Sfr6.50, 17 minutes) or car to Capolago. From there, jump on the rack-and-pinion **train** (☑ 091 630 51 11; www.montegeneroso.ch; return adult/reduced Sfr42/21; ⊙ up to 9 a day mid-Mar–mid-Oct).

Montagnola

German novelist Hermann Hesse (1877–1962) chose to live in this small town in 1919 after the horrors of WWI had separated him from his family. As crisis followed crisis in Germany, topped by the rise of the Nazis, he saw little reason to return home. He wrote some of his greatest works here, at first in an apartment in Casa Camuzzi. Nearby, in Torre Camuzzi, is the **Museo Hermann Hesse** (☑ 091 993 37 70; www.hessemontagnola.ch; Torre Camuzzi; adult/reduced Sfr8.50/7; ⊙ 10am-6.30pm Mar-Oct, to 5.30pm Sat & Sun Nov-Feb). Personal objects, some of the thousands of watercolours he painted in Ticino, books and other odds and ends help recreate something of Hesse's life.

From Lugano, take the Ferrovia Ponte Tresa train to Sorengo and change for a postal bus (Sfr3.75, 20 minutes).

Melide

Melide is a bulge of shore from which the A2 motorway slices across the lake. The main attraction is one that is bound to be a hit with most kids (and a few kids in grown-ups' clothes). **Swissminiatur** (☑ 091 640 10 60; www.swissminiatur.ch; Via Cantonale; adult/reduced Sfr19/15; ⊙ 9am-6pm mid-Mar–mid-Nov) is a miniature wonderland where you'll find finely rendered 1:25 scale models of more than 120 national attractions. It's the quick way to see Switzerland in a day if you don't have time to see the real thing. Castles such as the Château de Chillon in Montreux vie for attention with the only foreign interloper – the Duomo in Milan. All the models are numbered – make sure they give you the brochure with the full list when you enter.

Morcote

With its narrow cobblestone lanes and endless nooks and crannies, this peaceful former fishing village clusters at the foot of Monte Abostora on Lake Lugano. Narrow stairways lead to **Chiesa di Santa Maria del Sasso**, a 15-minute climb. The views are excellent and the church has 16th-century frescoes and carved faces on the organ. From there, continue another 20 minutes upstairs to **Vico di Morcote**, a pleasant high-altitude hamlet with a baroque church and vineyards. About 5km further is Carona, which is worth a visit for the **Parco Botanico San Grato** (admission free).

Four hundred metres left (west) from the boat stop, **Parco Scherrer** (☑ 091 996 21 25; adult/reduced Sfr7/6; ⊙ 10am-5pm mid-Mar–Oct, to 6pm Jul-Aug, closed Nov-Feb) offers a bustling range of architectural styles, including copies of famous buildings and generic types (eg Temple of Nefertiti, Siamese teahouse). It's all set in subtropical parkland.

The small **tourist office** (☑ 058 866 49 69; Riva dal Garavell; ⊙ 8.30am-12.30pm & 1.30-5.30pm Mon-Fri, 10am-noon & 1-5pm Sat & Sun late Mar–mid-Oct) has useful information about the village and entire Lugano region.

Meride

It's of specialised interest, but for those who are keen on prehistory, Meride, situated about 15km south of Lugano and just west off the A2 motorway, is worth a stop. The recently remodelled **Museo dei Fossili** (Fossil Museum; ☑ 091 640 00 80; www. montesangiorgio.ch; Via Bernardo Peyer 9; adult/ reduced Sfr12/8; ⊙ 9am-5pm Tue-Sun) displays vestiges of the first creatures to inhabit the region – reptiles and fish dating back more than 200 million years. It may sound dry, but the finds are important enough to warrant Unesco recognition of the area around nearby Monte San Giorgio (1096m), where they were uncovered, as a World Heritage Site. According to Unesco, the mount is the 'single best known record of marine life in the Triassic period'.

Near the town is a circular **nature trail**. You can reach Meride from Lugano by taking the train to Mendrisio and then the postal bus (Sfr12).

Bellinzona (Switzerland)

POP 17,544

Where several valleys leading down from the Alps converge, Bellinzona has always been an important crossroads. The most visible landmarks to this history are three grey-stone, medieval, Unesco World Heritage–listed castles that have attracted everyone from Swiss invaders to painters like William Turner.

The rocky, central hill upon which rises the main castle, Castelgrande, was a Roman frontier post and site of a Lombard defensive tower, and was later developed as a heavily fortified town controlled by Milan. The three castles and valley walls could not stop the Swiss German confederate troops from overwhelming the city in 1503, thus deciding Ticino's fate for the following three centuries.

◎ Sights

The city's three imposing castles are the main drawcard. Read up on them at www. bellinzonaunesco.ch. Although you could walk between the three, the top two castles can also be reached by car.

Castelgrande   CASTLE
(Monte San Michele; ☑ 091 825 81 45; www.cas telgrande.ch; grounds admission free, museum & towers adult/child Sfr5/2; ⊙ 10am-7pm Fri-Wed 10am-9pm Thu Jul & Aug, 10am-6pm Apr-Jun, Sep & Oct, 11am-4pm Nov-Mar) Castelgrande is the biggest fortification and rises above the town

centre. The first fortress on this site dates from the 4th century, but what you see today was built during and after the 13th century. It's worth paying the admission ticket here for the fine 18-minute video on Bellinzona's history, the fascinating museum, and the chance to climb to the summit of Torre Bianca (the climb begins in its twin Torre Neri).

The museum's highlights are the 15th-century decorations taken from the ceiling of a former noble house in central Bellinzona. The pictures range from weird animals (late medieval ideas on what a camel looked like were curious) to a humorous series on the 'world upside down'. Examples of the latter include an ox driving a man-pulled plough and a sex-crazed woman chasing a chaste man(!). The uncomfortable black seats you sit on for the audiovisual on the castle's history were designed by Mario Botta and cost around Sfr1000 a pop!

To get here, walk up Scalinata San Michele from Piazza della Collegiata, or take the lift, buried deep in the rocky hill in an extraordinary concrete bunker-style construction, from Piazza del Sole.

Castello di Montebello   CASTLE
(☑ 091 825 13 42; castle admission free, museum adult/concession Sfr5/2; ⊙ castle 8am-8pm Apr-Oct & 8am-5pm Nov-Mar, museum 10am-7pm Fri-Wed & 10am-9pm Thu Jul & Aug, 10am-6pm Mar-Jun,

---

ⓘ COMBINED CASTLE TICKET?

If you plan to visit all three of Bellinzona's castles, you might be tempted by the combined ticket (adult/child Sfr15/7.50), also known as the 'Cultura Pass', which allows entry to all three castles' museums and the Museo Villa dei Cedri. But you have to be sure of what you're getting. We strongly recommend visiting the outstanding musuem at Castelgrande where the ticket also entitles you to climb the castle's towers. In Castello di Montebello, however, the best views and more interesting section of the castle are accessible for free and the museum exhibition will appeal only to those with a specialist archaeological interest. Up at the Castello di Sasso Corbaro, access to the tower and best views is through whatever temporary exhibition they have on at the time, so it's probably worth paying to enter.

Bellinzona (Switzerland)

It also has a smaller museum of archaeological finds from medieval Bellinzona.

Castello di Sasso Corbaro CASTLE
(☏ 091 825 59 06; castle admission free, museum & tower adult/child Sfr5/2; ⊙ castle 8am-7pm Fri-Wed, 8am-9pm Thu Jul & Aug, 8am-6pm Apr-Jun, Sep & Oct, 8am-6pm Nov-Mar; museum 10am-7pm Fri-Wed & 10am-9pm Thu Jul & Aug, 10am-6pm Mar-Jun, Sep & Oct, closed Nov-Feb) The highest of the three castles at 250m above the city, Sasso Corbaro was built in just six months in 1479 on the orders of the Duke of Milan. On a clear day, the views from here are sweeping and spectacular.

Churches RELIGIOUS
Wandering south from the train station, you'll first see the **Chiesa Collegiata dei SS Pietro e Stefano** (Piazza della Collegiata; ⊙ 8am-1pm & 4-6pm), a Renaissance church with baroque touches and rich in frescoes inside. Nearby is the **Chiesa di San Rocco**

Sep & Oct, closed Nov-Feb) Slightly above the town and arguably the prettiest of the three castles, Castello di Montebello dates largely from the 15th century and has fine views from the ramparts and grassy castle grounds.

(Piazza dell'Indipendenza; ⊙ 7-11am & 2-5pm), with its huge fresco of St Christopher, and a smaller one of the Virgin Mary and Christ adorning the facade. Similarly decorated is the 14th-century **Chiesa di San Biagio** (Piazza San Biagio; ⊙ 7am-noon & 2-5pm), the difference being that these frescoes are not 20th-century restorations.

Situated west over the railway line is the **Chiesa di Santa Maria delle Grazie** (Via Convento; ⊙ 7am-6pm), a 15th-century church with an extraordinary fresco cycle (recently restored after being damaged by fire in 1996) of the life and death of Christ. The centrepiece is a panel depicting Christ's Crucifixion.

Festivals & Events

Rabadan   CARNIVAL
(www.rabadan.ch) Bellinzona's rowdy carnival starts on a Thursday seven-and-a-half weeks before Easter Sunday.

Piazza Blues Festival   MUSIC
Four days of international blues are brought to the city in summer (June/July). Entry is free except to the main stage on the last two days (Sfr15).

✗ Eating

Manor   CAFETERIA €
(☑ 091 823 86 99; Viale della Stazione 5; meals Sfr20-25; ⊙ 9am-6.30pm Mon-Wed & Fri, to 9pm Thu, 8.30am-6pm Sat) In this town of fairly pricey eating options, this no-nonsense cafeteria is a local favourite with large pasta dishes and daily specials, or you can just order a salad. Queues form here at lunchtime.

Osteria Zoccolino   SWISS €€
(☑ 091 825 06 70; Piazza Governo 5; meals Sfr30-40; ⊙ 11.30am-2pm & 5-9pm Mon-Fri) A photographer runs this slightly chaotic but cheery eatery that fills at lunchtime, especially. You never quite know what to expect here: a set lunch of Indian food, concerts on Thursday nights...and you may find he opens at night only if he has enough bookings. Otherwise, there are several alternatives along Via Teatro and Via Orico.

Locanda Orico   SWISS €€
(☑ 091 825 15 18; Via Orico 13; meals Sfr70-80; ⊙ 11.45-2pm & 6.45-10pm Tue-Sat) Behind the lace curtains of this low-slung temple to good food you come across such creations as *gnocchetti di patate alla zucca in una dadolat di camoscio in salmì* (little pumpkin gnocchi in jugged chamois meat).

★ Castelgrande   ITALIAN, TICINESE €€€
(☑ 091 826 23 53; www.castelgrande.ch; Castelgrande; meals restaurant Sfr80-100, grotto Sfr50-60; ⊙ restaurant 7-10pm Tue-Sat, noon-2pm Sun, grotto 11.30am-2pm & 7-9.30pm) It's not often you get the chance to eat inside a Unesco World Heritage Site. The restaurant itself is an elegant mix of classic and modern tastes, including white linen and black leather chairs. Cuisine changes with the seasons but is always a mix of Ticino and Italian, with flights of inventive fantasy. Try the five-course tasting menu for Sfr85.

❶ Information

Tourist Office (☑ 091 825 21 31; www.bellinzonaturismo.ch; Piazza Nosetto; ⊙ 9am-6.30pm Mon-Fri, to noon Sat Apr-Oct, 9am-noon & 1.30-6.30pm Mon-Fri, to noon Sat Nov-Mar) Located in the restored Renaissance Palazzo Civico (town hall).

❶ Getting There & Around

BUS
Postal buses for destinations around the region depart from beside the train station.

CAR
The A2 motorway from Lugano passes here – of the two autostrada exits, 'Bellinzona Nord' is marginally the best for the town centre. Most of the town centre is pedestrianised or has metered parking only. There's an **underground car park** (Piazza del Sole; per hr Sfr2) beneath Piazza del Sole.

TRAIN
Bellinzona is on the train route connecting Locarno (Sfr8.50, 20 to 25 minutes) and Lugano (Sfr10.50, 25 to 30 minutes). It is also on the Zürich–Milan route.

LAKE COMO & AROUND BELLINZONA (SWITZERLAND)

Bergamo, Brescia & Cremona

Includes ➡

Best Places to Eat

➡ Ristorante Gualtiero Marchesi (p146)

➡ Da Vittorio (p141)

➡ Hosteria '700 (p155)

➡ Osteria al Bianchi (p151)

➡ Colleoni & Dell'Angelo (p140)

Best Places to Stay

➡ Da Vittorio (p202)

➡ Albergo Orologio (p202)

➡ Delle Arti Design Hotel (p202)

➡ Agriturismo Casa Clelia (p201)

➡ Hotel Piazza Vecchia (p201)

Why Go?

Medieval towns, gentle lakes hemmed in by steep hillsides, vast plains, prehistoric rock art and mighty mountains make this part of the Lombard region one of northern Italy's most underrated corners. You'd need a couple of weeks to cover the area well, so you need to make choices. Bergamo, with its medieval Città Alta (Upper Town), is a must, and it's an inspired choice if this is your point of arrival in Italy. Townies and church lovers might concentrate on the main centres (Brescia, Cremona, Crema and Lodi) which all have fascinating medieval cores. An alternative tour of plains settlements will turn up palaces, castles and forts. Wine buffs may prefer touring the Franciacorta, south of Lake Iseo. North of Bergamo, several valleys lead deep into the picturesque Orobie Alps.

Road Distances (KM)

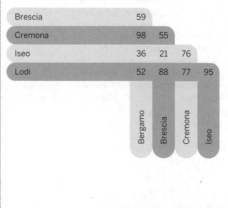

	Bergamo	Brescia	Cremona	Iseo
Brescia	59			
Cremona	98	55		
Iseo	36	21	76	
Lodi	52	88	77	95

Getting Around

Bergamo, Brescia and Cremona are all well connected to each other by train, road and bus. Services also connect Brescia and Bergamo with the valleys and mountains of the north – easily the most scenic area. But the prettiest drive is across the plains where medieval forts and churches await.

3 PERFECT DAYS

Day 1: Old Bergamo
Like an eagle's eyrie, the Città Alta (Upper Town) of Bergamo sits a world apart, looking down almost with condescension on the great Lombard plains to the south. Discover its lanes, the Renaissance Piazza Vecchia, the medieval Basilica di Santa Maria Maggiore, the Venetian defensive walls and La Rocca fortress. The Città Alta is jammed with fine eateries and several romantic places to sleep over.

Day 2: Brescia & Cremona
There are plenty of options in the Lombard plains south of Bergamo. You could make a whistle-stop tour of Brescia for its old centre and Roman ruins, then shoot south to Cremona to enjoy the magnificent Piazza del Comune and its monuments and search out some of the city's violin-makers. On the return leg to Bergamo, scoot by Pizzighettone for its impressive fortress walls.

Day 3: Northern Mountains
North of Bergamo, various valleys lead into the pre-Alpine hills and mountains of the Orobie Alps, while routes east head to Lake Iseo, the jewel of which is the island of Monte Isola. Hill valley highlights include San Pellegrino Terme, of mineral water fame; Ardesio and its pretty centre; Branzi and its hill walks to glacial lakes; Valbondione and the nearby Serio waterfalls; and, quite simply, the chance to admire some beautiful mountain country.

Where to Stay

With the exception of Bergamo, especially in the Città Alta, the Lombard cities of the plains are not heavily touristed. Lake Iseo can be busy in July and August. In the mountain valleys, options can be scarcer, except at towns serving as ski bases in winter.

DON'T MISS

The violin-making traditions of Cremona (p154).

Best Churches

➡ Basilica di Santa Maria Maggiore (p138), Bergamo

➡ Chiesa di San Tomè (p141), Almenno San Bartolomeo

➡ Duomo (p152), Cremona

➡ Tempio Civico dell'Incoronata (p156), Lodi

➡ Santuario di Santa Maria della Croce (p157), Crema

Best Escapes

➡ Val Taleggio (p141)

➡ Lake Iseo (p144)

➡ Orobie Alps (p141)

➡ Franciacorta wine region (p148)

➡ Crema (p157)

Resources

➡ **Brembana Valley** (www.vallebrembana.org) Info about the Valle Brembana north of Bergamo.

➡ **Rupestre.net** (www.rupestre.net) Useful site covering the region's prehistoric rock art.

➡ **Strada del Vino Franciacorta** (www.stradadelfranciacorta.it) One-stop guide to the Franciacorta wine region.

➡ **Lago d'Iseo** (www.lagodiseo.org) Info on accommodation and activities.

➡ **Bergamo** (www.turismo.bergamo.it) Excellent tourist office site.

BERGAMO, BRESCIA & CREMONA

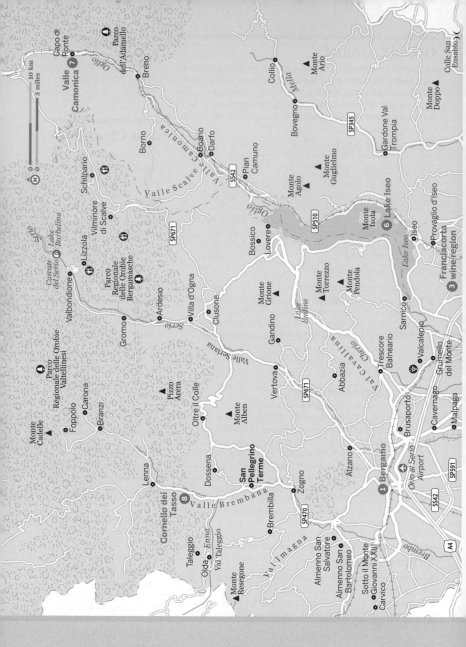

Bergamo, Brescia & Cremona Highlights

1 Wandering endlessly through the medieval lanes of Bergamo's Città Alta, beginning in the **Piazza Vecchia** (p138).

2 Tracking down the fascinating violin-making tradition of **Cremona** (p152) in the midst of the quiet old town.

3 Going for a drive around the **Franciacorta wine region** (p148) then stopping for lunch at **Ristorante Gualtiero Marchesi** (p146).

4 Enjoying the distinctive circular Romanesque cathedral, Roman ruins and the fabulous Museo della Città in **Brescia** (p148).

5 Exploring one of Italy's most underrated castles in the village of **Pizzighettone** (p156), west of Cremona.

6 Dropping off the tourist trail for a day by driving around **Lake Iseo** (p144), one of the least-known of the northern Italian lakes.

7 Embarking on a quest to find the Unesco World Heritage–listed rock art of **Valle Camonica** (p147).

8 Heading into the valleys north of Bergamo in search of ancient villages like **Cornello dei Tasso** (p144).

BERGAMO

POP 119,551

This eastern Lombard city offers a wealth of art and medieval Renaissance and baroque architecture, a privileged position overlooking the southern plains, breathtaking views and some fine dining. Bergamo is one of northern Italy's most beguiling cities.

The city's defining feature is a double identity. The ancient hilltop Città Alta (Upper Town) is a tangle of tiny medieval streets, embraced by 5km of Venetian walls.

Bergamo

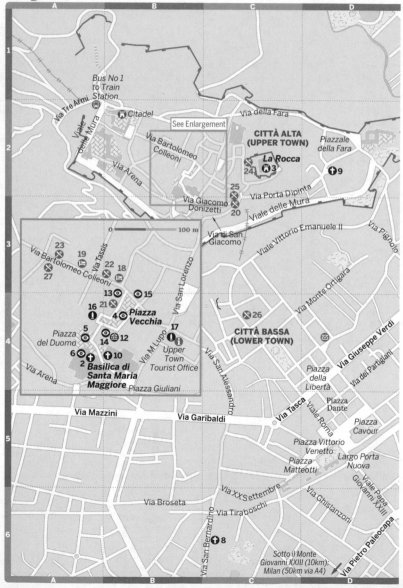

It lords over the largely modern Città Bassa (Lower Town), connected by a funicular.

History

It is thought Gauls and Etruscans had some sort of presence here, though they left nothing behind to indicate permanent settlement. The Romans, on the other hand, left a deeper mark. The hill settlement of Bergamo is strategically placed on a lonely rise south of the Lombard pre-Alps between the Brembo and Serio river valleys and was no doubt appreciated not only as a trade centre but as a handy lookout position over the vast Lombard plains to the south. As was typical in Roman settlements, the main roads were the intersecting *decumanus* (east–west road; Via Gombito) and *cardo* (north–south road; today Via Lupo and Via San Lorenzo).

Although Milan's skyscrapers to the southwest are visible on a clear day, historically Bergamo was more closely associated with Venice, which controlled the city for 350 years until Napoleon arrived. Medieval Bergamo was an industrious (textiles and metals) town that was incorporated into the Venetian empire in 1428, remaining under the domination of the Serenissima

BERGAMO, BRESCIA & CREMONA BERGAMO

(Venetian Republic) until the latter's fall to Napoleon in 1797.

◉ Sights

The best way to explore Bergamo's old town is to simply wander without haste. Via Bartolomeo Colleoni and Via Gombito are lined with all sorts of curious shops and eateries. Wander along the perimeter streets of the old town too, for rewarding panoramas from the city's Venetian-era defensive walls.

Piazza Vecchia   PIAZZA
(Old Square) The Upper Town's beating heart is the cafe-clad Piazza Vecchia, lined by elegant architecture that is a testament in stone and brick to Bergamo's long and colourful history. Its highlights include the Palazzo Nuovo, Palazzo del Podestà, Palazzo della Ragione and the Torre del Campanone. Tucked in behind the secular buildings of Piazza Vecchia, **Piazza del Duomo** is the core of Bergamo's spiritual life

Le Corbusier apparently described Piazza Vecchia as the 'most beautiful square in Europe' – good thing they didn't let him try out any of his ideas on it. Had he done so, he'd have been following a certain precedent. The Renaissance square was created by bulldozing the huddle of medieval housing that once stood there.

The white porticoed building on Via Bartolomeo Colleoni, which forms the northern side of the piazza, is the **Palazzo Nuovo**. Designed in 1611 by a brilliant architectural mind from Vicenza, Vincenzo Scamozzi (1548–1616), it was not actually completed until 1928. Long the seat of the town hall, it has been a library since 1873. Diagonally opposite, on the northwest side of the

square, the **Palazzo del Podestà** was long home to Venice's representative in Bergamo.

Turn south and you face the imposing arches and columns of the **Palazzo della Ragione**, built in the 12th century. The lion of St Mark is a reminder of Venice's long reign here. It's an early 20th-century replica of the 15th-century original, which was torn down when Napoleon took over in 1797. Note the sun clock in the pavement beneath the arches and the curious Romanesque and Gothic animals and busts decorating the pillars of the arches. Until the Accademia Carrara (p139) reopens, a selection of its masterpieces is on show in Palazzo della Ragione.

Across the square from the palace, the colossal, square-based **Torre del Campanone** (adult/child €3/free; ⊙ 9.30am-6pm Tue-Fri, 9.30am-8pm Sat & Sun Apr-Oct, 9.30am-1pm & 2.30-6pm Tue-Fri, 9.30am-6pm Sat & Sun Nov-Mar) tolls the old 10pm curfew. Originally raised in the 12th century and partly used as a jail in the 14th, it has undergone numerous alterations. In 1486, cheerful citizens lit a bonfire atop the tower to celebrate a religious holiday. Oddly, they didn't foresee that this would lead to the timber roof catching and burning to a crisp, leading to one of the many renovations. Lighting fires is no longer allowed but you can take a wheelchair-accessible lift to the top, from where there are splendid views.

Duomo   CATHEDRAL
(☑ 035 21 02 23; Piazza del Duomo; ⊙ 7.30-11.45am & 3-6.30pm) Roman remains were discovered during renovations of Bergamo's baroque cathedral. A rather squat maroon building, it has a brilliant white facade. Among the relics in a side chapel is the one-time coffin of the beatified Pope John XXII.

Museo e Tesoro Della Cattedrale   MUSEUM
(☑ 035 24 87 72; Piazza del Duomo; adult/reduced €5/3; ⊙ 9.30am-1pm & 2-6.30pm Tue-Sun) Down the steps right next to the Duomo, this glittering museum is filled with sacred art and reliquary from the cathedral's collection, as well as displays on the cathedral's architectural history.

Basilica di Santa Maria Maggiore   BASILICA
(Piazza del Duomo; ⊙ 9am-12.30pm & 2.30-6pm Apr-Oct, shorter hrs Nov-Mar) Begun in 1137, the Basilica di Santa Maria Maggiore is quite a mishmash of styles. To its whirl of Romanesque apses (on which some external frescoes remain visible), Gothic additions were slapped on. A more obvious addition

ⓘ BERGAMO CARD

The Bergamo Card (www.turismo-bergamo.it; 24-/48-/72-hour card €10/15/20) is a worthwhile investment to save a few euros. In addition to free funicular and bus transport (including the airport bus), the card entitles you to free entry to 21 museums, among them La Rocca, Torre del Campanone, Galleria d'Arte Moderna e Contemporanea and Museo e Tesoro Della Cattedrale. Cards can be bought at the airport, bus station, funicular station, participating museums and some hotels.

IN SEARCH OF LORENZO LOTTO

One of the great names of the late Venetian Renaissance, Lorenzo Lotto worked for 12 years in and around Bergamo from 1513. Today, three of his works remain in situ in three churches scattered about the city. Seeing them is largely a matter of luck, as finding these churches open is hit-or-miss. Just off Via Porta Dipinta at the eastern end of the Città Alta (Upper Town), the diminutive **Chiesa di San Michele al Pozzo** (St Michael at the Well; Via Porta Dipinta, Città Alta; ⊘ 9am-5pm) is home to a chapel filled with a cycle of paintings known as the *Storie della Vergine* (Stories of the Virgin), starting with her birth and culminating with the scene of her visiting Elisabeth (her cousin and soon-to-be mother of St John the Baptist). In two churches in the Città Bassa (Lower Town), the **Chiesa del Santo Spirito** (Church of the Holy Spirit; Via Torquato Tasso) and **Chiesa di San Bernardino** (Via San Bernardino), you can observe how Lotto treats the same subject in quite different fashion in altarpieces dedicated to the *Madonna in trono e santi* (The Madonna Enthroned with Saints). The latter is done with great flair and freedom, full of vivid colour, while the former seems more subdued.

is the busy Renaissance **Cappella Colleoni** (⊘ 9am-12.30pm & 2-6.30pm Mar-Oct, 9am-12.30pm & 2-4.30pm Tue-Sun Nov-Feb), on the side facing the Piazza del Duomo. Detached from the church is the octagonal **baptistry**.

Influences seem to come from afar, with dual-colour banding (black and white, and rose and white) typical of Tuscany, and an interesting trompe l'œil pattern on part of the facade.

The Cappella Colleoni, which was tacked on to the side facing the square between 1472 and 1476, was built as a magnificent mausoleum-cum-chapel for the Bergamese mercenary commander Bartolomeo Colleoni (c 1400–75), who led Venice's armies in campaigns across northern Italy. He lies buried inside in a magnificent tomb. Venetian rococo master Giambattista Tiepolo (1696-1770) did some of the frescoes below the central dome.

The baptistry was built in 1340 but plonked in its present spot in 1898.

La Rocca
FORTRESS

(Piazzale Brigata Legnano; adult/child €3/free; ⊘ 9.30am-1pm & 2.30-6pm Tue-Fri, 9.30am-7pm Sat & Sun Jun-Sep, 9.30am-1pm & 2.30-6pm Tue-Sun Oct-May) This impressive fortress is dominated by a round tower that dates from Bergamo's days as a Venetian outpost. La Rocca houses part of the city's **history museum** and is surrounded by a park with lovely views over lower Bergamo. The views are even better from the tower's summit.

Torre di Gombito
TOWER

(Via Gombito 13; ⊘ 2.30-4.30pm Mon & Fri, 10am-noon & 2.30-4.30pm Sat & Sun Mar-Sep) **FREE**

For a wonderful view from one of the highest points in the old town, climb the 12th-century Gombito Tower. Visits must be reserved in advance at the tourist office (p141), which is at the base of the tower, and leave every 45 minutes.

Accademia Carrara
ART GALLERY

(📞 035 39 96 40; www.accademiacarrara.bergamo.it; Piazza Carrara 82a) Just east of the old city walls is one of Italy's great art repositories, although it has been closed for major renovations since 2007. The reopening has been pushed back numerous times over the years, but May 2014 was the latest target at the time of our visit. Until it reopens, a selection of its masterpieces is on show in Palazzo della Ragione in the Città Alta.

Founded in 1780, it contains an exceptional range of Italian masters. Raphael's *San Sebastiano* is a highlight, but other artists represented include Botticelli, Canaletto, Mantegna and Titian.

Galleria d'Arte Moderna e Contemporanea
ART GALLERY

(GAMeC; 📞 035 27 02 72; www.gamec.it; Via San Tomaso 53; ⊘ 10am-1pm & 3-7pm Tue-Sun) **FREE** Facing across the square from the Accademia Carrara is this gallery, which displays the academy's small permanent collection of modern works by Italian artists such as Giacomo Balla, Giorgio Morandi, Giorgio de Chirico and Filippo de Pisis. A contribution from Vassily Kandinksy lends an international touch. Admission prices and opening hours vary for temporary exhibitions.

🗲 Tours

Guide Turistiche Città di Bergamo   TOUR
(📞 035 24 95 53; www.bergamoguide.it) Half- and full-day tours of Bergamo and further afield.

✗ Eating

Il Fornaio   PIZZA BY SLICE, BAKERY €
(Via Bartolomeo Colleoni 1; pizza slices €1.10-2; ⊗8am-8pm Mon-Sat, 7.30am-8pm Sun; 🖶) Bergamo's best coffee is part of the attraction here, but we also love it for the large and steaming-hot pizza slices that are packed with ingredients – the seafood variety has more on it than entire pizzas served in many restaurants.

Polentone   ITALIAN €
(📞 348 804 60 21; Piazza Mercato delle Scarpe 1, Città Alta; meals €10-15; ⊗11.30am-3.30pm & 6-9.30pm Mon-Thu, 11.30am-3.30pm & 6pm-1am Fri, 11.30am-1am Sat, 11.30am-9pm Sun) Styling itself as Italy's first polenta take-away (although it's more street food to be eaten nearby than true take-away), Polentone serves up steaming bowls of polenta in the sauce of your choice (including wild boar, venison and other unusual tastes). Choose between *gialla* (simple, corn polenta) or *taragna* (with cheese and butter). It's under the arches opposite the Upper Town Funicular Stop, with a few wooden stools strewn around.

Antica Hosteria del Vino Buono   BERGAMESE €
(📞 035 24 79 93; Piazza Mercato delle Scarpe, Città Alta; meals €20-25; ⊗7-10.30pm Tue, noon-2.30pm & 7-10.30pm Wed-Sun) Feast on typical dishes like cheese-sprinkled *casoncelli* (homemade pasta cushions filled with a spicy sausage meat and laced with a buttery sage sauce) followed by a plate of *stinco al forno con polenta* (baked pork shank with polenta) at this authentic inn. A typical Bergamese antipasto served up here is *schisöl* (polenta cooked with cheese and mushrooms).

La Cantina di Via Colleoni   BERGAMESE
(📞 035 21 58 64; www.lacantinadiviacolleoni.it; Via Bartolomeo Colleoni 5; meals €25-30; ⊗10am-3pm & 6-midnight) Still going strong after 10 years, this laid-back, casual eatery and bar serves up fine local dishes (such as cured meats, local cheeses and *casoncelli*) in a warm, brick-lined space and with a carefully chosen and very cool musical soundtrack. The excellent lunch *menu Bergamasco* (Bergamo menu) for €15 includes water, wine and two courses. Otherwise, mains include codfish with polenta.

Ristorante a Modo   ITALIAN €€
(📞 035 21 02 95; www.ristoranteamodo.com; Viale Vittorio Emanuele II 19; meals €35; ⊗noon-3pm & 8pm-midnight Mon-Sat) Inventive takes on modern Italian cooking make this our pick of the restaurants down in the Lower Town. Try their ravioli stuffed with pumpkin or walnuts or seabass carpaccio with crustaceans of the day. The weekday lunch menu is excellent value at €13/17/22 for one/two/three courses.

Officina dei Sapore   ITALIAN, SEAFOOD €€
(📞 035 24 76 86; www.officinaesapori.it; Via Solata 7; meals €35-40, set menu €40-45; ⊗noon-3pm & 7-11pm Mon-Sat) Marta and Stefano oversee this welcoming place with its intimate, old-world dining area and fine seafood-dominated menu. Dishes include lobster medallions or pheasant with citrus and thyme, while after their six-course tasting menus (divided into meat or fish) you may never want to eat again, but it's a marvellous way to go out.

Vineria Cozzi   ITALIAN €€
(📞 035 23 88 36; www.vineriacozzi.it; Via Bartolomeo Colleoni 22, Città Alta; meals €35-45; ⊗10.30am-3pm & 6.30pm-midnight Thu-Tue) Things have changed little since the original wine dealer started here in 1848. Elegant tables with delicate wrought-iron-backed chairs and a parchment-yellow paint scheme ensure a welcoming atmosphere and seem much as they were all those years ago. You can taste from the extensive wine list by the glass, and dine inside or in the tiny courtyard. Several pasta and rice options lead the way.

★ Colleoni & Dell'Angelo   ITALIAN €€€
(📞 035 23 25 96; www.colleonidellangelo.com; Piazza Vecchia 7, Città Alta; meals €50-60, tasting menus €75; ⊗noon-2.30pm & 7-10.30pm Tue-Sun) Piazza Vecchia provides the ideal backdrop to savour inventive local cuisine. Grab an outside table in summer or opt for the noble 15th-century interior, with its polished tile floors, rich linen, occasional fresco and the odd suit of armour standing about. Meals range from takes on strictly local dishes through to more generally Italian dishes and occasional use of products from further afield.

❶ Information

There's another tourist office at the **airport** (📞 035 32 04 02; www.turismo-bergamo.it; Airport arrivals hall; ⊗8am-9pm).

Lower Town Tourist Office (☎035 21 02 04; www.turismo.bergamo.it; Piazzale Marconi; ⏱9am-12.30pm & 2-5.30pm)

Upper Town Tourist Office (☎035 24 22 26; www.turismo-bergamo.it; Via Gombito 13; ⏱9am-5.30pm)

❶ Getting There & Around

AIR

Orio al Serio (☎035 32 63 23; www.sacbo.it), 4km southeast of Bergamo train station, has regular flights to/from the UK and other European destinations, as a result of which Bergamo is increasingly one of the most popular entry points into northern Italy.

ATB buses (☎035 23 60 26; www.atb.berga mo.it) to/from Orio al Serio airport depart every 20 minutes from Bergamo bus and train stations (€2.10, 15 minutes). Direct buses also connect the airport with Milan and Brescia.

BUS

ATB bus 1 connects the train station with the funicular to the Upper Town and Colle Aperto (going the other way not all buses stop right at the station but at the Porta Nuova stop). From Colle Aperto, either bus 21 or a funicular continues uphill to San Vigilio. Buy tickets, valid for 75 minutes' travel on buses, for €1.25 from machines at the train and funicular stations or at newspaper stands.

The main **bus station** (☎035 28 90 00, 800 139392; www.bergamotrasporti.it) for provincial services is across Piazzale Marconi from the train station.

CAR

From Milan or Brescia, take the A4 motorway and follow the Bergamo exits.

Traffic is restricted in the Città Alta, although you can approach and find limited parking outside the city walls. Otherwise, use metered parking or car parks in the Lower Town.

TRAIN

One or two trains run every hour between Milan (not all stop at Stazione Centrale) and Bergamo (€5.25, 50 to 65 minutes). Every 30 to 60 minutes a train runs to/from Brescia (€4.55, one to 1½ hours). Change there for Cremona or Mantua.

BERGAMO'S VALLEYS

The series of tranquil valleys that works its way like a hand of bony fingers into the mountains north of Bergamo rank among the region's best-kept secrets. Here the hills rise to the status of mountains in the Orobie Alps, which throw up a mix of jagged

> **WORTH A TRIP**
>
> ## DA VITTORIO
>
> Bergamo's acclaimed **Da Vittorio** (☎035 68 10 24; www.davittorio.com; Via Cantalupa 17, Brusaporto; set menus €70-230; ⏱12.30-2.30pm & 7-10pm Thu-Tue Sep-Jul) is set in a country house 9km east of town and is up there with the best restaurants in Italy, not the least on account of its truffle dishes (a special truffle menu can cost €230). The guiding thought behind the cuisine is the subtle use of the freshest possible seasonal products to create local dishes with inventive flair.

peaks, gentler, snow-covered slopes, thickly wooded dales and open high-country pasture. All sorts of little gems await discovery, from the Cascate del Serio waterfall outside Valbondione to the medieval stone hamlets of Cornello dei Tasso and Gromo. Serious hikers have endless opportunities in the Orobie Alps.

❶ Getting Around

From Bergamo's bus station, **SAB** (☎035 28 90 00; www.sab-autoservizi.it) operates services to just about every village in the valleys, albeit not with great frequency. Timetables are available at the station.

Your own vehicle makes touring the valleys a great deal easier. The S road heads north from the city along the Valle Brembana, while the S takes you northeast along the Valle Seriana.

Bergamo Hills to Taleggio

From Bergamo's Città Alta, several minor roads lead through the pleasant **Colli di Bergamo** (Bergamo Hills) and drop down into plains around Almenno San Salvatore (follow the S road). In the country between this town and **Almenno San Bartolomeo** is a wonderful example of early Lombard Romanesque, the circular **Chiesa di San Tomè** (⏱2.30-6pm Sat, 10am-noon & 2.30-6pm Sun & holidays). The exterior of this unusual stone church boasts some pleasing decorative patterns and the play of circular and semicircular spaces inside is testimony to the aesthetic sensibility of medieval builders.

A possible driving route from Almenno San Salvatore would lead 5.5km northeast along the S and then north up the S into the

BERGAMO, BRESCIA & CREMONA BERGAMO'S VALLEYS

Val Brembilla. North of the town of Brembilla, the wooded hill country makes for a fine scenic drive that brings you back to the S through the little-visited **Val Taleggio**, the home turf of one of Lombardy's signature cheeses. The valley passes through the 3km-long **Gola dell'Enna**, a narrow rocky gorge at the bottom of which surges the Enna river.

✖ Eating

La Collina LOMBARDY €€
(☑035 64 25 70; www.ristorantecollina.it; Via Ca' Paler 5, Almenno San Bartolomeo; meals €35-40; ⊘noon-2pm & 7-10pm Wed-Sun) With several dining areas, an outdoor pergola for summer meals, and a privileged position overlooking the surrounding territory, La Collina (aptly, The Hill), is a stylish setting for carefully prepared and beautifully presented Lombard cooking with international flair. First courses range from fish ravioli to a risotto that changes with the caprices of the chef. It subscribes to the slow-cooking philosophy, which seems perfectly suited to the surrounds.

Ristorante della Salute BERGAMESE €€
(☑0345 4 70 06; www.albergodellasalute.it; Costa d'Olda 73, Olda (Taleggio); meals €25-30; ⊘12.30-2.30pm & 6.30-9.30pm Tue-Sun) This agreeable country hotel about halfway along the wild and woolly Taleggio valley has a simple restaurant downstairs where a good number of the excellent home-cooked dishes feature the local speciality, taleggio. It also offers views of the surrounding greenery and dishes like *strozzapreti ai spinaci con crema di Taleggio* (a kind of spinach gnocchi bathed in a thick, creamy taleggio sauce).

San Pellegrino Terme

They first started bottling lightly sparkling mineral water in San Pellegrino Terme, 25km north of Bergamo along the **Valle Brembana**, at the beginning of the 19th century.

Thermal baths tourism began late that century and local investors decided to spend big on new facilities in the early 1900s, creating the massive, seven-storey **Grand Hotel** (1904) and the exuberant **Casinò Municipale** (1907). They face each other over the Brembo river and together form a treasure trove of *stile liberty* (Italian art nouveau). The Casinò Municipale, especially, is full of whimsical detail. The facade

⚐ Driving Tour
Castle Circuit & the Good Pope

START & FINISH BERGAMO
LENGTH 105KM; ONE DAY

The plains south of Bergamo are dotted with interesting towns and villages, some of them dominated by castles and palaces that stand as eloquent testament of their colourful history.

Take the SS42 east out of Bergamo, or drop south to the A4 motorway and head a short way east, turning south at the Seriate exit, taking the S provincial road for ❶ **Cavernago**, a village presided over by one of several forts built by the mercenary commander Bartolomeo Colleoni. **Castello Colleoni**, a turreted, stone hulk, looms up on the right as you trundle south into Cavernago. It was raised in the Middle Ages but substantially overhauled in the 17th and 18th centuries. You can peek through slits at the entrance to see the frescoed gallery around the courtyard.

Barely 3km southwest, on a farming estate, lies the crenellated brickwork ❷ **Castello di Malpaga**, another Colleoni residence. He had the original 14th-century castle expanded, turning the original defensive walls into a kind of interior courtyard. Some original frescoes still remain in place.

Picking up the S again, you wind up in ❸ **Romano di Lombardia** after 12.5km. The **Rocca** is a castle built just beyond the old town under Milan's Visconti clan. Its four high walls are topped by square-based towers at each corner. Partly overgrown with greenery and in need of restoration, it houses a library and offices. You can wander into the courtyard in office hours – note the fresco of the lion of St Mark.

From Romano, the next objective is ❹ **Caravaggio**. Aside from the impressive **Chiesa dei Santi Fermo e Rustico**, with its brick Gothic facade, fine frescoes and imposing 16th-century bell tower, and its claim to fame as the birthplace of the like-named artist, the town's main attraction lies along a tree-lined boulevard about 1.5km southwest of the centre. The **Santuario della Madonna di Caravaggio**

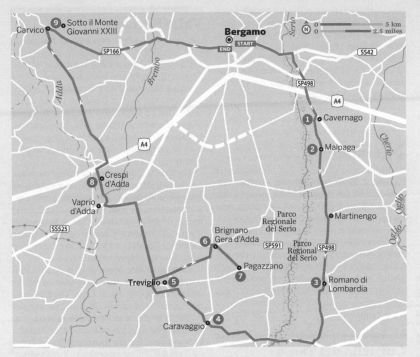

is a grandiose building started at the orders of Filippo Maria Visconti, Duke of Milan, after an alleged sighting on this spot of the Virgin Mary in 1432. With its fine dome and richly decorated 18th-century interior, it remains a major object of pilgrimage today.

A short hop northwest brings you to **5 Treviglio** (pop 25,000), at whose centre rises the **Collegiata di San Martino**, a brick Gothic church with a deep baroque makeover and typically impressive tower. A minor country road leads northeast out of Treviglio for **6 Brignano Gera d'Adda**, home to one of several Visconti castles in the area. Now a baroque residence jammed with frescoes and backed by an overgrown garden, the Palazzo Visconti (Via Vittorio Emanuele II) is undergoing renovation. Barely 3km southeast, in **7 Pagazzano**, stands yet another Visconti castle, the **Castello di Pagazzano**, this one decidedly more fortress-like and surrounded by a (filled) moat. The museum inside recounts rural life and includes a 1736 wine press.

8 Crespi d'Adda, some 20km northwest along various country roads, is a perfect example of the workers' town and factory

built by enlightened industrialists in various parts of Europe in the late 19th century. Here, the Crespi textile dynasty built cotton mills (which only closed in 2004), modest but pleasant housing for employees, a rather boisterous castle for the family and various services. The whole was declared a World Heritage Site in 1995. The village (www.villaggiocrespi.it) is still inhabited so there are no formal visiting hours. If hunger strikes, make for **Osteria da Mualdo**.

From Crespi, follow the Adda river north 15km to Carvico. Two kilometres east is **9 Sotto il Monte Giovanni XXIII**. Angelo Roncalli was born in this hamlet in 1881, which, as its name suggests, lies at the foot of a vineyard-draped mount that is topped by a medieval tower. In 1958, he become Pope John XXIII. In his five years as pontiff, he changed the face of the Catholic Church through the Vatican II Council reforms. You can visit his humble birthplace in the centre of town and a small museum set up in a house he used on summer holidays as cardinal.

From here, it is an 18km drive east back into Bergamo along the S road.

bears reliefs and sculptures of mythological figures and naturalistic forms (from laurel leaves to beetles), as well as two giant, wrought-iron lamp holders. Both buildings could only be seen from the outside at the time of writing as restoration work progresses to restore them to their original glory, although the Casinò was partially (and briefly) opened for summer crowds in 2013 – whether that's a precursor to more extensive opening hours remains to be seen.

✖ Eating

Cà Bigio BERGAMESE €€
(☑0345 2 10 58; www.bigio.info; Via Papa Giovanni XXIII 60, San Pellegrino Terme; meals €35-40; ⊙noon-2.30pm & 6.30-9.30pm) The Bigio family invented the archetypal Bergamese dessert, *polenta e osei* (cakes filled with jam and cream, topped with sweet polenta and chocolate birds). At their restaurant, though, it's the savouries that will win you over. Grab a table at the back for views up through the garden to the Casinò Municipale and order their tasting menu (€46) for a true taste of the mountains.

Cornello dei Tasso

Eight kilometres north of San Pellegrino Terme, Cornello dei Tasso (signposted off the S) is a compact time warp, a golden stone medieval hamlet high above the Brembo river that seems to have stood still, unconcerned by the passing of the centuries. You can park down near the main road and climb a pretty path (with great valley views). The heavy stone houses seem to huddle together, and the main lane is shielded from the elements by a series of protective vaults.

Northern Valle Brembana

From Cornello dei Tasso, the valley road proceeds north and splits deltalike into a series of valleys, some of which culminate in small winter ski towns, such as **Foppolo**, in the Orobie Alps. Hikers should note **Branzi** and **Carona**, which can make bases for walks up to a series of glacial lakes. Scenic-drive enthusiasts might opt for a different route, a minor road linking the Valle Brembana with the Valle Seriana via the villages of **Dossena** and **Oltre il Colle**. Territory ranges from dense forest to some fine open views north to the Orobie mountains from around Oltre il Colle.

Valle Seriana

As you wind out of Bergamo to the northeast, the Valle Seriana starts as a broad affair, pierced by a busy road (the S) and lined with towns and some industry.

Along the way, 25km northeast of central Bergamo, the town of **Gandino** is well worth a stop for its impressive **Basilica di Santa Maria Assunta** (Piazza della Emancipazione; ⊙8am-noon & 3-6pm), a baroque beauty with a richly decorated interior atop a sloping square.

Back on the main S road, things continue much as before. Then, quite suddenly, it all changes at **Ardesio**. The gushing Serio river is crowded in by lush green mountains and traffic drops to a trickle. Three kilometres north of Ardesio, **Gromo** is a charming medieval hamlet, with twisting lanes and stone houses topped by slate roofs.

Another 12km leads you north to **Valbondione**, a town used as a base by hikers and winter-sports enthusiasts. The highlight here is a 2½-hour hike to the **Cascate del Serio**, a triple cascade of 300m that constitutes one of Europe's tallest waterfalls. Follow signs for the nearby **Rifugio Curó** (☑0346 4 40 76; www.antoniocuro.it; dm without/with half-board €24/42; ⊙Fri-Sun May, Oct & Nov, every day Jun-Oct), which sits at 1915m near a pretty glacial lake and offers beds and meals. Check ahead for opening times. A 7km drive along a series of hairpin bends leads east up to **Lizzola**, another hiking base at 1256m, with magnificent views of the surrounding mountains and back south down the valley.

✖ Eating

Posta al Castello ITALIAN €€
(☑0346 4 10 02; www.postalcastello.it; Piazza Dante Alighieri 3, Gromo; meals €25-30; ⊙noon-3pm & 6.30-10pm Tue-Sun) Spread about inside what remains of the one-time castle at the heart of Gromo, the various rooms (some with frescoes) have a convivial air. Mushrooms are the speciality and you'll find them in many of the dishes, starting with the *zuppa di funghi* (mushroom soup) or *la delizia del Posta* (a kind of cheese-and-mushroom pancake).

LAKE ISEO & AROUND

Less than 100km from both Bergamo and Brescia, Lake Iseo (aka Sebino) is one of the least known Lombard lakes. Shut in by

WINNING WINE REGIONS

The plains around Bergamo, Brescia and Cremona are home to some respected, if little-known, wine-producing regions, which include the following:

➡ **Botticino** A small area 9.5km east of Brescia, where reds are made using barbera and marzemino grapes.

➡ **Cellatica** Another tiny area just northwest of Brescia, with similar reds to Botticino.

➡ **Franciacorta** South of Lake Iseo is this area celebrated for its sparkling white and rosé wines; look out also for *satèn*, a blanc de blanc almost exclusively made of chardonnay grapes.

➡ **San Colombano al Lambro** Family-run wineries produce small quantities of surprising reds and whites from a tiny enclave 15km south of Lodi.

➡ **Valcalepio** This up-and-coming area east of Bergamo produces merlot–cab sauv blends and a good white.

soaring mountains, it's a magnificent sight. About halfway along the lake, a mountain soars right out of the water.

With the exception of the south shore and a series of tunnels at the northeast end of the lake, the road closely hugs the water on its circuit around Lake Iseo and is especially dramatic south of Lovere. Various back roads also lead high up behind Lovere for magnificent views.

To the lake's north stretches the Valle Camonica, famed for its Stone Age rock carvings. To the south stretches the rolling Franciacorta wine country and, to the west, the picture-book-pretty Lake Endine.

ℹ Getting Around

BOAT

Navigazione sul Lago d'Iseo (☎ 035 97 14 83; www.navigazionelagoiseo.it) ferries zigzag their way along the length of the lake with stops around Monte Isola. There are also fairly regular runs between Lovere and Pisogne in the north.

Up to eight daily services (only two from September to April) run the whole way from Sarnico to Pisogne (a trip that can take two to three hours depending on stops, €6.65) and vice versa. Small boats make the quick crossing (10 minutes, every half-hour) from Sale Marasino and Sulzano, on the east shore, respectively to Carzano and Peschiera Maraglio on Monte Isola (€2.20/3.60 one way/return).

BUS

From Bergamo, **SAB** (☎ 035 28 90 00; www.sab-autoservizi.it) operates services (Line E) to Sarnico (€3.30, 50 minutes) and Tavernola Bergamasca. Line D also goes to Sarnico, while Line C runs via Lake Endine to Lovere and on to Boar-io in the Valle Camonica. The same company also has a service along the Valle Camonica.

CAR

From Bergamo or Brescia you can take the A4 motorway then turn north to Sarnico. Otherwise, the SS42 road east out of Bergamo leads past Lake Endine to Lovere, while the S from Brescia follows the eastern shore of the lake. They merge north of the lake as the SS42 and proceed up the Valle Camonica.

TRAIN

Trains run from Brescia to Iseo (€3.25, 30 minutes, hourly), up the east shore of the lake, and on up the Valle Camonica as far as Edolo, 56km north of the lake (up to 2½ hours).

Monte Isola

The towering island at the south end of Lake Iseo is easily the lake's most striking feature and merits an effort to get to know. Francesco Sforza granted the people of Monte Isola special fishing rights in the 15th century. Its people, whose ancestors may have lived here in Roman times, were also known for their handmade fishing nets. Perched on Europe's biggest lake island (4.28 sq km), they were largely self-sufficient in basic land produce. A handful of villages are scattered around the island. From **Carzano**, in the northeast (where many boats land), you can climb rough stairs to scattered rural settlements and follow a path to the top of the island (599m). The town hall is in **Siviano**, on the northwest shore. A 15km trail allows you to walk or cycle right around the island.

✗ Eating

Ristorante Monte Isola　　　ITALIAN €€
(☑030 982 52 84; www.ristorantemonteisola.it;
Località Carzano 144, Carzano; meals €25-35;
☺noon-3pm Tue, noon-3pm & 7-10pm Wed-Sun)
It's worth jumping on a boat in Sale Marasino just to get across to Monte Isola and
plonk yourself down in this restaurant.
Those with their own boat can tie up at the
restaurant's landing. The deal here is simple
enough: nicely prepared meals dominated
by lake fish, both in first and second courses. And when you're not eating, you can just
gaze outside over the water.

Iseo

POP 9205

At the lake's southeast edge, the sun sets
directly in front of the lakefront promenade
in Iseo and the string of squares just behind
the waterfront is wonderful for hanging
about in cafes and people-watching.

About 500m west of the old centre, you
can hire canoes and pedalos for about €6 an
hour. At **Iseobike** (☑340 39 62 095; www.iseo
bike.com; Via Colombera 2; bike rental per hour/
day €4.50/12, helmet €3; ☺9.30am-12.15pm &
2.30-7pm May-Aug, Fri-Sun Sep-Apr) Franco rents
bikes, but will also put together tailor-made
cycling tours around the lake and amid the
vineyards of the Franciacorta wine area
immediately to the south. There's also an
IAT Iseo (☑030 98 02 09; www.agenzialagoiseof
ranciacorta.it; Lungolago Marconi 2, Iseo; ☺10am-
12.30pm & 3.30-6.30pm Easter-Sep, 10am-12.30pm
& 3-6pm Mon-Fri, 10am-12.30pm Sat Oct-Easter)
tourist office.

Sarnico

POP 6652

Approaching Lake Iseo from the southwest
brings you to Sarnico, prettily located on a
corner of the lake and the Oglio river. It is
characterised by several lovely *stile liberty*
villas, many of them designed by Giuseppe
Sommaruga. Among them, his lakeside
Villa Faccanoni (Via Veneto) is the most
outstanding.

The heart of the old town, known as La
Contrada, straggles back from its pretty
riverside location on the mouth of the Oglio
river and is perfect for a wander after a
morning coffee along the riverside. Head
up Via Lantieri, lined with shops and eateries,
and along which you can make out vestiges

> **WORTH A TRIP**
>
> ### CASTELLO DEL GRUMELLO
>
> A 9km detour southwest of Sarnico
> brings you to Grumello del Monte,
> dominated by the partly overgrown
> **Castello del Grumello** (☑348 30 362
> 43; www.castellodigrumello.it; adult/child
> €10/5; ☺by appt), now part of a winery
> where you can book guided tours with a
> glass of produce thrown in. Indeed, this
> is one of northern Italy's lesser-known
> wine areas, the **Valcalepio**.

of the past. Via Scaletta, which runs down to
the lake, is where you'll find most evidence
of Sarnico's medieval past, with the remnants of towers and stout surviving walls.

Set in L'Albereta hotel in Erbusco 11.5km
south of Sarnico, **Ristorante Gualtiero
Marchesi** (www.marchesi.it; meals €150-200;
☺noon-2.30pm & 7.30-10pm Tue-Sat, noon-2.30pm
Sun) is possibly one of the best-known names
in contemporary Italian dining. Gualtiero Marchesi (once bemedalled with three
Michelin stars, which he tossed overboard
in a tiff with the French arbiters of taste at
table) continues to experiment and create
dishes that win the approval of the happy
few that manage to dine here. The setting
is as breathtaking as is the cuisine – as their
motto goes: 'cooking is in itself a science it's
the chef's job to turn it into an art'... If you
can't decide, try the tasting menu for €200.

For information, head for **Pro Loco Sar-
nico** (☑035 91 09 00; www.prolocosarnico.it; Via
Lantieri 6, Sarnico; ☺9.30am-12.30pm & 3-6.30pm
Tue-Sat, 9.30am-12.30pm Sun).

Lovere & Bossico

POP 5601 (LOVERE), 997 (BOSSICO)

Perched on the lake's northwestern tip, the
port town of **Lovere** is a gem, with a working harbour and a wealth of walking trails
nearby. Its cobbled old town, punctuated
by the occasional medieval tower, curves
around the harbour, shadowed by a leafy
lakefront promenade. Those in need of an
art shot should consider the waterfront
Accademia Tadini (☑035 96 27 80; www.
accademiatadini.it; Via Tadini 40; adult/concession
€7/5; ☺3-7pm Tue-Sat, 10am-noon & 3-7pm Sun &
holidays May-Sep, 3-7pm Sat, 10am-noon & 3-7pm
Sun & holidays Apr & Oct), home to a considerable art collection with works by Jacopo

Bellini, Il Parmigiano, Giambattista Tiepolo, Francesco Hayez, Antonio Canova and more.

Those with vehicles might want to drive 12km out of town and up into the hills behind Lovere to the hamlet of **Bossico** (900m). Several panoramic viewpoints offer great vistas over Lake Iseo from the village and nearby. Esmate, reached by Riva di Solto, 6km south of Lovere, offers further great lookout points over the lake.

There's a **tourist office** (✆035 96 21 78; Piazza XIII Martiri 34, Lovere; ⊙9.30am-12.30pm Mon-Thu, 9.30am-12.30pm & 2-5pm Fri, 9am-12.30pm & 2-5.30pm Sat & Sun) in Lovere.

Valle Camonica

Running northeast of Lake Iseo and marked by the course of the Oglio river, the Valle Camonica is best known locally for easy skiing at its northern extremity, but internationally as the sight of some quite extraordinary rock carvings, a Unesco World Heritage Site.

The rock carvings are concentrated in several sites around the small town of **Capo di Ponte** (www.capodiponte.eu), which sits on the Oglio river. The main site is the **Parco Nazionale delle Incisioni Rupestri** (✆0364 4 21 40; www.arterupestre.it; Località Naquane; admission €4; ⊙9am-5.30pm Mar-Oct, 9am-4pm Nov-Feb), on a rise just 1km out of the town centre on the east side of the river. It is a 30-hectare open-air museum containing a representative array of rock engravings going as far back as the Bronze Age. Colour-coded paths lead you past vast rock slabs that seem to have been created specifically for people to clamber around and chisel in their artistic talent. While engravings on some are barely distinguishable, on others you see a wealth of imagery, including animals (among them an extravagantly antlered deer) and people in various poses. Especially rich is Rock No 1 (aka Roccia Grande). If driving, you'll be charged €2 by enterprising local villagers to park at the start of the path.

Capo di Ponte is home to two other such parks, west of the river. One is closed for excavation, but the **Parco Archeologico Comunale di Seradina Bedolina** (✆334 657 5628; adult/child €2/1; ⊙10am-5pm Fri-Wed) is also rich in engravings. To get here, head for the town cemetery in **Cemmo** (you can drive or walk up from the centre), from where it's a 10-minute walk.

Also near the cemetery in Cemmo is one of the finest examples of Lombard Romanesque, the 11th-century **Pieve di San Siro** (⊙3-6pm Sat-Mon), or country church. Evidence suggests there may even have been a site of worship here in Roman times. Perched upon a rock ledge, the triple apse looks like it could easily topple into the Oglio river below. The geometric, animal and floral relief decoration on the entrance and inside is enchanting.

The riverside town of **Breno** (www.prolocobreno.it), 13km south of Capo di Ponte, is worth a stop for its extensive hilltop castle ruins. It is in fact a huddle of buildings built over centuries but consolidated as a defensive complex under Venetian rule from the 15th century on.

Visit **Pro Loco Capo di Ponte** (✆0364 4 20 80; www.proloco.capo-di-ponte.bs.it; Via Briscioli 42, Capo di Ponte; ⊙9.30am-12.30pm Sun, Mon & holidays, 9am-noon & 2.30-4.30pm Tue-Sat) for tourist information.

Lake Endine

The Cherio river runs from the south into lovely, mirror-still Lake Endine, surrounded by woods and reed banks, and where motorboats are banned – what an enlightened law! A minor road leads northeast off the main SS42 road to **Monasterolo del Castello**, a quiet medieval village on the south bank of the lake. The Monasterolo castle, turned into a country mansion in the 16th century, is just outside to the southwest. A lakeside path makes for pleasant strolls around Monasterolo. Or you can hire canoes (€6 an hour) at the Centro Nautico in **Spinone al Lago** on the opposite shore.

The 4km road north off the SS42 to **Bianzano** offers panoramic views of the lake. Bianzano's **Castello Suardo** can occasionally be visited by guided tour. Better still, the whole hamlet becomes the scene of **Rievocazione Storica** (www.cortedeisuardo.com), a medieval feast, for a long weekend around the end of July, with parades, activities and some 300 locals going about their business in medieval dress.

Valle del Fredo & Esmate

Around 2km northeast of Lake Endine is the **Riserva Naturale Regionale Valle del Freddo** (✆035 434 98 17; www.parks.it/riserva.valle.del.freddo), a short walk north of tiny

BERGAMO, BRESCIA & CREMONA VALLE CAMONICA

ⓘ WINE TOURING

You could easily spend days exploring the vineyards of the Franciacorta region (www.stradadelfranciacorta.it). To that end, most tourist offices in the region should have a copy of the *Franciacorta Wine Route* brochure. It details numerous hiking and cycling itineraries through the region (some of which are possible by car), and includes a pull-out list with contact details for over 100 local wineries.

Lake Gaiano. The Cold Valley has a unique microclimate, with a particularly cold subsoil (stick your hands into some of the holes in the ground) that allows 24 species of Alpine flowers (including edelweiss) and plants to flourish at an altitude of just 360m.

From there, head on foot or by car to the hamlet of **Esmate**, from where you can enjoy splendid views of the northern end of Lake Iseo. The views are good from the churchyard but breathtaking if you follow Via Cerrete about 2.5km from the church (it changes names several times). Where it narrows amid thick woods, several brief trails (20m or so) lead out to magnificent, wild viewpoints high above the lake.

Franciacorta

South of Lake Iseo and stretching towards Brescia are the rolling fields, low hills and flourishing vineyards of the greatly applauded Franciacorta wine region. This is perfect cycling country, with no mountain rises to worry about and plenty of villages to explore. The **Iseo tourist office** (☏030 98 02 09; Lungolago Marconi 2; ◷10am-12.30pm & 3.30-6.30pm Easter-Sep, 10am-12.30pm & 3-6pm Mon-Fri, 10am-12.30pm Sat Oct-Easter) can provide brochures with routes and wineries. The catch is that few wineries actually open their doors to passers-by. During the year, some open on certain weekends but tasting visits generally have to be booked.

Provaglio d'Iseo, 3.5km south of Iseo, is dominated by the Romanesque **Monastero San Pietro in Lamosa** (www.sanpietroinlamosa. org). The 11th-century church was donated to the Cluniac order of monks, who later expanded the area into a monastery. You can see the outside but visits inside are by appointment only. The complex sits above a 2-sq-km protected wetland, the **Riserva Naturale Torbiere del Sebino** (www.torbiere. it), formed from 18th-century peat beds. In late spring the pools are smothered in water lilies. Getting in is hit and miss, although there is a walking path around it.

About 7km southeast of Provaglio, in **Rodengo Saiano**, is the impressive **Abbazia di San Nicola**, set at the end of a short, cypress-lined avenue. The abbey in its present form dates largely from the 15th century and boasts a gracious Renaissance cloister. It is inhabited by Olivetan monks, and getting in just seems to be a matter of finding the doors open, or not.

Five kilometres south of Provaglio, in the hamlet of **Bornato**, stands a 13th-century castle, inside which was built a Renaissance villa. The castle's owners possess local vineyards around here and sell their wine at the castle – a tasting is part of the visit.

BRESCIA

POP 193,879

Brescia's core takes the form of a fascinating old town, which more than compensates for the city's rather ugly urban sprawl. The old town's narrow streets are home to some of the most important Roman ruins in Lombardy, and an extraordinary circular Romanesque church.

History

Brescia already had centuries of (now obscure) history behind it when the Romans conquered the Gallic town in 225 BC. In 89 BC, the inhabitants of Brixia, as the Romans called it, were granted Roman citizenship and the town began to grow in importance as a centre for the production of bronze implements. With Rome long gone, the Carolingians took over in the 9th century, and were followed by a millennium's worth of outside rulers including the Venetians. The city rebelled against the decision to hand it over to Austria in 1797, and again in 1848, when it was dubbed the 'Lioness' for its 10-day uprising against the Austrians.

◉ Sights

In addition to the sights covered below, don't forget to admire **Il Broletto** (Piazza Paolo VI), the medieval town hall with an 11th-century tower, and the nearby **Torre dell'Orologio** (Clocktower; Piazza della Loggia); the latter's

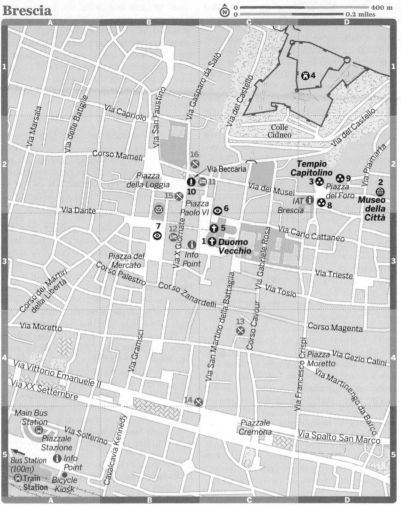

Brescia

Brescia

◎ Top Sights
1	Duomo Vecchio	C3
2	Museo della Città	D2
3	Tempio Capitolino	D2

◎ Sights
4	Castello	D1
	Civico Museo del Risorgimento	(see 4)
5	Duomo Nuovo	C3
6	Il Broletto	C2
	Museo delle Armi Antiche	(see 4)
7	Piazza della Vittoria	B3
8	Roman Forum	D2

9	Roman Theatre	D2
10	Torre dell'Orologio	B2

🛏 Sleeping
11	Albergo Orologio	C2
12	Hotel Vittoria	B3

✺ Eating
13	La Grotta	C4
14	La Sosta	B4
15	La Vineria	B2
16	Osteria al Bianchi	B2

exquisite astrological timepiece is modelled on the one in Venice's Piazza San Marco.

Museo della Città
MUSEUM, MONASTERY

(City Museum; ☑ 030 297 78 34; www.bresciamusei. com; Via dei Musei 81b; adult/child €10/free, temporary exhibitions extra; ☺ 10.30am-7pm Tue-Sun mid-Jun–Sep, shorter hrs rest of year) The jumbled **Monastero di Santa Giulia** and **Basilica di San Salvatore** is Brescia's single most intriguing sight. Inside this rambling church and convent complex, the Museo della Città houses collections that run the gamut from prehistory to the age of Venetian dominance.

The building of the monastery, which started as early as the 8th century, absorbed two *domus* (Roman houses), which were left standing in what would become the monk's garden (Ortaglia) near the north cloister. The remains have thus come to be known as the **Domus dell'Ortaglia** and have been protected by the monastery walls from outside interference or bulldozers through the centuries. Raised walkways allow you to wander round the **Domus di Dioniso** (so-called because of a mosaic of Dionysius, god of the grapevine) and the **Domus delle Fontane** (so-called because of two marble fountains in it). The beautiful floor mosaics and colourful frescoes in these two *domus* rank among the highlights of the monastery-museum.

The other star piece of the monastery collections is the 8th-century **Croce di Desiderio**, an extraordinary Lombard cross encrusted with hundreds of jewels.

Roman Brescia
RUIN

The most impressive of Brescia's Roman relics are the remains of the **Tempio Capitolino** (Via dei Musei; adult/concession €4/3, free entry with ticket to Museo della Città; ☺ 11am-4pm Tue-Sun), a Roman temple built by the Emperor Vespasian in AD 73. Six Corinthian columns stand before a series of cells. About 50m to the east, cobbled Vicolo del Fontanon leads to the overgrown ruins of a **Roman theatre** (off Via di Musei). Limited remains of the **Roman Forum** (Piazza del Foro) are nearby.

Duomo Vecchio
CATHEDRAL

(Old Cathedral; Piazza Paolo VI; ☺ 9am-noon & 3-6pm Wed-Sat, 9-10.45am & 3-6pm Sun) The most compelling of all Brescia's religious monuments is the 11th-century Duomo Vecchio, a rare example of a circular-plan Romanesque basilica, built over a 6th-century church. The inside is surmounted by a dome borne by eight sturdy vaults resting on thick pillars. Interesting features include fragmentary floor mosaics (some think from a thermal bath that might have stood here in the 1st century BC) and the elaborate 14th-century sarcophagus of Bishop Berado Maggi.

Duomo Nuovo
CATHEDRAL

(New Cathedral; Piazza Paolo VI; ☺ 7.30am-noon & 4-7pm Mon-Sat, 8am-1pm & 4-7pm Sun) Next door to the Duomo Vecchio, the Duomo Nuovo dates from 1604 (but was not finished until well into the 19th century). It dwarfs its ancient neighbour but is of less interest.

Castello
CASTLE

(Via del Castello; ☺ 8am-8pm) **FREE** Brescia's historic centre is dominated by a hill, **Colle Cidneo**, crowned with the rambling castle that for centuries was at the core of the city's defences. **Torre Mirabella**, the main round tower, was built by the Viscontis in the 13th century. The main reason to come up is to amble around the grounds, but the castle hosts two mildly diverting museums.

Within the castle grounds, the **Museo delle Armi Antiche** (☑ 030 29 32 92; www. bresciamusei.it; adult/reduced €5/4 incl admission to Civico Museo del Risorgimento; ☺ 3.30-7pm Tue-Sun) has an extensive collection of vintage weaponry, while the **Civico Museo del Risorgimento** (☑ 030 4 41 76; adult/reduced €5/4 incl admission to Museo delle Armi Antiche; ☺ 3.30-7pm Tue-Sun) is dedicated to the history of Italian reunification (Risorgimento).

Piazza della Vittoria
PIAZZA

Perhaps beautiful is not the word, but this nonetheless fascinating piazza is a leftover of Il Duce's dreams of grandeur. Designed by Marcello Piacentini and opened in 1932, the square is lined with a compendium of Fascist architecture – imposing, Big Brotherish, some would say even boorish.

At one end, the post office, with its soaring, right-angled columns, looks like some fear-inspiring ministry. Insurance companies with giant marble-faced porticoes line the square's sides. Perhaps most curious of all is the *arengario*, a rather small, rose-marble structure used to harangue the cheering crowds. One shudders to think what medieval jewels were swept away to make way for Piazza della Vittoria (Victory Sq).

Museo Mille Miglia MUSEUM
(✆030 336 56 31; www.museomillemiglia.it; Viale della Rimembranza 3; adult/reduced €7/5; ⏰10am-6pm) The Mille Miglia is a classic Italian car race that ran over 1000 miles between 1927 and 1957. It started and ended in Brescia and took around 16 hours to complete. It was cancelled after 11 spectators died in an accident in 1957, although nowadays nostalgia races are still held. The colourful museum is loaded with some of the great cars to cross the finish line.

The museum is housed outside central Brescia in the sprawling 11th-century Monastero di Sant'Eufemia della Fonte. Exhibits include racing cars, old-style petrol pumps and there's audio material and archive video footage race films. Bizarrely, the museum is also home to a **Beatles Museum** (Via della Rimembranza 3; admission incl with entry to Museo Mille Miglia; ⏰10am-6pm), which is dedicated to George Harrison.

✖ Eating

Risotto, beef dishes and *lumache alla Bresciana* (snails cooked with Parmesan and fresh spinach) are common in Brescia. Via Beccaria is the small but fiercely pumping heart of central Brescia's evening action. By day, you'll find no shortage of cafes, pizzerias and the like, especially along Corso Cavour and Via Gabriele Rosa, as well as Piazza Paolo VI.

★ Osteria al Bianchi OSTERIA €
(✆030 29 23 28; www.osteriaalbianchi.it; Via Gasparo da Salò 32; meals €20-25; ⏰9am-2pm & 4.30pm-midnight Thu-Mon) Crowd inside this classic old bar, in business since 1880, and try for a seat where you might be tempted by the *pappardelle al taleggio e zucca* (broad ribbon pasta with taleggio cheese and pumpkin), followed by anything from *brasato d'asino* (braised donkey) to *pestöm* (minced pork meat served with polenta).

La Grotta ITALIAN €€
(✆030 4 40 68; www.osterialagrotta.it; Vicolo del Prezzemolo 10; meals €25-30; ⏰11am-3pm & 7-11pm Thu-Tue) Tucked down Parsley Lane off pleasant pedestrianised Corso Cavour, this is a hidden gem for good home cooking served at tables dressed in gingham. Frilly curtains and cheerful frescoes (food and wine-making scenes) watch over chattering diners. You can't go wrong with *casoncelli al burro e salvia* (typical local meat-filled pasta with butter and sage).

La Vineria ITALIAN €€
(✆030 28 05 43; lavineria.jimdo.com; Via X Giornate 4; meals €25-30; ⏰11.30am-3pm & 6.30-11pm Mon-Sat) Bargain set lunches (€10) from Monday to Friday on the footpath tables or downstairs in the classy cellar, La Vineria ticks all the boxes. Try dishes like *polenta taragna e fungha porcini trifolati* (cheese polenta served with porcini mushrooms). The bread comes in a brown paper bag – a nice, if unusual, touch.

La Sosta ITALIAN €€€
(✆030 29 25 89; www.lasosta.it; Via San Martino della Battaglia 20; meals €45-55; ⏰12.30-2pm & 7.30-10pm Tue-Sat, 12.30-2pm Sun, closed Aug) Set partly in the stables of a 1610 palace, flanked by columns, La Sosta excels at finely tuned gastronomic creations using the freshest regional produce. The *griglia di pesce* (grilled fish platter) is perfectly executed and might be preceded by one of their creamy risottos.

ℹ Information

Info Point (✆030 240 03 57; www.brescia tourism.it; Via Trieste 1; ⏰9.30am-1pm & 1.30-5.30pm) The city's main tourist office has detailed brochures (not all of which are on display) on the city's churches, museums and piazzas. There's another, smaller Info Point (✆030 837 85 59; Piazzale Stazione) at the station.

IAT Brescia (✆030 374 99 16; www.provincia.brescia.it; Piazza del Foro 6; ⏰10am-6pm) Covers the wider Brescia region.

ℹ Getting There & Around

BICYCLE
You can pick up a bicycle (€1/10 per two hours/day) from the **bicycle kiosk** (✆030 306 11 00; Piazzale Stazione; ⏰7am-7.30pm Mon-Fri, 7.30am-1.30pm Sat) in front of the train station on Piazzale Stazione.

BUS
From Brescia's **main bus station** (✆030 4 49 15; Via Solferino) buses operated by **SAIA Trasporti** (✆030 288 99 11, 800 883999; www.saiatrasporti.it) serve destinations all over Brescia province. Some leave from another station off Viale della Stazione.

CAR
Brescia is on the A4 motorway between Milan and Verona. The A21 runs south to Cremona.

Driving in the old centre is restricted and monitored by camera. People staying in hotels in the centre need to give the hotel reception their number plate on arrival. You have 15 minutes to unload/load the vehicle before exiting again and parking elsewhere. There are car parks outside the old centre, where street parking is also possible.

TRAIN

Regular trains run to and from Milan (€7 to €20.50, 45 minutes to 1½ hours) and Verona (€6.25 to €17, 40 minutes). Hourly trains connect with Cremona (€5.25, one hour) and Bergamo (€4.55 to €6.45, one to 1½ hours).

CREMONA

POP 72,147

A wealthy, independent city-state for centuries, Cremona boasts some fine medieval architecture. The Piazza del Comune, the heart of the city, is where Cremona's historic beauty is concentrated. It's a wonderful example of how the religious and secular affairs of cities were divided neatly in two. The city is best known around the world, however, for its violin-making traditions.

Cremona was thought to have been founded by Celts, but the oldest archaeological finds date to the creation of a Roman outpost here around 218 BC. The city's glory days came as an independent *comune* (city-state) from the 11th century, until it was occupied by Milan in 1334. It would remain largely under the jurisdiction of the Duchy of Milan until the latter fell under the thumb of Spain in 1525.

◎ Sights

Piazza del Comune PIAZZA

This beautiful, pedestrian-only square is considered one of the best-preserved medieval squares in all Italy. To maintain the difference between the secular and spiritual, buildings connected with the Church were erected on the eastern side of Piazza del Comune, and those concerned with secular affairs were constructed across the way.

The business of city government was and still is carried out in the **Palazzo Comunale** (Piazza del Comune). Begun in the 13th century, the arcaded walkways and courtyards of the palazzo were gradually extended and embellished through the centuries. On the central pillar of the main facade, a marble *arengario* (balcony from which decrees were made and speeches given) was added in 1507. South across a lane, the **Loggia dei Militi** (Piazza del Comune) was the headquar-

ters of the long arm of the law. A delightful little Gothic gem built in 1292, it was where the captains of the citizen militia would meet.

On Sunday, the piazza is filled with antique stalls.

Duomo CATHEDRAL

(Piazza del Comune; ◎8am-noon & 3.30-7pm Mon-Sat, noon-12.30pm & 3.30-7pm Sun) Across the square from the Palazzo del Comune, Cremona's cathedral started out as a Romanesque basilica, but the simplicity of the Romanesque style later gave way to an extravagance of styles – the interior frescoes in this church are utterly overwhelming. One of the chapels contains what is said to be a thorn from Jesus' crown of thorns.

The Duomo was finished in 1107 but badly damaged by an earthquake in 1117 and rebuilt by 1190. In subsequent centuries, various embellishments left traces of Gothic, Renaissance and baroque taste. The facade reflects this mix. Romanesque sculptures from the prequake church adorn the facade, whose upper part is largely the result of Renaissance renovation. Even the lower part, while retaining something of a Romanesque flavour, is the result of work in the early 16th century – notably replacing the timber frontage with marble. The brick north facade is a fine example of Lombard Gothic.

The central nave and apse, in particular, flaunt a series of rich frescoes and paintings, with scenes dedicated to the lives of the Virgin Mary and Christ. The local, Ferrara-born Renaissance master Boccaccio Boccaccino carried out many of them. Elegant though his compositions are, it is the *Storie di Cristo* (Stories of Christ) by Pordenone that stand out. His *Crocifissione* (Crucifixion) and *Deposizione* (Deposition) are especially powerful, filled with curvaceous movement and voluptuous colour. Other masters who contributed to the church's decoration include local boys Giulio Campi and Gian Francesco Bembo.

The cathedral's most prized possession is the *Sacra Spina* (Holy Thorn), allegedly from the crown of thorns worn by Jesus Christ, which was donated to the church by Cremona-born Pope Gregory XIV in 1591. It's kept behind bars in the **Capella delle Reliquie**, in the left transept. In the **crypt**, the robed and masked body of Cremona's 12th-century patron saint, San Omobono Tucenghi, is on show in a glass casket.

Cremona

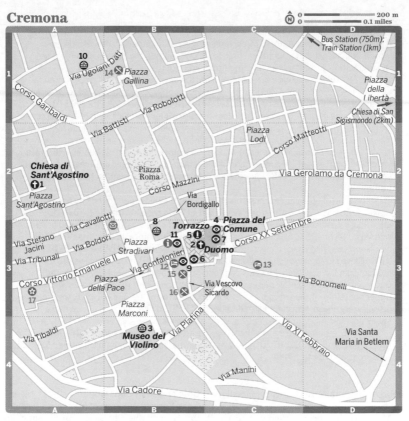

⊙ 0 ————— 200 m
0 ————— 0.1 miles

Torrazzo   TOWER
(Piazza del Comune; adult/child €5/4, incl baptistry €6/5; ⊙10am-1pm & 2.30-6pm Tue-Sun Mar-Nov) The 111m-tall torrazzo (bell tower, although 'torazzo' translates as something like 'great,

fat tower') is connected to the Duomo by a Renaissance loggia, the **Bertazzola**. It is fronted by a beautiful zodiacal clock, 8m wide and installed in 1583. A total of 502 steps wind up to the top of the tower. The

CREMONA'S VIOLINS

It was in Cremona that Antonio Stradivari lovingly put together his first Stradivarius violins, helping establish a tradition that continues today. Other great violin-making dynasties that started here include the Amati and Guarneri families.

Some 100 violin-making workshops occupy the streets around Piazza del Comune but very few accept casual visitors. To visit a workshop, you generally need to be looking to buy a violin, but the **Consorcio Liutai Antonio Stradivari** (☑ 0372 46 35 03; www.cremonaliuteria.it; Piazza Stradivari 1; ⊘ 11am-1pm & 4-6.30pm Tue-Sat), which represents the workshops (they have a list of over 100), can sometimes make appointments for visits. The Consorcio also has a small display of violins.

Various events dedicated to violin-making take place each year, while the **Triennale Internazionale degli Strumenti ad Arco** (International Stringed Instrument Expo; www.entetriennale.com) is held in Cremona every third year in September/October; the next one is in 2015.

At the time of our visit, Cremona had two museums dedicated to the city's violin-making traditions. The **Collezione Gli Archi di Palazzo Comunale** (☑ 0372 40 70 33; http://musei.comune.cremona.it; Piazza del Comune 8; adult/reduced €6/4, combined ticket with Museo Civico €11/6; ⊘ 9am-5pm Tue-Sun) featured instruments from the Stradivari workshop. North of the old town, the **Museo Civico** (☑ 0372 3 12 22; Via Ugolani Dati 4; adult/reduced €7/5, combined ticket with Collezione Gli Archi di Palazzo Comunale €11/6; ⊘ 10am-5pm Tue-Sun) held drawings and tools, as well as instruments by Amati and Guarneri. But not long after our visit, the two collections were to be brought together under one, state-of-the-art roof at the **Museo del Violino** (☑ 037 280 18 01; www.museo-delviolino.org; Piazza Marconi; adult/reduced €10/7; ⊘ 10am-6pm Tue-Sun). We've had a sneak preview and it promises to be a world-class museum.

To hear Cremona's violins in action, the season at the 19th-century **Teatro Amilcare Ponchielli** (☑ 0372 02 20 01; www.teatroponchielli.it; Corso Vittorio Emanuele II 52) runs from October to June.

---

effort is more than repaid with marvellous views across the city.

The clock has been tinkered with considerably over the years (the last time in the 1970s) but remains an extraordinary example of European clockwork, designed not only to tell the time but to measure the phases of the moon and seasons as well as present astrological information.

Baptistry
RELIGIOUS

(Piazza del Comune; adult/child €3/2, incl torrazzo €6/5; ⊘ 10am-1pm & 2.30-6pm Tue-Sun) The 12th-century baptistry houses some architectural fragments, including a 12th-century figure of the Archangel Gabriel that once perched on the roof of the baptistry.

Chiesa di Sant'Agostino
CHURCH

(Piazza Sant'Agostino) Inside the Chiesa di Sant'Agostino, the **Cappella Cavalcabò** (third chapel on the right) is a stunning late-Gothic fresco cycle by Bonifacio Bembo and his assistants. One of the altars is graced with a 1494 painting by Pietro Perugino, *Madonna in trono e santi* (The Madonna Enthroned with Saints).

Chiesa di San Sigismondo
CHURCH

(Largo Visconti) A couple of kilometres outside the old city, the Chiesa di San Sigismondo was built between 1463 and 1492 to commemorate the wedding of Francesco Sforza to Bianca Maria Visconti in 1441. The fresco cycle was painted from 1530 on and is a great example of Mannerist painting. All the big names of the Cremona art scene contributed, including all the Campi brothers and Camillo Boccaccino, son of Boccaccio. Camillo did the entire presbytery, with images including *Adultera* (Adultress) and *Risurrezione di Lazzaro* (Resurrection of Lazarus).

✬ Festivals & Events

Festival di Cremona Claudio Monteverdi
MUSIC

(www.teatroponchielli.it) A month-long series of concerts centred on Claudio Monteverdi and other baroque-era composers, held in the Teatro Amilcare Ponchielli early May to early June.

Festa del Torrone FOOD
(www.festadeltorronecremona.it) For a weekend in late autumn, the people of Cremona gather in the city centre for various exhibitions, performances and tastings all dedicated to that toffee-tough Christmas sweet and Cremona speciality, *torrone* (nougat).

✖ Eating

Plenty of charming eateries, some with a long history, offer a mix of local and more general Lombard dishes. Cremonese delicacies include *bollito* (boiled meats), *cotechino* (boiled pork sausage) and *mostarda* (fruit in a sweet mustard sauce).

★ **Hosteria '700** CREMONESE €€
(✑ 0372 36175; www.hosteria700.it; Piazza Gallina 1; meals €30-35; ☉ noon-3pm & 7.30-10pm Wed-Mon) Behind the dilapidated facade lurks a sparkling gem. A series of vaulted rooms, each with different colour scheme and some with ceiling frescoes, winds off from the entrance and past the kitchen. There is something noble about the atmosphere, with the antique cupboards and dark timber tables and chairs. The hearty Lombard cooking also comes in at a refreshingly competitive cost.

Ristorante Duomo ITALIAN €€
(✑ 0372 45 83 92; Via Gonfalonieri 13; meals €25-30; ☉ noon-3pm & 6.30-10pm) A few steps from the Piazza del Comune, this place is full every night with a happy mix of tourists and locals with more of the latter – always a good sign. The pizzas are good, while the *risotto ai fruta di mare* is chockful of shellfish. Large complimentary foccacia and a bruschetta round out an excellent overall package.

La Sosta OSTERIA €€
(✑ 0372 45 66 56; www.osterialasosta.it; Via Vescovo Sicardo 9; meals €30-35; ☉ 12.15-2.30pm & 7.15-10pm Tue-Sat, 12.15-2.30pm Sun) Surrounded by violin-makers' workshops, this is a beautiful place to feast on regional delicacies such as local cheeses and baked snails. The entrance is plastered with so many approving restaurant-guide stickers that you can't see through the glass.

Il Violino ITALIAN €€
(✑ 0372 46 10 10; www.ilviolino.it; Via Vescovo Sicardo 3; meals €40-45; ☉ 12.30-2.30pm Mon, 12.30-2.30pm & 6.30-10pm Wed-Sun) Il Violino is Cremona's timeless class option. Smooth service is key to this elegant spot, where you might start with one of a number of risotto

options or the *tortelli alle erbette al burro spumoso* (stuffed pasta in herbs and frothy hot butter).

ℹ Information

Tourist Office (✑ 0372 40 63 91; www.turismocremona.it; Piazza del Comune 5; ☉ 9am-1pm & 2-5pm Sep-Jun, closed Sun afternoon Jul & Aug)

ℹ Getting There & Around

BUS
Buses to surrounding towns leave from the bus station on Via Dante, near the train station.

CAR
From Milan, take the A1 motorway and then the A21 to Cremona. The A21 proceeds north to Brescia. The S heads northwest to Crema and on to Milan.

Driving through the old town is a no-no – obey signs that talk of a 'zona limitato' or you'll be captured on camera and forced to pay a €120-plus fine. Street parking becomes easier as you move away from the centre, and there is huge car-park space near the bus station.

TRAIN
The city can be reached by train from Milan (from €7, one to two hours, several daily) and Brescia (€5.25, one hour, hourly).

AROUND CREMONA

The plains around Cremona are dotted with interesting towns. Pizzighettone boasts great defensive walls and Soncino a fine Sforza-era fortress. The more substantial towns of Crema and Lodi have interesting old centres, the former dominated by the pretty Piazza del Duomo and the latter by the Incoronata church. Lodi and Pizzighettone, both settled on the banks of the Adda river, are within the boundaries of the **Parco**

> ## ℹ CREMONA CITY CARD
>
> At just €5, the Cremona Card is worth considering because it entitles you to discounts (you pay the concession instead of full admission rates) at a number of sights, hotels and theatres around Cremona and Crema. It can be purchased at the tourist office, where they have a list of participating museums, hotels etc.

Adda Sud (www.parcoaddasud.it) nature reserve. You can get some walking and cycling route ideas from the park's website. With your own transport, you could easily make a loop in a day from Cremona.

ℹ Getting Around

BUS

Buses run to Soncino from Bergamo, Cremona and Crema. There are also buses to Crema from Bergamo with **SAB** (☑ 035 28 90 00, 800 139392; www.sab-autoservizi.it).

CAR

The S main road northwest out of Cremona runs 38km to Crema, from where the S road heads 18km northeast to Soncino. For Pizzighettone, take the minor S road west out of Cremona. From there you can continue via Codogno until you hit the SS9 highway, which leads northwest to Lodi. Lodi is linked to Crema by the S road.

TRAIN

Pizzighettone (from €2.75, 45 minutes), Lodi (€5.25, 40 minutes) and Crema (€4.55, 40 minutes) are reached easily by train from Cremona. The former two are on the line from Milan to Cremona.

Pizzighettone

POP 6730

Just a 22km train ride west of Cremona, the walled town of Pizzighettone sits astride the Adda river. The bulk of the town, with its impressive defensive **walls** (☑ 0372 73 03 33; www.gvmpizzighettone.it; guided tours in Italian adult/child €3/free; ☺ tours 9.30pm Sat, 4pm & 5.30pm Sun & holidays Jul-Aug, 3pm Sat, Sun & holidays Sep-Jun), rests on the east bank.

The walls had been largely engulfed by vegetation until a volunteer organisation 'released' them from this green captivity in the 1990s, restoring them to their full majesty. Begun in the 12th century and constantly improved and expanded in the following centuries, especially under Visconti and Sforza rule, the walls are laced with passages and huge vaulted halls, some of which have been set aside as a small museum dedicated to the trades and traditions of local farmers. The most imposing part of the walls is known as the Rivellino, a series of casemates once used to house artillery and dating to the 15th century. You can wander much of the area any time.

Across the river from the main part of town is the pretty hamlet of **La Gera**.

✗ Eating

Cascina Valentino   AGRITURISMO **€€**
(☑ 0372 74 49 91; http://lnx.cascinavalentino.it; Cascina Valentino 37, Pizzighettone; meals €25-35; ☺ 7-10pm Mon-Sat & 12.30-2.30pm Sun) On a working farm where cows are raised and asparagus is grown, the owners also offer up fine local cooking with only the freshest in-season ingredients – this is a real rural eating experience. Booking ahead is compulsory.

The menu changes often but you might, if you're lucky, be offered a strawberry risotto. Mains are mostly from the farm's own meat stocks. The dining area, with dark timber furniture, in the main farmhouse, is a treat in itself. It's 2km away from central Pizzighettone. Cross the bridge east to La Gera and turn right along the river, then follow the signs along a dirt track past a dairy farm until you reach this second dairy farm.

Lodi

POP 44,401

Capital of an essentially agricultural province, Lodi was founded in the 12th century on the south bank of the Adda river after the original town (Lodi Vecchio, about 7km west) was destroyed by the Milanese army.

The old town centre, unknown to the majority of travellers, is well worth a half day of your time. From the train station, head north about 300m to Piazza Castello. The castle alluded to is largely gone, excepting a tall round **tower** built on Francesco Sforza's orders. Corso Vittorio Emanuele II leads another 300m into the enormous, cobbled Piazza della Vittoria, fronted by the city's **Duomo** (Cathedral), **Palazzo Comunale** (Town Hall) and multicoloured houses atop sheltering porticoes. Work on the cathedral began in 1160 and its towering brick facade betrays Romanesque, Gothic and Renaissance elements (the rose window being the clearest sign of the latter). Through an arch on its left flank you reach shady Piazza Mercato, tucked behind the cathedral's haughty triple apse.

Attractive though the cathedral is, Lodi's real gem lies about 50m away on Via Incoronata. The **Tempio Civico dell'Incoronata** (Via Incoronata, btwn Nos 23 & 25; ☺ 9am-noon Mon, 9am-noon & 3.30-6pm Tue-Sun) was built in the late 15th century at the prompting of the local citizenry, apparently after a sighting of the Virgin Mary with crown (hence the church's name 'Civic Temple of the Crowned One') on the spot, close to an infamous brothel. The church is a splendid, octagonal Renaissance affair, the inside of which is a riot of gold leaf, frescoes and paintings. Almost all the art, mostly depicting New Testament scenes, was done by Lodi's Piazza clan of artists (Callisto, Fulvio, Alberto and Scipione) over three decades in the first half of the 16th century.

✖ Eating

La Coldana   ITALIAN €€
(📞0371 43 17 42; www.lacoldana.it; Via del Costino, Lodi; meals €30-35, 2-course lunch €12; ⊘noon-2.30pm & 8-10.30pm Sun-Fri, 8-10.30pm Sat) A sprawling, yellow, 18th-century farmhouse, La Coldana seats its guests in bustling dining rooms or out in a quiet garden. The kitchen is a cauldron of ideas. Save room for a main of rack of lamb or wild salmon. Head southeast along Corso Mazzini from Porta Cremona, in the southeast corner of the old centre. Turn left at Via Friuli and left again into Via del Costino.

Crema

POP 34,144

Huddled up against the Serio river and 15km northeast of Lodi, Crema retains its late-medieval and Renaissance core largely intact. Even parts of the Venetian-built defensive walls are still in place. The local tourist office organises tours. Indeed, in 1449, Crema was one of the many Lombard cities to pass under Venetian suzerainty. The following centuries brought peace and prosperity, until Napoleon arrived to upset the apple cart in 1797.

At the heart of the city is enchanting, porticoed Piazza del Duomo, a Venetian renovation of the early 16th century dominated by the brick facade of the medieval **Duomo** (⊘7am-noon & 4-7pm). Completed in 1341, the cathedral sports a giant *facciata a vento* (wind facade) and is of typically Lombard Gothic style, which uses Romanesque devices (especially the semicircular arch) but on a far grander scale. To the left of the cathedral rises the **Torre Pretoria**, a family watchtower dating to 1286 that bears a sculpture of the lion of St Mark. The porticoes across the way belong to the early 16th-century **Palazzo Comunale** – as ever, the secular arm of power looks the Church straight in

the eye. The **Torrazzo** (Big Tower) had a defensive role but was reworked in baroque form in the 17th century and became purely decorative.

Crowning a Crema visit is one of the most striking Renaissance structures in Lombardy, the **Santuario di Santa Maria della Croce** (Piazza Papa Paolo Giovanni II; ⊘7am-noon & 2.30-7pm Mon-Sat, 8am-7pm Sun), built between 1490 and 1500 and about 1.5km north of the old town along Viale di Santa Maria della Croce. The graceful circular central body of the church has wedding-cake layers of increasingly delicate arches, and four bronze-domed chapels push out from it below, forming a cross. The octagonal interior is brimful of frescoes.

✖ Eating

Osteria del Rumí   OSTERIA €€
(📞0371 25 72 89; Piazza Trento e Trieste 12, Crema; meals €30-35; ⊘7-9.30pm Fri, noon-2pm & 7-9.30pm Sat-Wed) Just off Piazza del Duomo, this Tuscan-style eatery offers bags of boisterous atmosphere at timber tables beneath low-slung brick and stone vaults. You could start with a selection of bruschetta or choose from a range of first courses that include local risottos, followed by *stufato d'anatra con polenta* (stewed duck in polenta).

❶ Information

Pro Loco Crema (📞0373 8 10 20; www. prolococrema.it; Piazza Duomo 22) Organises guided tours of the defensive walls.

Soncino

POP 7767

With its four stout towers, crenellations, moat and drawbridge, you can almost see the **Rocca** (📞0374 84 88 83; www.prolocosoncino.it; Largo Salvini 1; adult/reduced incl Casa degli Stampatori €4.50/3 ; ⊘9am-1pm Tue-Fri, 10am-12.30pm & 2.30-7pm Sat, Sun & holidays Apr-Oct, closes earlier Nov-Mar) of Soncino under siege by some enemy of Milan's Sforza clan, which had it built on the site of a more rudimentary fort in 1473. There's a modest history museum in rooms of two of the towers, while from the courtyard you can visit various underground rooms. Parts of the later Venetian city walls (Venice was in control for a brief decade from 1499) remain intact too.

Another curiosity is the **Casa degli Stampatori** (Museo della Stampa; ☑0374 8 31 71; Via Lanfranco 6; adult/reduced incl entry to Rocca €4.50/3; ⊗9am-1pm Tue-Fri, 10am-12.30pm & 2.30-7pm Sat, Sun & holidays Apr-Oct, closes earlier Nov-Mar). A Jewish family on the run from persecution in Germany wound up here in the mid-15th century, changed the family name to Sonsino and began a trade that, at the time, was entirely new – book printing. The Sonsino family soon established a Europe-wide reputation and printed the first Bible in Hebrew. On show in this charming, three-storey brick house are various printing machines from the 19th and early 20th centuries, a remake of a 15th-century model, and other tools of the trade.

✕ Eating

Antica Rocca   ITALIAN €€
(☑0374 8 56 72; www.ristoranteanticarocca.it; Via Cesare Battisti 1, Soncino; meals €25-30; ⊗12.30-2.30pm & 7-10pm Tue-Sat, 12.30-2.30pm Sun) Local products are the name of the game in this busy family-run eatery, barely a five-minute walk from the Rocca fortress, just over a canal. Inside, the muted tangerine decor, timber furniture and quality linen lend the place a peaceful quality in which to savour a *risotto con asparagi e crema di formaggi* (risotto with asparagus and cream of cheeses).

❶ Information

Pro Loco Soncino (☑0374 8 44 99; www.prolocosoncino.it; Via Carlo Cattaneo 1) Opening hours are irregular.

Lake Garda & Around

Includes ➡

Why Go?

Covering 370 sq km, Lake Garda is the largest of the Italian lakes, straddling the border between three regions: the Lombard plains to the west, Alpine Trentino Alto-Adige to the north and the rolling hills of the Veneto to the east. Look around and you'll be surprised to see a Mediterranean landscape of vineyards, olive groves and citrus orchards that is thanks to the lake's uniquely mild microclimate.

Like the best Italian lunch, exploring this region can't be rushed. You'll want to linger in Sirmione's thermal pools, amble around Roman ruins and ferry-hop between villages. Then you might consider touring vineyards that feature in many sommeliers' top 10s: Valpolicella, Soave and Bardolino. Further south, in incurably romantic Verona, sit beneath the stars and enjoy world-class opera; and, in Mantua, feast on Renaissance frescoes. Uncork it, savour it, then come back for more.

Best Places to Eat

➡ Dal Pescatore (p192)

➡ Locanda 4 Cuochi (p183)

➡ Osteria Le Servite (p173)

➡ Agriturismo i Vegher (p167)

➡ Locanda San Vigilio (p178)

Best Places to Stay

➡ Villa Arcadio (p204)

➡ Agriturismo San Mattia (p205)

➡ Dimora Bolsone (p203)

➡ Sanzenetto (p205)

➡ Armellino (p206)

Road Distances (KM)

	Verona	Mantua	Desenzano del Garda	Salò
Mantua	59			
Desenzano del Garda	98	55		
Salò	36	21	76	
Riva del Garda	52	88	77	95

Best Tours

➡ **Isola del Garda** (p168) A tour of Garda's only private island.

➡ **Allegrini** (p187) Savour Valpolicella reds in a palatial setting.

Advance Planning

➡ **Three months** Book tickets for headline operas.

➡ **One month** Plan activities and secure equipment, guides or courses.

➡ **One week** Book to see Mantegna's *Camera degli Sposi* to ensure you're one of the 1500 people allowed to visit each day.

➡ **One day** Reserve wine tastings to ensure someone is in.

Resources

➡ **Visit Garda** (www.visitgarda.com) A one-stop shop for Lake Garda.

➡ **Strada del Valpolicella** (www.stradadelvalpolicella.com) Valpolicella's wine roads.

➡ **Tourism Verona** (www.tourism.verona.it) Covers Verona and eastern Lake Garda.

Getting Around

Having a car here can be both a blessing and a curse. It opens up the wine regions and allows an escape from the tourist trail, but summertime traffic around Lake Garda's perimeter road is best avoided, and traffic limitations in central Verona and Mantua make a car unnecessary. An extensive ferry network and excellent region-wide rail and bus links mean you can go largely car free, only getting behind the wheel for day trips into the vineyards and hills.

3 PERFECT DAYS

Day 1: Culture-Fix Verona

Exploring the art-packed halls of the Museo di Castelvecchio could easily take all morning, while Verona's architecture-rich piazzas are perfect for a post-lunch stroll. Countless wine cellars offer a different slice of cultural life; Antica Bottega del Vino and Osteria del Bugiardo are great places to start. If you've booked for the opera in the Roman Arena, it starts around 9pm – take your seats after a gourmet bite at Locanda 4 Cuochi.

Day 2: Adventurous Lake Garda

With its mountain hinterland, regular winds and enormous expanse, Lake Garda is the perfect outdoor playground. Come summer you'll find climbers clinging to Arco's rock faces like brightly coloured lizards, paragliders sailing off Monte Baldo's summit and bikers racing down its slopes. In Riva, windsurfers launch off the lakefront in large flocks of neon sails, and in the Valtenesi families ride out through vineyards and olive groves. At the end of the day, sore muscles can be soothed in Sirmione's thermal spa.

Day 3: Renaissance Mantua

Afloat in the watery hinterland of the Mincio river, fog-bound Mantua is known locally as *La Bella Addormentata* (Sleeping Beauty). Sleepy it may seem today, but in the 1500s this was one of Italy's greatest Renaissance courts where Mantegna, Guilio Romano and Raphael came to work for the ostentatious, art-loving Gonzagas. The result is some of Italy's finest frescoed palaces and perfectly preserved medieval piazze.

Getting Off the Beaten Track

➡ Hike the Ponale Road (p172) from Riva del Garda for a bird's eye view of Lake Garda.

➡ Barge and cycle down the Mincio river with Avemaria (p206).

➡ Swim in icy melt waters in the Valle delle Cartiere (p170).

➡ Cycle through the evergreen woods around the Rocca di Manerba (p166).

➡ Scale the Alto Garda plateau on horseback with Scuderia Castello (p170).

LAKE GARDA

Poets and politicians, divas and dictators, they've all been drawn to captivating Lake Garda (Lago di Garda). In fact, 7% of all tourists to Italy head for the lake's shores, taking to its wind-ruffled waters in the north and village- and vineyard-hopping in the south. Surrounded by three distinct regions – Lombardy, Trentino Alto-Adige and the Veneto – the lake's cultural diversity attracts a cosmopolitan crowd. Mittleeuropeans colonise northern resorts such as Riva del Garda and Torbole, where restaurants serve air-dried ham and Austrian-style *carne salada* (salted beef), while in the south, French and Italian families bed down in Valtenesi farmhouses and family-friendly spa towns such as Sirmione and Bardolino.

ⓘ Getting There & Away

Verona-Villafranca airport (p184) is 20km from the lake. Regular buses link the airport with Mantua and Verona; Peschiera del Garda is 15 minutes by train from Verona.

ⓘ Getting Around

BOAT

Ferries are run by **Navigazione Lago di Garda** (☑ 800 551801; www.navigazionelaghi.it; Piazza Matteotti 2, Desenzano del Garda). Fares range from €3 for short hops (such as Salò to Gardone Riviera) to €15.10 for the four-hour Riva–Desenzano run. The Alto Garda ticket costs €34.30/17.60 per adult/child and covers Salò, Limone, Riva and Malcesine. The Basso Garda ticket costs €27.40/16.40 and covers Salò, Sirmione, Garda and Bardolino.

Car ferries yo-yo between west-bank Toscolano-Maderno and east-bank Torri del Benaco, and seasonally between Limone sul Garda and Malcesine. A small car costs €10.70 one way.

BUS

APTV (☑ 045 805 78 11; www.aptv.it) Runs buses around the lake. In the west buses run between Desenzano train station and Riva del Garda (two hours, up to six daily). In the east hourly services run between Riva del Garda and Peschiera del Garda train station (1½ hours).

Trasporti Brescia (☑ 030 440 61; www.trasportibrescia.it; Via Cassale 3/a, Brescia) Operates the Riva del Garda–Brescia (two hours, four daily) route.

Trentino Trasporti (☑ 0461 821 000; www.ttesercizio.it) Hourly buses between Riva del Garda, Arco (20 minutes) and Trento (1¾ hours).

TOP MARKETS

⟶ **Monday** Torri del Benaco

⟶ **Tuesday** Desenzano del Garda, Limone sul Garda (first and third of the month)

⟶ **Wednesday** Gargnano, Lazise, Riva del Garda (second and fourth of the month)

⟶ **Thursday** Bardolino

⟶ **Friday** Garda

⟶ **Saturday** Malcesine, Salò

CAR

Lake Garda sits just north of the A4 Milan–Venice autostrada, and just west of the A22 Modena–Trento route. A single-lane road circles the lake shore and is heavy with traffic in summer. Local tourist offices can advise about car hire.

TRAIN

Desenzano del Garda and Peschiera del Garda are both on the Milan–Venice train line and have hourly trains in each direction. Excellent connections with Verona make the city an easy day trip.

Lake Garda South Bank

Easily accessible from the A4 autostrada, the southern shore of Lake Garda is the most developed and can get extremely busy in summer, especially around Peschiera del Garda, Sirmione and Desenzano. The latter is known as the *porta del lago* (gateway to the lake) and is a major transport hub, while Peschiera is a base for families keen on visiting the lake's enormous amusement parks.

Sirmione

POP 7420

Over the centuries impossibly pretty Sirmione has drawn the likes of Catullus and Maria Callas to its banks, and today millions of visitors follow in their footsteps for a glimpse of Lake Garda's prettiest village and a dip in its only hot spring.

◉ Sights & Activities

To get even the slightest glimpse of Sirmione's legendary natural beauty, come out of season (April or October) or in the evening when most day trippers have departed. Then you can snap the fortified bulwark of the Rocca Scaligera without dozens of gelati-licking visi-

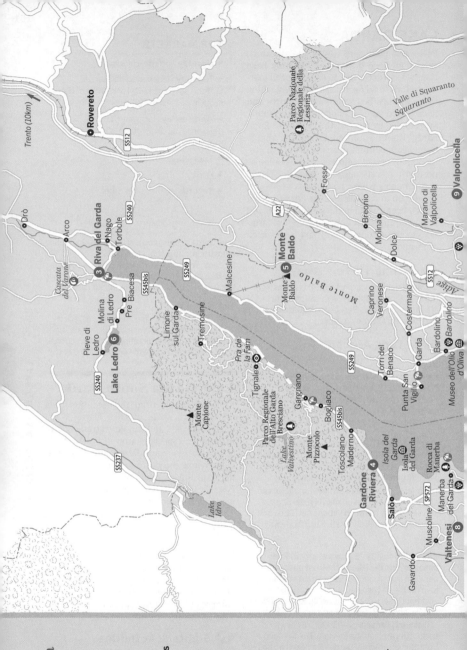

Lake Garda & Around Highlights

1 Enjoying an evening of opera beneath the stars in Verona's **Roman Arena** (p181).

2 Marvelling at Mantegna's **frescoes** (p188) in Mantua and deciphering coded meanings in the pleasure palace, **Palazzo Te** (p191).

3 Taking to the azure water by boat, windsurf or catamaran beneath the snow-capped peaks of **Riva del Garda**.

4 Finding new meaning in the word kitsch at the bombastic **mansion** (p169) of poet-turned-soldier Gabriele D'Annunzio.

5 Hiking, biking and paragliding on **Monte Baldo** (p175) for a bird's-eye view of the lake.

6 Taking the high road (and a picnic) and discovering the timeless rural landscape of **Lake Ledro**.

7 Watching the sunset over the lake through the rising steam of Sirmione's **thermal spa** (p164).

8 Sampling Italy's finest olive oil cultivated with passion for over 500 years at Valtenesi's **Comincioli** (p167).

9 Savouring world-class wines on a **Valpolicella** vineyard tour.

Soave (7km)

Zevio

Grezzana

A4

1 Verona

Parona di Valpolicella

Gargagnano
San Pietro in Cariano

San Giorgio

A22

Castelnuovo del Garda

Lazise

CanevaWorld

Gardaland

Peschiera del Garda

Verona-Villafranca Airport

Villafranca

Isola della Scala

A22

Mantua North

2 Mantua

Lake Mezzo

Lake Inferiore

Valeggio sul Mincio

Volta Mantovana

Goito

River Mincio

Lake Superiore

River Mincio

Lake Garda

Moniga del Garda

Padenghe sul Garda

Sirmione 7

Colombare

Desenzano del Garda

San Martino

Solferino

Castiglione delle Stiviere

Asola

Marcaria

Canneto sull'Oglio

Lonato

Montichiari

A4

SS11

Chiese

Brescia (11km);
Bergamo (65km)

N

0   10 km
0   5 miles

SOLFERINO & SAN MARTINO

A 19km drive south from Sirmione takes you to Solferino, a small village which played a huge part in Italian history – and helped spawn a global aid agency. On 24 June 1859, as part of the Risorgimento (Italian unification), Solferino and nearby San Martino were the scene of two battles where the combined 135,000 Piedmontese and French forces took on and defeated 140,000 Austrians. Almost 980 cannons were on the battlefields, along with 19,000 horses. Casualties were horrendous: 9800 soldiers died, 20,000 were wounded, 11,400 went missing or were taken prisoner. A Swiss businessperson, Henry Dunant, witnessed the aftermath of the battle and was so appalled by the lack of care for the casualties that he set up the organisation that became the international Red Cross and Red Crescent movements.

The **Musei di Solferino** (☑0376 85 40 19; www.solferinoesanmartino.it; Via Ossario di Solferino; adult/child €2.50/1; ☺9am-12.30pm & 2.30-7pm Tue-Sun Mar-Sep) displays small cannons, uniforms and gilt-framed paintings of the conflict, while the tower of the village's castle provides panoramic views of the battlefields. There is also a Red Cross monument, and a chilling ossuary in the church of San Pietro where the bones of more than 7000 soldiers are kept.

tors in the foreground and stroll around the 4km peninsula along the panoramic pathway. The Grotte di Catullo stays open until 8pm and the spa is open until 10pm.

Rocca Scaligera
CASTLE

(Castello Scaligero; adult/reduced €4/2; ☺8.30am-7pm Tue-Sun) Expanding their influence northwards, the Scaligeri of Verona built this enormous square-cut castle right at the entrance to the island. It guards the only footbridge into Sirmione, looming over it with impressive crenellated turrets and towers. There's not a lot inside, but the climb to the top (146 steps to the top of the tower) affords beautiful views over Sirmione's rooftops and the enclosed harbour.

Grotte di Catullo
HISTORIC SITE

(☑030 91 61 57; adult/reduced €4/2; ☺8.30am-8pm Tue-Sat, 9.30am-6.30pm Sun Mar-Oct, 8.30am-2pm Tue-Sun Nov-Mar) Occupying 2 hectares at Sirmione's northern tip, this ruined, 1st-century AD Roman villa is a picturesque complex of teetering stone arches and tumbledown walls, some three storeys high. It's the largest domestic Roman villa in northern Italy and wandering its terraced hillsides offers fantastic views.

Despite the name, there's no evidence Catullus lived here, although the poet did have a home in the village. Significantly, the living quarters were on the top floor offering 360-degree views of the surrounding waters.

★ Aquaria
SPA

(☑030 91 60 44; www.termedisirmione.com; Piazza Don Angelo Piatti; pools day/evening €33/27, treat-

ments from €25; ☺pools 2-10pm Mon, 10am-10pm Tue-Sun Mar-Dec, hours vary Jan & Feb) Sirmione is blessed with a series of offshore thermal springs that pump out water at a natural 37°C. They were discovered in the late 1800s and the town has been tapping into their healing properties ever since. At the Aquaria spa you can wallow in two thermal pools – the outdoor one is set right beside the lake.

Other treatments – including mud sessions (€50) and massages (€80) – must be booked in advance, but for the pools you just turn up with your swimsuit and flip-flops, and towels and robes will be provided. Swimsuits and thongs are also available for purchase at the spa if you don't have yours.

✖ Eating

La Fiasca
TRATTORIA €€

(☑030 990 61 11; www.trattorialafiasca.it; Via Santa Maria Maggiore; meals €30; ☺noon-2.30pm & 7-10.30pm Thu-Tue) Serving up the kind of sauces you can't help dunking your bread in, this authentic trattoria is tucked away in a back street just off the main square. The atmosphere is warm and bustling, and the dishes are packed with traditional Lake Garda produce. Prepare for some gutsy flavours: tagliatelle with perch and mushrooms, pappardelle with boar *ragù,* and duck with cognac and juniper.

La Rucola
GASTRONOMIC, GARDESE €€€

(☑030 91 63 26; www.ristorantelarucola.it; Vicolo Strentelle 7; meals €75-120; ☺noon-2.30pm & 7-11pm Sat-Wed, 7-11pm Fri) Sirmione's most elegant eatery is a refined affair. Modern art adds splashes of colour to the stone walls, while the chefs add a touch of class to a menu strong on sea and lake fish. Expect sea bass, prawns and the catch of the day to feature in numerous risotto, pasta and grilled guises, combined with flavour-enhancing confits, pâtés and marinades.

ⓘ Information

Tourist Office (☑030 91 61 14; iat.sirmione@tiscali.it; Viale Marconi 8; ⊙9am-12.30pm & 3-6.30pm) Located on the main road just before the castle drawbridge next to Sirmione's bus station.

Desenzano del Garda

POP 26,850

An easygoing commuter town 9km southwest of Sirmione, Desenzano del Garda is not as pretty as some of Garda's other lakeside villages, but its ancient harbour, broad promenades and vibrant Piazza Matteotti and Piazza Malvezzi make for pleasant wanderings. It is also a hub for summer nightlife.

◉ Sights

Villa Romana VILLA
(☑030 914 35 47; Via Crocifisso 2; adult/reduced €2/1; ⊙8.30am-7pm Mar-Oct, to 5pm Nov-Feb)

Before the Versaces and George Clooney, wealthy Roman senators and poets had holiday homes on the shores of Italy's northern lakes. A case in point is Desenzano's Roman villa, with its holiday-themed mosaic floors that once extended over a hectare of prime lakeside property.

Built over 2000 years ago, it was remodelled in the 2nd century, but continual renovations meant the interiors weren't complete until the 4th century. Wooden walkways snake through the villa above a colourful collage of black, red, olive and orange mosaic, many of them depicting scenes of hunting, fishing and chariot riding, garlanded by Garda's abundant fruits and flowers. A short video explains the layout of the villa and is worth watching before walking around the site.

✕ Eating & Drinking

★La Goccia Trattoria SEAFOOD €€
(☑030 910 31 94; Via Montonale Basso 13; meals €40-50; ⊙noon-2.30pm & 7.30-11pm) Positioned well back from the lakefront, La Goccia is a fantastic find, especially for fish lovers. With a chef who hails from Puglia you can expect the freshest seafood carpaccio followed by fragrant homemade pasta tossed with razor clams and shrimp. The *fritto misto* (fried

LAKE GARDA & AROUND LAKE GARDA SOUTH BANK

LAKE GARDA'S OLIVE OIL

Lake Garda's microclimate resembles the Mediterranean's, ensuring ideal olive-growing conditions. The lake's banks produce a tiny 1% of Italy's olive oil, but the product is renowned for being light, soft and sweet. Some 15 varieties of olives are grown here; the local black fruit produces subtler tasting oil, while the green olives are spicier – the oil makers' skill lies in achieving the perfect blend. Lake Garda's lighter oils work well with fish, the medium blends are delicious drizzled over mozzarella, and the stronger, spicier varieties are superb with grilled meats and soup. Locals advise not to use the best oils for salads, arguing if you're adding vinegar it ruins the taste.

Among the places you can tour the olive groves, sample and purchase the oil are Frantoio San Felice del Benaco (p167) and Comincioli (p167) in the Valtenesi and the Consorzio Olivicoltori di Malcesine (p175) in Malcesine.

seafood platter) is also a delight. Pair with the local Lugana 'Muntunal.' Perfect.

Caffè Italia   CAFE
(☑ 030 914 12 43; www.ristorantecaffeitalia. it; Piazza Malvezzi 19; meals €25-35; ☺ 12.30-2.30pm & 7.30-10.30pm) A perennial favourite on a busy piazza, Caffè Italia is popular for its outdoor seating, light lunches and psychedelic cocktails.

ℹ Information

Tourist Office (☑ 030 914 15 10; Via Porto Vecchio 34; ☺ 9.30am-noon & 3-6pm Mon-Sat)

Lake Garda West Bank

The western Lombard shore of Lake Garda is the most beautiful, lined with historic towns, stately villas, mountain-backed roads and frothing flower-filled gardens. North of Gardone, much of the shore is encompassed within the Parco Alto Garda Bresciano (www.parcoaltogarda.net), where it's easy to escape the summer crowds and find yourself amid some truly stunning scenery.

Valtenesi

The Valtenesi stretches languidly between Desenzano and Salò, its rolling hills etched with vine trellises and with olive groves. The main lake road heads inland, allowing for gentle explorations of an array of wineries and small towns, including Padenghe sul Garda, Moniga del Garda, Manerba del Garda and San Felice del Benaco.

The area also constitutes the Garda Classico DOC wine region, its vineyards producing the light, rose-coloured chiaretto, the rare, autochthonous groppello and the full-bodied rosso superiore. Olives also thrive here and you can sample the light, spicy oils at many wineries and *agriturismi* (farm-stay accommodation). The tourist office in Desenzano stocks the best information on the region.

◉ Sights & Activities

Away from the lake's shores this rural hinterland is zigzagged by narrow lanes and dotted with some fine local restaurants. It is perfect cycling country, so pick up a bike (or have one delivered) from **Cicli Mata** (☑ 0365 55 43 01; www.matashop.it; Via Nazionale 63, Raffa di Puegnago; half-/full-day €18/25; ☺ 9am-1pm & 2.30-7.30pm Tue-Sat, 2.30-7.30pm Sun & Mon) and select one of the well-charted routes on the community website www.pisteciclabili.com. Another resource is the mobile app **Garda Bello e Buono** (www.gardabelloebuono.it), which you can download for iPhones and Android. It details cycling routes, sights and restaurants.

★ Parco Archeologico
Rocca di Manerba   NATURAL RESERVE
(www.parcoroccamanerba.net; ☺ 10am-8pm Apr-Sep, to 6pm Thu-Sun Oct-Mar) **FREE** Protected by Unesco and now a natural reserve, the 'rock of Minerva' (so named after a long-gone Roman temple dedicated to Minerva) juts out scenically into the lake just north of Moniga del Garda. Now all that remains are the low rubble walls of a medieval castle and a restful nature reserve of evergreen woods and orchid meadows, criss-crossed with cycling and walking trails.

The shore around here features some of the best beaches on the lake. Strolling from Pieve Vecchia to Porto del Torchio via Punta del Rio reveals glorious views and idyllic spots for a dip or a paddle.

LAKE GARDA & AROUND LAKE GARDA WEST BANK

Santuario della Madonna
del Carmine
MONASTERY

(🗷 0365 6 20 32; www.santuariodelcarmine·sanfe
lice.it; Via Fontanamonte 1, San Felice del Benaco;
⊙ 7am-noon & 3-6pm; P) **FREE** In the tiny
village of San Felice del Benaco you'll find
the frescoed sanctuary of the Madonna del
Carmine, which dates from 1452. The simple
Gothic-Romanesque exterior does little to
prepare you for the Technicolour frescoes inside, depicting images of Christ and the Virgin and scenes resonant with the Carmelite
Order, who have been here since 1460.

Although the provenance of the 15th-
century frescoes is unknown, a number of
them are thought to be the work of Mantegna, Paolo Uccello and Vicenzo Foppa, such is
their quality and depth of perspective. You
can stay in the adjoining **complex** (www.car
minesanfelice.it; rooms s/d €44/78).

Comincioli
WINERY

(🗷 0365 65 11 41; www.comincioli.it; Via Roma 10,
Puegnago del Garda; ⊙ by reservation 9.30am-noon
& 2.30-7pm Mon-Sat) 🖉 **FREE** Despite modest appearances, Gianfranco Comincioli's
winery and olive press are behind some
truly groundbreaking oils and engaging and
unusual wines. Combining over 500 years of
traditional knowledge (the family tree traces its roots back to 1552) and €1 million in
technological investments, Comincioli now
produce what is Italy's finest olive oil, the
Numero Uno.

The secret to these elegant, well-defined
oils is a near-maniacal attention to every detail and a cutting-edge pitting process that
removes the stones before pressing and thus
avoids the often violent bitterness and oxi-
dative nuttiness that affect regular oils. The
other factor is the speed with which the olives are harvested – a process that takes no
more than 80 minutes, meaning that when
you break that wax seal you're tasting the
fullest, freshest expression of the fruit.

Comincioli is located in the small village
of Puegnago del Garda, which is in the heart
of the Valtenesi, 9.5km south of Salò and
15.5km north of Desenzano del Garda.

Frantoio San Felice
del Benaco
OLIVE OIL PRESS

(🗷 0365 623 41; www.oliveoil-lakegarda.com;
Via delle Gere 2, San Felice del Benaco; ⊙ shop
9am-noon & 3-6pm, happy hour 5.30-8pm; 🖪)
FREE With over 350 members, this DOP-
accredited cooperative is a great place to
sample Garda Breciano oils in a gorgeous

rural setting. It's also possible to rock-up for
tastings without reservations during the daily 'happy hour' and keep an eye out on Facebook for impromptu farmyard feasts when
you can enjoy spit-roast and live music.

La Basia
HORSE RIDING

(🗷 0365 55 59 58; www.labasia.it; Via Predefitte
31, Puegnago del Garda; half-/1hr lesson €15/25)
Just above the Viale Panoramico between
Puegnago and Salò is Elena Parona's extensive vineyard and riding school. While
the adults sample wines and wild honey
on the terrace, kids can enjoy structured
riding lessons in one of the two schools
with Simone and Irene or rides in the surrounding vineyards. Between March and
September you can also bed down in one
of their family-sized apartments (€345 to
€550 per week).

Azienda Agricola Zuliani
WINERY

(🗷 030 990 70 26; www.vinizuliani.it; Via Tito Speri
28, Padenghe sul Garda; ⊙ 9am-1pm & 2.30-7pm
Mon-Sat) **FREE** This family-run vineyard has
been producing wine since 1589 and is an
aristocratic Valtenesi brand. Of the farms' 22
hectares, 13 are devoted to vineyards while
the other nine are covered in meadows, olive
groves and pasture. Make a reservation for a
tour and a tasting in the historic farmhouse
kitchen.

✕ Eating

La Dispensa
MODERN ITALIAN €€

(🗷 0365 55 70 23; Piazza Municipio 10, San Felice
del Benaco; meals €25-40; ⊙ 7-11.30pm) This
fun and colourful wine bar and restaurant
(with accompanying shop, VinoeLino) offers a mouthwatering modern Italian menu
with a focus on sensational fish and handsome charcuterie platters. Ingredients are
top-notch, market-fresh and locally sourced
and sometimes come accompanied by live
jazz.

★ Agriturismo i Vegher
AGRITURISMO €€

(🗷 0365 65 44 79; www.agriturismovegher.it; Via
Mascontina 6, Puegnago del Garda; meals €25-35;
⊙ 7-10pm Wed-Mon, noon-2.30pm Sun & public
holidays; P🖪) As you bump down the un-
surfaced lanes between vines and olive trees
you may think you're lost, but don't give up. I
Vegher is worth the persistence and the long
booking lead times (book at least a month
in advance for holiday weekends, otherwise
about two weeks). Also, you'll want to come
with a hungry group who can do justice to

the 12 to 15 delicious antipasti courses, the homemade pasta course and the meat *secondi*. All of it is made with local produce, much of it from the farm.

Ristorante Fior di Loto   STEAKHOUSE €€€

(☑0365 65 42 64; www.ristorantefiordiloto.it; Via Dei Laghi 8, Puegnago del Garda; meals €40-50; ☺7.30-10pm Tue, 12.30-2pm & 7.30-10pm Wed-Sun; P🖶) Describing Fior di Loto as a steakhouse is criminal given the Rolls Royce selection of meat cuts aged between 25 and 40 months. Ten different cuts of meat are displayed in the counter like finely veined pieces of marble. Take the chef's advice when selecting and then sit back on the patio overlooking Lake Sovenigo and wait for your succulent steak to appear.

Salò

POP 10,350

Wedged between the lake and the foothills of Monte San Bartolomeo, Salò exudes an air of courtly grandeur, a legacy of its days as Garda's capital when the Venetian Republic held sway over the lake. Devoid of any singular sights, Salò's lovely historic centre is lined with fine Liberty-style buildings and small, ordinary shops and restaurants. In 1901 an earthquake levelled many of its older *palazzi*, although a few fine examples remain: the Torre dell'Orologio (the ancient city gate), the late Gothic *duomo* with its Renaissance facade and the grand porticoed Palazzo della Magnifica Patria.

In 1943 Salò was named the capital of the Social Republic of Italy as part of Mussolini and Hitler's last efforts to organise Italian Fascism in the face of advancing American forces. This episode, known as the Republic of Salò, saw more than 16 public and private buildings in the town commandeered and turned into Mussolini's ministries and offices.

The tourist office has an English-language map and booklet featuring significant locations in town and you can also look out for multilingual plaques around town. The Palazzo della Magnifica Patria (now the town hall) was the Interpreters' Office HQ, where foreign dispatches were translated. Bar Italia was the Casa del Fascio, home to Mussolini's guards, and the local primary school became the base for Agenzia Stefani, the notorious news agency for Fascist propaganda.

✖ Eating

★ Ristorante Papillon   PIZZERIA €

(☑0365 4 14 29; www.ristorantepapillon.it; Lungolago Zanardelli 69/70; pizza €8-14; ☺8am-10pm Tue-Sun; 🖶) Surprisingly good thin-crust pizza straight from the wood-fired oven. Enjoy them lakeside beside the weeping willow, but watch out for the pushy, pizza-loving ducks!

Osteria di Mezzo   OSTERIA €€

(☑036 529 09 66; Via di Mezzo 10; meals €32; ☺noon-11pm Wed-Mon) At this intimate *osteria* a constant stream of hearty meals heads into a dining room lined with antique mirrors and weathered stone. Pumpkin gnocchi, grilled perch, and rabbit with smoked ham and prunes are just some of the delights to choose from.

Antica Trattoria alle Rose   MODERN ITALIAN €€€

(☑0365 432 20; www.trattoriaallerose.it; Via Gasparo da Salò; meals €45-65; ☺noon-2.30pm & 7.30-11pm Thu-Tue) Go with the flow in this elegant trattoria where Rosanna Faè and Gianni Briarava have been turning out contemporary, local cuisine for 25 years. Say yes to the parade of mixed antipasti – the zucchini souffle in a puddle of melted mountain cheese is delicious – and the homemade pastas with seasonal finferli mushrooms. Then you'll have to agonise over the rabbit in cognac or the grilled lake sardines, before crashing out at dessert and petit fours.

Its sister restaurant, **Osteria dell' Orologio** (☑0365 29 01 58; www.osteriadel lorologio.it; Via Butturini 26; meals €25-35; ☺noon-2.30pm & 7.30-10.30pm Thu-Tue), is equally good but less formal.

❶ Information

Tourist Office (☑0365 2 14 23; www.rivieradeilimoni.it; Piazza Sant'Antonio 4; ☺10am-12.30pm & 3-6pm Mon, Tue & Thu-Sat, 10am-12.30pm Wed)

Isola del Garda

It's not often you get to explore a serene private island in the company of its aristocratic owners, so a trip to **Isola del Garda** (☑328 384 92 26; www.isoladelgarda.com; tour incl boat ride €25-30; ☺Apr-Oct) is a treat. Floating just off Salò, this speck of land is crowned with impressive battlements, luxuriant formal gardens and a sumptuous neo-Gothic Venetian villa. It's owned by the Contessa

Cavazza, and she and her seven children still live on the island with their families.

Visits to the island are by guided tour only (in Italian, English, French and German) and last one and a half to two hours. Boats depart from Salò, Gardone Riviera, Garda and Sirmione, but they only leave each location one or two times a week, so plan ahead.

Gardone Riviera

POP 2700

Once Lake Garda's most prestigious corner, Gardone is flush with belle époque hotels, opulent villas and extravagant gardens. They tumble down the hillside from the historic centre, Gardone Sopra, complete with tiny chapel and piazza, to the cobbled *lungolago* (lakefront promenade) of Gardone Sotto, which is lined with cafes and other tourist paraphernalia. Although the haute glamour of Gardone's 19th-century heyday is long gone, it is a pleasant enough place for a stroll and drink, although you'll probably want to base yourself elsewhere on the lake.

An hour of so uphill from Gardone is the pretty mountain village of San Michele, from where you can pick up a number of panoramic walking trails. Ask at the tourist office in Gardone Sotto for details.

⊙ Sights

★ Il Vittoriale degli Italiani   MUSEUM
(📞 0365 29 65 11; www.vittoriale.it; Piazza Vittoriale; gardens & museums adult/reduced €16/12; ⊗ grounds 8.30am-8pm Apr-Sep, to 5pm Oct-Mar, museums to 7pm Tue-Sun Apr-Sep, 9am-1pm & 2-5pm Tue-Sun Oct-Mar; 🅿) Poet, soldier, hypochondriac and proto-Fascist, Gabriele d'Annunzio (1863–1938) defies easy definition, and so does his estate. Bombastic, extravagant and unsettling, it's home to every architectural and decorative excess imaginable and the decor helps shed light on the man. In the 1920s d'Annunzio became a strong supporter of Fascism and Mussolini, while his affairs with wealthy women were legendary.

By 1914 d'Annunzio was an established poet, but his fame was cemented by a series of daring military adventures in WWI. His most dramatic exploit was an unsanctioned occupation of Fiume, now Rijeka, on the Adriatic. Outraged that it was about to be handed over to Yugoslavia, not Italy, at the end of the war, he gathered a mini-army, invaded the port and proclaimed himself the ruler. Despite eventually surrendering he was hailed a national hero.

In his main house, the Prioria, black velvet drapes and stained glass windows cast an eerie light on gloomy rooms (he had an eye condition that made exposure to sunlight painful) crammed with classical figurines, leather-bound books, leopard skins, gilded ornaments, lacquer boxes and chinoiserie. Highlights include the bronze tortoise that sits on the guests' dining table (in admonition of overeaters, it was cast from a pet that died of overeating); the bright blue bathroom suite with over 2000 pieces of bric-a-brac; his spare bedroom where he would retire to lie on a coffin-shaped bed and contemplate death; and his study with its low lintel – designed so visitors would have to bow as they entered. Guided visits, in Italian only, tour the house every 10 minutes and last half an hour.

If you aren't already overwhelmed by d'Annunzio's excesses, the estate's Museo della Guerra is housed nearby in the art nouveau Casa Schifamondo ('Escape from the World'). It is full of mementoes, banners and medals of d'Annunzio's war-time exploits, while the gardens offer the chance to wander the deck of the full-sized battleship *Puglia*, which d'Annunzio used in the Fiume adventure.

✗ Eating

Antico Brolo   OSTERIA €€
(📞 0365 214 21; www.ristoranteanticobrolo.it; Via Carere 10; tasting menu €38, meals €35-45; ⊗ noon-2.30pm & 7.30-10.30pm Tue-Sun) If you're considering a date night, Antico Brolo is the place for you, with seating in an intimate walled courtyard or better still on a tiny balcony frothing with pink geraniums overlooking Gardone. The food is as elegant as the surroundings, serving tiny amuse-bouche and nouvelle plates of steamed fish and truffle pasta.

Locanda Agli Angeli   GARDESE €€
(📞 0365 2 08 32; Piazza Garibaldi 2; set menu €20, meals €35; ⊗ 11am-11pm Wed-Mon) A shaded terrace, rattan chairs and burgundy tablecloths set the scene for some classic Lake Garda cooking. Tempting choices include veal ravioli, sardines with potatoes and herbs, and fettucine with smoked eel. As Agli Angeli is tucked into the hillside on the way to Il Vittoriale, it makes an ideal post-sightseeing stop.

Toscolano-Maderno

POP 8000

Straddling the Toscolano torrent are the twin hamlets of Toscolano and Maderno, strung together by a mile-long beach, the largest on Lake Garda. To the southwest, pretty, pastel-coloured Maderno marks the location of Benacum, the principal Roman town on the lake, while once industrial Toscolano, to the northeast, once supplied nails for Venetian galleys and thick, creamy paper for Martin Luther's Bible. For more info see www.prolo cotoscolanomaderno.com.

Aside from its picturesque setting on a nubby headland at the foot of Monte Pizzocolo (1582m), the villages retain some fine period churches, the 12th-century **Chiesa di Sant'Andrea** (Piazza San Marco) and the Renaissance sanctuary and church of the **Madonna del Benaco** (Piazza Caduti) and **Santi Pietro e Paolo** (Piazza S Maria del Benaco), both of which are frescoed. Down by the water, the long promenade is backed by a shady camping area and is well supplied with bike and boat hire outlets like **Garda Yachting Charter** (www.gyc.it).

The Toscolano torrent upstream fed numerous paper mills in the Middle Ages and you can follow the riverside road up the wooded **Valle delle Cartiere** and explore their peaceful ruins. The largest of them is now the **Museo della Carta** (www.valledel lecartiere.it; Via Valle delle Cartiere; adult/reduced €5/3; ☉10am-6pm May-Sep, to 6pm Sat & Sun Mar-May & Oct). Further up, towards the top of the valley, there are plenty of opportunities for swimming.

Also set back from the lakeside are the two idyllic villages of **Gaino** and **Cecina**. In the former you'll find **Agriturismo Scuderia Castello** (☑0365 64 41 01; www.scuderiacas tello.it; Via Castello 10, Gaino; s €45-50, d €70-80; ℗) ✆, where you can spend the night overlooking the lake, or join one of its mountain horse treks (€20/160 per half/full day).

Gargnano

POP 3000

Although they loom on the horizon for much of the lake, it's around Gargnano that the mountains really kick in. They rear so steeply it's overwhelming – you don't just look at views like these, you step into them. Thanks to its awkward location (at the point when the road north becomes a tortured set of dynamite-blasted tunnels), Gargnano has been spared the worst excesses of the tourism industry and it retains a pleasant, local feel. It is linked with the hamlets of Bogliaco and Villa, through which you pass before you reach Gargnano proper. It's a perfect spot to spend a couple of days relaxing and exploring off-the-beaten-track nature trails. For more information on walking itineraries around Gargnano visit www.gargnanosul garda.com.

In September, Gargnano hosts the lake's most prestigious sailing regatta, the **Centomiglia** (www.centomiglia.it), which starts in Bogliaco and circumnavigates the lake. It attracts international sailors and throughout the week the village celebrates with markets and open-air concerts.

◎ Sights & Activities

Like Gardone, Gargnano has some impressive Liberty villas and has attracted its fair share of artists and aristocrats. DH Lawrence stayed at **Villa Igea** in 1912–13 and wrote *Twilight in Italy,* and now the tourist office recommends walking itineraries in his footsteps so you, too, can see the source of Lawrence's inspiration. The enormous **Villa Bettoni** (not open to the public), which is now spliced in two by the Gardesana road – such is the scale of the property – was modelled on the Schönbrunn Palace in Vienna and Benito Mussolini kept house at **Villa Feltrinelli**, now an opulent hotel, when things started to take a downturn for the Axis powers in 1943.

Chiesa di San Francesco   CHURCH

(☉8am-noon & 4-7pm) The Franciscans were Gargnano's first inhabitants, and their modest 13th-century Romanesque church is the village's main monument. They were also some of the first farmers to cultivate citrus fruits in Europe, and you'll find an array of lemons, oranges and melons carved lovingly into the capital's inside.

Parco la Fontanella   BEACH

(Via Rimembranze 18; ☉9am-9pm mid-Mar–mid-Sep, 10am-5.30pm mid-Sep–mid-Mar; ♿) A 300m stroll north from the ferry landing brings you to a beach where gleaming white pebbles fringe shallow crystalline waters. The shore, bar and restaurant are backed by olive groves which look out directly at the craggy heights of Monte Baldo opposite. If you're here in late spring, the mountain often still has snow clinging to its tip.

Popular with families, the beach is well equipped with a shaded picnic area, ping pong tables, volleyball courts, and water sports hire outlets. **OKSurf** (www.oksurf.it; Parco Fontanella) offers a range of windsurfing courses for adults and children.

✖ Eating

Osteria del Restauro   OSTERIA €€
(✆0365 726 43; Piazza Villa 19, La Villa; meals €25-30; ⊘noon-2.30pm & 7-10pm Thu-Tue; ⛟) This one-time restoration studio is located by La Villa's tiny harbour with outdoor seating adjacent to the pier. The highly seasonal menu includes treats like zucchini flowers stuffed with ricotta, chilled gazpacho or hand-cut salmon, and the fish practically hops right out of the water on to your plate.

Ristorante Lido   CONTEMPORARY ITALIAN €€
(✆0365 79 10 42; Via Colletta 61, La Villa; meals €30-50; ⊘noon-3pm & 7.30-11pm Wed-Mon) The sleek, modern Lido is a perfect lunch location, its terrace thrust out over the lake shaded by a pergola and ancient olive tree. Gramatica's dishes are similarly simple and pared back: fish carpaccio drizzled with Limone lemons, homemade ravioli in sage and butter and grilled lake fish. At night, fairy lights add to the romance.

La Tortuga   GASTRONOMIC €€€
(✆036 57 12 51; Via XXIV Maggio 5; tasting menu €80, meals €60-100; ⊘noon-2.30pm & 7-10pm Wed-Mon) Despite its homey appearance Michelin-starred La Tortuga serves a sophisticated menu without undue pomp and ceremony. Appreciative diners at its handful of tables enjoy Garda classics such as pasta with lake perch in a fragrant slow-cooked broth and veal fillet with truffles or morelles. Wines from the encyclopaedic wine list are generously priced, with classics like Allegrini's La Grola a mere €35.

The Upper Lake Road

Heading north from Gargnano the SS45bis climbs steeply, its cliff-edge bends interspersed with long, dark tunnels and signs warning of rock falls. Around 8km north of Gargnano, a turn-off on the left leads via an ultra-steep detour to the atmospheric village of **Tignale**, some 500m above the water. Somehow clinging to a spur of rock above the nearby hamlet of Gardola is the 16th-century **Santuario di Montecastello** (✆036 57 30 19; ⊘9am-7pm Easter-Oct), which has a 15th-century gilded wooden altar, frescoes of the Giotto school and extraordinary views down the whole lake.

From here you can continue higher, over the mountain pass to the 400m-high plateau of **Tremosine** for more tremendous views of the lake. Seventeen small villages huddle on this Alpine plateau, the main one being Pieve di Tremosine. In June you can join the five-mile gourmet walk, the **Cinquemiglia del Ghiottone**, through woods, meadows and pastures sampling speciality dishes in seven Tremosine villages. For more information check out www.infotremosine.it.

To descend from the plateau, pick up the snaking SP38 through the sheer-sided **Brasa Gorge**. One of the most spectacular roads in Italy, Winston Churchill dubbed it 'the eighth wonder of the world.'

Back on the main SS45bis lake road, the route from Gargnano passes **Tignale Porto**, a popular windsurfers' hang-out. A couple of

---

LAKE GARDA'S LEMON INDUSTRY

It's thought monks from Genoa brought lemons to Gargnano when they arrived at the town's monastery of St Francis in the 13th century. Lake Garda's temperate climate provided good conditions for a fruit normally grown further south, and by the 18th century hundreds of *limonaie* (lemon houses) were being built. These kept the frosts off the trees by laying sheets of glass over a wooden latticework supported by ranks of tall, thin stone pillars. Hundreds of thousands of lemons were exported annually to Germany and Russia, providing a crucial local income. But by the second half of the 19th century the industry fell into terminal decline due to disease and the discovery of artificial citric acid.

Today, terraces of weathered stone pillars are evidence of this lost industry. You can visit restored lemon houses at **Pra de la Fam** (✆036 57 14 49; Tignale Porto; ⊘3-5pm Wed & Sat, 10am-noon Sun Apr-Oct, 3-5pm Wed Nov-Mar) ᖴᖇᕮᕮ in Tingale Porto and **Limonaia del Castèl** (✆0365 95 40 08; Via Capitelli; adult/child €1/free; ⊘10am-6pm Apr-Oct) in Limone sul Garda on the west bank of the lake, and at Torri del Benaco's Il Castello Scaligero (p176) on the east bank.

kilometres further, the cliff-backed beaches at Campione del Garda provide views of fleets of windsurfers skimming the lake surface at exhilarating speeds.

Eight kilometres further north, Limone sul Garda is the last town in Lombardy. Here, stone houses tumble down steep slopes and cobbled lanes meander towards a waterfront lined with pastel-painted houses. Inevitably in the summer it's besieged by tourists (nearly 10,000 a day) and the trinket sellers and snack bars are there in force.

Lake Garda North Bank

The northern tip of Lake Garda lies across the border from Lombardy in the Alpine region of Trentino-Alto Adige. Fjord-like, the glassy water lies in the shadow of the lake's highest peaks. Currents of air, swooping off their sheer slopes ensure the towns of Riva, Torbole and Malcesine attract windsurfers and sailors, and shoreside towns and hotels are well equipped with rentals and surfing schools.

Riva del Garda & Around

POP 15,800 / ELEV 73M

Encircled by towering rock faces and a looping landscaped lakefront, Riva's appealing historic core is arranged around handsome Piazza III Novembre and is a medley of maze-like streets and period facades.

For centuries Riva's position at the northern tip of the lake, a key access for northern armies into Italy, lent it a vital strategic role. In the Middle Ages the town was a port for the Prince-Bishops of Trento, and throughout its history Riva was much fought over,

ruled at various times by the Republic of Venice, Milan's Visconti and Verona's Della Scala families. In 1815 it became part of the Austrian Empire (Trentino itself is still considered the Südtirol) and soon became a holiday resort for the Archduke and the northern European intelligentsia. Stendhal, Thomas Mann and Kafka all summered here, drawn by Goethe's evocative descriptions in his 1786 bestseller, *Italian Journeys*.

◎ Sights & Activities

Riva makes a natural starting point for a host of activities, including hiking and biking trails around Monte Rocchetta (1575m), climbing in Arco and canyoning in the Val di Ledro. One of the town's top highlights is the easy 7km hike along La Strada del Ponale (www.ponale.eu), the old lakeside road, which rises up to Pregasina offering stunning lake views the entire route.

Along the gorgeous landscaped lakefront more gentle pursuits are possible, such as swimming, sunbathing and cycling the 3km lakeside path to Torbole. The water here is safe for small children, and there are numerous play areas set back from the water. Like its neighbour Torbole, Riva is well known for windsurfing and has several schools that hire out equipment on Porfina Beach.

Museo Alto Garda   MUSEUM
(La Rocca; ☑ 0464 57 38 69; www.museoaltogarda. it; Piazza Cesare Battisti 3; adult/child €3/1.50; ⊙ 10am-6pm Tue-Sun Mar-Nov, to 5pm Dec-Feb) Housed in Riva's stunted medieval castle, known locally as La Rocca, the civic museum features a modest selection of local archaeology, frescoes from Roman Riva, historical documents and paintings. Perhaps the most revealing exhibits are the antique maps dating from 1579 and 1667 and a 1774 *Atlas Tyrolensis,* which evocatively convey the area's shifting boundaries.

Cascata del Varone   WATERFALL
(www.cascata-varone.com; adult/reduced €5.50/ 2.50; ⊙ 9am-7pm May-Aug, to 6pm Apr & Sep, to 5pm Mar & Oct) This 100m waterfall thunders down sheer limestone cliffs through an immense, dripping gorge. Walkways snake 50m into the mountain beside the crashing torrent, and strolling along them is like walking in a perpetual thunderstorm. You'll find it signposted 3km northwest of Riva's centre. It's also possible to walk there from Riva's waterfront.

LAKE GARDA'S WINDS

Lake Garda has an unusual meteorological quirk – the winds that blow over its surface are almost as regular as clockwork. The Pelèr (also called Suer or Vento) gusts gently from the north, lasts 12 hours and is normally done by 10am, while the Ora blows from the south between noon and sunset and is felt mainly in the central and northern parts of the lake. Their predictability has ensured Riva, Torbole, Campione and Malcesine are magnets for windsurfers and sailors.

Riva del Garda

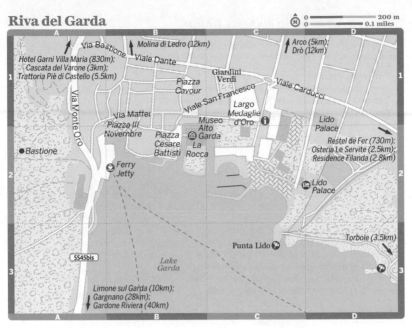

Bastione   LANDMARK

From the centre of Riva, the Bastione is the chalk-white castle clinging to sheer cliffs high above the west edge of town. The 3.5km hike to this picturesque ruin is as steep as it looks and leads up hairpin bends past oleanders, cypresses and wayside shrines. The castle was built by the Venetians in a desperate, and doomed, bid to hold onto power.

Pick up the signed path where Via Bastione joins Via Monte Oro.

Arco   TOWN

No doubt avoiding the summer tourists, Archduke Albrecht preferred to build his winter palace 5km north of Riva in pretty Arco in 1872. Around it he created a magnificent arboretum, now the **Parco Arciducale** (Via Lomego; ⊙ 8am-7pm Apr-Sep, to 4pm Oct-Mar) **FREE**, planted with huge holm-oaks, sequoias and dagger-sharp cypresses. His neighbours did the same and now Arco blooms beautifully throughout the summer.

Above the tips of the cypresses you'll spot the dramatically sighted **Castello di Arco**. Originally built by the Goths over a thousand years ago, it guarded the Valle di Sarca and was controlled by the Counts of Arco from the 12th century until 1703, when the French finally breached the walls.

From Arco, you can cycle north towards Drò to view the rocky desert of the **Marocche** – an area of huge mountain boulders which have tumbled down the steep slopes and now cover a desert-like area of 15 square kilometres between Drò, Drena and Lake Cavedine.

✖ Eating

Riva is an unashamed holiday resort catering to a large number of sports enthusiasts, many of whom have little time to spare for fine dining. As a result you'll find a plethora of pizza places and trattorias serving generic 'Italian' dishes. To seek out something more authentic you'll have to search further afield in Arco, Tenno and the surrounding mountains.

★**Osteria Le Servite**   OSTERIA, GARDESE €€
(☑ 0464 55 74 11; www.leservite.com; Via Passirone 68, Arco; meals €30-45; ⊙ 7-10.30pm Tue-Sun Apr-Sep, 7-10.30pm Thu-Sun Oct-Mar; P ♿) Tucked away amid Arco's vineyards is this elegant little *osteria* where Alessandro and his wife serve mimosa gnocchi, tender *salmerino* (Arctic char) and pork fillet with grape must. In summer you can sit on the patio sipping small-production DOC Trentino wines.

ACTIVITIES AROUND RIVA DEL GARDA

Though you can ride, cycle, hike and sail your way around Garda, the real hub of the lake's activities is the triangle of towns Riva, Arco and Torbole.

Water Sports

Fleets of operators provide equipment hire and tuition along the lakefront in Riva and Torbole. One of the largest is **Surfsegnana** (☑0464 50 59 63; www.surfsegnana.it; Foci del Sarca, Torbole), which operates from Lido di Tòrbole and Porfina Beach in Riva. It runs lessons in windsurfing (€72), kitesurfing (€110) and sailing (€75), as well as hiring out all the windsurf kit (€40 per half-day), sail boats (€32 to €52 per hour) and kayaks (€9/14 for one-/two-person kayaks). Other operators include www.sailingdulac.com, www.pierwindsurf.it and www.vascorenna.com.

Climbing

Surrounded by perfect waves of limestone, Arco is one of Europe's most popular climbing destinations and is the location of the **Rockmaster festival** (www.rockmasterfesti val.com) in September.

With hundreds of routes of all grades to choose from, Arco climbs are divided between short, bolted, single-pitch sports routes and long, Dolomite-style climbs, some extending as much as 1400m. The 300m **Zanzara** is a world classic, a 7a+ climb directly above the Rockmaster competition wall.

For information on climbing courses and routes contact **Friends of Arco** (www.friend sofarco.it). **Guide Alpine Arco** (www.guidealpinearco.com) is another good resource.

Canyoning

Thanks to glacial meltwaters, which have worn smooth the limestone mountains surrounding Riva and the Val di Ledro, canyoning here is a fantastic experience offering lots of slides, jumps and abseiling. Both Friends of Arco and Guide Alpine Arco arrange trips to the Palvico and Rio Nero gorges in the Val di Ledro (€69 each) and the Vione canyon in Tignale (€125); as does **Canyon Adventures** (www.canyonadv.com).

Trattoria Piè di Castello TRENTINO €€
(☑0464 52 10 65; www.piedicastello.it; Via al Cingol Ros 38, Tenno; meals €20-25; ⊘noon-2.30pm & 7-10pm Wed-Mon; P 🐾) If you're looking for a real local experience, book a table at this travellers inn on the road to Tenno. It's been run by the same family for the last 80 years and prepares the typical Trentino dish, *carne salata*. Although ostensibly salted beef, the dish requires a laborious preparation: the meat must be tenderised in herb-infused brine in a ceramic dish for several days and is then served with various pickled side dishes. It's been around since the Middle Ages.

Restel de Fer OSTERIA €€
(☑0464 55 34 81; www.resteldefer.com; Via Restel de Fer 10, Riva del Garda; 4/6 courses €35/50; ⊘noon-2.30pm & 7-11pm Jul-Aug, Thu-Tue only Sep-Oct & Dec-Jun; P) The restaurant at this family-run *locanda* (inn) feels like dropping by a friend's rustic-chic house: expect worn leather armchairs, copper cooking pots and glinting blue glass. The menu might feature seasonal, local delicacies such as rabbit wrapped in smoked

mountain ham, char with crayfish, and veal with Monte Baldo truffles.

ℹ Information

Tourist Office (☑0464 55 44 44; www.gardatrentino.it; Largo Medaglie d'Oro; ⊘9am-7pm May-Sep, to 6pm Oct-Apr)

Lake Garda East Bank

Sitting in the Veneto region, the eastern shore of Lake Garda has a different character again. Its nickname, the Riviera degli Olivi comes from the silvery olive groves that line the shoreline and the lower reaches of Monte Baldo (2130m), a massive, muscular limestone ridge that stretches 40km between Lake Garda and the Adige valley.

Malcesine

POP 3647

With the lake lapping right up to the tables of its harbourside restaurants and the vast ridge of Monte Baldo looming behind, Malcesine is quintessential Lake Garda. Alas, it's picturesque setting attracts thousands of holidaymakers and day trippers, who flood the town's tiny streets and drive locals into the hills. The best beach is located south of the town centre in the pretty cove of the Val di Sogno.

◉ Sights

A startling 90% of Malcesine's income comes from tourism and its streets, paved with lake pebbles, are almost impassable such is the number of visitors.

Palazzo dei Capitani
PALACE
(Via Capitanato; ⊘10am-5pm) **FREE** This palace was home to Malcesine's governor when it was ruled by the Republic of Venice, largely between 1405 and 1797. A single, large hall leads onto a secluded waterfront terrace through an archway that frames a beautiful lake view.

Castello Scaligero
CASTLE
(Via Castello; adult/child €6/2; ⊘9.30am-6.30pm Tue-Sun) From Via Capitanato winding lanes lead to the chalky-white Castello Scaligero. This late-6th-century fortress was built by the Franks and consolidated by the Della Scala family, who ruled Malcesine between 1277 and 1387. The poet Goethe thought the castle so beautiful he sketched it, was mistaken for a spy and temporarily thrown into its cells.

★ Funivia Malcesine–Monte Baldo
FUNICULAR
(☑045 740 02 06; www.funiviedelbaldo.it; Via Navene Vecchia; adult/reduced return €19/15; ⊘8am-7pm Apr-Aug, to 6pm Sep, to 5pm Oct) Jump aboard this cable car and glide 1760m above sea level for spectacular views – rotating cabins reveal the entire lake and the surrounding mountains spread out like a brightly coloured, textured map. For the first 400m the slopes are covered in oleanders and olive and citrus trees – after that, oak and chestnut take over.

Getting off the cable car at the intermediate station of San Michele (Malcesine to San Michele one way/return €5/7) opens up some excellent hikes; pick up a map from the tourist office before you set out. The hour-long walk back to Malcesine reveals a rural world of hillside houses and working farms.

There are also several panoramic mountain biking trails down from the summit.

Consorzio Olivicoltori di Malcesine
OLIVE OIL COOPERATIVE
(☑045 740 12 86; Via Navene 21; ⊘9am-1pm & 4.30-7pm; P) **FREE** Olives harvested around Malcesine are milled into extra-virgin olive oil by this local consortium, where you can enjoy mini olive oil tastings. The 550 members all come from Malcesine's hills and produce 400,000kg of olives and 75,000L of oil annually. Prices of the cold-pressed extra virgin DOP oil range from €11 for 0.5L to €52 for 5L.

✖ Eating

Speck Stube
BARBECUE €
(☑0457 40 11 77; www.speckstube.com; Via Navene Vecchia 139, Campagnola; meals €8-20; ⊘noon-midnight Mar-Oct; P ⌖) Wood-roast chickens, sausages and pork on the bone are the speciality at this family-friendly place 2.5km north of Malcesine. Chow down on hearty portions and mugs of beer at trestle tables

LAKE GARDA & AROUND LAKE GARDA EAST BANK

WORTH A TRIP

LAKE LEDRO

From Riva, first the S then the SS240 wind their way west up the mountains. The road signs here speak volumes, warning of low cloud, rockfalls and ice. It's an ear-popping drive past rural villages with an Alpine feel; detouring off the main road into villages such as **Biacesa** and **Pré** provides an insight into mountain life. Around 11km from Riva the road flattens and **Lake Ledro** (www.vallediledro.com) comes into view.

Only 2.5km long and 2km wide, this diminutive lake sits at an altitude of 650m, set in a bowl of tree-covered mountains. **Molina di Ledro** is at the lake's eastern end, where tiny thatched huts line up beside a string of beaches and boat-hire pontoons. Like Riva, Lake Ledro is the springboard for numuorous outdoor activities ranging from hiking and canyoning to paragliding. It also has 200km of mountain-bike trails. The Riva del Garda **tourist office** (☑0464 55 44 44; www.gardatrentino.it; Largo Medaglie d'Oro; ⊘9am-7pm May-Sep, to 6pm Oct-Apr) can provide more information.

Malcesine

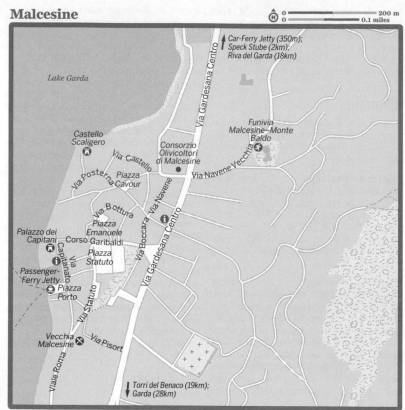

Lake Garda

Car-Ferry Jetty (350m);
Speck Stube (2km);
Riva del Garda (18km)

Via Gardesana Centro

Funivia Malcesine–Monte Baldo

Castello Scaligero

Via Castello

Consorzio Olivicoltori di Malcesine

Via Navene Vecchia

Piazza Cavour

Via Posterna

Via Navene

Via Bottura

Piazza Emanuele

Palazzo dei Capitani

Corso Garibaldi

Via Capitanato

Piazza Statuto

Via Boccara

Via Gardesana Centro

Passenger-Ferry Jetty

Piazza Porto

Via Statuto

Vecchia Malcesine

Via Pisort

Viale Roma

Torri del Benaco (19km);
Garda (28km)

beneath the olive trees, while kids and pets amuse themselves in the play area and park.

Vecchia Malcesine   GASTRONOMIC €€€
(☏045 740 04 69; www.vecchiamalcesine.com; Via Pisort 6; meals €45-100; ☉noon-2.30pm & 7-10.30pm Thu-Tue) Set far above the town with a bird's eye view over the rooftops and lake is this Michelin-starred restaurant. Dine out on the covered terrace on a six-course earth, lake or mountain menu paired with two local wines. Artful dishes include wild garlic and snail risotto, marinated prawns with gin and tonic, and dainty 'meteorites' of chocolate filled with Garda olive oil.

ℹ Information

Tourist Office (☏045 740 00 44; www.tourism. verona.it; Via Gardesana 238; ☉9.30am-12.30pm & 3-6pm Mon-Sat, 9.30am-12.30pm Sun) The main tourist office is set back from the lake beside the bus station on the main road through town. There's a second **tourist**

office (☏045 658 99 04; www.malcesinepiu. it; Via Capitanato 6) with the same hours that's convenient for visitors arriving by ferry.

Torri del Benaco

POP 2850

Picturesque Torri del Benaco is one of the most appealing stops on the eastern bank. Another 14th-century Scaligero castle, remodelled from the town's 10th-century walls, overlooks a pint-sized harbour filled with swaying yacht masts. Arranged around a single, cobbled street, Corso Dante, are ivy-draped, 16th-century *palazzi*, relics of a past prosperity when Torri del Benaco was a thriving financial centre, levying customs duties on lake traffic.

◎ Sights

Castello Scaligero   MUSEUM
(☏045 629 61 11; Viale Frateli Lavanda 2; adult/ child €3/1; ☉9.30am-12.30pm & 2.30-6pm Apr–

mid-Jun & mid-Sep–Oct, 9.30am-1pm & 4.30-7.30pm mid-Jun–mid-Sep) This atmospheric museum packs a wealth of history into the rough stone walls of a 14th-century castle. The fortification was built in 1338 as part of the Della Scala family's attempts to fend off the Venetian Republic. Exhibits scattered around the castle's rooms explore traditional industries such as fishing, olive oil production and lemon growing.

Most interesting is the *limonaie* (lemon glasshouse), the oldest on the lake, which dates from 1760 – it's crowded with fragrant citrus trees and windfalls litter the floor.

✖ Eating

Restaurant Gardesana   HOTEL RESTAURANT
(📞045 722 54 11; www.gardesana.eu; Piazza Calderini 20; pizzas €5-7, meals €35; ⊘noon-2.30pm & 7-10pm) The artfully lit arches of Hotel Gardesana's restaurant make a romantic spot for dinner as the sun sinks over a pink-tinged lake and the distant mountains beyond. The food is understated but excellent – try the perch in white wine with brioche croutons – although you may be distracted by the views.

ℹ Information

Tourist Office (📞045 722 51 20; Viale Fratelli Lavanda; ⊘9.30am-4.30pm Mon & Thu-Sat, 10am-3pm Sun)

Garda & Punta San Vigilio

POP 4000
Situated in the shade of the Rocca del Garda is the 10th-century fishing village that gave the lake its name. Sadly, the picturesque town is now cut through by the main perimeter road around the lake, making summer traffic overwhelming. Out of season, Garda's perfectly curved bay and fine shingle beaches make it a great lunch spot. Boat trips to Isola del Garda (p168) leave from Garda (in front of Hotel Miralago) on Wednesday morning.

◉ Sights

Punta di San Vigilio   BEACH
The leafy headland of Punta San Vigilio curls out into the lake 3km north of Garda. An avenue of cypress trees leads from the car park towards a gorgeous crescent of bay backed by olive groves. The privately owned **Parco Baia delle Sirene** (📞045 725 58 84; www.parcobaiadellesirene.it; Punta San Vigilio; adult/child €9/6, reduced admission after

4.30pm; ⊘10am-7pm Apr-May, 9.30am-8pm Jun-Aug; 🅿) has a beach with sun loungers beneath the trees; there's also a children's play area. Prices range from €5 to €9 per adult (€4 to €6 per child) per day between April and September, with reduced admission after 4.30pm. Outside of these months you can enjoy the beautiful location free of charge.

Alternatively, from the parking place walk north a short distance and head off down the paths to a couple of smaller, quieter public coves. The tiny headland is home to the plush Locanda San Vigilio, housed in the Villa Guarienti, designed by star Venetian achitect Sammicheli, and set within a formal Renaissance garden. Its excellent restaurant is at the foot of a cobbled lane, which winds to the lake from the end of the cypress avenue.

Market   MARKET
(Piazza Catullo) It's worth timing a visit to Garda to coincide with its exuberant Friday market, one of the biggest on the lake's eastern bank. Look out for Lake Garda lemons and jars of golden local honey.

✖ Eating

Bar-Taverna San Vigilio   GARDESANA €€
(📞045 725 51 90; Punta San Vigilio; mains €14-25; ⊘10am-5.30pm; 🅿) With tables strung out along Punta di San Vigilio's tiny crab-claw

---

DON'T MISS

HORSE TREKKING ON MONTE BALDO

For a totally unique experience, saddle up one of **Ranch Barlot's** (📞348 2313055; www.ranchbarlot.com; Località Porcini, Caprino Veronese; treks per person per day €110-150) sweet Appaloosa or Argentinian ponies and ride Western-style up Monte Baldo or through the lushly forested Adige valley. Treks from two- to eight-days are possible and prices include everything from your mount and guide to accommodation in mountain refuges. Back at the ranch you can take expert lessons in Western-style riding at the school watched by the farm's friendly deer herd.

You'll find the ranch 14.5km northeast of Garda, up a steep, narrow country road just beyond the village of Caprino Veronese.

harbour, this is one of the most atmospheric bars on the lake. The salad-based menu includes lobster, veal and prosciutto with mozzarella. The candle-lit buffets (Friday and Saturday from mid-June, booking required, €45) feature a gourmet spread accompanied by live music.

★ **Locanda San Vigilio** GASTRONOMIC €€€
(☑045 725 66 88; www.locanda-sanvigilio.it; Punta di San Vigilio; meals €80; ☺12.30-2pm & 7-10.30pm; P) In the restaurant of the Locanda San Vigilio the setting almost upstages the food. Dark beams, rustic tables, elegant tableware and crisp fabrics combine to bewitching effect. The sophisticated menu includes rabbit with wild fennel, lake-fish risotto, and quail with polenta and caramelised onion. For a special touch ask for a table in the open-sided loggia.

Bardolino

POP 6700

Prosperous Bardolino is a town in love with the grape. More than 70 vineyards and wine cellars grace the gentle hills that roll east from Bardolino's shores, many within DOC and the even stricter DOCG quality boundaries. They produce an impressive array of pink Chiaretto, ruby Classico, dry Superiore and young Novello.

Bardolino is at its most Bacchic during the **Festa dell'Uva e del Vino** in early October, when the town's waterfront fills with food and wine stands, as well as musicians and dancers. The tourist office stocks a map of local producers on the **Bardolino Strada del Vino** (www.stradadelbardolino.com). Otherwise, plan your visit on a Thursday in order to catch the weekly market.

Bardolino is also also a big spa town and the springboard for the ancient walled village of Lazise.

◉ Sights & Activities

Museo del Vino MUSEUM
(☑045 622 83 31; www.zeni.it; Via Costabella 9; ☺9am-1pm & 2.30-7pm Mar-Oct, 8.30am-12.30pm & 2.30-6.30pm Jan-Mar) FREE The Museo del Vino is set inside the Zeni winery on the outskirts of Bardolino. The museum visit includes free tastings of Zeni's red, white and rosé wines or you can pay to sample the more expensive vintages, including barrel-aged Amarone.

Museo dell'Olio d'Oliva MUSEUM
(☑045 622 90 47; www.museum.it; Via Peschiera 54, Cisano; ☺9am-12.30pm & 2.30-7pm Mon-Sat year-round, 9am-12.30pm Sun Mar-Dec) FREE In this slick museum, 2km south of Bardolino in Cisano, audiovisual displays chart the history of olive oil production on Lake Garda and explain how the crop is harvested today. Highlights include the huge mule-driven presses.

Aqualux Hotel Spa SPA
(☑045 622 99 99; www.aqualuxhotel.com; Via Europa Unita 24; adult Mon-Fri €28, Sat & Sun €32, child free; ☺9am-7pm Mar-Dec) Treat yourself to a day at Bardolino's four-star Aqualux spa where over 1000 sq metres, eight pools and a fitness room are dedicated to your well-being. A circulating whirlpool, hydromassage jets and warm waterfalls get the circulation going and double as fairground rides for older kids, while designated children's pools and play areas keep little ones amused.

Guerrieri Rizzardi WINE TASTING
(☑045 721 00 28; www.guerrieri-rizzardi.com; Via Verdi 4; tastings €15; ☺5pm Wed May-Oct) One of the most atmospheric ways to savour Bardolino's bitter cherry flavours is a tutored tasting at Guerrieri Rizzardi. After a tour of wine cellars full of cobweb-laced bottles, relaxed tastings take place in the ancient walled kitchen garden. Bookings required.

✖ Eating & Drinking

★ **Il Giardino delle Esperidi** GARDESE €€
(☑045 621 04 77; Via Goffredo Mameli 1; meals €35-50; ☺7-10pm Wed-Fri & Mon, noon-2.30pm & 7-10pm Sat & Sun) Bardolino's gourmets head for this intimate little osteria where sourcing local delicacies is a labour of love for its sommelier-owner. The intensely flavoured baked truffles with parmigiano reggiano (Parmesan) are legendary, and the highly seasonal menu may feature rarities like goose salami or guinea fowl salad.

Osteria Al Capitel VERONESE €€
(☑348 598 19 72; www.osterialcapitel.it; Via Gardesana Dell'Acqua 5; meals €20-30; ☺noon-2.30pm & 7-10pm) Despite its roadside situation, Al Capital features a lovely shady garden, a warm rustic interior and serves a commendable Veronese menu. Lake fish are well represented alongside Venetian and Veronese specialities such as sarde e soar (sardines in wine vinegar).

LAKE GARDA & AROUND LAKE GARDA EAST BANK

LAKE GARDA'S AMUSEMENT PARKS

For adrenalin-sparking rides and stunt shows, it's hard to beat northern Italy's Lake Garda. The lake's eastern bank is home to larger-than-life dinosaurs, pirate ships, roller coasters and a dolphinarium at the kid-oriented **Gardaland** (☑ 045 644 97 77; www.gardaland.it; Via Dema 4, Castelnuovo del Garda; adult/reduced €37.50/31; ☺ 10am-11pm mid-Jun–mid-Sep, 10am-6pm Apr–mid-Jun & last 2 weeks Sep, 10am-6pm Sat & Sun Oct, late Dec & early Jan).

To its north, **CanevaWorld** (☑ 045 696 99 00; www.canevaworld.it; Via Fossalta 1; adult/reduced €25/19) features an **aqua park** (☺ 10am-6pm mid-May–Jun & Sep, to 7pm Jul & Aug) and **medieval shows** (adult/reduced dinner & show €29/19; ☺ 2 shows daily May–mid-Sep) complete with medieval banquet. Within the same sprawling park is CanevaWorld's **Movieland Studios** (☺ 10am-6pm Easter–mid-Sep, to 6pm Sat & Sun Apr & Oct), featuring stunt-packed action shows. Opening times vary slightly throughout the year, so check the website for details. Cheaper deals and family tickets are also available online.

Both parks are just off the main lake road. Gardaland is 2km from Peschiera del Garda; CanevaWorld is a similar distance from Lazise. Free buses shuttle visitors to both parks from Peschiera del Garda train station.

La Bottega del Vino WINE BAR
(☑ 348 604 18 00; Piazza Matteotti 46; snacks €5, glass of wine from €2; ☺ 10.30am-2pm & 5pm-2am Tue-Sun) To experience some authentic Bardolino atmosphere head to this no-nonsense bar in the centre of town. Inside, walls are lined with bottles four deep and a stream of lively banter passes between locals and staff.

ℹ Information

Tourist Office (☑ 045 721 00 78; www.tourism.verona.it; Piazzale Aldo Moro; ☺ 9am-1pm & 2-6pm Mon-Sat, 10am-4pm Sun Sep-May, 9am-7pm late Jun-Aug) Operates a hotel booking services and provides tons of information on the surrounding wine region.

Lazise

The picturesque town of Lazise, some 5km south of Bardolino, preserves its encircling walls. On the harbour's south side (opposite the ferry jetty) the Romanesque Chiesa di San Nicolo sits beside Via Castello. This heads right, towards the five towers of the privately owned **Rocca Scaligera** – look out for the huge hole in the north wall of its main tower, made by a canon during the 15th-century wars between Venice and Milan. The town's south gate, known as the **Porta dei Leon** due to the bas-relief of the Venetian lion carved on it, is alongside.

Via Rocca continues east beside the weathered town walls, leading away from the main tourist drag and towards the town's eastern gate, which is dedicated to San Zeno; his images feature in a mosaic on the outer side. At the neighbouring neo-classical **Chiesa di San Martino** leave the walls temporarily, head a few steps down Via Chiesa, then right into Via Francesco Feliciano Scolari, through a couple of small squares and into Corso Cangrande, which again hugs the walls.

Lazise's final gate is **Porta Nuova**, 'new' in that it was built by the ruling Della Scala family in the 14th century. Look out for the mosaic of San Martino, complete with the castles of Lazise in the background. A few metres more leads back to the harbour. You could do the whole circumnavigation in 10 minutes flat, but picturesque alleyways, squares and shops provide plenty of appealing detours.

VERONA

POP 263,950

Shakespeare placed star-crossed Romeo Montague and Juliet Capulet in Verona for good reason: romance, drama and fatal family feuds have been the city's hallmark for centuries.

From the 3rd century BC, Verona was an important Roman trade centre, with ancient gates, a forum (now Piazza delle Erbe) and a grand amphitheatre – but Shakespearean tragedy came with the territory. In the Middle Ages, the city flourished under the fratricidal Della Scala family, who were as much energetic patrons of the arts as they were murderous tyrants. After Mastino della Scala (aka Scaligeri) lost re-election to Verona's

Verona

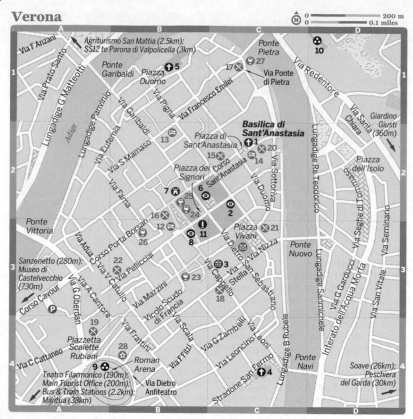

Verona

◎ Top Sights

◎ Sights

🛏 Sleeping

⊗ Eating

⊖ Drinking & Nightlife

⊛ Entertainment

commune in 1262, he claimed absolute control, until murdered by his rivals.

His son, Cangrande I (1308–28), went on to conquer Padua and Vicenza, with Dante, Petrarch and Giotto benefitting from the city's patronage. But the fratricidal rage of Cangrande II (1351–59) saw the family run out of town in 1387, leaving behind them a host of elaborate family tombs, the Arche Scaligere. Between 1405 and 1797, Venice took definitive control, before briefs spells under Napoleon and Austria, prior to the Unification of Italy in 1861.

◉ Sights

Many sights are closed, or only open for a half-day, on Monday. The excellent-value **VeronaCard** (www.veronacard.it; 2/5 days €15/20) covers free entry into the main attractions and churches. It's available at sights and tobacconists and includes free use of the town's buses.

Roman Arena ARCHAEOLOGICAL SITE
(⌨ 045 800 32 04; www.arena.it; Piazza Brà; opera tickets €21-220, adult/reduced €6/4.50, or with VeronaCard; ⊘ 8.30am-7.30pm Tue-Sun, 1.30-7.30pm Mon) This Roman-era arena, built of pink-tinged marble in the 1st century AD, survived a 12th-century earthquake to become Verona's legendary open-air opera house, with seating for 30,000 people. You can visit the arena year-round, though it's at its best during the June-to-August opera season. You'll find the **ticket office** (⌨ 045 800 51 51; Via Dietro Anfiteatro 6b) nearby.

Museo di Castelvecchio MUSEUM
(⌨ 045 806 26 11; Corso Castelvecchio 2; adult/reduced €6/4.50, or with VeronaCard; ⊘ 8.30am-7.30pm Tue-Sun, 1.30-7.30pm Mon) Bristling with battlements along the River Adige, Castelvecchio was built in the 1350s by Cangrande II. The fortress was so severely damaged by Napoleon and then WWII bombing that many feared it was beyond repair. But instead of erasing the past with restorations, Venetian architect Carlo Scarpa reinvented the building for a new museum, adding bridges over exposed foundations, filling gaping holes with glass panels and balancing a statue of Cangrande I above the courtyard on a concrete gangplank.

Scarpa's revived castle is now a fitting home for Verona's largest museum, with a diverse collection of medieval statuary, 14th-century frescoes, jewellery and paintings by Pisanello, Giovanni Bellini, Tiepolo and Veronese. In Room 17, look out for the clearly recognisable Verona landmarks of the Piazza di Signori and the Della Scala palaces in the painted *predella* (altarpiece) depicting the *Storie di Santa Barbara* (Trials of St Barbara).

Basilica di San Zeno Maggiore BASILICA
(www.chieseverona.it; Piazza San Zeno; adult/child €2.50/free, combined Verona church ticket €6 or with VeronaCard; ⊘ 8.30am-6pm Tue-Sat, 12.30-6pm Sun Mar-Oct, 10am-1pm & 1.30-5pm Tue-Sat, 12.30-5pm Sun Nov-Feb) A masterpiece of Romanesque architecture, the striped brick and stone basilica was built in honour of the city's patron saint. Enter through the flower-filled cloister into the nave, a vast space lined with 12th- to 15th-century frescoes, including Mary Magdalene modestly covered in her curtain of golden hair. Painstaking restoration has revived Mantegna's 1457–59 *Majesty of the Virgin* polyptych altarpiece, painted with such astonishing perspective and convincing textures that you actually believe there are garlands of fresh fruit hanging behind the Madonna's throne.

ROMEO & JULIET IN VERONA

Shakespeare had no idea what he'd start when he set his (heavily derivative) tale of star-crossed lovers in Verona, but the city has seized the commercial possibilities with both hands – everything from *osterie* and hotels to embroidered kitchen aprons get the R&J branding. While the play's depiction of feuding families has genuine provenance, the lead characters themselves are fictional. Undaunted, in the 1930s the authorities settled on a house in Via Cappello (think Capulet) as Juliet's and added a 14th-century-style balcony and a bronze statue of our heroine. You can squeeze through the crowds at this **Casa di Giulietta** (Juliet's House; ⌨ 045 803 43 03; Via Cappello 23; adult/reduced €6/4.50 or with VeronaCard; ⊘ 8.30am-7.30pm Tue-Sun, 1.30-7.30pm Mon) onto the balcony itself, or see the circus from the square below, a spot framed by a slew of scribbled love graffiti that doesn't compare well to the bard's sonnets.

An eerie **crypt** is located beneath the main altar, with faces carved into medieval capitals and St Zeno's corpse glowing in a transparent sarcophagus.

Chiesa di San Fermo
CHURCH

(www.chieseverona.it; Stradone San Fermo; combined Verona church ticket/single entry €6/2.50; ⊘10am-1pm & 1.30-5pm Tue-Sat, 1-5pm Sun) Chiesa di San Fermo is actually two churches in one: Franciscan monks raised the 13th-century Gothic church right over an original 11th-century Romanesque structure. Inside the main Gothic church, you'll notice a magnificent timber *carena di nave*, a ceiling reminiscent of an upturned boat's hull. In the right transept are 14th-century frescoes, including some fragments depicting episodes in the life of St Francis. Stairs from the cloister lead underground to the spare but atmospheric Romanesque church below.

Piazza delle Erbe
HISTORICAL SITE

(btwn Piazza XIV Novembre & Piazza dei Signori) Originally a Roman forum, Piazza delle Erbe is ringed with buzzing cafes and some of Verona's most sumptuous buildings, including the 18th-century baroque **Palazzo Maffei**, now a corporate headquarters, at its northern end. Separating Piazza delle Erbe from Piazza dei Signori is the monumental gate known as **Arco della Costa**, hung with a whale's rib that, according to legend, will fall on the first just person to walk beneath it. So far, it remains intact, despite visits by popes and kings.

On the northern side of Piazza dei Signori stands Verona's early-Renaissance **Loggia del Consiglio** (Piazza dei Signori), the 15th-century city council (not open to visitors). Through the archway at the far end are the open-air **Arche Scaligere** (Via Arche Scaligere; admission incl Torre dei Lamberti by lift/on foot €4/3; ⊘9.30am-7.30pm Tue-Sun, 1.45-7.30pm Mon Jun-Sep) – elaborate Gothic tombs of the Scaligeri family where murderers are interred next to the relatives they killed.

Dividing the two piazzas, the striped **Torre dei Lamberti** (☎045 927 30 27; adult/reduced €6/4.50; ⊘8.30am-7.30pm) rises a neck-craning 85m. Begun in the 12th century and finished in 1463 – too late to notice invading Venetians – this watchtower still offers panoramic views of the city and nearby mountains, which are snowcapped in winter. A lift whisks you up two-thirds of the way.

★**Basilica di Sant'Anastasia**
BASILICA

(www.chieseverona.it; Piazza di Sant'Anastasia; adult/reduced €6/2, or with VeronaCard; ⊘9am-6pm Tue-Sat, 1-6pm Sun Mar-Oct, 1.30-5pm Tue-Sat, 1-5pm Sun Nov-Feb) Dating from the 13th to 15th centuries, the Gothic Chiesa di Sant'Anastasia is Verona's largest basilica and a showcase for local art. The multitude of frescoes is overwhelming, but don't overlook Pisanello's storybook-quality fresco *St George Setting out to Free the Princess from the Dragon* in the Pisanelli Chapel, or the 1495 holy water font featuring a hunchback carved by Paolo Veronese's father, Gabriele Caliari.

Duomo
CATHEDRAL

(☎045 59 28 13; www.chieseverona.it; Piazza Duomo; adult/reduced €2.50/2, or with VeronaCard; ⊘10am-5.30pm Mon-Sat, 1.30-5.30pm Sun Mar-Oct, 10am-1pm & 1.30-5pm Tue-Sat, 1.30-5pm Sun Nov-Feb) Verona's 12th-century cathedral is a striking, striped Romanesque building, with polychrome reliefs and the bug-eyed statues of Charlemagne's paladins Roland and Oliver, crafted by medieval master Nicolò, on the west porch. Nothing about this sober facade hints at the extravagant interior, frescoed over during the 16th to 17th centuries with angels aloft amid *trompe l'oeil* architecture. At the left end of the nave is the **Cartolari-Nichesola Chapel**, designed by Renaissance master Jacopo Sansovino and featuring a vibrant Titian *Assumption*.

Teatro Romano e Museo Archeologico
ARCHAEOLOGICAL SITE

(☎045 800 03 60; Regaste Redentore 2; adult/reduced €4.50/3, or with VeronaCard; ⊘8.30am-7.30pm Tue-Sun, 1.30-7.30pm Mon) Just north of the historic centre you'll find a Roman theatre. Built in the 1st century BC, it is cunningly carved into the hillside at a strategic spot overlooking a bend in the river. Take the lift at the back of the theatre to the former convent above, which houses an engaging collection of Roman-era bronzes, beautifully carved friezes and brightly coloured mosaics.

★**Giardino Giusti**
GARDEN

(☎045 803 40 29; Via Giardino Giusti 2; adult/reduced €6/5; ⊘9am-8pm Apr-Sep, to 7pm Oct-Mar) Across the river from the historic centre, these lush gardens, considered a masterpiece of Renaissance landscaping, are well worth seeking out. Named after the noble family that has looked after them since opening them to the public in 1591, the gardens have lost none of their charm over the centuries. The vegetation is an Italianate mix of the sculpted and natural, graced by soaring cypresses, one of which the German poet Goethe immortalised in his travel writings. At the back of the garden, a short but steep climb rewards with sweeping views over the city.

Tours

Pagus Valpolicella   WINE TOURS
(045 751 44 28; www.pagusvalpolicella.net) If you don't want to bother renting a car, Pagus offers half- and full-day tours of Valpolicella and Soave, leaving regularly from Verona. Tours include visits to unusual rural sites, impromptu rambles, lunches in local restaurants and, of course, wine tastings. Tours can also be customised.

Festivals & Events

Verona's Opera Festival   OPERA
(045 800 51 51; www.arena.it; Via Dietro Anfiteatro 6) There are around 50 performances during Verona's opera season, featuring all the classics, particularly those of home-grown talent Giuseppe Verdi. Prices range from €18 to €21 on unreserved stone steps and €183 to €198 on the central gold seats. In winter months, concerts are held at the adjacent 18th-century Ente Lirico Arena.

Estate Teatrale Veronese   THEATRE, JAZZ
(www.estateteatraleveronese.it) One of the best ways to experience the hillside Roman amphitheatre is during Verona's summer festival, when a program of theatre (with a clear preference for Shakespeare and Goldoni), dance and jazz are performed at the archaeological site. Sit back in the gathering dusk and enjoy the show and the sparkling lights of the city below.

VinItaly   WINE FAIR
(www.vinitaly.com) Held in April, the country's largest wine expo is open only to food and wine professionals. The event includes tastings, presentations about winemaking and unmatched insight into the breadth and depth of Italian wines.

Eating

The historic centre teems with *osterie* and wine bars serving hearty country cooking with its emphasis on meats and thick sauces. For picnic supplies or pre-opera snacks, pick up fresh fruit and veg from market stalls in

PONTE PIETRA

At the northern edge of the city centre, this bridge is a quiet but remarkable testament to the Italians' love of their artistic heritage. Two of the bridge's arches date from the Roman Republican era in the 1st century BC, while the other three were replaced in the 13th century. The ancient bridge remained largely intact until 1945, when retreating German troops blew it up. Locals fished the fragments out of the river, and painstakingly rebuilt the bridge stone by stone in the 1950s.

Piazza delle Erbe. Nearby, **De Rossi** (045 800 24 89; Corso Porta Borsari 3) sells fresh bread and pastries. For meats and cheese, stroll 50m northeast to **Albertini** (045 803 10 74; Corso Sant'Anastasia 41).

Gelateria Ponte Pietra   GELATO €
(340 471 72 94; Via Ponte Pietra 23; 2.30-7.30pm Sep-Oct & Mar-May, to 10pm Jun-Aug, closed Nov-Feb) Impeccable gelato is made on the premises, with flavours like *bacio bianco* (white chocolate and hazelnut), candied orange with cinnamon, and *mille fiori* (cream with honey and bits of pollen gathered from local hillsides).

Pizzeria Du de Cope   PIZZERIA €
(045 59 55 62; www.pizzeriadudecope.it; Galleria Pellicciai 10; pizzas €6-12; noon-2pm & 7-11pm) This fashion-forward pizzeria manages to blend refinement with relaxed ease in its airy and vividly coloured dining space. You can peek over the counter and watch your pizza bubbling in the wood-fired oven, or ease up on the carbs with one of the high-quality salads.

Osteria Sottoriva   OSTERIA €
(045 801 43 23; Via Sottoriva 9a; meals €15-20; 11am-10.30pm Tue-Tue) The last of the historic *osterie* that once lined this riverside alley, Sottoriva still draws local crowds to rough-hewn tables under the arcade, with wine by the glass at fair prices, and traditional pork sausages and horse meatballs.

★ **Locanda 4 Cuochi**   MODERN ITALIAN €€
(045 803 03 11; www.locanda4cuochi.it; Via Alberto Mario 12; meals €30-40; 12.30-2.30pm & 7.30-10.30pm Wed-Sun, 7.30-10.30pm Tue) With its open kitchen, impeccable presentation

and four hot-shot chefs designing the seasonal menu and manning stations, you're right to expect great things from the *locanda*. Don't disregard the simpler dishes; some of them are genuinely inspired such as the mushroom *velouté* (a velvety soup made from stock, egg yolks and cream) on a bed of smoked potato, with such a flavour punch you'll wonder if you've ever truly tasted a mushroom before.

La Taverna di Via Stella   VERONESE €€
(☑045 800 80 08; www.tavernadiviastella.com; Via Stella 5c; meals €20-30; ☺11.30am-2.30pm & 6.30-11pm Thu-Sun & Tue, 11.30am-2.30pm Mon) Brush past the strings of garlic and haunches of prosciutto dangling over the deli bar and make your way into a dining room, decorated Tiepolo-style with rustic murals. This is the place you'll want to sample traditional Veronese dishes such as horse *pastissada* (stew), bigoli with duck *ragù* and DOP Lessinia cheeses from Monte Veronese.

★Pescheria I Masenini   SEAFOOD €€€
(☑045 929 80 15; www.imasenini.com; Piazzetta Pescheria 9; meals €50; ☺12.30-2pm Wed-Sun, 7.30-10pm Tue-Sun)   Located on the piazza where Verona's Roman fish market once held sway, Elio Rizzo is quietly serving up traditional Veronese dishes with an elegant, modern twist. Mullet tartare comes in a fresh tomato and basil puree, octopus is roasted with broccoli and anchovies, and scallops come gratinated with baked endives.

🍷 Drinking & Nightlife

Piazza delle Erbe is ringed with cafes and bars and fills with a fashionable drinking crowd come early evening. Most of them gather outside historic **Caffè Filippini** (☑045 800 45 49; Piazza delle Erbe 26; ☺4pm-2am Thu-Tue Sep-May, daily Jun-Aug) and hip **Casa Mazzanti Caffè** (☑045 800 32 17; www.casamazzanticaffe.it; Piazza delle Erbe 32; ☺8am-2am).

★Osteria del Bugiardo   WINE BAR
(☑045 59 18 69; Corso Porta Borsari 17a; ☺11am-11pm, to midnight Fri & Sat) On busy Corso Portoni Borsari, traffic converges at Bugiardo for glasses of upstanding Valpolicella bottled specifically for the *osteria*. Polenta and *sopressa* make worthy bar snacks for the powerhouse Amarone.

Antica Bottega del Vino   WINE BAR
(☑045 800 45 35; www.bottegavini.it; Vicolo Scudo di Francia 3; 3 tasting plates €27; ☺noon-11pm)

Wine is the primary consideration at this historic *enoteca* (wine bar) with beautiful wood panelling and backlit bottles of Valpolicella vintages. The sommelier will gladly recommend a worthy vintage for your lobster *crudo* (raw) salad or Amarone risotto – some of the best wines here are bottled specifically for the Bottega. Note they sometimes close in November and February.

Terrazza Bar al Ponte   BAR
(☑045 927 50 32; www.terrazzabaralponte.eu; Via Ponte di Pietra 26; ☺9am-2am) Join hip, young locals for a *spritz* beneath the giant chandelier in this retro-cool bar. Come early enough and you might even nab a table on the tiny terrace overlooking the river and the Ponte Pietra.

☆ Entertainment

Teatro Filarmonico   DANCE
(☑booking 045 800 51 51; www.arena.it; Via dei Mutilati 4; ☺opera & ballet season Nov-May) This 18th-century theatre, just south of Piazza Brà, has a program of ballet and opera that dominates proceedings (rub shoulders with the likes of Anne Boleyn, Macbeth and even Cinderella), but you might just as easily come across a jazz night.

ℹ Information

MEDICAL SERVICES
Guardia Medica (☑045 807 56 27; ☺8pm-8am) A locum doctor service; doctors usually come to you.
Ospedale Civile Maggiore (☑045 807 11 11; Piazzale Stefani 1) The main city hospital.

TOURIST INFORMATION
Tourist Office (www.tourism.verona.it) Main tourist office (☑045 806 86 80; www.tourism.verona.it; Via degli Alpini 9, Piazza Brà; ☺9am-7pm Mon-Sat, to 5pm Sun); Verona-Villafranca airport (☑045 861 91 63; www.tourism.verona.it; Verona-Villafranca airport; ☺10am-4pm Mon & Tue, to 5pm Wed-Sat); Train station (☑045 800 08 61; www.tourism.verona.it; Porta Nuova station; ☺9am-7pm Mon-Sat)

ℹ Getting There & Away

Verona-Villafranca airport (☑045 809 56 66; www.aeroportoverona.it) has direct links with Italian and European cities. It is located 12km outside the city and is linked to Verona by **ATV bus** (Azienda Trasporti Verona; ☑045 805 79 22; www.atv.verona.it). Shuttles to the airport run between 5.15am and 11pm (€6, 20 minutes, every 20 minutes from 6am to 11pm) and depart from Porta Nuova train station. A taxi costs €30.

ⓘ Getting Around

BUS

Verona's bus and main train stations are both at Porta Nuova. ATV bus numbers 11, 12, 13 and 51 (numbers 90, 92, 93 and 98 on Sunday) shuttle between the train station and Piazza Brà (hourly tickets €1.50). Buy tickets onboard (correct change required).

CAR

Verona is at the intersection of the A4 auto-strada between Milan and Venice (exit at Verona East) and the A22 between Modena and Trento (exit at Verona North). Southern Lake Garda is 30km away.

The centre of Verona is restricted to traffic. Useful car parks fringe the city, some as cheap as €5 a day. The nearest car park to the city centre is 400m south of Piazza Brà at Piazza Cittadella (per hour/day €2/14).

Tourists staying within the limited traffic zone (ZIL) need to obtain a permit from their hotel or B&B in order to park within the historic centre.

TRAIN

Verona's rail links include those with Milan (€11.55 to €21.50, 1½ to 2 hours depending on service), Mantua (€3.45, 40 minutes), Bologna, Florence and Rome. Regular services also connect with Austria, Switzerland and Germany. Lake Garda is only a short hop away, with hourly links to Desenzano del Garda (€3.80, 25 minutes).

AROUND VERONA

The Veneto produces more DOC (*denominazione di origine controllata*) quality-controlled wines than any other region in Italy, with the most productive vineyards – Soave and Valpolicella – within easy reach of Verona. Northwest, Valpolicella is celebrated for Amarone, an intense red made from partially dried grapes, while Soave delivers its crisp, namesake whites amid storybook medieval walls.

Valpolicella

The 'valley of many cellars,' from which Valpolicella (www.valpolicella.it) gets its name, has been in the business of wine production since the ancient Greeks introduced their *passito* technique (the use of partially dried grapes) to create the blockbuster flavours

we still enjoy in the region's Amarone and Recioto wines.

◉ Sights

Seven comuni compose the DOC quality-controlled area: Pescantina, San Pietro in Cariano, Negrar, Marano di Valpolicella, Fumane, Sant'Ambrogio di Valpolicella and Sant' Anna d'Alfaedo. For tourist information and biking and hiking itineraries, visit the **Valpolicella tourist office** (☑ 045 770 19 20; www.valpolicellaweb.it; Via Ingelheim 7; ☺ 9am-12.30pm Mon-Fri, 3-6pm Tue & Thu-Sun, 9.30am-12.30pm Sat & Sun).

Villa della Torre　　　　HISTORIC BUILDING
(www.villadellatorre.it; Via della Torre 25, Fumane; guided tour of the villa/with wine tasting/with lunch €10/30/60; Ⓟ) The jewel in the Allegrini crown, this historic villa dates back to the 16th century and was built by intellectual and humanist Giulio della Torre. Architects such as Giulio Romana (of Palazzo Te fame), Michele Sanmicheli and Bartolomeo Ridolfo all contributed to its construction, and now Allegrini wine tastings are held in the peristyle.

But don't let the wine and Ridolfo's magnificent gaping-mouthed, grotesque fireplaces distract you completely from the garden, which is the earliest example of a Mannerist garden in Italy: its multi-layered meaning and hell's-mouth grotto hinting at the powerful, primitive forces that lurk beneath the polished veneer of the villa.

✕ Eating

★L'Antica Osteria Le Piere　　OSTERIA €
(☑ 045 884 10 30; Via Nicolini 43, Mizzole; meals €15; ☺ noon-2.30pm & 7-10pm) In this large stone mansion in the village of Mizzole, self-trained chef Maurizio Poerio serves hearty three-course lunches to villagers and vineyard workers. Seasonal wild asparagus, wild game and smoky cured ham accompany a 250-bottle wine list.

★Osteria Numero Uno　　OSTERIA €€
(☑ 045 770 13 75; www.osterianumero1.com; Via Flaminio Pellegrini 2, Fumane; meals €15-30; ☺ noon-2.30pm & 7-10.30pm Thu-Mon, noon-2.30pm Tue) The archetypal *osteria* with a wooden bar packed with overall-clad vintners and delicious aromas wafting out of the kitchen. Glasses of valpolicella range from just €2 to €5 for a good Amarone. Pair them salty speck and belly-filling duck with wild garlic and gnocchi.

LAKE GARDA & AROUND VALPOLICELLA

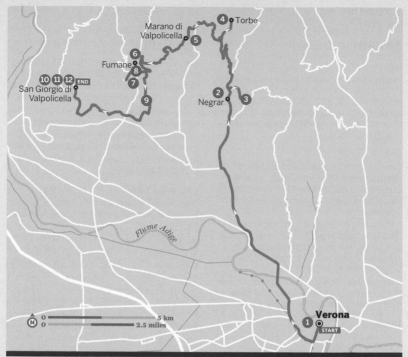

Driving Tour
Valpolicella

START VERONA
END SAN GIORGIO DI VALPOLICELLA
LENGTH 43KM; SIX HOURS

Wine has been made in these hills since Roman times and today Valpolicella produces some of Italy's most renowned reds. Situated within easy striking distance of Lake Garda's shores and an easy 20-minute drive from Verona, a tour of the wineries makes a pleasant day trip.

From ❶ **Verona**, pick up the SS12 highway northwest out of town. At the turning for Parona di Valpolicella a warren of narrow country lanes straggle north. Turn on to the Via Valpolicella (SP4) and drive into the hills towards ❷ **Negrar** and ❸ **Fratelli Vogadori** (p187). Here the eponymous brothers (*fratelli*) produce just 10,000 bottles of Valpolicella, Ripasso, Amarone and Recioto wines adhering to the strictest organic production techniques. If you choose to lunch at ❹ **Trattoria Caprini** (p187), 5km further

north in Torbe, you can sample them with homemade *sopressa* (salami).

From Torbe loop over the ridge along Via Scandola, through Valle and Fava and drop down to ❺ **Marano di Valpolicella**, with its large-domed Romanesque church. From here take the SP33b to ❻ **Fumane** and ❼ **Allegrini** (p187), where wine tastings are held in the 16th-century Villa della Torre. Locals flock to ❽ **Osteria Numero Uno** (p185) for superb *cucina casalinga* (home cooking). From Fumane detour to ❾ **Valentina Cubi** (p187) to sample the area's only certified organic wines.

Then head southwest first on SP33 and then SP4 to pretty ❿ **San Giorgio di Valpolicella** situated on a hilltop in the heart of Amarone country. Here you'll find the early Romanesque ⑪ **Pieve di San Giorgio** with frescos dating from the 11th century and a wonderfully crooked cloister. Book in to ⑫ **Trattoria dalla Rosa Alda** for a memorable evening meal before collapsing upstairs on an antique bed in one of the ten bedrooms.

TOP TIPPLES

Allegrini (☑ 045 683 20 11; www.allegrini.it; Via Giare 9/11, Fumane; tours €12-60; ⊙ by appointment; Ⓟ) Valpolicella aristocracy, the Allegrini family have been producing grand crus from corvinia and rondinella grapes since the 16th century.

Fratelli Vogadori (☑ 328 941 72 28; www.amaronevalpolicella.org; Via Vigolo 16, Negrar; ⊙ by appointment) 🌿 Producing just 10,000 bottles each year, the eponymous Vogadori brothers use organic methods and unusual native varieties such as Oseleta and Negrara.

★ **Massimago** (☑ 045 888 01 43; www.massimago.com; Via Giare 21, Mezzane di Sotto; ⊙ 9am-3.30pm Mon-Fri) Breaking the traditional mould, Camilla Chauvet concentrates on a limited range of lighter, more modern valpolicellas at her winery-come-relais, including a rosé and an unusual sparkling variety.

Valentina Cubi (☑ 045 770 18 06; www.valentinacubi.it; Località Casterna 60, Fumane; ⊙ by appointment) 🌿 This teacher-come-winemaker is blazing a trail with one of the few certified organic wineries in the region. The San Cero is one of few 'natural' valpolicellas, which includes no sulphates at all.

Trattoria Caprini TRATTORIA €€
(☑ 045 750 05 11; www.trattoriacaprini.it; Via Zanotti 9, Negrar; meals €25-30; ⊙ noon-2.30pm & 7-10pm Thu-Mon) A family-run trattoria in the centre of Negrar serving homemade *lasagnetta*, with hand-rolled pasta and a *ragù* of beef, tomato, porcini and finferli mushrooms. Downstairs, beside the fire of the old *pistoria* (bakery), you can sample some 200 Valpolicella labels.

Soave

From the reds of Valpolicella and on to the whites of Soave, a village and wine district some 30km east. The Della Scala family expanded Soave's medieval **Castello** (☑ 045 68 00 36; adult/child €4.50/3; ⊙ 9am-noon Tue-Sun year-round, 3-6.30pm Tue-Sun Apr–mid-Oct, 3-5pm Tue-Sun mid-Oct–Mar), a magnificent, soaring storybook ramble of crenellated walls, courtyards and a central tower. It's a short, signed walk from the village centre through gardens and vineyards.

You can sample some of Soave's lemon-zesty DOC Classico across from the old-town church at **Azienda Agricola Coffele** (☑ 045 768 00 07; www.coffele.it; Via Roma 5, Soave; ⊙ 9am-12.30pm & 2.30-6.30pm Mon-Sat & by appointment), alongside the more nutty, and faintly bubbly DOCG Recioto di Soave. The family also rents out rooms among their vineyards a few kilometres from town.

For more information on Soave's vineyards contact the local **tourist office** (☑ 045 768 06 48; www.prolocosoave.it; Via XXV Aprile 6, Soave) or check out www.stradadelsoave.com.

MANTUA

POP 46,550

As serene as the three lakes it sits beside, Mantua (Mantova) is home to sumptuous ducal palaces and a string of atmospheric, cobbled squares. Settled by the Etruscans in the 10th century, it has long been prosperous, the Latin poet Virgil was born just outside the modern town in 70 BC, Shakespeare's Romeo heard of Juliet's death here and Verdi set his tragic, 19th-century opera, *Rigoletto*, in its melancholy fog-bound streets.

Mantua's 400-year heyday, however, began in the 14th century when the city passed to the fast-living, art-loving Gonzaga dynasty, one of Italy's great Renaissance families. It rapidly became an important buffer state between the expansionist ambitions of Milan and Venice, and attracted leading lights such as writer Petrarch, Renaissance teacher Feltre and artists Mantegna, Rubens and Romano. Even now, and despite a worrying wobble after the earthquake of 2012, the city preserves its illustrious and antique history in its fabulous art and architecture. The golden days of 'La Gloriosa' ceased when Austria took control in 1708 and ruled (aside from the Napoleonic interlude in the late 1700s) until 1866, when Mantua joined Italy.

⊙ Sights

The tight-knit centre of Mantua is like an alfresco architectural museum – the interlocking piazze a series of medieval and Renaissance rooms, comprising from north to

Mantua

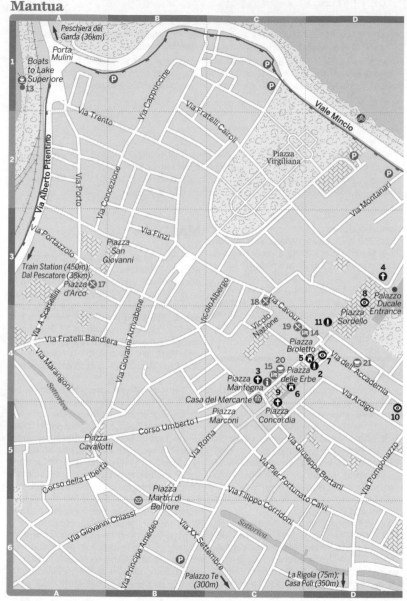

south: Piazza Sordello, Piazza Broletto, Piazza delle Erbe and Piazza Mantegna. All four fill with market stalls at the weekends and come early evening, waves of promenading Mantuans ebb and flow between them.

★ Palazzo Ducale

PALACE

(☎0376 22 48 32, bookings 041 241 18 97; www.mantovaducale.benicultura.it; Piazza Sordello 40; adult/reduced €6.50/3.25; ☺8.15am-7.15pm Tue-Sun) For over 300 years the enormous Palazzo Ducale was the seat of the Gonzaga – a

Mantua

adorned with over 2000 artworks. Sadly the collection, with the exception of the frescoes and gilt ceilings, was auctioned off by Vicenzo II to Charles I of England in 1627, just prior to the collapse of the family's fortunes in 1630.

A visit to the palace, for which you should budget several hours, takes you through just 40 of the palace's finest rooms. The biggest draw, however, is the mid-15th-century fresco by Mantegna, the **Camera degli Sposi** (Bridal Chamber). Executed between 1465 and 1474, the room, which is entirely painted, shows the Marquis, Lodovico, going about his courtly business with family and courtiers in tow. Painted naturalistically and with great attention to perspective, the arched walls appear like windows on the courtly world – looking up at the Duke's wife Barbara, you can even see the underside of her dress as if she's seated above you. Most playful of all though is the trompe l'œil oculus featuring bare-bottomed putti balancing precariously on a painted balcony, while

family of wealthy horse breeders who rose to power in the 14th century to become one of Italy's leading Renaissance families. At the height of their power, the palace's 500-plus rooms, three squares and 15 courtyards, occupying 34,000 square metres, were

---

ℹ️ MANTUA MUSEUM CARD

The Mantova Musei 8 Card (adult/reduced €17/14.45) covers free entry to all the main attractions, plus reductions to other regional museums such as those in Sabbioneta. The Mantova Musei 5 card (adult/reduced €15/12.75) covers the Palazzo Ducale, Palazzo Te and the Bibiena theatre. They are available at the tourist office.

---

smirking courtly pranksters appear ready to drop a large potted plant on gawping tourists below.

Other palace highlights worthy of attention are Domenico Morone's *Expulsion of the Bonacolsi* (1494), in Room 1, depicting the Gonzaga coup d'état of 1328, and Rubens' vast *Adoration of the Magi* in the **Sala degli Arcieri** (Room of Archers), which Napoleonic troops brutally dismembered in 1797. In Room 2, the **Sala del Pisanello**, fragments and fascinating preliminary sketches of Pisanello's frescoes of Arthurian knights remain, while the cream-and-gold **Galleria degli Specchi** (Gallery of Mirrors) is actually a complete 17th-century Austrian reworking – under the Gonzaga the gallery housed prized paintings, including Caravaggio's radical *Death of the Virgin* (which is now in the Louvre).

Look up for some of the palace's finest remaining features, its frescoed and gilt ceilings including, in Room 2, a labyrinth, prophetically predicting the capricious nature of good fortune. Below it, as if in illustration, are two portraits of Eleanor Gonzaga (1630–86), who rose to marry a Habsburg Emperor, and Vicenzo II (1594–1627), who lost the entire family fortune and one of Europe's most enviable art collections.

Last, but not least, in Rooms 34 to 36, the **Stanze degli Arazzi**, are some of the only original artworks commissioned by the family: nine 16th-century Flemish tapestries reproduced from Raphael's original designs for the Sistine Chapel. Woven in Brussels using the finest English wool, Indian silk and Cypriot gold and silver thread, they represent the cosmopolitan sophistication of the Gonzaga court at the height of its power.

Piazza Sordello   PIAZZA

Piazza Sordello is the oldest square, and was probably the location of the Etruscan town. The existing layout is thanks to the Gonza-

gas whose immense living quarters, fronted by the Palazzo Ducale, frame the east side. Sideways onto the palace, the towering, creamy **cathedral** (Piazza Sordello 16; ⏰ 7am-noon & 3-7pm) **FREE** sports three styles: a late-baroque facade (c 1750), a Gothic left side and a Romanesque belfry. At the square's southwest corner the flat-fronted, red-brick **Torre della Gabbia** (Cage Tower; Piazza Sordello) dates from the 13th century. Look out for the *gabbia* (cage) dangling from one side – people who'd offended the authorities were incarcerated in it.

Piazza Broletto   PIAZZA

Once home to the city's highest official and adorned with a coat of arms, the **Palazzo del Podestà** is located in Piazza Broletto. The square also features a white stone shrine dedicated to Virgil, depicting the poet sitting at his desk. The brick arch to the left, the **Arengario**, bears evidence of more medieval Mantuan punishments. Prisoners were suspended from the iron rings in the ceiling and the ropes pulled taught, a torture known as *squassi di corda*.

Piazza delle Erbe   PIAZZA

Once the location of the town's vegetable market, Piazza delle Erbe is Mantua's most lively piazza. Its 13th-century **Palazzo della Ragione** (Town Hall; ☎ 0376 22 00 97; Piazza delle Erbe; ⏰ 10am-1pm & 4-7pm Tue-Sun during temporary exhibitions) **FREE** sports a 15th-century clock tower at its south end which marks the phases of the moon and signs of the zodiac.

Mantua's oldest church, the 11th-century **Rotonda di San Lorenzo** (☎ 0376 32 22 97; Piazza delle Erbe; ⏰ 10am-1pm & 3-6pm Mon-Fri, 10am-6pm Sat & Sun) **FREE**, sits just below street level alongside Palazzo della Ragione. Narrowly missing destruction during the frenetic Gonzaga refurbishment of the town, this weathered, red-brick sanctuary once sat within the heart of the Jewish ghetto and its walls are still decorated with the shadowy remains of 12th- and 13th-century frescoes.

Basilica di Sant'Andrea   BASILICA

(☎ 0376 32 85 04; Piazza Andrea Mantegna; ⏰ 8am-noon & 3-7pm Mon-Fri, 10.30am-noon & 3-6pm Sat, 11.45am-12.15pm & 3-6pm Sun) This towering basilica safeguards the golden vessels said to hold earth soaked by the blood of Christ. Longinus, the Roman soldier who speared Christ on the cross, is said to have scooped up the earth and buried it in Mantua after leaving Palestine. Today, these containers rest beneath a marble octagon in front of the altar and are paraded around Mantua in a grand procession on Good Friday.

Ludovico II Gonzaga commissioned Leon Battista Alberti to design the basilica in 1472. Its vast, arched interior is free from pillars and has just one sweeping central aisle, which is dotted with frescoes, gilded ceiling bosses and columns cleverly painted to look like carved stone.

The first chapel on the left contains the tomb of Andrea Mantegna, the man responsible for the splendours in the Palazzo Ducale's *Camera degli Sposi*. The chapel is beautifully lit and also contains a painting of the Holy Family and John the Baptist, attributed to Mantegna and his school.

⭐ **Palazzo Te**   PALACE
(🖉 0376 32 32 66; www.palazzote.it; Viale Te; adult/reduced €8/5; ☉ 1-6pm Mon, 9am-6pm Tue-Sun; Ⓟ) Hardly more modest in scale than the Palazzo Ducale, Frederico II's (1500–1540) suburban villa where he escaped for love trysts with his mistress Isabella Boschetti, is decorated in playboy style with stunning frescoes, playful motifs and encoded symbols. A Renaissance pleasure-dome, it is the finest work of star architect Giulio Romano, whose sumptuous Mannerist scheme fills the palace with fanciful flights of imagination.

Having escaped a Roman prison sentence for designing pornographic prints, Romano, Raphael's most gifted student, was the perfect choice for the commission, which represents one of the great Mannerist buildings in Italy. Using the trompe l'œil technique, he eschewed the cool classicism of the past in favour of wildly distorted perspectives, a pastel colour palette and esoteric symbols.

The second room, the **Camera delle Imprese** (Room of the Devices), sets the scene with a number of key symbols: the salamander, the symbol of Federico, the four eagles of the Gonzaga standard and Mt Olympus, the symbol of Charles V, Holy Roman Emperor, from whom the Gonzaga received their titles and in whose name they ruled Mantua. The purpose of Renaissance devices was to encode messages, mottos and virtues so that visitors to the palace could 'read' where loyalties lay and navigate political power structures. Federico's device, the salamander, is accompanied by the quote: 'quod hic deest, me torquet' (what you lack, torments me), alluding to his notoriously

passionate nature when compared to the cold-blooded salamander.

The culmination of the symbolic narrative, however, comes together masterfully in the **Camera dei Giganti** (Chamber of the Giants), a domed room where frescoes cover every inch of wall with towering figures of the rebellious giants (disloyal subjects) clawing their way up Mt Olympus (symbol of Charles V) only to be laid low by Jupiter's (Charles') thunderbolt. The effect is spectacular. As the viewer you are both spectator and participant, standing in the centre of the scene, the worried faces of Olympian gods stare down at you, would-be presumptuous giant or loyal subject?

The symbolism was not lost on Emperor Charles V who visited the palace in 1530 and afterwards raised Federico up from a marquis to a duke.

Teatro Bibiena   THEATRE
(🖉 0376 32 76 53; www.societadellamusica.it; Via dell'Accademia 47; adult/child €2/1.20; ☉ 9.30am-12.30pm & 3-6pm Tue-Sun) If ever a theatre was set to upstage the actors, it's the 18th-century Teatro Bibiena. Its design is highly unusual: a bell-shaped four storeys of intimate, stucco balconies arranged around curving walls. The theatre's shape was specifically intended to allow its patrons to be seen – balconies even fill the wall behind the stage. Just a few weeks after it opened in 1769, the theatre hosted a concert by the 14-year-old Wolfgang Amadeus Mozart.

🏃 Activities

Lakefront Promenades   WALKING
On a sunny day the people of Mantua head for the waterfront, where grassy banks are thronged with fishermen and picnicking families. Each of the three lakes has a distinct style. The shore of **Lake Mezzo**, complete with the child-friendly gadgets of the **Parco dell Scienza** (outdoor science park), is the most crowded; the quieter path beside **Lake Superiore** meanders amid reed beds and wading birds; while the shore of **Lake Inferiore** brings broad views.

Cycle Routes   CYCLING
(www.parcodelmincio.it) The tourist office stocks the excellent, English-language booklet, *Mantova in Bici*, detailing cycling itineraries around the lakes, along the Po river and in the Parco del Mincio (www.parcodelmincio.it). The shortest route (a couple of hours) takes cyclists around Lago Superiore to the

DAL PESCATORE

Petals of egg pasta frame slices of guinea fowl caramelised in honey saffron while silky tortellini are stuffed to bursting with pumpkin, nutmeg, cinnamon and candied mostarda – you can practically eat the Mantuan countryside in Nadia Santini's internationally acclaimed restaurant **Dal Pescatore** (📞0376 72 30 01; www.dalpescatore.com; Località Runate, Canneto sull'Oglio; meals €150-250; ⏱noon-4pm & 7.30pm-late Thu-Sun, 7.30pm-late Wed; 🅿🍴). What's even more surprising is that Italy's best female chef (2013) is entirely self-taught and has only ever cooked in this singular restaurant, originally the modest, family trattoria of her husband's family. Beneath the tutelage of her now 84-year-old mother-in-law, who still cooks in the kitchen, Nadia learnt to cook Mantuan cuisine deftly and creatively – venison comes soaked in a cabernet and blueberry sauce, lake eel is pickled with ginger and served with osetra caviar. Despite a background in food science the food isn't remotely high-tech, but rather quietly brilliant, focusing on the essentials and balancing simplicity with the very finest natural produce.

The restaurant is located 40km west of Mantua in a green glade beside the Oglio river. Nearby, **9 Muse B&B** (📞335 800 76 01; www.9muse.it; Via Giordano Bruno 42/a, Canneto sull'Oglio; s/d €45/75; 🅿🍴@) provides elegant and charming accommodation.

Santuario di Santa Maria delle Grazie, while longer routes meander south to the abbey of San Benedetto Po and Gonzaga town of Sabbioneta Hire bikes from **La Rigola** (📞0376 36 66 77; Via Trieste 7; per day from €10).

👣 Tours

For more extended exploration of the Mincio and Po rivers, Avemaria (p206) is a barging hotel offering four-day or week-long cultural cruises complete with onboard bikes.

Boat Tours   BOAT TOUR

Short one- to two-hour tours on Lake Superiore are offered by two competitor companies **Motonavi Andes** (📞0376 36 08 70; www.motonaviandes.it; Via San Giorgio 2) and **Navi Andes** (📞0376 32 45 06; www.naviandes.com; Lago di Mezzo jetty) between April and October (Monday to Saturday €9, Sunday €10, 1½ hours). They skirt lotus flowers, reed beds and heron roosts, and provides great city views.

Both companies also offer longer trips to San Benedetto Po (one-way/return Monday to Saturday €13.50/19, Sunday €15.50/20; 2½ hours one-way) through the Mincio park. The trip leaves Mantua from the jetty on Lungolago dei Gonzaga.

🍴 Eating

With its pumpkin ravioli and apple relish, spiced pork risotto and cinnamon-flavoured *agnoli* (ravioli stuffed with capon, cinnamon and cloves), Mantua has a marvellous culinary tradition dating back to the Renaissance when sweet and sour

flavours were *de rigeur*. Pumpkin and pork are the order of the day, unsurprisingly given that for every Mantuan there are at least eight pigs in the province. Frogs-leg pasta, rabbit and duck *ragù* and soft-stewed donkey in red wine are designed for melancholy Mantuan winters. Bakeries stock wonderful *torta di tagliatelle* (an unusual blend of crunchy tagliatelle, sugar and almonds) and *sbrisolona* (a hard biscuit with almonds).

Zapparoli   DELICATESSEN €

(📞0376 32 33 45; Via Cavour 49; ⏱8.15am-1pm & 4.30-7.30pm Tue-Sun, 8.15am-1pm Mon) A one-stop-shop for all your picnic needs. The counters of this deli are crammed with delights, from the mounds of marinated olives, oil-soaked artichokes and local cheese to salamis, roast chickens and hanging hams.

Osteria delle Quattro Tette   MANTUAN €

(📞0376 32 94 78; Vicolo Nazione 4; meals €10-15; ⏱12.30-2.30pm Mon-Sat) Take a pew at rough-hewn wooden tables beneath echoing barrel-vaulted ceilings and order up pumpkin pancakes, pike in sweet salsa or *risotto alla pilota* (risotto with spiced sausage). It is spartan, rustic and extremely well priced, which is why half of Mantua is in here at lunch time.

Fragoletta Antica   MANTUAN €€

(📞0376 32 33 00; www.fragoletta.it; Piazza Arche 5; meals €35; ⏱noon-3pm & 7-11.30pm Tue-Sun; 🍴) Wooden chairs scrape against the tiled floor as diners eagerly tuck into Slow

Food–accredited *culatello di Zibello* (lard) at this friendly local trattoria. Other Mantuan specials such as *risotto alla pilota* (rice seasoned with sausage meat) and perfectly seasoned steaks feature on the menu. Dine in the back room with its bright homemade art amid stacks of wine crates.

★ Il Cigno
MANTUAN €€€

(☑ 0376 32 71 01; www.lesoste.it; Piazza d'Arco 1; meals €55-65; ⊙12.30-2.30pm & 7-11pm Wed-Sun, closed Aug) The building is as beautiful as the food: a lemon-yellow facade dotted with faded olive-green shutters, and dining rooms adorned with Venetian glassware. Inside Mantua's gourmets tuck into delicately steamed risotto with spring greens, poached cod with polenta or gamey guinea fowl with spicy Mantuan *mostardo* (relish).

🍷 Drinking

Bar Caravatti
CAFE, BAR

(☑ 0376 32 78 26; Portici Broletto 16; ⊙7am-8.30pm) All of Mantua passes through Caravatti at some point during the day for coffee, *spritz* or Signor Caravatti's 19th-century *aperitif* of aromatic bitters and wine.

Le Pupitre
CAFE, BAR

(Via dell' Accademia 18; snacks €5-10; ⊙8am-10pm) Come early if you want to stand any chance of elbowing your way through the cool crowd to Pupitre's bountiful *aperitivo* bar laden with punchy salami snacks, hot *pizzette*, *frittate* and sweet Mantuan-style salsa dips.

ℹ Information

Tourist Office (☑ 0376 43 24 32; www.turismo.mantova.it; Piazza Mantegna 6; ⊙9am-1.30pm & 2.30-6pm Mon-Fri, 10am-6pm Sat & Sun)

ℹ Getting There & Around

BUS
APAM (☑ 0376 230346; www.apam.it; ⊙ticket office 7.30am-12.45pm & 3-5.45pm Thu-Tue, 7.30am-12.45pm Wed & Sat) operates city-wide buses, although they're hardly necessary given that it takes only about 20 mintues to walk across town.

At the weekend, a special service leaves from outside Palazzo Ducale to the Gonzaga's smaller country fiefdom of Sabbioneta (€8 return, one hour, 3pm Sat, 9am & 1.15pm Sun).

A new express service also operates from Piazza Sordello and Piazza don Leoni for Verona airport (adult/child €5/free, 45 minutes, four daily).

CAR
Mantua is just west of the A22 Modena–Verona–Trento autostrada; the best exit is Mantua North. The city is 45km south of Verona and around 50km south of Lake Garda.

Much of old Mantua is a traffic-restricted zone. There is free parking along the city's northern lake road (Viale Mincio) and to the south of the city along Viale Isonzo, near Palazzo Te.

TRAIN
Direct trains link Mantua with Verona (€3.45, one hour, hourly) and Milan (€11.05, two hours, every two hours). The trip to Lake Garda's Peschiera del Garda train station (€5.40, 1½ hours, hourly) involves a change in Verona.

Accommodation

Best Places to Sleep

➡ Brera Apartments (p195)

➡ Grand Hotel des Iles Borromees (p197)

➡ Da Vittorio (p202)

Best Agriturismi

➡ Agriturismo Casa Clelia (p201)

➡ Agriturismo Munt de Volt (p199)

➡ Agriturismo San Mattia (p205)

Best for Romance

➡ Grand Hotel Majestic (p197)

➡ Hotel Leon d'Oro (p198)

➡ Locanda San Vigilio (p205)

Where to Stay

Accommodation around the Italian Lakes ranges from mountain huts and grand lakeside villas to fashion-conscious design digs in Milan. Given the popularity of the region, genuine value can be hard to come by so in this chapter we've focused on independent accommodation options that offer charm, good value and a heartfelt welcome.

Although it is always preferable to stay as close to key sights as possible, striking out into the countryside offers its own rewards and some of the regions best experiences in small *locande* (inns) and charming *agriturismi* (farmstays), which often offer a range of family-friendly activities, such as a swimming pool, horse riding and bikes. They proliferate in the hillsides and mountains back from the lakes and in wine regions such as the Valtenesi, Franciacorta and Valpolicella. B&Bs are an increasingly popular alternative to hotels in regional towns, although there is a dearth of quality options in Milan.

For those looking for a base for a week or two, there is an enormous variety of apartments and villas around the lakes. Campgrounds, too, can be a good option for families, particularly around Lake Garda, where some boast stunning locations and offer large resort-style facilities.

Pricing

The price indicators refer to the cost of a double room with private bathroom and include breakfast unless otherwise noted. Where half board (breakfast and dinner) is included, this is mentioned in the price. All hotels in the region now apply a tourist tax to overnight stays (€0.60 to €3.50 per person per night).

	ITALY	SWITZERLAND
€	less than €100	less than Sfr120
€€	€100 to €220	Sfr120 to Sfr300
€€€	more than €220	more than Sfr300

MILAN

The tourist office distributes *Milano Hotels,* a free annual listings guide to Milan's 350 plus hotels. Good value is difficult to come by in most budget ranges, and downright impossible during large fairs. That said, booking ahead and comparison-shopping online for 'special rates' can result in unexpected deals.

Don't forget to factor in location. For those visiting during Expo 2015 proximity to the red line (MM1) will put you in prime position.

Ostello Burigozzo 11   HOSTEL €

(Map p46; ☑02 5831 4675; www.ostelloburigoz-zo11.com; Via Burigozzo 11; dm/s/d €21/50/80; P @ 훅; ⊕9, 29, 30) A spartan but spotless hostel decked out with a dash of design brio. Bunks are in single-sex dorms, each with their own shower; doubles, triples and quads are also available. There's a communal TV room, laundry and large kitchen.

Euro Hotel   HOTEL €

(Map p46; ☑02 3040 4010; www.eurohotelmilano. it; Via Giuseppe Sirtori 24; d €75-120; P ✽ @ 훅; Ⓜ Porta Venezia) This large, well-serviced hotel near Porta Venezia offers a huge variety of comfortable, modern rooms and efficient, friendly service. Given its competitive price point it is popular with groups and fills up fast during events and fairs. Book ahead online for the best rates and deals.

SEASON MATTERS

Around the lakes prices can fluctuate considerably depending on season, with Easter, summer and the Christmas/New Year period being the typical peak tourist times. Indeed, many lakeside hotels only open from Easter to October, going into hibernation once the colder weather sets in.

Milan is a case of its own, with price variations linked to the trade-fair and events calendar – the bigger the fair, the higher the price and the greater degree of difficulty in locating a room. During the Salone del Mobile prices can increase 200%. Likewise, Verona's summer opera festival and large-scale concerts put pressure on prices and availability. August, though, is low season for Milan as everyone escapes to the lakes for annual holidays.

★ Brera Apartments   APARTMENT €€

(Map p50; ☑02 3655 5708; www.breraapartments. com; Via San Fermo 1; d apt €110-200; ✽ @ 훅; Ⓜ Moscova, Lanza) These six super stylish apartments dotted around Brera, Moscova and Montenapoleone are decorated with the design-conscious in mind: sleek wooden floors, hanging mezzanines, design fixtures and fittings, and a soothing white and dove-grey palette. Kitchens are small but well equipped, and all the apartments come with satellite TV, a DVD and CD collection, and iPod docks. Children over four years and additional adults cost €50 to €100 per day.

★ Maison Borella   BOUTIQUE HOTEL €€

(Map p46; ☑02 5810 9114; www.hotelmaison-borella.com; Alzaia Naviglio Grande 8; d €140-220; ✽ @ 훅; Ⓜ Porta Genova) With geranium-clad balconies overhanging the Naviglio Grande and striking black, white and grey decor and pinstriped bedlinen, Maison Borella brings a much-needed touch of class to Navigli and is, amazingly, the first canalside hotel. The hotel is a converted house arranged around an internal courtyard, while the historic rooms feature parquet floors, beamed ceilings and elegant *boiserie* (sculpted panelling).

Guests staying in the suites have access to the Maison Borella Club, which offers a free shuttle to Monza, San Siro tickets and a personal shopper for fashion show attendees.

Foresteria Monforte   B&B €€

(Map p46; ☑02 7631 8516; www.foresteriamonforte.it; Piazza del Tricolore 2; d €150-250; ✽ @ 훅; Ⓜ San Babila) With Philippe Starck chairs, flat-screen TVs and a communal kitchen, the three classy rooms in this upmarket B&B are just a short walk from the Duomo. The ceilings are high, the rooms are filled with natural light and the bathrooms are dizzyingly contemporary.

Hotel Gran Duca di York   HOTEL €€

(Map p50; ☑02 87 48 63; www.ducadiyork.com; Via Moneta 1; d €160-205; ✽ @ 훅; Ⓜ Duomo) This lemon-yellow palazzo, literally a stone's throw from the Duomo, was once a residence for scholars working in the nearby Ambrosiana library. Now it offers smiley service and 33 small, breezy rooms (some with balconies) with plump beds and neat, marble bathrooms. Our advice is to skip the rather dull breakfast and opt for five-star pastries at Princi a few blocks away.

Tara Verde
B&B €€

(☑ 02 3653 4959; www.taraverde.it; Via Delleani 22; d €110-120; ❋ @ ☜; Ⓜ De Angeli) This painted palazzo in a quiet residential street offers three exotically coloured rooms in rag-rolled lime green, lemon yellow and raspberry red. Owner Roberta has a designer's eye for details with decor ranging from antique brass lamps and ethnic coverlets to bright Moroccan tiles in the bathrooms. Other thoughtful touches are luggage racks, orthopaedic mattresses and complimentary mini-bars.

Antica Locanda Leonardo
HOTEL €€

(Map p46; ☑ 02 4801 4197; www.anticalocandaleonardo.com; Corso Magenta 78; s €80-120, d €90-200; ❋ @ ☜; Ⓜ Conciliazione) Rooms here exude homey comfort, from the period furniture and parquet floors to the plush drapes. Take breakfast in the quiet, scented interior garden of this 19th-century residence.

Bulgari Hotel
BOUTIQUE HOTEL €€€

(Map p50; ☑ 02 805 80 51; www.bulgarihotels.com; Via Privata Fratelli Gabba 7b; d €590-750; Ⓟ ❋ @ ☜ ≋; Ⓜ Montenapoleone) Just as the adjacent Botanical Gardens were used to develop medicines, the first Bulgari hotel serves up a rejuvenating tonic, with its cool, calming decor, peaceful gardens and divine spa. Located on a private road behind Milan's Quadrilatero d'Oro fashion district, this hotel was exquisitely designed down to the last detail by Antonio Citterio, best known for his work for furniture company B&B Italia.

The result is a wonder of wood, marble and granite that defines Milano cool and exudes warmth at the same time. There's an excellent gym and spa with a gorgeous lap pool, but the best bit is just hanging out in the gardens and lounge areas.

Hotel Principe di Savoia
HISTORIC HOTEL €€€

(Map p46; ☑ 02 623 01; www.hotelprincipedisavoia.com; Piazza della Repubblica 17; d €290-700; Ⓟ ❋ @ ☜ ≋; Ⓜ Repubblica) Every major city in the world needs an unrepentantly ostentatious hotel and this is Milan's, attracting a who's who of movers and shakers and an international celebrity clientele. Why? Because despite its location – it's a cab ride away from major sites – this is an exquisite property where everything, from the beautiful chandeliers in the lobby to the writing desks in the suites, is a collectable.

Service, too, is exemplary with room service arriving on linen covered trolleys, olive oil pressed exclusively for hotel guests and a spa staffed by the city's best beauticians.

Antica Locanda dei Mercanti
B&B €€€

(Map p50; ☑ 02 805 40 80; www.locanda.it; Via San Tomaso 6; d €195-240, ste €260-650; ❋ @ ☜; Ⓜ Cairoli) This B&B doesn't have a sign out the front, making it feel like you're visiting a friend's place. What it does have is lots of character in its 14 individually decorated, flower-filled rooms. While the Classic and Master rooms are fine, the Terrace rooms (each with their own private balcony) are the pick of a lovely bunch.

Next door, at number 8, **Alle Meraviglie** (Map p50; ☑ 02 805 10 23; www.allemeraviglie.it; Via San Tomaso 6; d €225-295; Ⓟ ❋ ☜) is run by the same people.

Oltrepò Pavese

Villa I Due Padroni
APARTMENT €

(☑ 0385 9 92 55; www.duepadroni.it; Frazione Spagna 9, Montecalvo Versiggia; d €70-95, apt €595-975 per week; @ ☜ ≋) This sunny, two-bedroom apartment in Nico and Stef's hilltop villa is the perfect base for exploring Oltrepò Pavese wine country. Enjoy their great company along with your own private terrace, a pool, cookery classes and long lazy walks and cycle rides.

LAKE MAGGIORE & AROUND

Lake Maggiore has a reputation for glamour, for the kind of grand belle époque hotels on the lakeshore that have drawn Europe's rich and famous for a century. Many of these hotels remain, but there are plenty of enticing midrange options to even things out a little.

Lake Maggiore West Bank

Hotel Elena
HOTEL €

(Map p77; ☑ 0323 3 10 43; www.hotelelena.com; Piazza Cadorna 15, Stresa; s/d €60/85; Ⓟ) Adjoining a cafe, the old-fashioned Elena is slap-bang on Stresa's central pedestrian square. Wheelchair access is possible, and all of Elena's comfortable rooms, with parquet floors, have a balcony, many overlooking the square.

Hotel Belvedere
HOTEL €

(☑0323 50 32 02; www.pallanzahotels.com; Viale Magnolie 6, Verbania Pallanza; d without/with lake view from €99/110; ❄☎) Set in a lovely waterfront, 19th-century building right next to the Verbania Pallanza boat landing, the Belvedere is a fine Lake Maggiore base. The rooms are well-sized, come with free wi-fi, and service is at once friendly and professional. It's worth paying extra for a room with a view. It also has a couple of other hotels nearby that set a similar standard.

★Hotel Pironi
HOTEL €€

(☑0323 7 06 24; www.pironihotel.it; Via Marconi 35, Cannobio; s €110-120, d €150-190; P☎) In a 15th-century mini-monastery (later home of the noble Pironi family) high in Cannobio's cobbled maze, Hotel Pironi is a charming choice. Behind its thick-set stone walls lurks a beautifully restored excursion into the past, with antiques sprinkled about, frescoed vaults, exposed timber beams, stairs climbing off in odd directions, a frescoed breakfast room and an assortment of tastefully decorated rooms, some with lake views.

Hotel Cannobio
HOTEL €€€

(☑0323 73 96 39; www.hotelcannobio.com; Piazza Vittorio Emanuele III 6, Cannobio; s €120-145, d €195-210, ste €240-285; ☎) This four-star place sits at the southern end of the waterfront with excellent views from many rooms. The rooms have a mock-antique style with heraldic symbols adorning the bedheads, strong colour schemes and wood furnishings

Grand Hotel Majestic
LUXURY HOTEL €€€

(☑0323 50 97 11; www.grandhotelmajestic.it; Via Vittorio Veneto 32, Verbania Pallanza; r without/with lake view from €164/231; P❄@☎⊠) With its private boat landing, private little beach, wellness centre, bars and restaurants, you may never feel inclined to venture out into the world. Even some of the smaller, cheaper rooms have lake glimpses, while many of the more generously appointed rooms and suites, draped in fine textiles and equipped with marble-faced bathrooms, have balconies looking straight over the lake.

Grand Hotel des Iles Borromees
HISTORIC HOTEL €€€

(Map p77; ☑0323 93 89 38; www.borromees.it; Corso Umberto I 67; s €378-451, d €479-597; P❄@☎⊠) One of Lake Maggiore's most celebrated hotels (it makes an appearance in Ernest Hemingway's *A Farewell to Arms*), this place exudes an extravagant, old-world charm with luxurious rooms, attentive service and and a front-row perch overlooking the lake.

Borromean Islands

Albergo Ristorante Belvedere
HOTEL €€

(☑0323 3 22 92; www.belvedere-isolapescatori.it; Isola Superiore; r €99-199; ❄) Perfectly located at the serene northeast end of the island, this cheerful little hotel-restaurant has eight modern, comfortable rooms, most with a balcony or terrace offering lake and mountain views. The restaurant has two pleasant garden areas. It's open mid-March to October.

Albergo Verbano
HOTEL €€

(☑0323 3 04 08; www.hotelverbano.it; Via Ugo Ara 2, Isola Superiore; s €100-120, d €150-185; ☎) If you want to stay on the Isola Superiore, and doing so is one of Lake Maggiore's most memorable experiences as it allows you to enjoy the island without the crowds, the romantic Albergo Verbano has a dozen rooms with wrought-iron bedsteads, and half- and full-board options. Most of the rooms have views towards Isola Bella or Isola Madre. The hotel will send out its own boat free for guests once the ferries have stopped running. It's open March to December.

Lake Maggiore East Bank

Lido Angera
HOTEL €€

(☑0331 93 02 32; www.hotellido.it; Viale Libertà 11, Angera; s €82-90, d €112-128; P❄) In a stout orange building set amid greenery and just back from a modest sandy beach just north of central Angera, this hotel is an excellent deal. Rooms are generally spacious, mostly decorated in creams and whites and, in some cases, with windows or balconies opening up right over the lake.

Varese & Around

Al Borducan
HISTORIC HOTEL €€

(☑0332 22 29 16; www.borducan.com; Sacro Monte del Rosario; s €80-130, d €90-150, ste €170-230; ❄@) This building, home to a local herbs-and-orange based elixir, has been standing high in the medieval hamlet of the Sacro Monte del Rosario since 1924. Inside are nine enchanting rooms with art nouveau furniture. Room styles vary – the smallest is a little tightly packed, while the suites, with their hardwood floors and high ceilings, will warm the heart. Downstairs is a recommended restaurant.

Lake Orta

★ Locanda di Orta
HOTEL €

(Map p91; ☑ 0322 90 51 88; www.locandaorta.com; Via Olina 18; s/d/ste from €60/70/150; ☎) This new place is outrageously good value, effortlessly combining medieval touches with modern design flair. Most of the rooms have exposed stone walls, which offset nicely the classy and contemporary decor all dressed in white. It's also in the heart of the old town and feels like you should be paying a whole lot more than you are. They also offer packages that include dinner and boat tickets to Isola San Giulio.

Hotel Leon d'Oro
HOTEL €€

(Map p91; ☑ 0322 91 19 91; www.albergoleondoro.it; Piazza Mario Motta 42, Orta San Giulio; s €100, d €110-180, ste €200-280; ⊙ Feb-Dec; ❄) Any closer to the lake and you'd be in it. A centuries-old building on Piazza Motta, this hotel is ideally located and irresistibly romantic, with its more expensive doubles looking directly across to Isola San Giulio. Sunny yellows and deep blues dominate the decor, with heavy window curtains, timber furniture, tiled floors and, in some rooms, jacuzzi-style baths. It also has some smallish suites.

Piccolo Hotel Olina
HOTEL €

(Map p91; ☑ 0322 90 56 56; www.ortainfo.com; Via Olina 40, Orta San Giulio; s €64-75, d €90-105; ❄) Artistically decorated with contemporary prints, bright colours and light-wood furniture, this ecofriendly hotel with a touch of modern design right in Orta San Giulio's medieval heart is a gem. It also has a fine, somewhat avant-garde restaurant downstairs, and they have other hotel options scattered around the old town if this one is full.

Villa Crespi
HISTORIC HOTEL €€€

(Map p91; ☑ 0322 91 19 02; www.hotelvillacrespi.it; Via Giuseppe Fava 18, Orta San Giulio; s €200-300, d €240-390, ste €350-800; ⊙ Apr-Dec; ℗❄@ ☎☒) Staying at this Moorish extravaganza, which is topped with an aqua-coloured onion-dome spire, is to enter the madcap design dream of the family (a rich textile clan) that built this caprice. Think velvet walls, four-poster beds in some rooms and otherwise opulent interiors and sprawling gardens, all designed for cotton trader Benigno Crespi in 1879.

Locarno & Around

Vecchia Locarno
HOTEL €

(Map p96; ☑ 091 751 65 02; www.vecchia-locarno.ch; Via della Motta 10; s/d with shared bathroom from Sfr55/90, with private bathroom Sfr120/140; ☎) Rooms are gathered around a sunny internal courtyard, evoking a Mediterranean mood, and some have views over the Old Town centre and hills. The digs are simple enough, but comfortable (heaters are provided in the colder months).

Hotel Garni Muralto
HOTEL €€

(Map p96; ☑ 091 735 30 60; www.hotelmuralto.ch; Via Sempione 10; s Sfr99-129, d Sfr149-215; ℗ ❄☎) On a gentle rise above the station, but within a 10-minute walk of the old town, this excellent place is worth considering for its large, modern rooms that punch above their three-star rating. It's worth paying a little extra for the balcony rooms which are large and light-filled; those on the back side of the building are smaller.

Schloss Hotel – Albergo Castello
HOTEL €€

(Map p96; ☑ 091 751 23 61; www.schlosshotellocarno.ch; Via Bartolomeo Rusca 9, Locarno; s Sfr97-150, d Sfr172-228; ℗@☒) Tucked in behind the Visconti clan castle, this hotel has something of the bearing of a castle itself, with its five storeys, fine arches and Mediterranean feel. Inside, grand fireplaces, heavy rugs and the 16th-century restaurant all chime in to add atmosphere, and the pool adds to the Med mood. Rooms are somewhat simpler, the occasional four-poster bed notwithstanding.

★ Caffe dell'Arte
BOUTIQUE HOTEL €€€

(Map p96; ☑ 091 751 93 33; www.caffedellarte.ch; Via Cittadella 9; d Sfr269-289; ☎) Styling itself as a B&B, this charming place above a cafe and art gallery weds personal attention to a designer aesthetic. Some rooms have mock frescoes, others sport leopard-print sofas and all have Nespresso coffee machines. Highly recommended.

Ticino's Western Valleys

Antica Osteria Dazio GUESTHOUSE €
(☑ 091 755 11 62; www.osteriadazio.ch; Valle Maggia; dm/s/d from Sfr49/70/85; ☺Mar-Nov) This guesthouse is a beautifully renovated place to sleep, with loads of timber and Alpine charm. The more you spend on the doubles, the more charming the room. It has a restaurant, too.

Osteria Vittoria GUESTHOUSE €€
(☑ 091 746 15 81; www.osteriavittoria.ch; Lavertezzo, Valle Verzasca; s Sfr70-100, d Sfr120-140) Stay at riverside Osteria Vittoria, a bustling family lodge with its own restaurant and garden. Most rooms have balconies with views over the Verzasca, although they're simpler than the price suggests.

LAKE COMO & AROUND

Booking ahead is always recommended in this area, but that's particularly the case in Como, Bellagio on weekends, and Varenna. Elsewhere there is good accommodation all along Lake Como's West Bank and Lugano; we suggest using the latter as a base for Bellinzona.

Como

Le Stanze del Lago APARTMENT €
(Map p104; ☑ 339 5446515; www.lestanzedellago.com; Via Rodari 6; 2-/4-person apt €100/130; ✳) Five cosy apartments, nicely decked out in modern but understated fashion, make for a good deal in the heart of Como. For stays of five days or longer you can use the kitchen too. All apartments feature double bed, sofa bed, timber ceiling and tiled floor.

★ **Avenue Hotel** BOUTIQUE HOTEL €€
(Map p104; ☑ 031 27 21 86; www.avenuehotel.it; Piazzole Terragni 6; d/ste from €170/220; ✳☎) Combining a quiet location deep in the old town with ultra-modern rooms in which bold colours offset a minimalist white background, Avenue Hotel is deservedly popular. The free bicycle rental is a nice touch, as is the laptop safe box and flat-screen TVs. The service, too, is warm but discreet.

Albergo Firenze HOTEL €€
(Map p104; ☑ 031 30 03 33; www.hotelfirenzecomo.it; Piazza Volta 16; s €92, d without/with piazza view €125/145; ✳☎) Tucked above a women's fashion boutique on Piazza Volta, this attractive hotel has bright, spotless rooms, including several with access for wheelchairs. Don't be put off by the somewhat gloomy reception area, but do pay extra for a superior room with a piazza view as those out the back are a little dark.

Albergo del Duca HOTEL €€
(Map p104; ☑ 031 26 48 59; www.albergodelduca.it; Piazza Mazzini 12; s/d €75/130; P ✳ @) Set on a peaceful square in central Como, the hotel occupies a renovated 17th-century building with a pleasant internal courtyard. Rooms, which exude the warmth that comes from hardwood floors, look either onto the square or the courtyard.

Triangolo Lariano

Agriturismo Munt de Volt RURAL INN €
(☑ 031 91 88 98; www.muntdevolt.altervista.org; Via Monti di Là 3, Pian del Tivano; r per person €20) It would be difficult to feel more deeply ensconced in the rural world. Off the Pian del Tivano, a high country plain some 7km from lakeside Nesso, this farm in dairy country offers four simple rooms. To the front of the house are views over thickly forested valleys, while behind, spring flowers carpet the slopes (where there are some swings for kids). It lies 1km off the main road (look for Via Battista Longoni, opposite the helipad and the sign to Albergo Dosso, 1.5km east of Zelbio). It serves meals too (€20 per person).

Hotel Aurora HOTEL €€
(☑ 031 91 46 45; www.hotelauroralezzeno.com; Via Sossana 2, Lezzeno; d €90-175; P @☎) In the heart of Lezzeno (the longest village on Lake Como), 11km southwest of Bellagio, this is a comfy family hotel in a village off the mainstream tourist radar. Singles look inland but the best doubles have balconies with lake views. Across the road, take breakfast with a lake breeze in the hotel restaurant. Just below the restaurant, the hotel has sun loungers along a wooden boardwalk and access to a whole range of water activities. It operates April to October.

Hotel La Pergola HOTEL €€
(☑ 031 95 02 63; www.lapergolabellagio.it; Piazza del Porto 4, Pescallo, Bellagio; s/d €75/125; ☎) A 15-minute (1km) walk from Bellagio along cobbled lanes leads to sheltered Pescallo, a tiny port. Pescallo's quiet hotel is right on the water (and the pergola referred to

shades a fine restaurant jutting out over it). The 16th-century one-time convent has pleasant rooms, some of which look directly over the lake.

★ **Hotel Silvio** HOTEL €€
(☑ 031 95 03 22; www.bellagiosilvio.com; Via Carcano 10-12, Bellagio; d from €180; ☺ Mar–mid-Nov & Christmas; ᴾ ❋ ☒) Located above the small fishing hamlet of Loppia, a short walk from the centre of Bellagio through the gorgeous Villa Melzi gardens, this family-run hotel is Bellagio's best-value accommodation. From the contemporary Zen-like lakefront rooms you look out over the 10th-century church of Santa Maria, the gardens of Villa Melzi and across to Villa Carlotta on the western shore. The hotel restaurant with its outdoor terrace is also well regarded locally (meals €30 to €40). The hotel has recently obtained the lease for Bellagio's public *lido* (beach) so hotel guests have free use of the pool, complete with diving board over the lake.

Lake Como West Bank

Alberghetto della Marianna GUESTHOUSE €
(☑ 0344 4 30 95; www.la-marianna.com; Via Regina 57, Cadenabbia di Griante; d €80-95; ❋ ☜) About 200m north of the ferry landing in Cadenabbia, this rambling house on the lakeside road offers eight rooms. The place, with dark wooden beams and a charmingly chaotic feel to it, is nothing at all like the grander affairs further down the road. Rooms have parquet floors, tasteful wood furniture and soothing decor. It has a great place to eat too.

★ **Hotel La Perla** HOTEL €€
(☑ 034 44 17 07; www.laperlatremezzo.com; Via Romolo Quaglino 7, Tremezzo; d €125-145, with lake view €140-160, family ste €185-235; ❋ ☜ ☒) It's rare that hotels are as universally acclaimed as this one. Rooms are immaculate, service is warm and friendly, and the vantage point from Tremezzo is one of the loveliest on Lake Como. It's all housed in an artful reconstruction of a 1960s villa. Definitely pay extra for a room with a view.

★ **Villa Mirabella** HOTEL €€
(☑ 034 44 30 90; www.villamirabella.com; Via Regina 13, Cadenabbia; d with garden/lake view from €125/145, ste with lake view €190; ❋ ☜ ☒) Rooms in this lovely converted 19th-century villa looking out across the water towards Bellagio are quite simple but they're fresh

and lovingly maintained with parquet floors. The public areas have plenty of antiques and the service is friendly and professional. Highly recommended.

Albergo Centrale HOTEL €€
(☑ 031 51 14 11; www.albergo-centrale.com; Via Regina 39, Cernobbio; s €70-90, d €80-160; ᴾ ❋ ☜) Situated just 50m back from the water on Cernobbio's main street, the cosy, wood-shuttered hotel has a flowery terrace, a red-brick cellar, and a tavern serving pizzas baked in a wood-fired oven. The early-20th-century building has 22 rooms with parquet floors, muted pastel colours and high ceilings.

Hotel Villa Marie HOTEL €€
(☑ 0344 4 04 27; www.hotelvillamarie.com; Via Regina 30, Tremezzo; d with garden/lake view from €100/130; ᴾ ❋ ☜ ☒) The 19th-century Hotel Villa Marie has a charming lakeside terrace (where you take breakfast) and spacious, light-filled rooms. The variety of rooms explains the broad price range – the two *stile liberty* (Italian art nouveau) suites could be part of a museum visit.

Relais Regina Teodolinda LUXURY HOTEL €€€
(☑ 031 40 00 31; www.relaisreginateodolinda.it; Via Vecchia Regina 58, Laglio; r €180-520; ᴾ ❋ @ ☜ ☒) Want to stay in a villa on the waterfront near George Clooney's place? This charming villa, just north of central Laglio, 200m short of where Via Vecchia Regina meets the more modern SS340, could be the place for you. You can approach by boat if you want, as it has a private landing. Either way, you'll be greeted by pleasant gardens. Most rooms, decorated tastefully in muted colours, offer lake views. It's open March to October.

Lake Como East Bank

Albergo Conca Azzurra HOTEL €
(☑ 0341 93 19 84; www.concazzurra.com; Via per l'Abbazia di Piona 19, Colico Olgiasca, Lecco; s €46-65, d €70-85; ᴾ ❋ @ ☜) One kilometre short of the Abbazia di Piona Cistercian abbey, on a verdant promontory jutting into the lake close to Lake Como's southeastern corner, this bucolic, three-storey hotel is a peaceful hideaway, with gardens and wooden shutters, in a lovely location. It offers a variety of rooms, many with balconies and lake views, and has its own restaurant-bar. A cobblestone path runs down to the abbey.

Albergo Milano
HOTEL €€

(☑ 0341 83 02 98; www.varenna.net; Via XX Settembre 35, Varenna; s €115-125, d €140-180; ✳ @ ☎) In the middle of Varenna on the pedestrian main street (well, lane), Albergo Milano is high up the slope and opens onto a terrace with magnificent lake vistas. Most of the 12 rooms have some kind of lake view and balcony, and are tastefully appointed, with gaily painted iron bedsteads, dark-wood wardrobes and creamy white linen. You can dine on the terrace (p121) or just sip a cocktail. It's open March to November.

Lake Lugano

Hotel & Hostel Montarina
HOTEL, HOSTEL €€

(Map p124; ☑ 091 966 72 72; www.montarina.ch; Via Montarina 1; dm Sfr29, s Sfr82-92, d Sfr112-132; P ☎ ✳) The Hostel Montarina has simple rooms with four to 16 bunk beds. A buffet breakfast is available for Sfr12. There is also a hotel on the site; the best rooms are airy, with timber floors and antiques. Some rooms have a private kitchen. The pool is set in pleasant gardens.

Locanda del Giglio
LODGE €

(☑ 091 930 09 33; www.locandadelgiglio.ch; Roveredo, Capriasca; dm Sfr35-45, s/d Sfr95/150) A lovely place to stay is the Locanda del Giglio, in Roveredo, Capriasca, 12km north of Lugano. It is a warm timber building powered by solar energy. Rooms have balconies offering mountain views and even lake glimpses. Take a bus from Lugano to Tesserete (30 minutes) and change there for another to Roveredo (about 10 minutes).

Hotel International au Lac
HOTEL €€

(Map p124; ☑ 091 922 75 41; www.hotel-international.ch; Via Nassa 88; s Sfr125-185, d Sfr195-390; ☺ Apr-Oct; ✳ ☎ ✽) From the balconies of the front rooms you look straight out over Lago di Lugano – some of the best hotel-room views in the city. There are other cheaper rooms scattered about the hotel. Rooms are comfortable, with some antique furniture.

★ Hotel Gabbani
BOUTIQUE HOTEL €€€

(Map p124; ☑ 091 921 34 70; www.hotel-gabbani.ch; Piazza Cioccaro 1; s Sfr190-390, d Sfr220-470) Run by the respected local Gabbani food family and within sight of their signature shop, this gorgeous place has individually styled rooms, each with their own colour scheme built around food and the use of wood and marble – the 'Chocolate' room

is dark brown, the 'Honey' room yellow, 'Chili' has splashes of fiery red, and so on. Fittings are ultra-modern and the service excellent.

BERGAMO, BRESCIA & CREMONA

There are excellent accommodation possibilities everywhere here, especially in the three main cities. There are some good choices around Lake Iseo and its hinterland, but fewer than the other lakes in the region.

Bergamo

Nuovo Ostello di Bergamo
HOSTEL €

(☑ 035 369 23 76; www.ostellodibergamo.it; Via Galileo Ferraris 1, Monterosso; dm/s/d €18/35/50; P @) Bergamo's state-of-the-art HI hostel is about 4km north of the train station. Its 27 rooms offer views over Bergamo's Città Alta old centre. Take bus 6 from Largo Porta Nuova near the train station (get off at Leonardo da Vinci stop) or bus 3 for Ostello from the Città Alta.

★ Hotel Piazza Vecchia
HOTEL €€

(Map p136; ☑ 035 428 42 11; www.hotelpiazzavecchia.it; Via Bartolomeo Colleoni 3; s/d from €120/145; ✳ @ ☎) Carved out of a 13th-century building a few steps off Piazza Vecchia, this charming hotel's 13 rooms are all quite different. All have parquet floors and baths set in stone, but the decor varies. Some have exposed beams, some a balcony, some a king-size bed.

Albergo Il Sole
HOTEL €€

(Map p136; ☑ 035 21 82 38; www.ilsolebergamo.com; Via Bartolomeo Colleoni 1; s/d €70/90) The picture windows and colourful bedspreads at Albergo Il Sole lend its otherwise fairly straightforward but immaculately maintained rooms a countrified air. This is perhaps odd, given that it is jammed deep inside the medieval rabbit warren of the Città Alta.

Agriturismo Casa Clelia
RURAL INN €€

(☑ 035 79 91 33; www.casaclelia.com; Via Corna 1/3, Sotto il Monte Giovanni XXIII; s/d from €60/100; ☎) Barely a 10-minute stroll from the centre of Sotto il Monte Giovanni XXIII, and 18km from Bergamo's airport, this working farm offers 10 spacious, beautiful rooms in the carefully restored 16th-century main farmhouse, set amid gardens and outhouses. Exposed stone and brick, timber beams and dark wood furniture characterise the rooms.

Da Vittorio
BOUTIQUE HOTEL €€€

(☑035 68 10 24; www.davittorio.com; Via Cantalupa 17; s €250-300, d €350-400; P❄@🛈) Not only is Da Vittorio a noteworthy gourmet hideout (p141) 9km east of town, it also offers 10 quality suites in its low-slung country estate. Each of the generous rooms enjoys its own sumptuous decor, with beautifully woven fabrics and marble bathroom. Indulge in a tasting menu breakfast, with a series of miniportions of various sweet and savoury options. The place looks over a park and vineyard. It's open September to July.

Lake Iseo & Around

Hotel Milano
HOTEL €

(☑030 98 04 49; www.hotelmilano.info; Lungolargo Marconi 4, Iseo; s €42-47, d €84-92; ❄@🛈) One of only two hotels in the centre of Iseo, the lakefront Milano is an excellent deal. It's definitely worth paying fractionally more for the pleasant rooms with lake views (one-week minimum stay mid-July to mid-August) – so you have a front row seat for sunset behind the mountains over the lake.

L'Albereta
HOTEL €€€

(☑030 776 05 50; www.albereta.it; Via Vittorio Emanuele 23, Erbusco; s/d from €220/310; P❄@🛈🏊) This country estate, sheathed in creeping ivy, has been converted into luxury Relais & Châteaux digs. Set on a rise overlooking the surrounding Franciacorta wine country and with a state-of-the-art spa (with Henri Chenot products) and gym, it's perfect for a pamper. The rooms are spacious and tastefully decorated and the grounds and public spaces impeccable. You can round off the experience by dining at Marchesi (p146).

Brescia

★ Albergo Orologio
BOUTIQUE HOTEL €€

(Map p149; ☑030 375 54 11; www.albergoorologio. it; Via Beccaria 17; s €85-150, d €110-200; ❄@🛈) Right by its namesake clock tower in the pedestrianised old town, fine art and artefacts, and soft gold, brown and olive furnishings and terracotta floors make this boutique ho-

tel a gem. It has just 16 varied rooms carved out of a medieval building that combine warmth in the decor with contemporary design in the bathrooms.

Hotel Vittoria
HOTEL €€

(Map p149; ☑030 28 00 61; www.hotelvittoria. com; Via X Giornate 20; s €100-150, d €150-170, ste €250; ❄@🛈) Given this grand 1938 hotel's chandeliers, extravagant ballrooms and luxurious guest rooms, resting your head here represents unexpectedly good value. After sweeping through the grand hall and public spaces, which drip with marble and walnut, you'll see the rooms have a restrained elegance and mostly enjoy plenty of natural light.

Cremona

Albergo Duomo
HOTEL €

(Map p153; ☑0372 3 52 42; www.hotelduomo cremona.com; Via Gonfalonieri 13; s/d €60/85; P❄🛈) Just a few steps from Cremona's cathedral and ablaze with wrought-iron flower boxes in spring, Albergo Duomo was given a complete overhaul in 2013 and now offers decent rooms with contemporary flair than you can usually expect for this price. It's even better value when you consider the location.

Delle Arti Design Hotel
DESIGN HOTEL €€

(Map p153; ☑0372 2 31 31; www.hoteldellearti. com; Via Bonomelli 8; s/d from €109/139; ❄🛈) This rather self-consciously hi-tech vision of glass, concrete and steel has rotating displays of more contemporary paintings and photographs, a Turkish bath, gym and suitably chic rooms with clean lines, bold colours and artistic lighting. For those who want to feel like they never left the fashion crowd in Milan, this could be the place.

Around Cremona

La Casa di Oliver
B&B €

(☑0371 41 17 77; www.lacasadioliver.it; Via Defendente 60, Lodi; s/d €50/80; P❄) Set in a two-storey early 1900s *stile liberty* (Italian art nouveau) building about a five-minute walk from the centre of Lodi, this charmer has three spacious rooms overlooking an extensive garden. Parquet floors and soft decor make the nicely renovated rooms welcoming.

LAKE GARDA & AROUND

Poets and politicians, divas and dictators, they've all been drawn to the sunny shores of Lake Garda. Opulent art nouveau villas line the western shore, many of them converted to luxury hotels. To the north the lake narrows between soaring mountains, making the resorts of Gargnano and Riva an excellent base for activity holidays, while to the east and south, rolling vineyards and olive groves offer plenty of farmstay accommodation and resort spas.

Lake Garda South Bank

Hotel Grifone   HOTEL €
(☑ 030 91 60 14; www.gardalakegrifonehotel.eu; Via Bocchio 4, Sirmione; s/d €45/90; ❄) The rustic rooms of this two-star *albergo* (hotel) look directly onto the lake and Sirmione's waterfront castle. The only other place with views this good is the 5-star Grand Hotel Terme opposite.

Il Giardino Segreto   B&B €€
(Map p165; ☑ 030 917 22 94; www.relaisilgiardino-segreto.it; Via Curiel 2, Desenzano del Garda; d €95-140; ℗❄@☎) The Secret Garden is a B&B with a boutique feel. Six double rooms in Mediterranean colours feature vast beds, playful modern furnishings and works of art. Many have patios fronting the luxuriant garden where breakfast is served in summer.

Hotel Marconi   HOTEL €€
(☑ 030 91 60 07; www.hotelmarconi.net; Via Vittorio Emanuele II 51, Sirmione; s €45-75, d €80-135; ℗❄) Blue and white striped umbrellas line the lakeside deck at this stylish, family-run hotel. The restrained rooms are all subtle shades and crisp fabrics, and the breakfasts and homemade pastries are a treat.

Lake Garda West Bank

Agriturismo La Breda   AGRITURISMO €
(☑ 0365 622 00; www.agriturismolabreda.com; Via Benaco 15, San Felice del Benaco; d €59-125, qd €65-180; ℗@☎) Run by the Cavazza family of Isola del Garda, La Breda enjoys an unspoilt location. The old farmhouse accommodates five apartments kitted out in pine fittings and furniture and checked linens. In addition, you have use of the pool at La Fornella, access to the Baia Verde boat centre and can enjoy the exclusive privilege of picnicking on Isola del Garda. Open April to September.

Albergo Tiziana   HOTEL €
(☑ 0365 7 13 42; www.albergotiziana.com; Via Dosso 51, Gargnano; s €43, d €60-72; @) This classic, green-shuttered villa just above Gargnago offers large, light-filled rooms with cool terrazzo floors and views over the lake. Furnishings are retro and unfussy, but the pretty garden and prime location more than make up for the lack of frills.

★Campeggio Fornella   CAMPGROUND €
(☑ 0365 6 22 94; www.fornella.it; Via Fornella 1, San Felice del Benaco; pitches €13-37, bungalows €45-198; ℗❄@☎) This luxury, four-star campground comes complete with private beach, lagoon pool, Jacuzzi, children's club, boat centre, restaurant, bar and pizzeria. All you have to do is pick a scenic pitch, mobile home or bungalow.

Dimora Bolsone   B&B €€
(☑ 0365 2 10 22; www.dimorabolsone.it; Via Panoramic 23, San Michele; s €170, d €200; ℗) Lose yourself amid woodlands and wildflowers in the picturesque hamlet of San Michele. Host Raffaelle is passionate about the lake and eagerly recommends walks high in the hills to follow your spectacular breakfast served on the terrace. Not suitable for children under 12.

Locanda Agli Angeli   RURAL INN €€
(☑ 036 52 08 32; www.agliangeli.com; Piazza Garibaldi 2, Gardone Riviera; s €45-70, d €80-180; ℗❄☎) A delightful renovation has produced an 18th-century *locanda* (inn) of old polished wood, gauzy fabrics and bursts of lime, orange and aquamarine. The terrace has a compact pool and views across rooftops to the lake beyond. The owners offer similar but slightly simpler rooms (singles/doubles €55/95) next door.

Hotel Laurin   HISTORIC HOTEL €€
(☑ 0365 2 20 22; www.laurinhotelsalo.com; Viale Angelo Landi 9; d €155-250; ℗❄@☎☎) An art nouveau gem with some real history behind it, the Hotel Laurin (formerly the Villa Simonini) was the Foreign Ministry during Mussolini's short-lived Republic. Downstairs salons retain wonderful details: frescoes by Bertolotti, intricate parquet floors and wood inlay and wrought-iron volutes. Even the furnishings are faithful Liberty reproductions and antiques. A piece of history at a surprisingly affordable price.

LAKE GARDA'S HISTORIC HOTELS

Basking in year-round sunshine, the shoreline between Gardone and Gargnano is the location of some of Lake Garda's most prestigious, historic hotels. Staying at one of these beauties will set you back anywhere from €300 to €2000 per night.

Grand Hotel Fasano (www.ghf.it) This 1892 hunting lodge, once home to the Austrian royal family, has its own private beach and park.

Villa del Sogno (www.villadelsogno.it) Built by a Viennese tycoon in 1904, the 'house of dreams' affords spectacular views from its lofty perch.

Villa Fiordaliso (www.villafiordaliso.it) In the last days of the Salò Republic, Mussolini installed his mistress Clara Petacci in this 1903 neoclassical extravagance.

Villa Feltrinelli (www.villafeltrinelli.com) An 1892 pink, Venetian palazzo once owned by the Feltrinelli brothers and occupied by Field Marshal Rommel and Mussolini.

★**Villa Arcadio**   HISTORIC VILLA €€€
(☏ 0365 4 22 81; www.hotelvillaarcadio.it; Via Palazzina 2, Salò; d €230-350, ste €300-450; P🅿️❄️@ 🛜🏊) Perched above Salò on the wooded hillside, this converted convent is the essence of lakeside glamour. Enjoy the vista of glassy lake and misty mountains from the panoramic pool or retreat inside to frescoed rooms and ancient wood-beamed halls.

Villa Giulia   HOTEL €€€
(☏ 036 57 10 22; www.villagiulia.it; Viale Rimembranze 20, Gargnano; s €155, d €235-350; P❄️@ 🛜🏊) Lakefront gardens dotted with palm and olive trees make this 18th-century villa feel like a Mediterranean hideaway. Bedrooms are either snazzy and modern, or rich in antiques, thick rugs and soft gold fabric. Service is faultless and your biggest dilemma will be whether to swim in the pool or the lake after that spell in the sauna.

Lake Garda North Shore

Hotel Garni Villa Maria   APARTHOTEL €
(☏ 0464 55 22 88; www.garnimaria.com; Viale dei Tigli, Riva del Garda; s €35, d €60-100, apt €280-340; P❄️🛜) A small, spruce hotel with a Scandinavian vibe sporting all-white linens, sleek modern bathrooms and zesty lime green and orange accents. Situated just outside Riva's historic town centre, balconied rooms offer views of soaring mountains.

★**Residence Filanda**   APARTHOTEL €€
(☏ 0464 55 47 34; www.residencefilanda.com; Via Sant'Alessandro, 51 ; d €105-135, qd €165-210; P❄️@🏊) Located two kilometres outside Riva, this bright, burnt-orange residence situated amid olive groves and vineyards is a haven for families. Rooms and apartments overlook lush grounds that include a heated pool, tennis and volleyball courts and 2.5 acres of child-friendly gardens. Facilities are top-notch, too, with satellite TV, fully equipped kitchenettes, laundrette and all the necessary paraphernalia for young children.

Reception staff can arrange discounts on bike and windsurf rental as well as windsurfing and climbing courses.

Lido Palace   LUXURY HOTEL €€€
(Map p173; ☏ 0464 02 18 99; www.lido-palace.it; Viale Carducci 10, Riva del Garda; d €270-380, ste €450-550; P❄️@🛜🏊) If you're going to splash the cash, this is the place to do it. Riva's historic Lido Palace dates back to 1899 and is an absolute stunner. Sensitive renovations have installed uncompromisingly modern interiors within the grand Liberty-style palace, complete with Michelin-starred restaurant, peerless views over lawns and lake, and sumptuous spa facilities (open to nonguests by reservation).

Lake Garda East Shore

Hotel Al Molino   HOTEL €
(☏ 045 740 02 99; www.hotelalmolino.com; Via Gardesana 382, Malcesine; d €76-90; P) With direct access to the beach and an olive garden equipped with swings, Al Molino is a rare budget find. Valentina Manzana and her family have been running the place for over 30 years providing breezy blue-and-white rooms and excellent home-cooked meals. There are discounts for weekly bookings.

Albergo Gardesana   HOTEL €€
(☑ 045 722 54 11; www.hotel-gardesana.com; Piazza Calderini 20, Torri del Benaco; s €95-185, d €110-200; P ❈ 🕾) The guest list at this gorgeous 15th-century hotel has featured actors, writers, statespeople and kings. Painted wood and antiques fill the bedrooms, while the vine-fringed breakfast terrace has delightful harbour views. Ask for Room 123 with its wraparound balcony – Winston Churchill and King Juan Carlos of Spain no doubt enjoyed their stay in it too.

Hotel La Vittoria   HOTEL €€
(☑ 045 627 04 73; www.hotellavittoria.it; Lungolago Regina Adelaide 57, Garda; d €92-150, ste €104-178; P ❈) This chic little three-star spot sits right on Garda's waterfront promenade. Spacious lake-view rooms are done out in delicate cream and gold, while free mini-antipasti and afternoon tea – best sampled on the palm-dotted terrace – add to the appeal. The room price includes free entry to the new wellness centre, **Gardacqua** (www.gardacqua.it).

★**Locanda San Vigilio**   BOUTIQUE HOTEL €€€
(☑ 045 725 66 88; www.punta-sanvigilio.it; Punta San Vigilio; d €270-375, ste €440-890; P ❈ @ ≋) Hidden away on a headland, this 16th-century *locanda* is a place to remember. It feels like a stately English home: discreet, understated and effortlessly elegant. Dark woods, stone floors and plush furnishings ensure an old-world-meets-new-luxury feel.

For those looking for an equally comfortable country inn away from the lake try San Vigilio's sister hotel, **Locanda San Verolo** (☑ 045 720 09 30; www.sanverolo.it; d €195-260, ste €280-320; P ❈ @ 🕾 ≋), located in Costermano in the hills above Garda.

Verona

★**Agriturismo San Mattia**   FARMSTAY €
(☑ 045 91 37 97; www.agriturismosanmattia.it; Via San Giuliana 2; s €60-€85, d €85-95, apt per week €550-€1150; P ❈ 🕾) Make friends with the chickens, ducks and horses as you wander through San Mattia's olive groves, orchards and vineyards, then sit back on the patio and soak up the stunning views of Verona. Host Giovanni Ederle is the tour de force behind this 14-room farm, its popular slow-food focused restaurant and valpolicella vintages (€8.50–€40). The lavish farm breakfast is an additional €5.

Sanzenetto   B&B €€
(☑ 392 982 59 86; www.sanzenetto.com; Vicolo Cieco Boscarello 3a; s €55-95, d €70-150; ❈ 🕾) Sanzenetto's mid-century modern style is a breath of fresh air in traditional Verona. Chantal is happy to provide unusual tips on what to see and where to eat. Make time for the splendid breakfast of fresh croissants, yoghurt, cereals and cold cuts served delightfully on the best china and silverware.

★**Corte delle Pigne**   B&B €
(Map p180; ☑ 333 758 41 41; www.cortedellepigne. it; Via Pigna 6a; s €60-90, d €90-130, tr & q €110-150; P ❈ 🕾) The toast of the historic centre, this three-room B&B is arranged around the quiet internal courtyard of a historic villa. Personal touches are everywhere: a communal sweet jar, luxury toiletries and even a Jacuzzi for one lucky couple.

Albergo Aurora   HOTEL €€
(Map p180; ☑ 045 59 47 17; www.hotelaurora.biz; Piazza XIV Novembre 2; s €90-135, d €100-160; ❈) Right off bustling Piazza delle Erbe yet cosy and blissfully quiet, this hotel has spacious, unfussy doubles, some with city views. There are cheaper single rooms with shared bathroom (€58 to €80). Head to the sunny terrace for drinks overlooking the piazza.

Due Torri Hotel Baglioni   HOTEL €€€
(Map p180; ☑ 045 59 50 44; www.baglionihotels. com; Piazza di Sant'Anastasia 4; s/d €430/486-750, ste €850; P ❈ @ 🕾) This former Della

---

WORTH A TRIP

ECOFRIENDLY HIDEAWAY
....
Stay near Lake Ledro amid apple trees of the Concei valley at the glass-and-timber ecolodge **Hotel Elda** (☑ 0464 59 10 40; www.hotelelda.com; Via 3 Giugno 3; s €70-120, d €94-160; P @ ≋) ✿ . Once a traditional inn, it has been converted by the family's prodigal son, who invited a team of architect-designers to reinvent the old building with five-star ecocredentials. The result is a happy combination of thermo-insulation and solar energy with state-of-the-art bathrooms and Philippe Starck furnishings. Do the eco-thing and immerse yourself in the landscape. You'll find bikes at reception and a fully fledged bio spa, which comes in handy after mountain walks.

A FLOATING HOTEL

Peek out of your porthole at cormorants sunning themselves on branches as you glide down the Mincio and Po rivers to Ferrara or Venice. **Avemaria** (☑ 0444 32 36 39; www.avemariaboat. com; Contrà Manin, Vicenza; per person weekend €160-250, week €955; 🚲) 🏊 is a barging hotel offering four-day or week-long cultural itineraries exploring the peaceful nooks and crannies of the delta. Onboard, 40 unisex bikes (child seats available on request) make for easy hop-on, hop-off explorations while the rooftop sundeck provides a superlative terrace for cocktails and romantic dining.

Scala palace exudes luxury from the velvet-clad sofas in the cavernous lobby to walls clad in tapestries. Suites feature burnished antiques, embossed leather books and monogrammed towels. Significant discounts (up to 70%) apply if you book online, in advance.

Mantua

★ Armellino
B&B €

(Map p188; ☑346 314 80 60; www.bebarmellino. it; Via Cavour 67; s €65, d €75-85; @🛜) Enjoy a touch of ducal splendour in Antonella and Massimo's fabulous *palazzo*. Grand rooms are furnished with 18th-century antiques and retain original wooden floors, fireplaces and ceiling frescoes. Not all bedrooms have a bathroom, but this has the feel of an exclusive private apartment rather than a B&B.

C'a delle Erbe
B&B €€

(Map p188; ☑ 0376 22 61 61; www.cadelleerbe.it; Via Broletto 24; d €130-160; ❄🛜) With an unbeatable location in the heart of old Mantua, this exquisite 16th-century townhouse teams exposed brick walls with lavish bathrooms and modern art. Ask for the room with the balcony overlooking Piazza delle Erbe.

Casa Poli
BOUTIQUE HOTEL €€

(☑0376 28 81 70; www.hotelcasapoli.it; Corso Garibaldi 32; d €110-180; ❄ @🛜) Expect a warm welcome, ultracool decor and boutique rooms full of soft greys, crisp lines and occasional splashes of orange. Imaginative touches are everywhere, from tucked-away TVs to room numbers projected on the floor.

Understand the Italian Lakes

The Italian Lakes Today

News flash: Italy was not cryogenically frozen six centuries ago. Lombardy is one of Europe's most creative corners, contributing 20% of Italian GDP and registering one third of the country's innovation patents. Look around you and you'll notice breakthrough ideas literally popping up: urban art projects, green-designed parks and state-of-the-art neighbourhoods. Wary of the future, though, savvy Lombards are now investing heavily in the knowledge-economy.

Best in Print

Promessi Sposi (The Betrothed; 1827) Alessandro Manzoni's tale of two lovers, and a country, longing to be united.
Design as Art (1966) Illuminating text by designer Bruno Munari.
Accidental Death of an Anarchist (1970) A sly, subversive comedy by Dario Fo.
Voices from the Plains (1985) Gianni Celati's arresting stories of chance encounters on the Po plains.

Best in Film

Miracolo a Milano (Miracle in Milan; 1951) Vittorio de Sica's fairy tale about a boy who unites the poor and is given the gift of miracles.
Rocco and His Brothers (1960) Luchino Visconti's take on southern immigration, boxing and brotherhood.
Teorema (1968) Pier Paolo Pasolini sets Terence Stamp loose on a haute-bourgeois Milanese family.
I Am Love (2009) Luca Guadagnino's drama about the suffocating power of family and tradition.
Che Bella Giornata (What a Beautiful Day; 2011) Gennaro Nunziante's comedy about a security guard from Brianza is Italy's most commercially successful film.

Ambitious Industrialists

Lombardy stands out in the European landscape for its diverse economy, industrial strength and productive agricultural sector. With a population of nearly 10 million there are more Lombards than Swedes and with 8.45 companies for each 100 inhabitants, the region's economy is larger than Belgium's with GDP per capita 35% higher and unemployment less than half the European average. Some 220,000 students in 15 universities keep the region and its cities young and full of ideas, while foreign immigrants (25% of all foreign immigrants in Italy) give Milan a cosmopolitan flavour. And in the face of global recession, Lombards have simply redoubled their efforts, engaging Kartell president Claudio Luti to rebrand the Salone del Mobile, attracting Qatari investment to Porta Nuova and planning the biggest, commercial enterprise in recession-plagued Europe: Expo 2015.

Reinventing the Future

As hardworking as the Lombards may be, if you hang out in Milan's piazzas and bars, you'll find plenty of Milanese who'll make time for conversation. They'll reveal that young Milanese are now taking jobs that interest them rather than positions with big salaries and career advancement. How Lombardy manages the transition from its traditional manufacturing and agricultural economy to specialist services and knowledge-intensive activities will be the key to maintaining its distinctive European position.

While multinational companies have a strong presence here, it is the 823,000 small- and medium-sized businesses that will have the largest role to play in this transformation. Employing more than 4.3 million people, they represent the life-blood of the region. And if they're to stand any chance in the changing global economy they will need to focus on differentiation and specialisation, much like the silk weavers of Como who now advise visiting Chinese manufacturers.

Among them are high-end technology companies and business services as well as value-added design, craft, food and fashion enterprises. After all, 15 million tourists flock to Milan annually for La Scala openings, shopping in some 650 fashion showrooms, the Milan film festival, art exhibits, football matches and international concerts, snapping up nearly 10 million tickets a year.

This strong streak of entrepreneurialism and creativity is Lombardy's biggest asset, but it needs a sturdy infrastructure to support it and at present the creaking transport system, traffic-clogged autostrade and surprisingly low level of university graduates (just 16%) are putting severe brakes on progress.

Expo 2015

The solution? The Expo 2015 world exhibition costing a cool €13.5 billion and forecast, by Bocconi University, to achieve €25 billion in investment and the creation of 200,000 new jobs. It's a bold vision and one that Enrico Letta, Italy's prime minister, is banking on to lift Italy out of its economic doldrums.

But there are fears that organised crime will infiltrate the bids (Letta vows it won't be tolerated); budgets will overrun painfully; the city won't be able to accommodate the 20 million expected visitors; and the trains simply won't run on time (of the three metro lines only MM5 is sure to be finished).

Still, the success of the Expo is vital not only to Lombardy, but to Europe as a whole, commercially, psychologically and politically. With 131 countries signed up, including economic powerhouses China, India, Brazil and Mexico, the prospects look hopeful. The theme, too, plays to Lombardy's agricultural, design, biotech and engineering strengths, *Feeding the Planet, Energy for Life*. And the conceptual master plan for a 1.1 sq kilometre 'planetary garden' from architects Jacques Herzog, Mark Rylander, Ricky Burdett, Stefano Boeri and William McDonough has been endorsed by former American vice president and environmentalist Al Gore. Now all that's required is some of that Lombard chutzpah to defy the naysayers and fulfil Expo president Diana Bracco's prophecy that Expo will be 'the first major event after the crisis'.

POPULATION **9.7 MILLION**

AREA **23,844 SQ KM**

GDP **€326 BILLION**

GDP PER CAPITA **€25,251**

UNEMPLOYMENT **5.8%**

EXPORTS TO EUROPE **70%**

if the Italian Lakes were 100 people

91 would be Italian
3 would be Romanian
2 would be Moroccan
2 would be Albanian
2 would be Other

employment rate
(% of population)

74   56

Men   Women

population per sq km

MILAN   LOMBARDY   ITALY

≈ 205 people

History

Northern Italy, with its head full of jagged Alpine teeth and its feet paddling in the swampy deltas of the Po river, has been both blessed and cursed by its geography throughout the centuries. Despite their awesome appearance, the Alps have been crossed without difficulty since the Bronze Age, and during the Roman Empire 17 of the 23 Alpine passes were already in heavy use. Carthaginian general Hannibal brought his army and elephants across the Alps, and Alaric and Attila marauded from the east. Yet those pearly white peaks and broad delta have also been the making of northern Italy.

Cisalpine Gaul

Lombardy's first designers set to zealously decorating their surrounds; the rocky Val Camonica to Milan's northeast is covered in 150,000 engraved petroglyphs dating back to 8000 BC, gleefully depicting figures hunting, farming, making magic and indulging in wild sexual antics. It was recognised as a World Heritage Site in 1979.

The Romans didn't consider wild Cisalpine Gaul (meaning Gaul on the near side of the Alps) part of Italy at all and stayed well away until the Gauls swept south through Etruria and sacked Rome in 387 BC. Then they sided with the Carthaginians in the Punic Wars (264–146 BC) so Rome marched north subduing Mediolanum (Milan) in 221 BC and establishing Roman garrisons at Piacenza, Como and Cremona. The Romanisation of the region was accomplished through a combination of military and political inducement: adversaries were disarmed by the grant of citizenship (which brought with it social, legal and economic privileges), while Roman culture wowed the masses with its impressive civic buildings, literature and philosophy.

Julius Caesar was made consul of northern Italy in 59 BC and found it a fruitful recruitment ground. He took his legions into neighbouring Gaul (modern France) on a campaign of conquests that would last until 51 BC. They provided him with a strong enough power base to cross the Rubicon and embark on the Italian civil war (49–46 BC) that would lead him to absolute power in 45 BC. None of this would have been possible without the loyalty of Cisalpine Gaul.

Mediolanum was by then a prosperous city astride key routes. The city supplied arms for the Empire's insatiable war machine, traded wool, hides and metal, and boasted a theatre, university, forum, mint and many fine temples and palaces, remnants of which survive in the Basilica di San Lorenzo and the palace ruins in Via Brisa. The lakes

TIMELINE	11,000 BC	c 600–400 BC	218 BC
	Accounts of Roman historian Titus Livius point to the invasion of the Lombard plains and Po valley by Gallic tribes from southern France as early as the 10th century BC.	According to legend, the Insubri Gauls chose the site of Milan when their greedy king glimpsed a bristle-backed boar across the plains. They call it Mediolanum (Middle of the Plains).	Carthaginian general Hannibal crosses the Alps into the Lombard plains and 50,000 Gauls join his forces. After several defeats, Rome emerges master of the Mediterranean.

became a favoured holiday destination for the Roman elite; it was to a villa in Sirmione that poet Catullus retreated when 1st-century-BC 'It girl' Clodia Metelli broke his heart. As the Empire crumbled in the 4th century, Mediolanum, with its strategic position by the Rhine frontier, became home to the imperial court.

Long Beards & Franks

Despite an unprecedented three centuries of relative tranquillity, Lombardy gets its name not from the Romans, but the *langobardi* (long beards). A Germanic people from across the Danube, they marched into northern Italy almost unopposed in 568. Led by King Alboino (c 530s–572), they rapidly captured all the cities of the Po valley, first taking Verona and then, over the next four years, besieging Bergamo, Brescia and Milan. In 572 they captured Pavia and made it their capital.

Between this Lombard kingdom in the north and the reduced Roman seat of power in Ravenna an uneasy peace survived for nearly 200 years, long enough for the heartlands of both to become known as Lombardy and Romagna. Much of this tenuous peace was based on a shared and growing Christian faith, championed by Milan's Archbishop Ambrose (c 340–97), Pope Gregory (540–604) and devout Queen Theodolinda (c 570–628). Married to two Lombard kings, and Queen Regent for her young son from 616, Theodolinda was instrumental in restoring mainstream (Nicene) Christianity to the northern provinces and routing its rival, Arianism. She patronised many new churches – the oratory at Modena, the cathedral at Monza and the first baptistery in Florence – and in 628 she donated the Lombard *Corrona Ferrae* (Iron Crown) to the Italian Church in Monza.

Despite history dismissing this period as Italy's Dark Age, the cathedral museum at Monza houses a spectacular collection of early medieval artworks, much of it collected by Theodolinda. It includes a rich stash of Barbarian and Carolingian art, Lombard gold jewellery and 16 6th century Palestinian ampullae sporting the earliest depictions of the Crucifixion and the Nativity in medieval art.

But with the fall of the Roman frontier at Ravenna to the Lombards in 727, when the city rebelled against a new edict banning icons, Pope Stephen II (715-57) became increasingly alarmed at expanding Lombard ambitions and turned to the Frankish ruler, Pepin, for military support. In return for Pepin's help and the assumption of conquered Lombard territories, Stephen named Pepin protector of the Church. It was Pepin's son, Charles, more famously known as Charlemagne (742–814), who eventually swept away the Lombard kingdom and was crowned King of Italy in 774 and Holy Roman Emperor in 800.

Roman Italia was a land of city-states that largely ran themselves. Yet the empire engendered loyalty and prosperity through free trade and a common currency, the provision of justice, and a broadminded attitude about race and class that modern Europe is having trouble emulating today.

49 BC	313	568	773–74
The Cisalpine cities of northern Italy are granted the right to declare *civis romanus sum* (I am a Roman citizen), the year Caesar marched on Rome.	Roman Emperor Constantine issues the Edict of Milan, declaring Christianity the official state religion. St Ambrose becomes Bishop of Milan 61 years later.	Germanic tribes known as Lombards (or Langobards) occupy northern Italy, making Pavia their capital and giving the Po valley its present name.	Charlemagne leads Frankish troops into Italy, defeats the Lombards and has himself crowned with the legendary Iron Crown. The Lombards pay homage to him at Pavia.

Frederick Barbarossa

By the 11th century the over-extended Holy Roman Empire was ill equipped to administer its thriving Italian colonies. The growth and prosperity of the cities gave their citizens the desire to run their own affairs. Unwilling to accept an absentee foreigner with doubtful rights of sovereignty, they were soon electing their own leaders, running their own courts and raising their own militias.

Frederick I (1122–90), Duke of Swabia, who became emperor in 1155, was determined to reverse this drift and restore the Empire to the powerful force it was under Charlemagne. A feted warrior, with grandiose notions of his rights, he became renowned as a symbol of Teutonic unity, a hero to German romantics and an inspiration for Adolf Hitler.

The defiance of anti-imperial Milan, the largest Italian city, and its subjugation of pro-imperial neighbours Pavia, Lodi and Como inspired Frederick to invade Italy. He captured Milan in 1162 and destroyed it utterly, earning his nickname Barbarossa (red beard) both for the colour of his beard and the ferocity with which he fought. He also obliterated the towns of Cremona and Crema, who likewise resisted him.

But these triumphs and the humiliations of the conquered, who were made to parade before Frederick barefoot with swords and ropes around their necks, were to be short-lived as his actions prompted the formation of the Lombard League (1167). Uniting 16 Lombard cities, the League promised to aid anyone threatened by Frederick's armies, and although a few member states dropped out in subsequent years, the League held long enough to rout Frederick's armies at Legnano in 1176. This historic defeat forced Barbarossa to the negotiating table, and at the Treaty of Constance in 1183 he conceded the rights of the *comune* (city-state) to elect their own leaders, make their own laws and administer their own territories.

Feminist Icons

Queen Theodolinda *Church builder and art collector*

Beatrice d'Este *Fashion icon and art patron*

Isabella d'Este *Political maven, intellectual and art patron*

Sofonisba Anguissola *Cremonese Renaissance painter*

Empress Maria Theresa *Civil rights champion*

A New Law & Order

Medieval Italians described their *comune* (city-state) as if it were an earthly paradise, where life was regulated by sublime statutes framed by learned lawyers. They were proud of their appearances, too. Since things were constructed in their name they could take proprietorial interest in the paving of streets, the layout of squares and the building of bridges.

Bonvesin de la Riva was a typical medieval citizen. A well-to-do Milanese, he belonged to an order of monks called the Umilati. Thanks to his magnus opus, *De Magnalibus Mediolani* (The Marvels of Medieval Milan), which he penned in the spring of 1288, we have quite an image of medieval Milan, the largest city of the peninsula in 13th century. Milan,

800	1098	1176	1329
Having conquered and Christianised Friuli, Saxony, Swabia, Bavaria, Hungary, Gascony and northern Spain, Pope Leo III crowns Charles Holy Roman Emperor on Christmas Day.	Milan becomes a *comune*, an increasingly independent city-state. Bergamo, Brescia, Como, Cremona, Mantua and Verona follow suit in the ensuing 30 years.	Defeated by the Lombard League, Frederick Barbarossa sues for peace. Peace between Frederick and Pope Alexander III is achieved in 1177 with the Treaty of Venice.	Azzone Visconti becomes the first strongman of Milan. In his 10 years as Lord of Milan he annexes Bergamo, Como, Crema, Cremona, Lecco, Lodi and Vercelli, among other territories.

THE IRON CROWN

Despite it's small size, the heavily jewelled *Corrona Ferrae* (Iron Crown) is one of the most significant symbols of royalty in Western Europe. It is called the Iron Crown because of the 'iron' band (revealed to be silver in later tests) that encircles the inside of the diadem, which, according to legend, was beaten out of a nail used at the Crucifixion. This makes the crown both a religious relic worthy of veneration, as well as a potent symbol of monarchy.

As with most medieval relics, the nail is said to have been discovered by St Helena, mother to Constantine, the first Christian Roman Emperor, who allegedly dispatched it to Theodolinda, regent of the Lombards, for her good work in converting her people to Christianity. Although no pre-12th century records survive, the crown was purportedly used in the coronation of Charlemagne and in 34 subsequent coronations, including those of Frederick Barbarossa, Charles V, Napoleon and Ferdinand I of Austria, who was the last Italian King to be crowned with it in 1838.

Before surrendering Lombardy to the newly unified Italian state, the Austrians removed the crown to Vienna. But in 1866, when they were finally defeated, the peace terms stipulated the return of the crown to Monza where it is now on display in the cathedral museum. The new Italian monarchs never held a coronation, but the Iron Crown was carried behind the funeral cortege of King Vittorio Emanuele II (1820–78), the first king of independent Italy.

he tells us, is exalted among cities 'like the eagle above birds'. He goes on to enumerate its admirable features: aside from its 'wondrous rotundity' it had 6km of city wall, six monasteries and 94 chapels, 80 farriers, 440 butchers and over 1000 tavern owners. The city Bonvesin loved had a population nearing 150,000. Florence and Venice were not far behind.

But left to itself the *comune* had a tendency to expand – to strengthen its borders, thwart its rivals and acquire land from weaker neighbours. By the 14th century, Milan and Venice controlled most of northern Italy and wars between the two rumbled on for decades. This endless internecine conflict, coupled with the devastating effects of the Black Death between 1348 and 1350, which killed more than 30,000 people in Milan, left people yearning for strong leadership even if losing some of their liberties was the price.

Comuni thus began inviting in strong men who could lead their cities out of crisis. The most successful of these 'temporary' leaders often refused to retire and instead became *signori*, founding long-lasting dynasties. Among the strongest were the Visconti in Milan, the Dalla Scala (or Scaliger) in Verona and the Gonzaga in Mantua. Under Azzone Visconti (who ruled from 1330–37), Milan took control of Bergamo, Brescia,

History on Show

Valle Camonica
Bronze Age rock art

Duomo (Monza)
Home of the Iron Crown

Science Museum (Milan) *Leonardo da Vinci's models*

Solferino *The 19th-century battle memorabilia*

Bellinzona *Massive borderland castles*

1386

Work begins on Milan's Duomo. The Candoglia marble quarries on Lake Maggiore are requisitioned in perpetuity and new canals are built to transport materials to the city.

1450

Soldier of fortune Francesco Sforza, married to Filippo Maria Visconti's daughter, grabs power in Milan. He aims to maintain a balance of power within Italy and keep the French out.

1495–98

At the behest of Ludovico Sforza, Leonardo da Vinci starts work on *Il Cenacolo*. He opts for an experimental new medium (oil paint), and robes Christ in a dazzling ultramarine cloak.

→ Francesco Sforza

Como, Cremona, Lodi, Novara, Piacenza and Sondrio, extending its influence from the Ticino and the Alps in the north to the Po river in the south. In 1395 Milan annexed Verona and Vicenza, as well as Bologna, Siena and Perugia.

Southeast along the Po valley were two small but vigorous principalities – the duchy of Ferrara and the marquessate of Mantua – which by the 1400s even challenged the cultural primacy of Florence. The success of Mantua's Gonzaga dynasty owed much to their skill in choosing the winning side in regional wars. It owed even more to the political talents of Isabella d'Este, a daughter of the Duke of Ferrara who became regent of Mantua in 1519 and so enhanced the prestige of her domain that her first son became a duke and her second a cardinal.

Ludovico & Leonardo

Ludovico Sforza (1452–1508) was as handsome, vigorous and cunning as a Renaissance prince could hope to be. Known to all as Il Moro (the Moor) thanks to his dark complexion, he became de facto ruler of Milan in 1481 after usurping his feckless nephew Giangaleazzo. Under his cultured and crafty rule, Ludovico turned the duchy into the 'most flourishing realm in Italy' according to the envious Holy Roman Emperor Maximilian I.

He married the brilliant Beatrice d'Este (1475–97), who is widely credited with luring high calibre Renaissance painters, musicians and architects to the court. Law and medicine flourished at the universities of Milan and Pavia. New buildings were commissioned from Bramante, and Ludovico laid the first stone of the beautiful church of Santa Maria dei Miracoli with his own hands. But Ludovico could not rest easy. Gian-

Ludovico Sforza's downfall in 1499 deprived Leonardo da Vinci of his most generous patron. Ironically, he and Ludovico were both to die barely 32km apart in the Loire valley in France: the duke imprisoned in the dungeon of Loches castle in 1508, and Leonardo in the manor house of Cloux at Amboise in 1519.

THE GOOD, THE GREAT & THEIR LEGACIES

➜ **Scaliger Clan** Verona's paranoid ruling *signori* who built the Castelvecchio and Arche Scaligeri.

➜ **Gonzaga Dynasty** Renaissance patrons of frescoes by Andrea Mantegna and Giulio Romano, and a grand cathedral by Leon Battista Alberti.

➜ **Giangaleazzo Visconti** The figure behind Milan's Duomo and the Certosa di Pavia.

➜ **Ludovico Sforza** Patron to Leonardo da Vinci and commissioner of *The Last Supper.*

➜ **Bartolomeo Colleoni** Venice's mercenary commander whose mausoleum is the Cappella Colleoni in Bergamo.

➜ **Empress Maria Theresa** The empress who ordered the building of La Scala in Milan.

➜ **Benito Mussolini** Creator of Milan's Fascist icon the Stazione Centrale and Brescia's Piazza della Vittoria.

1499	1510	1515	c 1550
A confederation of Swiss-German cantons wins independence from Austrian Habsburg control. Four years afterwards they take Bellinzona from the Sforzas.	Pliny, Ovid and Virgil all wrote about mulberry trees. In 1510 entrepreneur Pietro Boldoni realises their profit-making potential and established the first silk spinning mills on Lake Como.	Milanese and Swiss forces are defeated by François I at Marignano (modern-day Melegnano); the present-day border between Lombardy and Ticino is established.	Following Columbus' return from the New World in the late 1400s with maize, Lombard farmers take up corn production. Corn, in the form of polenta, becomes a staple.

galeazzo's father-in-law was Alfonso II, the king of Naples, whose daughter Isabella deplored Ludovico's scheming and did not fail to report her sufferings to her father. Ludovico was told to beware of assassins.

Among the brilliant courtiers in Ludovico's court was Leonardo da Vinci who was the same age as the duke. By the accounts of early biographers he, too, was strikingly handsome. He had long hair, long eyelashes and a very long beard. One itemised list of clothing notes a rose-coloured Catalan gown, dusty-rose hose, a purple cape with a velvet hood and another of crimson satin. He had brawn and vigour, too. During his absences from court, he climbed the barren peaks north of Lake Como seeking fossils and developing a taste for Valtellina wines. An epitome of masculinity he bore the title *pictor et ingeniarius ducalis*: the duke's painter and engineer.

He had come to Milan, aged 30, in the hopes of inventing and constructing fearsome war machines such as chariots, cannons and catapults. His hopes were no doubt bolstered by the fact that Milan was at war with Venice, with Ludovico spending almost 75% of his revenues on warfare. But although visions of war filled his head, he was set to work on more modest tasks such as designing costumes for weddings and banquets, decorating the halls of the castle, fashioning elaborate stage sets for pageants, and painting portraits of Il Moro's mistresses, Cecilia Gallerani and Lucrezia Crivelli.

But if Il Moro underused Leonardo, he at least offered the temperamental artist creative latitude and financial security. For the better part of two decades Leonardo was allowed to pursue his intellectual explorations through aeronautics, anatomy, architecture, mathematics and mechanics (the wonders of which are on display in Milan's Biblioteca Ambrosiana (p49) and Science Museum (p56)) and finally furnished the world with *The Last Supper*, an artwork of such unquestionable superiority it swept away the efforts of even the greatest masters before him. In 1489, commissioners for the decorations in Orvieto cathedral in Umbria declared Pietro Perugino the most famous painter in all of Italy. But when Perugino unveiled his altarpiece in 1505, he was ridiculed for his lack of ability and want of originality. By 1505, Leonardo had changed the way men saw the world.

Foreign Rule

As a relation of the Angevins, Charles VIII had a weak claim to the throne of Naples, which he was encouraged to revive by Ludovico Sforza who wanted to rid himself of the Neapolitan threat, Alfonso II. And so, in 1494, the French king marched down the peninsula unopposed and occupied Naples in February 1495.

In 1512 the Swiss helped Ludovico's son Massimiliano return to the ducal throne of Milan but a Franco-Venetian alliance soon reversed that situation. Beaten by the forces of François I at the Battle of Marignano (modern day Melegnano) in 1515, the Swiss retreated over the border and judged it prudent not to embark on foreign wars ever again.

1630–31	1713	1760s	1799
Neglected by Spanish governors, Lombardy sinks into provincial decay and a devastating plague sweeps across the region, killing almost half the population of Milan.	The Treaty of Utrecht ends the War of Spanish Succession and thwarts French ambitions. Spanish territories, including Lombardy, are given to Austria to restore the balance of continental power.	Milan, along with Venice, Turin, Florence and the lakes, becomes an essential stop for British aristocrats on the Grand Tour, a trend that continues until the 1840s.	Como's most famous son, Alessandro Volta (1745–1827), invents the electric battery. Professor at the University of Pavia, he is made a count by Napoleon in 1810.

After an enthusiastic welcome, Charles made himself popular slashing taxes and throwing banquets, but he was far too venal for his popularity to last. As the French army sickened from syphilis he found himself opposed by a Holy League that included Venice, Mantua, Florence, the Pope and Ludovico who, perturbed by the garrisoning of Charles' cousin and would-be claimant to the Milanese duchy, Louis of Orléans, at Asti, had switched sides.

Making a run for the north, troops of the Holy League, lead by Francesco II Gonzaga, caught up with Charles at Fornovo. Despite being outnumbered three to one and with their artillery rendered useless by the rain, the French were brutally exposed. But instead of inflicting a crushing defeat, the Italian troops broke rank and made straight for the booty-laden French wagons. Since the French continued retreating after the battle, Francesco claimed a dubious victory and even had Mantegna paint the *Madonna della Vittoria* (The Madonna of Victory) in commemoration.

Milanese journalist and politician Luigi Barzini (1908–84) considered the Battle of Fornovo a crucial event in Italian history. If the Italians had won, he theorised, 'Nobody would have ventured lightly across the Alps, for fear of being destroyed'. Instead, Charles' uncontested march on Naples showed how easy a conquest Italy was. It encouraged Charles' cousin, and the next king of France, Louis of Orléans, to emulate him in 1499 – leading an invasion which led to the overthrow and capture of Ludovico Sforza.

As the struggle for supremacy in western Europe escalated between the French and Spanish in the 16th century, the French invasions of Italy brought Spain into the northern half of the country. Lying directly between Naples, which Emperor Charles V inherited from his Spanish mother, and Germany, which he claimed through his Habsburg grandfather, Lombardy was the inevitable battleground. Following the death of the last Sforza duke in 1535, Charles took control of the duchy of Milan and gave it to his son Philip II (1527–98), the future Spanish king. Thus the political and cultural independence of Milan was extinguished forever.

The Five Day Revolt

Napoleon's greatest legacy as the king of Italy (1805–14) was a new-found sense of nationalism. When his adversaries gathered in Vienna in 1814 to restore Europe's pre-Napoleonic borders and Lombardy's previous Austrian rulers, many Milanese in the Italian contingent complained. One of them told Lord Castlereagh, the British foreign secretary, that Italians were no longer satisfied to languish beneath paternalistic Austrian rule. But the great powers of Europe – Britain, Russia, Prussia and Austria – weren't inclined to listen. If the Austrians were going to have to give

1805	1805–1814	1814–15	1848
Milan's Duomo is finished for the coronation of Napoleon Bonaparte, who crowns himself King of Italy with the Iron Crown and the words, 'God gives it to me, beware whoever touches it'.	Italy becomes a battleground between Napoleon, the Habsburgs and their Russian allies, thousands of Italians are conscripted and much of the region's cultural patrimony is stolen.	The Congress of Vienna re-establishes the pre-Napoleonic European borders with Lombardy and the Veneto joined as a single 'kingdom' beneath Austrian rule.	Revolts across Europe spark rebellion in Italy. King Carlo Alberto of Piedmont joins the Lombards against Austria, but within a year the latter recovers Lombardy and the Veneto.

up the Netherlands, then they wanted their northern Italian territories back.

Filled with prosperous industrialists and intellectuals, Milan now chafed under Austrian rule, not because it was bad, but because they were occupiers. Poet-prophet Vittorio Alfieri (1749-1803) and statesman Massimo d'Azeglio (1798-1866) were ashamed by Italy's subjugation and were convinced that the country's dignity could only be restored through martial ardour. Other artists and intellectuals joined Azeglio in searching history for material they could weave into their patriotic propaganda promoting unity and independence, but they had a hard time finding suitable examples (after all the Battle of Legnano was over 600 years ago). The only work of the era that has truly lasted is Alessandro Manzoni's *I Promessi Sposi* (*The Betrothed*; 1827), a book that acquired the status of national monument soon after its publication, written as it was in the new 'Italian' language.

Other idealogues like Milanese philosopher Carlo Cattaneo (1801-69) advocated for a federal system, arguing that Italy's 'ancient love of liberty' was more important that 'the cult of unity'. Cattaneo pointed out how medieval Italy had prospered from civic competition and he presciently argued that a political system that failed to take into account the communal ethos would not succeed.

In 1848, Italy began the year with revolution. First an uprising broke out in Sicily in January, where insurgents forced Ferdinand II to grant his kingdom a constitution. By March, constitutions had also been proclaimed in Tuscany, Piedmont and Rome and further insurrections were breaking out in Venice, Milan, Parma and Modena. When the Cinque Giornate di Milano (Five Days of Milan) broke out on 18 March, Cattaneo threw himself into the street fighting, joining rebels bent on forcing Austrian commander Marshal Radetzky out of the city. Together with democrats Enrico Cernuschi, Giulio Terzaghi and Giorgio Clerici, Cattaneo formed a council of war in Via Bigli from where he helped direct operations, refusing all offers of an armistice and insisting on the complete evacuation of Radetzky's forces from Lombardy.

The revolts in Milan and, more importantly, in Venice (where the rebels held out until well into 1849) may have failed but they provided essential fuel for those clamouring for Italian unification. The diplomatic offensive to this end came from the Duchy of Savoy, whose capital was in Turin. Ably led by prime minister Count Camillo Benso Cavour, the House of Savoy struck a deal with France's Napoleon III. In 1859, Savoyard and Napoleonic troops defeated the Austrians at Magenta (4 June) and Solferino (24 June) and within a year all of Lombardy had joined the nascent Italian kingdom. Venice would not do so until 1866 and unification was completed in 1870 with the taking of Rome.

1861	1870–1915	1915	1921–22
Two decades of insurrections culminate in a new Italian government, with a parliament. Vittorio Emanuele II is proclaimed king of a newly united Italy.	Milan booms, becoming the country's main railway hub and leading industrial centre. Milanese banks dominate financial markets and in 1883 one of Europe's first electric power stations is opened.	Italy enters WWI on the side of the Allies to win Italian territories still in Austrian hands. Austria had offered to cede some of these territories but Italy insists the offer is insufficient.	Mussolini forms the Fascist Party and marches on Rome. King Vittorio Emanuele III, fearful of the movement's popular power, asks Mussolini to form a government in 1922.

Bombs & Blackshirts

Milan hadn't yet recovered from its WWI losses when influenza struck in 1918, and the economy faltered. Benito Mussolini's political career began in Milan, swiftly moving from words to direct action at the hands of his paramilitary Blackshirts. His promises of strength and national unity had broad appeal and by 1922 he was prime minister (many turned a blind eye to his rapid assumption of absolute power until 1938, when at Hilter's behest, he introduced anti-Semitic 'race laws'). The city's Fascist monuments include San Siro, Stazione Centrale, the Triennale, Palazzo dell Arengario and the massive Armani shop on Via Manzotti.

During WWII, the Allied forces destroyed over a quarter of the city, leaving La Scala and the Palazzo Reale in ruins. The Italian Resistance and anti-Fascist trade unions paralysed Milan with strikes and demonstrations in 1943. Italy surrendered to Allied forces on 8 September, but two weeks later Mussolini declared a new Fascist republic in Salò on Lake Garda, forcing a long, bloody fight against the Allies and a civil guerrilla war. The partisans prevailed in 1945 and Brescia earned a Gold Medal for its brave resistance against the Fascists.

Mussolini was captured near Como as he tried to escape to the border. He was executed along with his mistress, their bodies brought to Milan and displayed at a petrol station. Journalist Rossana Rossanda recalled, 'I saw the bodies, Mussolini, Clara Petacci and the others, strung up by their feet in Piazzale Loreto. In front of them there thronged a furious mass of people, women shouting, men white-faced with indignation, screaming out their anger and their impotence: justice had been done by somebody else, on their behalf. There was some derision, but mostly rage. I turned away; it was a necessary ritual, perhaps, but terrible.'

> The Cimitero Monumentale contains a memorial to the Milanese who died in Nazi concentration camps. Designed by Studio BBPR, the pure form of a cube is traced in steel and slab marble, a response of reason and light to the horror of the war years. At its centre is earth from the camp where Gianluigi Banfi, one of BBPR's four partners, died.

Comebacks & Kickbacks

A postwar manufacturing boom produced yet another growth spurt and change was in the air. In 1963 Umberto Eco, chafing against the conformity and insularity of Italian intellectual life, co-founded the avant-garde literary group Gruppo 63. The year 1968 brought dissent, free love and psychedelic fashions to Milan's students. The Quadrilatero d'Oro became synonymous with the fashion industry. At the same time, growing income gaps and mass migration from southern Italy inflamed underlying tensions and old political rivalries. Brigade Rosse terrorism and repressive anti-terror laws created further turmoil, giving rise to extremist groups like the right-wing Lega Nord (Northern League).

The glamorous '80s and '90s brought stability to Milan, or so it seemed. Corruption and organised crime mushroomed behind closed doors until the Tangentopoli (or 'kickback city') scandals broke in 1992. Milanese

1940–43	1945	1946	1961
The Fascist Italian Empire joins Germany in declaring war. Italy surrenders in 1943; Mussolini refuses to comply and establishes the so-called Republic of Salò.	Partisans capture and execute Mussolini and his companion Clara Petacci on the shores of Lake Como. Their bodies are later strung up in Milan's Piazzale Loreto.	Italians vote to abolish the monarchy and King Umberto II leaves Italy, refusing to recognise the result. Sixty-three percent of Lombards vote for a republic.	With low salaries and a booming export business, Milan and its surrounding area attract vast waves of immigrants from the south – more than 80,000 settle in Milan in 1961.

judges opened investigations and trials implicating thousands of northern politicians and high-flyers in a panoply of white-collar crimes. Led by judge Antonio di Pietro, the trials came to be known as Mani Pulite (Clean Hands) and rocked the political and business establishment.

Many spoke of the coming of a new republic, as traditional parties such as the centre-right conservative Catholic Democrazia Cristiana and centre-left Partito Socialista Italiano (PSI) crumbled. PSI chief and former prime minister Bettino Craxi chose exile in Tunisia rather than face the courts. An old pal of his, Milan business magnate Silvio Berlusconi, saw his political opportunity and launched his Forza Italia (Go Italy!) campaign. He was elected prime minister in 1994 with the support of an equally colourful character from near Varese – Umberto Bossi.

Bossi's Lega Nord (Northern League), founded in the 1980s on a narrow anti-immigration, anti-Rome and pro-secession (now watered down to devolution) platform, quickly pulled the rug from under Berlusconi's feet by withdrawing from the coalition, but stood with him again in his election victories of 2001 and 2008. Although the Lega Nord often wins as much as 20% of the vote in northern Italy, most northern cities (apart from Milan) have tended to vote centre-left. Recent exceptions to that rule have been Verona and Brescia, although in 2013 elections Brescia swung back to the centre-left. Likewise, Milan voted in its first ever centre-left mayor Giuliano Pisapia (a former communist) in 2011, a result that dealt a devastating blow to Berlusconi who considers the city his home turf.

The Crisis

By mid-2009 the economic woes besetting the world were making themselves felt in Lombardy. From the silk business in Como, to tourism on the lakes, the crisis was beginning to bite. It was estimated that throughout Lombardy the contraction in business had cost companies some €12 billion in the first three months of 2009, while gross domestic product fell by 6.3%. The national debt rose to a dizzying 130% of GDP in 2013.

Assuming that the country can continue to borrow at the current 4% interest rate, the economy will have to grow by 5% annually to maintain the current debt ratio. This doesn't give newly elected prime minister Enrico Letta much time to implement reform, especially with a forced coalition of social democrats and conservative members of Silvio Berlusconi's party behind him. But economic realities are dictating radical change: Italy's debts are too high, its products are uncompetitive and investment is low. In northern Italy, the country has a significant industrial and creative asset, which is ripe for investment. Improving conditions for that investment and moving away from the polarising, media-driven, populist politics of Berlusconi is the key to getting Lombardy, and Italy, back to work.

Claudia Cardinale starred in the 1984 film *Claretta* about the racy life and tragic end of Clara Petacci, Mussolini's lover. Given the chance to flee when they were captured, she instead tried in vain to shield Il Duce from the partisan execution squad's bullets.

In 2013 Vodafone posted scorching £1.8 billion losses on its Spanish and Italian operations. While a nation's mobile phone bill might not be the last word in financial modelling, Italy has the highest mobile penetration in Europe (90.5% of 11 to 74 year olds) and that's an awful lot of people who simply can't afford to spend what they used to.

1982	2001	2011	2013
Umberto Bossi founds the right-wing, separatist Lega Lombarda movement, which in 1991 becomes Lega Nord and later an ally of prime minister Silvio Berlusconi.	Silvio Berlusconi's right-wing Casa delle Libertà (Liberties House) coalition wins an absolute majority in national polls. The following five years are marked by economic stagnation.	Berlusconi stands trial in Milan in April on charges of abuse of power and paying for sex with an under-aged Moroccan prostitute called Karima El Mahroug (aka 'Ruby Heart Stealer').	Campaigning on the slogan *prima il Nord* (the North first), Roberto Maroni's victory as President of Lombardy consolidates the Northern League's hold over the largest regional government in Italy.

The Arts

A young Michelangelo Merisi, now better known by the name of his Lombard home town Caravaggio, got noticed in Milan with his singular style of extreme realism in 1584, while art maverick and true Renaissance man Leonardo da Vinci hung around long enough to paint *The Last Supper* and install a system of locks and levees for the city's canals. Art and architecture in Milan have always been about innovation.

Medieval English poet Geoffrey Chaucer was linked with Milan's Visconti dukes through his patron, Lionel, Duke of Clarence, who married Violante Visconti in 1368. Chaucer mentions Bernabò Visconti ('God of delit and scourge of Lumbardye') in the exempla of tyrants in the *Monk's Tale*, while Pavia provides the setting for *The Merchant's Tale*.

Lingua Franca

Virgil (70–19 BC), son of Mantua, was poet laureate of Roman Italia, penning the national epic *The Aeneid* in which he promoted the idea of Italianism by fusing Greeks, Trojans and Italic peoples into a shared Roman ancestry. His poetry had an enduring and widespread influence, providing inspiration for medieval humanists like Petrarch, Boccaccio and Dante, who made Virgil his guide in his underworld peregrinations in the *Divina Commedia* (Divine Comedy; 1555).

Other northern luminaries included poet Catullus (84–54 BC), naturalist and philosopher Pliny the Elder (23–79), writer Pliny the Younger (61–112) and historian Tacitus (56–117). Through them Romanisation continued apace, carried to all corners of the Empire through its legionnaires, who spoke in Latin and retired to villas in the Po valley and around the lakes. To make them comfortable, extensive building projects were commissioned: a castrum at Como and Castelseprio, a grand arena in Verona, a forum, theatre and a multitude of basilicas and temples in Mediolanum (Milan) and Brixia (Brescia), and commodious country villas at Sirmione, Desenzano del Garda and Bellagio. Many of these, such as the well-preserved Domus dell'Ortaglia in Brescia's Museo della Città, were decorated with fine mosaics, elegant *peristyles* (internal courtyards) and frescoes.

This rash of building gave the peninsula a common (vernacular) architectural language. The red-brick basilica with its colonnaded interior, plain facade and semicircular apses is still discernable in many of Milan's oldest churches (Sant'Eustorgio, Sant'Ambrogio, Santa Maria delle Grazie, San Lorenzo). In Cremona, Lodi and Monza, and around the lakes, especially Lake Como, dozens of towns and villages boast Lombard Romanesque churches, distinguished by their plain facades, symmetrical layout, vaulted interiors and rounded, ornamental arcades. The Maestri Comacini (Como Masterbuilders) spread across Lombardy and Europe, some travelling as far as Catalonia (Spain) and St Petersburg (Russia).

Likewise, *volgare latino* (vernacular Latin) cut across diverse regional dialects providing Italy with its first lingua franca. From this, modern Italian was to finally emerge nearly 1800 years later, promoted over the centuries through the works of Virgil, Petrarch, Dante and Alessandro Manzoni, whose immense novel *I Promessi Sposi* (1827) is considered the first modern 'Italian' novel.

A Humanist View

Almost 200 years before da Vinci's *The Last Supper* came Giotto's Renaissance breakthrough: the moving, modern 1303–05 frescoes in Padua's Capella degli Scrovegni. Medieval churchgoers were accustomed to blank stares from flat, far-off saints perched on high golden Gothic thrones, but Giotto introduced Biblical figures as characters in recognisable settings, caught up in extraordinary circumstances. Onlookers gossip as middle-aged Anne tenderly kisses Joachim, and then late in life gives birth to miracle-baby Mary, and Jesus stares down Judas as the traitor puckers up with a fateful kiss.

Dante, da Vinci and Boccaccio all honour Giotto (1267–1337) as the artist who officially ended the Dark Ages. His humane approach changed how people saw themselves; not as lowly vassals but as vessels for the divine. This radical idea was the product of a new generation of Italian scholars who were rediscovering classical ideals. Poet Francesco Petrarch (1304–74) was just such a man. Like Giotto, Petrarch was patronised by Azzone Visconti, for whom he worked as an ambassador in Milan between 1353 and 1361, and where he spent his time writing to Boccaccio extolling the glories of Pavia's well-endowed library.

A seat of humanist scholarship and debate, Pavia's library contained many richly illuminated manuscripts in the *ouvraige de lombardie* tradition, a highly decorative style that emanated from Po valley workshops. At the time manuscript illumination led the visual arts agenda in Italy and Europe and many proponents of the style like Giovannino de'Grassi (c 1340–1398), a pupil of Giotto whose Sketch Book is the prized possession of Bergamo's Angelo Mai library, and the Zavattari brothers, who executed the frescoes in Theodolinda's chapel in Monza in 1444, were extraordinary artisans.

These artist-artisans specialised in manuscript illumination, fresco, stained glass and sculpture. In fact, Grassi was also a master builder on Milan's Duomo and a consultant on the building of Pavia cathedral. In their work they emulated Giotto's richness of colour, anecdotal representation of character and well-defined perspective. You can see the close connections between the frescoes in the Mocchirolo Oratory (reconstructed wholesale in the Pinacoteca di Brera) and the Oratory of Albizzate near Varese, and the exquisite detail in Grassi's illuminated Tarocchi Brambilla (Brambilla tarot cards) also in Brera (Room XXI), where the Lombard's greater decorative sensibility and attention to fashion are wonderfully rendered in the costumes of Milanese nobles and St Catherine's ermine-tasselled gown.

TRUMP CARDS

The Visconti-Sforza tarot deck (1463) is one of the oldest card decks in the world. When they were commissioned, the cards were still known as *Trionfi* ('triumphs', ie trump) cards, and used for everyday playing. They had a significant impact on the visual composition, card numbering and interpretation of modern decks.

Architecture of the Imagination

The Duomo may be the enduring symbol of Milan, but it is also one of the most famous and complex constructions of Italian Gothic architecture. Begun by Giangaleazzo Visconti in 1387, its ambitious design was considered impossible to build. Canals were constructed to transport marble to the centre of town and new technologies were invented to adapt to the never-before-attempted scale. And its slow construction – over 500 years – made its name a byword for an impossible task (*fabrica del Dom* in the Milanese dialect).

During his stint as King of Italy, Napoleon, never one to miss a chance to be associated with something monumental, offered to fund its completion in 1805. The appointed architect piled on the neo-Gothic details displaying a prescient use of fashion logic, ie everything old is new again. The organic ferment of petrified pinnacles, cusps, buttresses, rampant arches, cyma and acroteria are almost all products of the 19th century but pay faithful homage to the original design.

The choice of the Duomo's Gothic style was inspired by 14th-century European trends, reflecting the Visconti's close links with France, Germany and Bohemia, through marriage and alliance. Although the designer is unknown, we do know that Giovannino de'Grassi was listed among the engineers in 1389. In 1395 he was painting the sacristy sculpture, and from 1396 he was involved in illuminating the transcript of Beroldo's *Treatise on the Usage of Milan Cathedral*, which he decorated with swirling plants and pinnacles. In it the close relationship between organic forms and the cathedral's architectural detail are clear. The macrocosm of the Duomo and the microcosm of manuscript decoration were part and parcel of the same stylistic universe.

French, Flemish, Venetian, German and Alpine influences are evident throughout the enormous structure. Initially designed so Milan's then-population of around 40,000 could fit within, the cathedral's elegant, hysterical and sublimely spiritual architecture can even transport 21st-century types back to a medieval mindset. Inside, once your eyes adjust to the subdued light, how but not to stare up, and up, to the largest stained-glass windows in all of Christendom? In the north (left) transept the Trivulzio Candelabra is one of the cathedral's original decorations. Attributed to Anglo-Norman master Nicolas de Verdun, its roiling, writhing composition of Biblical figures, flora and fauna reflects the same naturalistic detail and simplicity of form that marks out Grassi's manuscripts and Baldassare degli Embriachi's extraordinary triptych (c 1390–1400) in hippopotamus ivory in the Duomo's only contemporary, the Certosa di Pavia.

Although nothing else of scale remains from the Gothic period, the era's highly decorative tradition, love of naturalism and representation of an anecdotal character captured the northern imagination and resonate across the centuries. Men like Grassi were forerunners to the burgeoning Renaissance talent of Stefano da Verona (c 1379–1438), Gentile da Fabriano (c 1370–1427) and the great Pisanello (1395–1455), who worked at the courts of Verona, Ferrara, Mantua, Milan, Rome and Naples. Pisanello foreshadowed the coming brilliance of the Renaissance with his naturalistic style so wonderfully captured in his fresco *St George and the Princess of Trebizond* in Verona's church of Sant'Anastasia, and the graphic cartoons in Mantua's Palazzo Ducale.

Better known as an architect, Bramante embarked on numerous architectural projects in the city, most notably the church of Santa Maria presso San Satiro. With a tiny plot to work on, Bramante used all his illusionistic skills as a painter to create the illusion of a grander space with his theatrical trompe l'œil apse.

Classicism

In 1452 the most important Renaissance treatise on architecture, *De Re Aedificatoria* (On the Art of Building; 1485) was written by Genovese polymath Leon Battista Alberti (1404–72). Like Petrarch before him, Alberti loved the classics and grasped how the lessons of ancient Rome

THE COURT PAINTER

The first Renaissance court painter was Andrea Mantegna, who was employed by the Gonzaga marquesses of Mantua from 1460 until his death in 1506. He was a good choice for a dynasty with political pretensions. With his understanding of perspective and knowledge of the classical world, Mantegna glorified his subjects, making his nobles seem like ancient heroes as well as contemporary men. Viewers of his powerful series *The Triumph of Julius Caesar* (1484–92; now at Hampton Court in London) can sense the implied connection between his patrons and the conquering Caesar. For his pains, Mantegna, a poor woodworker's son, received an extravagant income (75 lire a month), and the Gonzaga got their propaganda and the reputation they still enjoy today – that of being great patrons of the arts. Bramante, Leonardo da Vinci, Raphael and Michelangelo all followed in his footsteps and worked as court painters for powerful patrons.

were pertinent to the city-states of 15th-century Italy. Regarding mathematics as the common ground between art and the sciences, Alberti made an effort to explain his thinking in his earlier publication, *De Pictura* (On Painting; 1435), which formed the first scientific study of perspective. He dedicated the treatise to Gian Francesco Gonzaga, his generous Mantuan patron.

As the Pope's architectural advisor, Alberti had plenty of time to study ancient ruins and the writings of Roman architect and engineer Vitruvius (c 80–c 15 BC). His detailed observations appeared in the 10-volume *De Re Aedificatoria,* which was to become the major reference for Renaissance architects. Eager to put his theories into practice, Alberti then set about building things. His most notable projects are the church of Santa Maria Novella in Florence and the soaring cathedral of Sant'Andrea in Mantua.

In Mantua, Alberti was given free rein to create a monumental edifice to house the Gonzaga's most precious relic, two ampoules of Christ's blood. Alberti recreated an Etruscan temple with a huge barrel-vaulted nave fronted with a triumphal arch for a facade. Fittingly, in the first chapel on the left, rests that other great classical artist Andrea Mantegna (1431–1506), whose outstanding depiction of the *Dead Christ* (1480) is thought to have been created for this chapel.

Like Alberti, Mantegna was fascinated with the classical world and experimented widely with perspective. His painted room, the *Camera degli Sposi,* in the Gonzaga's Palazzo Ducale is the apotheosis of this study. Apprenticed in Padua, he would have come into contact with the work of Tuscans Paolo Uccello, Filippo Lippi and Donatello, and in 1453 he married Nicolosia Bellini, bringing him into the orbit of the celebrated Venetian Bellini brothers, Giovanni and Gentile. Synergies between their work are evident in Mantegna's gorgeous, garlanded Madonna in San Zeno Maggiore, in Verona, and the softer, more luminous *Madonna of the Cherubim* (c 1485), which sits next to Bellini's Mantegna-esque *Pietà* (1460) in the Brera gallery.

Donato Bramante (1444–1514) took his lead from Mantegna, producing the intensely poignant but restrained *Christ at the Column* (c 1490). Commissioned by Cardinal Ascanio Sforza for the Chiaravalle Abbey on the outskirts of Milan, the image demonstrates Bramante's research into perspective and the volumetric construction of a human body. Christ's profoundly tragic gaze, though, shows a clear dialogue with the work of Leonardo da Vinci who was working in Milan at the same time.

In the same way as Bramante, Brescian artist Vicenzo Foppa, who frescoed the Portinari chapel in Sant'Eustorgio, combined the perspective-based classicism of Mantegna with the intense compassion and realism of Leonardo.

Leonardo da Vinci

During the 15th century wealthy Lombards like the Della Scala family in Verona and the Gonzaga in Mantua played a key role in patronising and promoting the great artists of the day, and even wealthy merchants, abbots and bankers spent their hard-earned coin on frescoing their townhouses, fashioning extraordinary mausoleums and commissioning frescoes and portraits. Medici banker Pigello Portinari commissioned Vicenzo Foppa to paint his private chapel in Milan; Venetian commander Bartolomeo Colleoni engaged Pavian architect and sculptor Giovanni Amadeo to fashion his polychrome marble mausoleum, the Cappella Colleoni, in Bergamo; and Cardinal Castiglioni hired Florentine Masolino to paint the charming frescoes in Castiglione Olona in Varese province.

Top Frescoes

Il Cenacolo Vinciano, Milan

Chiesa di San Maurizio, Milan

Basilica di San Giulio, Lake Orta

Palazzo Te, Mantua

Chiesa di Santa Maria Foris Portas, Castelseprio

Basilica di Sant'Abbondio, Como

Collegiata, Castiglione Olona

Cremonese Sofonisba Anguissola (c 1561–1625) was one of the few professional female artists of the 16th century. She set a precedent for women to be accepted as students of art and she pursued an international career at the royal court in Madrid. Despite two marriages she worked as a professional artist her whole life, until she died aged 93 in 1625.

From the fruitful partnership between Ludovico Sforza and Leonardo, Milan's (and possibly the world's) most famous painting was to emerge. Leonardo's depiction of *Il Cenacolo* (*The Last Supper*; 1495–98), painted on a wall of the refectory adjoining the Chiesa di Santa Maria delle Grazie, shows Christ and his disciples at dinner during the dramatic moment when Christ reveals he is aware one of his followers will betray him. It is a masterful psychological study.

For Leonardo, painting was all about capturing the details, details which he tirelessly recorded in his famous sketchbook. In his treatise on painting he stated the artist had two goals: the first to represent man, and the second to capture the intentions of his mind. While the first had already been ably demonstrated by Pisanello, Mantegna, Bramante and Foppa, the second was much harder. Leonardo concluded the only way to do this was by capturing men's expressive 'gestures and movements'. It was this that he so masterfully translated into *The Last Supper*, where the drama of the scene is embodied in the disciples' reactions, both physical (upsetting glasses, recoiling backwards, lifting knives and leaning in) and in their varied facial expressions (mouths agape, brows furrowed, expressions incredulous).

So outstandingly good was Leonardo's composition that almost before the paint dried demand grew for copies. Princes, cardinals, churches and monasteries all wanted a replica, much in the way that everyone wanted a relic of the True Cross. *The Last Supper* was engraved as early as 1498 and Giampietrino executed the most faithful copy on canvas in 1520 and many other copies followed in fresco, panel, canvas, marble and tapestry. Copies were produced in Venice, Antwerp and Paris. The Certosa di Pavia even had two versions. But while the results were spectacular, Leonardo's choice of oil paint was flawed; unlike traditional egg tempera, the oil paint did not bond successfully with the plaster and within a few decades began to flake. After 22 years of diligent restoration (completed in 1999) conservators estimate that 80% of the original colour has been lost.

But the legacy remains. *The Last Supper* ushered in the High Renaissance with a flourish, influencing generations of Lombard artists (Giovanni Boltraffio, Marco d'Oggiono, Bernardino Luini, Salaino, Giampietrino, Cesare da Sesto, Andrea Solari and Cristoforo Solari, whose works are scattered through the collections of the Pinacoteca di Brera, the Accademia Carrara, the Museo di Poldi Pezzoli and the Certosa di Pavia) and laying the groundwork for Michelangelo and Raphael.

Accademies & Collectors

When Pope Clement XIV (1769–74) suppressed the Jesuit order, their grand palace and well-stocked library on Via Brera was appropriated by the ruling Austrian state. At the time, Maria Theresa and her son Joseph II were engaged in a wide-ranging program of reforms in Milan, which extended to the city's educational establishments. Giuseppe Piermarini, who had designed La Scala, was chosen to adapt the palace for use as a new art academy and in 1801 Giuseppe Bossi was appointed secretary. An ardent republican, artist, connoisseur and friend of Canova and Angelica Kauffmann, Bossi assembled the nucleus of Brera's art collection.

The *pinacoteca* (gallery) was to come later in 1809, under the direction of Viceroy Eugène de Beaubarnais, in fulfillment of Napoleonic policy intent on creating cultural repositories for public edification much in the same vein as the Louvre. Prestigious works of art, considered symbols of national identity, were confiscated from churches and monasteries in the Veneto, Mantua, Ferrara, Bologna, Ravenna, Urbino and the Papal States and brought to Brera. The focus, naturally, was on the Italians

Best in Print

Painters of Reality *(Andrea Bayer et al) Sumptuous, illustrated exploration of the Lombard Renaissance.*

Maurizio Cattelan *(Francesco Bonami, Massimiliano Gioni et al) Milan's bad boy artist, pocket-sized.*

Design City Milan *(Cecilia Bolognesi) Photographic tour of cutting-edge architecture.*

Giò Ponti *(Ugo La Pietra) Monograph from local publisher Rizzoli.*

Villas on the Italian Lakes *(Elizabeth Minchilli) Mouth watering villa interiors.*

AN ENLIGHTENED VISION

The great museum tradition for which Milan is famous can be traced back to the educational aims of Counter-Reformation cardinal Federico Borromeo (1564–1631). During his 36 years as Milan's cardinal, he distinguished himself through his incorruptible episcopal virtue, academic zeal and civic patronage, applying everywhere the reformed principles laid down by the Council of Trent (1545–63).

In 1609 he founded the Biblioteca Ambrosiana, which, along with Oxford's Bodleian, was one of the first public libraries in Europe. In 1618 he also donated his art collection to the Ambrosian academy and laid the foundation of a public institution that could work with the school training artists and supply them with models and examples to copy. Not only did he make his collection available, but he compiled a catalogue called the *Musaeum*, in which he gave an explanation of his tastes and ideas about art.

In contrast to the tradition of the time, Borromeo's collection included many anti-academic works like Caravaggio's *Basket of Fruit* (1599) along with genre paintings, still lifes by Breugel and Paul Bril, and miniatures, portraits and landscapes that reflected his scientific approach and interest in visual realism. Despite being struck by the plague while feeding the poor in 1630, which led to the closure of the academy for many years, the public tradition and universal intention introduced by him were to leave an indelible mark on Milan.

(Bellini, Bramante, Luini, Mantegna, Raphael and Titian), reflecting the museum's social context and role as a great workshop of art.

At the same time men like Count Giacomo Carrara (1714–96), descended from that long line of wealthy Lombard art patrons, sought to establish a similar institution in Bergamo. Well educated and well travelled, Carrara was an art connoisseur who believed passionately in the values of the Renaissance in northern Italy. By his death he had amassed 1300 works of art, all of which he bequeathed to his new Accademia Carrara in the hope of reviving the local Bergamo school, which boasted great talents such as portraitist Giovanni Moroni and Lorenzo Lotto. Although Venetian by birth, Lotto spent his most productive years in Bergamo and Brescia leaving the glorious *Pala Martinengo* in the church of San Stefano, frescoes in the Suardi chapel in Trescore and some 20 canvases commissioned by wealthy merchants and aristocrats, many of which now live in the Carrara collection.

Although the Carrara is the grandest expression of civic-minded private patronage in Lombardy, many other enlightened individuals formed smaller but equally impressive collections. Count Guglielmo Lochis (1789–1859), the pro-Austrian *podestà* (mayor) of Bergamo, donated many works from his collection to Carrara, as did art critic Giovanni Morelli (1816–91). In Milan, Gian Giacomo Poldi Pezzoli (1822–79) amassed one of the finest private collections in Europe and modelled his apartments on the house-museum that he had seen in London (which was later to become the Victoria & Albert Museum). His contempories, Fausto (1843–1914) and Joseph Bagatti Valsecchi (1845–1934), transformed their Milanese townhouse into a faithful copy of a Lombard-Renaissance palazzo and filled it with paintings, sculptures, glass, ceramics, textiles, books and crafts belonging to the Lombard Renaissance tradition. Other noble families, like the Melzi d'Eril, branched out into landscapes, such as those by Bernardo Bellotti, a student of Canaletto, who painted their villa at Gazzada on Lake Varese, while Napoleonic politician Count Giovanni Sommariva collected Canova statues and romantic Hayez paintings at Villa Carlotta in Tremezzo.

THE CLUE IS IN THE DETAILS

Brilliant art critic and anti-intellectual Giovanni Morelli (1816–91) devised the 'Morellian' technique of identifying authorship of a painting by studying the characteristic 'hands' of painters, by which the minor details of a portrait or scene, such as the painting of a subject's ears or hands, reveals the artist's subconscious shorthand.

The Morellian technique of finding hidden clues in the details was to have a much wider cultural influence, when the method was mentioned in Arthur Conan Doyle's best-selling series *Sherlock Holmes*, and in the work of Sigmund Freud.

GALLERIA

Stile Liberty

From the latter end of the 19th century, there was a boom in villa construction on the lakes, a symbol of self-worth among moneyed families at a time of confidence following Italian unification. The villas became the focus of a high-class dolce vita, as well as their gardens, which were seen as a kind of open-air salon where a coterie of socialites and artists were entertained.

It was the belle époque, and for some decades a fresh new wave in art and architecture had been spreading across Europe, taking its cue from applied arts and strong Japanese influences. Known as art nouveau in France, it came to be called *stile liberty* (liberty style) in Italy. Key points for identifying such buildings are the proud and visible use of materials previously considered 'ignoble', such as wrought iron, ceramics, stained glass, brick and, in some cases, cement. In addition, liberty and art nouveau designers and architects favoured curves and natural motifs (flowers, vines etc) over straight lines, particularly in decorative elements (from door handles to windows, sculptural reliefs to door frames). The style reached its apotheosis in the spa of San Pellegrino Terme and in the residential area around Corso Venezia in Milan, where there are many examples, like the exotic natural history museum and the civic aquarium, and Casa Galimberti, with its ceramic facade, on Via Malpighi.

Directly across from the Duomo sits Milan's other precocious feat of engineering, the Galleria Vittoria Emanuele. This soaring iron-and-glass neoclassical arcade heralded the new industrial Italy of the Risorgimento. Highly innovative for its time, the building has spawned countless imitators, right down to the glazed-roofed megamalls of today.

It is hardly surprising that many buildings in this style should have popped up on the lakes. They did so mainly in more popular resorts. Since the opening of the Sempione (Simplon) Pass from Switzerland and the arrival of rail connections, Stresa on Lake Maggiore had become a key holiday destination as had sunny Gardone Riviera on Lake Garda. Both are dotted with liberty villas like the Grand Hotel Borromees and Villa Barberis on Lake Maggiore and Villa Simonini (now Hotel Laurin) and Villa Feltrinelli (also a hotel) on Lake Garda. One of the great Italian liberty architects was Giuseppe Sommaruga, who left several villas in Sarnico (the most noteworthy is Villa Faccanoni) on Lake Iseo. On Lake Como, only the Villa Bernasconi is a clear liberty example, though it's one of the best.

Fascism & Futurism

With the advent of war the effete, decorative style of *stile liberty* was no longer fit for purpose in a world where Mussolini blustered about the Roman ideals of strength, masculinity and rationality. San Siro Stadium was built in 1926, embodying fascism's disconcerting mix of Rationalist modernity with Mussolini's fetish for the camper side of Imperial Rome. As Italy's biggest rail terminus, Mussolini commissioned a fitting palace for rail transport on Piazza Duca d'Aosta. Begun in 1912, but finally realised between 1925 and 1931, the extraordinary design is flush with national fervour. Most of the overtly fascist symbolism was removed or obscured but the deco-tinged neo-Babylonian architecture can hardly hide its intent. Milan's other former fascist monuments include the Triennale, Palazzo dell'Arengario and the massive Armani shop on Via Manzotti.

Contemporaneous with fascism was FT Marinetti's violent, history-hating Futurist credo, intent on dispatching the deadening weight of the past in order to speed Italy into the modern age. Futurist painter Gino Severini described the artistic atmosphere of early-20th-century Milan as 'messier and more destructive than you could imagine'. Launched by a gang of drawing-room revolutionaries, Marinetti's 1910 manifesto railed against museums, the past and even pasta, and looked presciently to a new century forged by violence, war, machines and speed. The movement was a broad church, ranging from Marinetti's card-carrying fascism to those more interested in aesthetic liberation and the search for a poetic of the industrial age. These included Giacomo Balla, Umberto Boccioni and a young Bruno Munari.

Post WWII, the Informels captured the frustrated but heady energy of the early boom years in paintings marked by 'formlessness'. Initially an Informel, Lucio Fontana went on to poke holes and slash canvases, and with Piero Manzoni, famous for exhibiting cans of 'Artist's Shit', was Italy's seminal conceptual artist. Crowded salon-style into the Piero Portaluppi–designed 1930s apartment of collector and Pirelli engineer, Antonio Boschi and his wife, Marieda di Stefano, are some 300 examples of Futurist and Informel works, where Fontana's slashed canvases hang side-by-side with Manzoni's surface-busting *Anchromes*.

The Contemporary Scene

Milan's creative reputation is usually linked to the fashion and design industry, but the city's contemporary art scene is, with neighbouring Turin, the most dynamic in Italy. The majority of Italy's living artists choose to call Milan home, at least between sojourns in New York or Berlin, and there's a network of commercial galleries gathered under the StartMilano (www.start-mi.net) umbrella. Most galleries once clustered in Brera, near the city's famous art school, though they are now spread around the city. Lambrate's Via Ventura is emerging with a handful of excellent galleries, including seminal Galleria Massimo De Carlo.

The Milanese often carp that despite claims they are Italy's most modern city, they've not been able to produce a significant building since Giò Ponti erected the Torre Pirelli. That's all about to change: the sound of jackhammers around Stazione Garibaldi signifies the emergence of the new Porta Nuova neighbourhood with César Pelli's shardlike skyscraper and apartments with hanging gardens by Stefano Boeri. In addition, the 420-acre CityLife and Expo site in Rho and Pero promises a futuristic new skyline from international archi-stars Zaha Hadid, Arata Isozaki, Pier Paolo Maggiora and Daniel Libeskind.

In addition to the private gallery scene, a number of dynamic private foundations champion some of the region's most avant-garde art. Prada (www.fondazioneprada.org), Trussardi (www.fondazionenicolatrussardi.com) and Hangar Bicocca (www.hangarbicocca.org) all stage programs of important, ground-breaking work. These shows are well worth looking out for; they're attention grabbing in scale and often competitive in the provocation stakes.

Villas & Gardens

First they fixed the drawing room and then they started on the garden: Italy's penchant for the 'outdoor room' has been going strong since wealthy Romans realised the benefits of regular rest and relaxation, and situated their holiday villas beside the tranquil northern lakes. Medieval humanists revived their interest in botany and pharmacology, and Renaissance princes used never-before-seen engineering techniques to mould Italian landscapes into dramatic and dynamic statements of wealth and power.

Classical poet Ovid records the myth that explains the association of the cypress with grief. The handsome boy Cyparissus, a favourite of Apollo, accidentally kills a beloved tame stag. He is so distraught that he asked to weep forever in punishment and so he is transformed into *cupressus sempervirens*, whose sap eternally weeps his tears.

Classical Ideals

As early as the 1st century AD (the rough date of the Grotte di Catullo, sited on the headland of Sirmione on Lake Garda), the garden landscape played a significant role in classical culture. Writers such as Ovid, Cicero, Pliny the Elder and Pliny the Younger set their stories in fantastical gardens full of grottoes and groves and wrote treatises on agriculture, outdoor dining, summerhouses and the pleasure of aviaries.

For the Romans, a garden was not only a practical place to cultivate vegetables, but also a place of relaxation and physical well-being. Pliny the Younger is known to have used his garden at Bellagio as a place of meditation, while Plato used a garden to host his philosophy lessons. Other ruins at Desenzano del Garda reveal an indoor-outdoor colonnaded peristyle and lavish mosaics, while the Domus dell'Ortaglia, in Brescia, overlooks a grassy viridarium, a contemplative space lined with fruit trees, laurel hedges and fragrant roses.

In the more cash-strapped Middle Ages, medieval gardeners seemed to lose the pleasure principle of the Roman *horti* (garden) and focused solely on a protected area or *hortus conclusus* (walled garden) for the production of food, fruit and medicinal herbs. Cloisters in medieval abbeys and churches were often cultivated in this way, and at the Basilica di Sant'Ambrogio in Milan, the monks allowed humanist scholar Francesco Petrarch (1304–74) to experiment with growing spinach, beets, fennel and laurels. Petrarch wrote extensively about these experiments and through his work, among others, the classical ideals of the garden as an aesthetic place began to be revived.

Renaissance Revival

In 1453, one of the Renaissance's most gifted men, polymath Leon Battista Alberti (1404–72), wrote a radical new treatise on architecture and the architecture of gardens. *De Re Aedificatoria* (On the Art of Building; published 1485) suggested that the Renaissance retreat should not look inwards, but instead sit in an elevated position so its inhabitants could both 'see' and 'be seen'. To create a beautiful garden in a magnificent landscape was to tame nature and introduce culture, something to be widely applauded. This new showiness appealed greatly to fashionable cardinals, princes and popes, who commissioned daring new pleasure gardens such as Bramante's Cortile del Belvedere (1484) and Raphael's Villa Madama (1518), both in Rome.

These ground-breaking commissions introduced new rules of proportion, perspective and symmetry to the garden. Off Alberti's central axis, the Renaissance landscaper divided up the garden with hedges and rows of trees, while open terraces created powerful architectural planes and loggias linked indoor and outdoor rooms. Hedges and topiary added sculptural possibilities and organised space, contrasting openness with enclosures. The neatly clipped labyrinth, serried ranks of cypresses and geometric axes of the Giardino Giusti (1580) in Verona and the two-storied loggia, Roman statuary and 'garden rooms' of Villa Guarienti (1538) at Punta San Vigilio provide classic examples.

Water, too, was a key component of the Renaissance garden. Still a luxury in the 16th century, it was vital in enlivening the garden, attracting both birds and animals in summer months. Ingenious new hydraulic engineering meant it was possible to pipe water further and in greater quantities, allowing for elaborate fountains and humorous *giochi d'acqua* (water tricks), which were liable to drench silk-clad guests at any moment to the great amusement of their hosts.

Such a garden was the Gonzaga's garden at their suburban villa, Palazzo Te, where Giulio Romano, Raphael's most gifted student, came to work after a dispute at Villa Madama. Although the planting schemes are long gone, the garden's structure remains: a square house, built around a cloistered courtyard where a formal garden divided by a central access would have been laid out. At the far end, a *giardino segreto* (secret garden) was added where Duke Federico could court his mistress in private. And beneath it is a shell-encrusted grotto complete with *giochi d'acqua,* which splashed visiting courtiers standing on the covered balcony.

Italian Villas and Their Gardens is Pulitzer Prize–winner Edith Wharton's pioneering collection of essays on Italian gardens. Written during a four-month tour of the country in 1903, it is one of the first books to explore Italian garden architecture and it influenced a generation of landscape architects.

Baroque Splendour

By the end of the 16th century the idea of the garden as a quiet, contemplative space had completely given way to an outdoor room expressing wealth and culture. The garden was now a place where new and ingenious hydraulic devices transported gallons of water to costly, elaborate fountains; where rare and expensive plants demonstrated a patron's knowledge and culture; and where artfully arranged sculpture imbued with layers of meaning carried symbolic messages and displayed refined artistic sensibilities. All these ingredients ultimately combined to form the bold gardens of the baroque era.

WHAT DOES IT ALL MEAN?

In the humanist tradition gardens were associated with the classical Golden Age, Arcadia and the Garden of the Hesperides, goddess Hera's mythical garden where the tree of golden apples grew. This tradition served Renaissance princes well, suggesting helpful comparisons that they were the heirs of classical virtues and the garden was a microcosm of the patron's kingdom, where skill, virtue and hard work triumphed over the chaotic landscape. This reflected the confidence of Renaissance men in their elevated position in the cosmic hierarchy.

To further this happy narrative, architectural features, statues, fountains and planting schemes formed a visual language, telling a clear story for the cultured guests who were likely to wander through. Often these narratives explored the relationship between art and nature or evoked classical mythology as a means of flattering powerful patrons.

The myth of Hercules was a favourite of the Este clan (whose daughters Beatrice and Isabella married dukes of Milan and Mantua respectively), thanks to family genealogists who amazingly found a means of claiming Hercules as a direct ancestor! Frequent statues of Hercules and images of his heroic feats and triumphs that were dotted around their gardens and villas glorified the entire Este dynasty.

SECRET GARDENS

Secret gardens abounded during the Renaissance, providing the celebrities of the day with one of their only truly private spaces. Aside from privacy, the secret garden was also a place for prized plants and exotic specimens, acting as an extension of the indoor cabinet of curiosities.

Isabella d'Este's apartments in the Corte Vecchia at the Palazzo Ducale in Mantua house the perfect example of this private space. Designed in 1522 by Mantuan architect Gian Battista Covo, the garden is completely surrounded by walls and can only be seen from Isabella's private rooms.

Classical features abound: Ionic columns line the walls and were originally interspersed with classical statuary lodged in the niches in the walls, while around the top runs an inscription singing Isabella's praises and reminding visitors that she is a daughter of the King of Naples and the powerful Este house, as well as a wife and mother of the Gonzaga dynasty. The garden adjoins Isabella's *studiolo* (study), where the walls are lined with inlaid cabinets stamped with Isabella's monogram. These cabinets housed her most precious jewels and treasures in countless tiny drawers. Likewise the design of the flowerbeds mirrors the compartmentalisation of the *studiolo*, divided into small sections sometimes called *cassettes* or boxes.

Around this time, the first great lakeside villas were being built or bought, designed as holiday pleasure domes for the wealthy. The Marquis Stanga acquired Villa Serbelloni, in Bellagio, and set about creating its gardens. Until then, here and in a handful of other older villas, the grounds had served as orchards and herb gardens, grown amid chestnut forests and freely running streams. All this was gradually cleared to make way for symmetrically laid-out lawns and topiary, pergolas and terraces. In 1565, work on what is now Villa d'Este began, and in around 1600 the Sfondrati family came into possession of what would be transformed into Villa Monastero.

Of these the Borromean garden of Isola Bella is Italy's finest example of the baroque garden. It was built between 1632 and 1671 on the instruction of Count Carlo Borromeo III, who wanted to transform a barren island in Lake Maggiore into his own version of the Garden of the Hesperides, that blissful orchard of classical mythology where immortality-giving golden apples grew.

His vision was for a pyramid of terraces that would mimic the shape of a baroque galleon at anchor in the lake. The island's handful of inhabitants, who were asked to relocate from their homes, understandably didn't share the Count's enthusiasms so plans had to be modified and the galleon lost its pointed prow and the central axis linking the garden to the palace.

Nevertheless, the garden wrought by an otherwise unremarkable architect from Milan, Angelo Crivelli, was nothing short of spectacular. Fountains, terraces, grottoes and a water theatre combine to form a theatrical and energetic space. Vast quantities of soil were ferried from the mainland, clothing the jagged rock with 10 sloping terraces. Marble from Baveno followed, as did stone from Viggiù. Later, boats packed with Spanish lemon trees, lilies and lotus flowers brought the flora for its rising galleries and, finally, statues of Agriculture and Arts, waving *putti* (boys) and the triumphant Borromeo unicorn were set atop Carlo Fontana's spectacular shell-encrusted water theatre. It is the perfect expression of the confidence and power of the Borromean family who had furnished Milan with two cardinals, one of whom was canonised by Pope Paul V in 1610.

Giovanni Battista Ferrari's *Flora overo cultura dei fiori* (1638) was the most influential florilegium of the 17th century. It was the first book ever written about plants cultivated for purely ornamental purposes and it tackles every detail, from the choice of garden guard dog to the modification of flower colour, scent and form.

French Influences

The most famous garden in the world isn't Italian, but French, yet 'garden' is hardly a word to apply to the vastness of Versailles. Designed by André Le Nôtre, gardener to Louis XIV, in the latter half of the 17th century, it came to epitomise a modern expression of wealth and power. Unlike Italian gardens it did away completely with any sense of enclosure, intimacy or humour. Vast avenues shoot out from the palace to distant horizons a perfect statement of illimitable power, while immaculate, geometrical parterres and wide open lawns give a sense of monumental, uncluttered space.

With the fashion for all things French taking Italy by storm in the 17th century, it wasn't long before Le Nôtre was making his way south with plans for the Palazzo Reale in Turin. Needless to say he thought little of Italian garden design, sniffily concluding, 'they have no taste in gardens'. But try as they might to imitate Le Nôtre, the monumental scale of his gardens was hardly possible in the cluttered, intensely cultivated landscape of northern Italy. Although imitated with some success at the Venaria Reale, the Savoy hunting lodge in Piedmont, the closest Lombardy came to the *jardin à la francaise* was the park at Monza and the exposed formal garden at Villa Olmo, which runs into a tree-filled park.

The English Garden

Other international influences were also gaining ground in the south at the Bourbon court in Naples, where English prime minister Sir John Acton was a favourite of Queen Maria Carolina (the daughter of Maria Theresia, Habsburg Empress and Duchess of Milan). Under the English influence a section of the fabulous new gardens at the Bourbon palace at Caserta, just outside Naples, were to be laid out in English style, that is under a seemingly 'natural' design of irregular paths and profuse plantings, rather than the more formal, geometric French or Italian style.

PARTERRE

A *parterre* is a formal garden constructed on a level surface, consisting of planting beds arranged to form a pleasing, usually symmetrical pattern, with gravel paths laid between. The beds are edged in stone or tightly clipped hedging and need not contain any flowers.

A BOTANICAL BENT

Renaissance gardens flourished against a backdrop of scientific discovery. With human dissection new on the syllabus at Padua University, students of medicine were rapidly gaining a greater understanding of anatomy and physiology and coming to terms with the shortcomings of existing medical texts, many of them dating back to the 1st century AD. What's more, merchant ships docking in Venice were starting to offload strange and exotic plants along with medicinal herbs, which were fetching prices just shy of gold and spices in the Rialto market.

This new interest in botany, and the fabulous specimens (such as maize) arriving from voyages of discovery such as those by Christopher Columbus in 1492 and 1493, captured the popular imagination of villa owners who coveted rare plants for display in their newly designed gardens. Aristocratic families like the Medici's, Este's and Borromee funded early botanic gardens and, through their patronage, plant collecting developed into a full-blown mania in the 17th and 18th centuries.

At Villa Monastero on Lake Como, African and American palms tower above groupings of agave and dragon trees. Aubergines were introduced from Asia and tulips from Persia and some 80,000 bulbs, representing 65 varieties, are planted at Villa Taranto on Lake Maggiore. Although there was a fashionable element to plant collecting, the trend was part of a wider intellectual landscape of discovery. Count Vitaliano IX Borromeo, who introduced species from China, New Zealand, India, the Himalayas and South America to Isola Madre, was a serious and passionate botanist, as was Baroness Antoinette Saint Leger who transformed San Pancrazio, the larger of the Isole di Brissago, with thousands of exotic specimens into an enormous island garden.

Garden Greats

Giardino Giusti
Renaissance rules

Villa Balbianello
Perfect lakeside promenade.

Isola Bella
Baroque theatrics.

Isola Madre *English informality*

San Pancrazio
Botanical blooms

In 1801 Ercole Silva published *Dell'arte dei giardini inglesi*, the first treatise on the English garden, advising the 'artist-gardener' to abandon the architectural approach which hampered true creativity and genius.

This romantic English tradition suited the awkward Italian landscape far better and appealed to Italian tastes with its element of surprise and delight in the changing perspectives. It was also easier to incorporate into traditional Italian schemes, and many gardens around the lakes are now a hybrid of Italian and English styles; a more formal Italianate layout fronting the villa or palace which gradually gives way to softer more varied planting schemes incorporating thickets and clearings set around curvaceous ponds and paths.

Villa Carlotta, built in the 17th century on Lake Como, follows just such a design. Around the villa itself the ordered layout suggests the Italianate approach, though as you explore this changes radically. At one part of the northern end of the garden is the cool and magical Valle delle Felci (Fern Valley), a dense forest full of ferns and trees, including towering sequoias. This 'wilderness' is perhaps the best example of the English ideal on the lakes. Villa Melzi d'Eril, in Bellagio, is another good example. Likewise, Villa Balbianello, the most visually striking of Lake Como's gardens, follows the same pattern. Perched on a promontory, the villa buildings have a neoclassical flavour with some lightly baroque elements while the surrounding terraced gardens are a mix of Italian and English plantings. But of all the gardens around the lakes, the most English is the romantic garden of Isola Madre.

Public Gardens

Plantsmen rather than architects were the heroes of 19th-century gardens thanks to gardeners such as the Rovelli brothers, who worked for the Borromean family. Experts in cultivation and hybridisation, the brothers ran a nursery on the side at Verbania Pallanza, where they sold some of the Count's 500 varieties of camellia.

It also became the fashion for aristocratic families to send their gardeners and landscapers on educational voyages around Europe. One of the earliest examples of this is the trip Archduke Ferdinand (1754–1806) took between 1783 and 1786 with Ercole Silva (1756–1840). Ercole was primarily a writer, but oversaw a number of garden designs in Milan, including the Palazzo Reale overlooking the Giardini Pubblici, Villa Litta in the suburb of Affori and Villa Reale at Monza.

This growing exchange of information popularised gardening as a pastime. The Rovelli brothers even published a catalogue on camellias while others, such as the Roda brothers working for the House of Savoy in Piedmont, wrote gardening manuals and features for monthly magazines. New horticultural societies were established in Piedmont and Lombardy, nurseries proliferated around Milan and Padua, and space was cleared for public parks in Milan, Turin and Venice. Finally, with the Unification of Italy in 1861, a new middle class began to emerge, keen on tending their own small patch of paradise.

The Lakes Kitchen

Is there a lake cuisine? No, not if you're looking for a homogenous gastronomic tradition. Northern Italy's political and cultural history and its varied terrain make it impossible to assign a single food style to the area. But Lombardy is divided naturally into distinct zones: the Po plain with its rice paddies, rivers, game birds, frogs and snails; the lakes teeming with freshwater fish; the foothills of the Alps where cows, goats and sheep graze, providing milk for Lombardy's fine cheeses and meat for sausages and salami; and the mountains with their chestnut forests, mushrooms and wild herbs. Eat your way around here and you'll learn much about Italy's history of city-states and changing tastes while savouring some of its richest flavours.

A Rich & Industrious Kitchen

Northern Italy was never a naturally rich or fertile region. Centuries of human labour and know-how have adapted the shifting Po Delta and shorn up the mountain sides, while a cosmopolitan outlook has incorporated and refined the endlessly varied flavours we delight in when we sit down to enjoy a meal.

But what is remarkable about Lombard cuisine is that despite industrialisation and the radical dietary changes in northern Italy's fast-paced modern cities (Italy's first supermarket opened in Milan in 1957 and its first fast-food outlet arrived in 1982), the food on the table remains largely local, seasonal and artisanal. Italians buy just a quarter of the frozen products that the British do, and 50% of their spending is still on fresh, unpackaged goods. Just check out the food markets in Milan, Mantua and Verona to witness the health of the local food economy.

But northern Italy is not some timeless land of peasant cooks, nonnas and mammas. There are over 70,000 registered agribusinesses in Lombardy, producing 15% of Italy's food and, together with Piedmont, 30% of Europe's rice crop. But many of these industrial-scale products are actually some of the country's most genuine: ham, cheese, salami and rice were designed for preservation, transport and trade. Northern Italy's agribusinesses may cater to the masses but they include 25% of Italy's DOP and IGP quality-assured meat and cheese products, and 60% of the nation's quality-assured wines.

'A good cook in a great city is more or less like a general in a vast theatre of war... It is not just that big cities are ever more bountifully provisioned with all sorts of fine ingredients. They have people whose job it is to supply you with the tiny things that may have little intrinsic importance, but which help to make your handiwork varied, elegant and precise.' *Science in the Kitchen and the Art of Eating Well*, Pellegrino Artusi

An Urban Kitchen

Northern Italian food is city food originating from one of the richest urban cultures on the planet. Peasants may have toiled in the fields, but they rarely had the means to eat anything more exciting than wild garlic, greens, leeks and polenta. The latter, a coarsely ground barley/farro/spelt/chestnut-meal (maize was not cultivated in Europe until the 16th century), has been a staple since Roman times and such was the consumption that regular outbreaks of pellagra (a devastating disease caused by niacin deficiency) were common. Baked, fried or grilled, modern variations include *polenta taragna* (with buckwheat flour), *polenta uncia* (made with cheese) and *missultin e polenta* (cooked with dried fish from Lake Como).

The people with the knowledge to transform the country's growing abundance of ingredients wasn't the peasantry but the inhabitants of wealthy and cosmopolitan cities like Milan, Pavia, Verona, Cremona, Brescia and Mantua. With the rise of Venice's mercantile empire in the 10th century, northern Italy was at the vanguard of Europe's transformation from an agricultural society to a medieval powerhouse of trade. As Venetian and Genoese seamen offloaded their cargoes of spices, sugar cane, saffron, figs, lemons, almonds and more from around the Mediterranean, so tradesmen distributed them via northern Italy's navigable network of rivers that connected Milan to Lake Maggiore and Como, Venice to Vicenza and Mantua to Ferrara, Parma and Piacenza. By the 13th century cartloads of wine were trundling over the Brenner pass into Austria.

Powerful clans such as the Della Scala family in Verona, the Gonzaga's in Mantua and the Sforza's in Milan competed for a slice of the profits, dividing up and taxing the countryside and establishing themselves as political dynasties. It was in this competitive, commercial environment that Italy's great cuisine was born.

The Marvels of Medieval Milan

De Magnalibus Mediolani (The Marvels of Medieval Milan) was written in 1288 by Milanese monk Bonvesin de la Riva. In his proud depiction of his home town's finest features, Bonvesin gives us a rare insight into one of Europe's largest medieval cities and its surprisingly rich diet.

Born in Dumenza on Lake Maggiore, Bartolomeo Scappi was one of the greatest cooks of the Italian Renaissance. In his six-volume *Opera di Bartolomeo Scappi* (1570) he left a meticulously illustrated monument to the aspirations of Italian Renaissance cuisine.

Butchers, fishmongers and bakers were important men, members of powerful organised guilds, and it's no wonder when you consider the animals, wild birds, poultry, fruits and fish they supplied. Dishes such as *nervetti* (veal cartilage), *busecca* (tripe stew), *bollito* (boiled meats) and *carpione* (fried, floured fish) were becoming standard and Bonvesin also lists damascene plums, early figs, hyssop and white horehound, exotic ingredients even by today's standards. And already land-locked Milan was one of the best places in Italy to eat fish, thanks to its access to the northern lakes. There was even an abundant supply of prawns from the city's moat.

To accompany this medieval city guide, Bonvesin wrote *Fifty Courtesies at Table*. With this in hand, city sophisticates could avoid such faux pas as sneezing into the communal plate, and were reminded to wipe their mouths before drinking from the communal goblet. Good manners were no longer the preserve of aristocrats, but a badge of success for the upwardly mobile middle class.

Cooking in the Renaissance

As with art, music and architecture, the Renaissance was a period of culinary creativity. Italy's urban food system became more sophisticated,

PROTECTED DESIGNATION OF ORIGIN

Like much bureaucratic legislation, DOP (Protected Designation of Origin) and IGP (Protected Geographical Indication) accreditation is boring but important: quite simply, there is a huge amount of money at stake. At last count, Italy had 221 DOP and IGP products, 20% of which are Lombard specialities, including a wide range of cheeses, *salame* and rice, but also Mantovan pears, peaches from Verona, asparagus, nuts, olive oil from Lake Garda, *bresaola* (air-cured beef) from the Valtellina and *cotecchino* (pork sausage). No other European country can boast as many accredited products. Together, these Italian products generate annual sales of around €8 billion. In a 'post-horsemeat-masquerading-as-beef' world where consumers are ever more sensitive to the quality of produce, and the price of anonymous ingredients, the little blue and yellow badge that signals a DOP pedigree is priceless.

BEYOND PASTA

Some 50 varieties of rice are grown in the Po valley, making rice the number one staple in northern Italy. Sure, pasta (an import from the south in the 17th century) abounds, but a risotto has more cachet than pasta ever will. Among the best known is *carnaroli*, a medium-grain rice mostly grown in Piedmont. Others, such as arborio (a short grain) and *vialone nano* (a thicker grain), are grown around Pavia – the rice capital of Italy.

How should we count the ways of preparing risotto? The Milan standard is with saffron and a meat broth. In Pavia a speciality is *risotto con le rane* (with crispy fried frogs). *Risotto al porcini* (with porcini mushrooms) is a universal favourite, while risottos done with wines as a base, such as Barolo or Amarone, are typical in wine regions. In Mantua, *risotto alla pilota* (with minced pork) is a signature dish and seafood variations from the Veneto include *risotto al nero* (with black octopus or squid ink).

and political power and wealth were increasingly displayed at the table. Sugar and spices became a European addiction, and saffron, nutmeg, cloves, cardamon and pepper entered the cooking repertoire, giving us sweet and sour dishes such as *agnoli* (ravioli stuffed with capon, cinnamon and cloves), *sbrisolona* (a hard biscuit with almonds) and *mostarda* (candied fruit and mustard relish).

Opulent banquets combined food with theatre, music and dance for the first time. Leonardo da Vinci was even drafted in to design sets for the wedding banquet of Milan's Gian Galeazzo Sforza and Isabella of Aragon in 1489. Cristoforo da Messisbugo's 1548 *Banquets* gives us some idea of their scale and extravagance. A record of the wedding feast of the Duke of Ferrara's son Ercole to Renée, the daughter of Louis XII of France, offers us an endless list of courses, gifts and entertainments – shocking in light of the plague that was decimating the countryside around Ferrara at the time.

At a rough calculation each of the guests had to plough through 18 large portions of fish, three whole birds, three portions of meat, sausage, salame and ham, 15 pastries and pies, as well as sweetmeats and an early morning collation of fruit in sugar and syrup. They were seated carefully, according to rank, their places affording access (or not) to the choicest dishes. The Duke's sister, Isabella d'Este (the Marchioness of Mantua, and one of the most esteemed dinner guests of the Renaissance), sat at his right hand, and the Venetian ambassador was prominently placed so he could report back on the costly spectacle.

In 1661 the first known law for the protection of a local Italian speciality was issued, protecting the heritage recipe for *mortadella* (pork cold cut).

Below stairs, a similar charade of political maneuvering was going on in the kitchen as the Este's cook brokered new relationships with possible patrons and suppliers. Unlike courtiers, cooks came from rural backgrounds. As the seasons and their employer's fancies changed, they networked constantly to find suppliers and discover new recipes. It was through cooks that an understanding of good food circulated between rich and poor, the country and the town.

The French & Austrian Influence

Between the 1600s and 1800s foreign influences brought new flavours to bear and spices went out of fashion. The French introduced butter and cream (*crema di asparagi*, a creamed asparagus soup, is typical) while the Austrians introduced a penchant for sausages and schnitzel (*scaloppina* and *cotoletto alla Milanese* are variations on the Austrian breaded cutlet, Wiener Schnitzel) and a tradition of *viennoisserie* that is still evident in Milan's glut of elegant *pasticcerie* (pastry shops).

A new centralised bureaucracy and a reformed tax system increased agricultural output, while new farming methods and crops (potatoes, tomatoes and maize from the New World) revolutionised the diet of the masses. From across the Alps came Grand Tourists, French recipe books and the fashion of eating *a la russe* (Russian style), in separate courses comprising individual plates. Piedmontese chefs trained in France were most in demand.

With new political ideas came new places to meet and eat. Cafes, serving a new drink - coffee - and Austrian doughnuts (*ciambella* and *castagnole*) and strudels, were hothouses of political debate and the rise of the restaurant democratised access to good food. New advances in medicine raised the profile of vegetables and fruit. Sweet peppers from the New World found their way into Voghera's version of risotto, the potato craze began (*gnocchi di patate* is now a Verona speciality) and herbs, lemon juice and olive oil became acceptable, even desirable, flavourings for delicate fish dishes.

Home Cooking

Up until the early 20th century, the only Italian cookery books in circulation were written by men: chefs, stewards and courtiers working in the wealthiest city households with the finest ingredients. *Cucina casalinga* (home cooking) had no place at this elite table. That is, until the deprivation of two world wars pushed middle-class housewives out of the kitchen and into print.

The first Italian cookery book written by a woman was *Come Posso Mangiar Bene?* (How Can I Eat Well?) by home cook Giulia Tamburini and published in Milan, by Hoepli, in 1900. She was to be the first in a long line of northern Italian housewives – including, most recently, Anna del Conte, whose biography, *Risotto With Nettles*, recalls her wartime Milanese childhood and its influence on her cooking – who valued good food but, by necessity, had to work within a limited budget.

Thanks to them, a simple, filling *primo* (first course) of *minestra* (soup), gnocchi or risotto now sits at the heart of the northern Italian meal. 'Make-do' classics such as *mondeghili* (Milanese meatballs made with leftover chopped, boiled meat), *minestrone* (a rich vegetable soup including rice and pancetta) *and pasta rasa* (egg pasta cooked in a soup with tomatoes, beans, potatoes, onions and garlic) were elevated. Whether it came in the form of soup, rice or pasta, *minestra* allowed middle-class families to live with a modicum of comfort. The more expensive

According to Futurist Filippo Marinetti food wasn't simply fuel for the body, but an aesthetic experience that affected the way people thought, dreamt and acted. In a modern era of molecular gastronomy, recipes from *The Futurist Cookbook* (1932) are no longer look quite so kooky.

LIVING WELL IN DIFFICULT TIMES: JEWISH SPECIALITIES

One surprising cookery writer working in Fascist Milan was Fernanda Momigliano, a middle-aged Jewish intellectual who lived with her ailing mother.

Her first book, *Vivere bene in tempi difficili: come le donne affrontano le crisi economiche* (Living Well in Difficult Times: How Women Face Up to the Economic Crisis), attempted to address the issues faced by housewives in the wake of the 1929 Wall Street crash. Advocating 'economy, not deprivation or waste', Momigliano's manual showed Italian women how they might eat well on their diminishing budget. As Italy lurched from deprivation to hunger in the wake UN sanctions in 1935, these reassuring tips on making ends meet, using cheaper cuts of meat and making home preserves put home-cooking firmly on the modern Lombard table.

But it was her follow-up book, *Eating Italian*, published in 1936, which is even more interesting not least because it includes 16 Jewish recipes, many of them typical of northern Italy. They range from carp with porcini mushrooms cooked in white wine to a saffron risotto prepared on the eve of the Sabbath, and goose ham and salami, a specialist product from Mortara that now holds the prestigious Slow Food badge of approval.

second course was a secondary concern: liver, or butter-fried eggs during the week, roast chicken or veal cutlets on Sundays.

The Perfect Cheeseboard

Counters in northern Italian *alimentari* (food stores) overflow with cheeses. They come in every possible size, form, colour and texture, which isn't surprising considering Lombardy produces nearly 40% of Italy's cheese.

One of the most widespread and best-known Lombard cheeses is *stracchino*. The name is derived from *stracca*, meaning tiredness. It is said that the milk of tired cows (during the seasonal move to and from Alpine pastures) is richer in fats and acids, giving this cheese its tang. It is usually eaten as a dessert cheese. *Bitto*, from the Valtellina, is similarly dry and sharp as it ages. Once known as green stracchino, gorgonzola is made of autumn cow's milk (collected after the return from the Alps) and is one of several cheeses made laced with blue mould.

Another popular autumn cheese is taleggio, a soft cheese originally made in the like-named valley north of Bergamo. It is a mild cheese matured in six to 10 weeks and regularly washed to prevent mould or a thick rind forming. Other mountain cheeses from the Val Brembana, north of Bergamo, are generically called *formai de mut* (cheese of the mountains).

Originating from the Lodi area is the soft cream cheese known as mascarpone, a versatile product obtained from milk cream and used to make desserts (most famously tiramisu). Lodi also produces *pannerone* (a soft, fatty cheese made without salt) and Grana Lodigiano. The latter is similar to Parmesan and Grana Padano, but 'weeps' a drop of whey when flakes of it are cut away.

From the province of Brescia comes *bagoss*, a well-matured, straw-coloured cheese traditionally made in cow herds' huts in the summer mountain pastures. Robiola is a soft pasteurised cow's milk cheese made in Lombardy and Ticino. It comes in small discs. A cool, fresh alternative in Ticino is *robiolino* (tubes of pasteurised cow's milk cheese often seasoned with herbs or pepper). Various types of *formaggella* (a semi-hard cheese with a greyish crust) are produced throughout the region.

Several goat cheeses, such as *cadolet di capra* (from the Valle Camonica north of Lake Iseo) and *fatuli*, are made in spring and summer and lightly smoked. Caprino Lombardo, a generic name, covers a range of such cheeses. True goat-milk cheese ranges from the fresh, soft white variety to those matured over several months in oil and laurel leaves. Cingherlin, from Varese and Como, is drizzled with olive oil and vinegar and served with beans

On The Wine Trail

The region around the northern Italian lakes has been producing wine since Roman times and today produces an enormous variety from fizzy red lambruscos to bombastic Sforzato and chilly, mineral-rich whites. The tradition of selling many of these modestly priced wines in local *osterie* (taverns), *cantine* (cellars) and *enoteche* (wine bars) has led to the impression that they are of lesser quality than wines from other areas, but the region claims five DOCG, 19 DOC and 15 IGT wines.

Franciacorta

DOCG *spumante* (sparkling) whites and rosés lead the way in Franciacorta (www.franciacorta.net), an area stretching between Brescia and Lake Iseo. Look out also for Satèn, a *blanc de blanc* almost exclusively made of chardonnay grapes. The Curtefranca DOC covers a series of

THE LAKES KITCHEN THE PERFECT CHEESEBOARD

At Italian unification in 1861 the average consumption of meat was 12kg per person per year, equivalent to 33 grams per day or half the weight of an egg. By 1989 Italians were more fond of meat that the British, consuming 91kg per person.

Tipicita or 'typicality' describes the magical aura that food acquires when local identity is invested in it. In Italian, *tipico* has become synonymous with *buono* – good, wholesome, delicious.

whites and reds, the latter dominated by cabernet franc and the local carmenere grape varieties.

Oltrepò Pavese

Riots broke out in the Middle Ages when Milan was cut off from Oltrepò, Lombardy's most renowned wine region (www.vinoltrepo.it). No fewer than 20 wines are classified as DOC in this area, and the Oltrepò Pavese spumante is a DOCG. Keep an eye out for reds like the Oltrepò Pavese Barbera and the Bonarda, among the stars of the area's DOC wines made from the local croatina grape. A curious sweet dessert red is the Sangue di Giuda (Judas' Blood).

Riviera del Garda & Bardolino

Along the west shore of Lake Garda, vineyards blanket the Valtenesi area all the way up to Lake Idro. Look for Garda DOC or Garda Classico DOC (www.gardaclassico.it). The reds predominantly use the local gropello grape.

On the southeastern shore, one of the Veneto's best-known reds is cultivated around the town of Bardolino. Of its namesake reds, the Bardolino Superiore DOCG is a delicate, dry drop that pairs well with meat and game. If you're looking for a fine white, try Lugana DOC (www.consorziolugana.eu).

Soave

West of Verona, the town of Soave (www.ilsoave.com) rests next to a castle-topped hill whose slopes are dense with vineyards. Some of Italy's finest white wines come from here. The local garganega grape dominates the area's two white DOCGs, Recioto di Soave and Soave Superiore.

Valcalepio

The Valcalepio wine region between Bergamo and Lake Iseo is just beginning to make a name for itself. Since the 1970s, small local holdings have been continually refining their two main DOC products: a red that blends merlot and cabernet sauvignon (and which also comes in an aged *riserva* version) and whites that combine pinot bianco and pinot grigio varieties. You will also come across a sweet dessert *passito* using moscato grapes, which is perfect as an accompaniment for pastries and dessert.

Alongside France, Italy is the largest wine producer in the world, processing 45 to 50 million hectolitres per year, around one-third of the world's contribution. Of this, 1.1 million hectolitres come from Lombardy.

Valpolicella

Led by the outstanding Amarone della Valpolicella DOC (using dried corvina, rondinella and molinara grapes), this region, which stretches north–northwest up the valleys parallel to Lake Garda from Verona, is one of the best-known names in northern Italian wine. While many Valpolicella reds are light, pleasant wines, the flagship Amarone (literally 'big sour one') is big, bold and dry. It is accompanied by another signature red, also made with dried grapes, the somewhat sweeter Recioto.

Valtellina

Like a well-behaved Milanese dinner companion, the Valtellina (www.consorziovinivaltellina.com) red is distinctive and rich without being too forward – Leonardo da Vinci loved the stuff. The area boasts two DOCG classifications, a general one (Valtellina Superiore DOCG) and one applied to a particular style of wine, the Sforzato (or Sfursat) di Valtellina DOCG. The nebbiolo grape (locally known as chiavennasca) is the most important.

Fashion & Design

Lombardy's creative reputation is inextricably linked to the fashion and design industries, which power the local economy and drive an endless round of influential and fabulous designer fairs. Today Milan is home to all the major showrooms and continues to be a centre of fashion and design education and publishing. Design isn't merely functional here; it is also suffused with emotion – expressive, inventive and humorous.

Fashion

Italians have strong opinions about aesthetics and aren't afraid to share them. A common refrain in Milan is *che brutta!* (How hideous!), which may strike visitors as tactless. But consider it from an Italian point of view – everyone in this fashion town is rooting for you to look good, and allowing you to step out in an unflattering get-up would be considered a serious failure of taste on their part. After all, Italy's centuries-old reputation for style is at stake.

Medieval Trendsetters

Northern Italian artisans and designers have been shoeing, dressing and adorning Europe's affluent classes since the early Middle Ages, when Venetian merchants imported dyes from the East and Leonardo da Vinci helped design Milan's canal system, connecting the wool merchants and silk weavers of Lake Maggiore and Lake Como to the city's market places. Further south, Florence's wool guild grew so rich and powerfulthat it was able to fund a Renaissance.

As this cultural reimagining transformed philosophy, art, music and literature, fashion flourished as a new expression of taste and status. Dresses and men's doublets grew shorter and fuller; impractical, pointy Gothic headdresses were tossed aside; and hair reappeared trimmed with golden ribbons and covered in fine Venetian lace. Patterned velvet and brocade were in vogue, and robes, sleeves and skirts were slashed to reveal shockingly bright silks and dainty jewelled shoes.

Promoted by the celebrities of the day – the Sforza's of Milan, the Este's of Ferrara, Mantua's Gonzaga dukes and the extravagant Florentine Medicis – they immortalised their style choices in newly commissioned portraits and public works. Da Vinci painted three of Ludovico Sforza's mistresses, and Mantegna's frescoes in the *Camera degli Sposi* depict the latest men's trend, pastel hose. On her wedding to Henry, Duke of Orleans (later King of France), in 1533 Tuscany's Catherine de'Medici (1519–89) single-handedly transformed French fashions, wearing the first pair of four-inch, high-heeled shoes. Some courtesans and trophy wives were so widely imitated that sumptuary laws were passed restricting necklines, stacked heels and trailing cauls.

In Venice and Milan, the advent of illustrated pamphlets, forerunners to Italian *Vogue,* sent these fashions global. What's more, as feudalism waned and northern city-states revelled in periods of relative peace and prosperity, new forms of mass culture emerged. In 1637 the first public opera house opened in Venice, with La Scala's precursor the Teatro Regio

The beret originated in Italy during the Renaissance. It was made of a circular piece of cloth gathered onto a band decorated with jewels or embroidery. Inside the band was a string, which could be tightened to fit any head.

Ducale opening in 1717. Regular public appearances required the careful cultivation of image and a gradually expanding wardrobe.

Como Silk

Smuggled out of China inside a bamboo pole, the first silkworms reached northern Italy in the 13th century. At the time, the majority of peasants around Lake Como were employed in woollen mills, but given the abundance of mulberry trees in the Po valley a few canny entrepreneurs, such as Pietro Boldone, spotted the potential for sericulture and established Como's first silk-spinning mill in the early 1500s.

Although nurturing the worms and harvesting the silk was brutally hard work, silk cultivation gradually became an annual sideline for lower- and middle-class families, many of whom risked their annual savings trying to capitalise on the rich harvest. Entire sections of farmhouses were turned over to the worms, which women and children tirelessly fed mulberry leaves by hand until they spun their silken cocoons.

Incorporating both the production and processing of silk, Como manufacturers, especially those around Lecco, produced some of the world's finest, most durable silks. The weavers had a knack for knowing a quality thread, which was both fine and elastic and wouldn't snap on the weaving rack. By the 18th and 19th centuries, Como was the third-largest silk-producing sector in the world (not far behind China and Japan) and silk constituted Italy's most important national export. So valuable was the trade that the export of silk represented a third of the value of all Italian exports.

Even after the devastating prebina epidemic of 1855, which all but wiped out the Italian moth species, necessitating the import of raw silk from the Far East, the Como weaving industry retained a significant world presence. It was only in the early 20th century, following the economic crash of 1929 and the advent of new synthetic fabrics, that the industry fell into terminal decline.

Today, raw silk is imported from China and only the finishing, dyeing and printing work is carried out in Como. Out of literally hundreds of silk houses only three big firms remain: Seteria Ratti (www.ratti.it), Mantero (www.mantero.com) and Canepa (www.canepa.it). They employ nearly one third of the Como population, while Como's Istituto Tecnico Industriale di Setificio, founded in 1869, continues to turn out world-class designers, printers and chemical-dyeing experts.

Global Powerhouses

Although Italy ceded ground as global tastemaker to France, Austria and even England between the 17th and 20th centuries, when foreign domination of the Italian peninsula sent power and vertigo-inducing pomaded wigs elsewhere, the streamlined look of Italian Futurism and the industrial revolution of the 19th century brought fashion back to Florence. Where once Italian cobblers, seamstresses and leatherworkers crafted only made-to-measure designs for aristocrats and royalty, in 1950s Florence the idea of a seasonal fashion show was born. Held in the Palazzo Pitti, these shows were an extraordinary success, launching some of world's most famous fashion empires.

But Milan literally stole the show in 1958 when it hosted Italy's first Fashion Week. Away from the constraints of the Florentine fashion establishment, where designers had to be invited to show, and shows were heavily formatted, the Milan Fashion Week gave designers creative power. Thanks to this, the first ready-to-wear collections aimed at mass markets were launched and fashion finally found a way to make money from the business of dressing people.

The price of raw silk recently reached its highest level. The reason? Chinese farmers are turning away from the arduous work to other more lucrative crops, and rapid industrialisation is consuming farmland in the silk-producing region of Shanghai.

FASHION WEEK

For a full timetable of Fashion Week shows, check the website Camera Nazionale della Moda Italiana (National Chamber of Italian Fashion; www. cameramoda.it).

LUISA CASATI

Before Lady Gaga's meat dress or Italian style-star Anna dello Russo's *Star Wars*–style feathered headgear, there was the Marquesa Casati (1881–1957). The first female style icon to realise the power of fashion in creating legend, the Marquesa proudly proclaimed, 'I want to be a living work of art'.

Born in Milan, the daughter of a wealthy cotton merchant, Luisa was one of Italy's wealthiest heiresses by the age of 15. She married well and all seemed to be going according to plan, until she met notorious Italian writer and war hero, Gabriele d'Annunzio, with whom she started a shockingly open love affair.

Unfettered by d'Annunzio's unorthodox nature Luisa began to transform her appearance, dyeing her hair flame red, highlighting her huge green eyes with droplets of poisonous belladonna, and dressing in lustrous Bakst velvets.

Luisa Casati is one of the most widely represented women in history. She has been painted, sculpted, drawn and photographed by some of the 20th centuries' most avant-garde artists (Boldoni, Singer Seargeant, Dalí, Epstein, Man Ray and Cecil Beaton, to name but a few). She played muse to many movements, including the Italian Futurists, and launched the careers of countless artists through her generous patronage. But her greatest impact was in the world of fashion, where she is considered the original female dandy. Buried in Brompton Cemetery with her false eyelashes, her tombstone reads: 'Age cannot wither her, nor custom stale her infinite variety'.

Recognising the huge potential of mass markets, designers like Armani, Missoni and Versace began creating and following trends, selling their 'image' through advertising and promotion. In the 1980s, Armani's power suits gave rise to new unisex fashions, Dolce & Gabbana became a byword for Italian sex appeal and Miuccia Prada transformed her father's ailing luxury luggage business with democratic, durable totes and backpacks made out of radical new fabrics like waterproof Pocone, silk faille and parachute nylon.

Even more ubiquitous was the sportswear and casual chic look of fashion houses like Diesel and Benetton – the provocative advertising campaigns of the latter broadcasting an image of an irreverent brand with a social conscience. Fashion, it seemed, had something to say and now had the power to say it on a global scale.

Fashion Mecca Milan

Milan's rise to global fashion prominence was far from random. No other Italian city, not even Rome, was so well suited to take on this mantle. First, thanks to its geographic position, the city had historically strong links with European markets. It was also Italy's capital of finance, advertising, television and publishing, with both *Vogue* and *Amica* magazines based here. What's more, Milan had always had a fashion and clothing industry based around the historic textile and silk production of upper Lombardy. And, with the city's postwar focus on trade fairs and special events, it provided a natural marketplace for the exchange of goods and ideas.

As a result, in just over 15 years Milan emerged as Italy's top (and the world's fourth-biggest) fashion exporter. Six of the world's top 10 fashion houses are Italian, and four of those are based in the Milan. The Quadrilatero d'Oro, that 'Golden Quad', is now dominated by over 500 fashion outlets in an area of barely 6000 sq metres. Such is the level of display, tourists now travel to Milan to 'see' the fashion.

If you feel so inclined, you can also drop by during one of the four fashion weeks (the 'week' is now nine days long) for male and female summer and winter collections. They are held, respectively, in January and February, and June and September.

Fashion Classics

Borsalino *Montecristi Panama*

Prada *Cashmere sweater*

Aspesi *Trench coat*

Gallo *Silk socks*

Car Shoe *Loafers*

Ermenegildo Zegna *Midnight-blue suit*

Design

Better living by design: what could be more Milanese? From the cup that holds your morning espresso to the bedside light you switch off before you go to sleep, there's a designer responsible, and almost everyone in Milan will know their name. Design here is a way of life.

Iconic Designs

Alessi Kitchen utensils designed by architects

Vespa Piaggio 1946 mini-motor

Cassina Furniture by Frank Lloyd Wright

Alfa Romeo Milan's sexy racing roadster

Mezzadro Castiglioni's cantilevered chair

Modern Italian Design

Italy's design roots are in 1930s Milan, with the opening of the Triennale, the founding of *Domus* and *Casabella* magazines, Rinascente's visionary commissions (Giorgio Armani started as window dresser here) and the development of the Fiera. Where elaborate French rococo and ornate Austrian art nouveau had captured the imagination of a genteel pre–world war Europe, the dynamic deco style of Italian Futurism was a perfect partner for the industrial revolution and thrusting Fascist philosophies.

Like cogs in a political wheel, Fascist propaganda co-opted the radical, neoclassical streamlining that Futurism inspired and put it to work in posters, architecture, furniture and design. Modern factories were needed to aid the war effort and Fascist tendencies to hierarchical organisation and centralised control boosted Italian manufacturing. Through an inherent eye for purity of line, modern Italian design found beauty in balance and symmetry. This refreshing lack of detail appealed greatly to a fiercely democratising war-torn Europe where minimalism and utility came to represent the very essence of modernity.

After WWII, the military industrial complexes in Turin and Milan became the centrepieces of a new, global consumer-centric economy. Turin's strength was industrial design, from Lavazza espresso machines to the Fiat 500 car; Milan focused on fashion and home decor. Italian films and pioneering magazines such as *Domus* showcased these newly mass-produced design objects, making them seem both desirable and, more importantly, attainable.

Alessi's famous bird-whistle kettle designer, American Michael Graves, once received a postcard from a French poet, who wrote, 'I'm always very grumpy when I get up in the morning. But when I get up now, I put the teakettle on, and when it starts to sing it makes me smile – goddamn you!' More than just a kettle, it captured the public imagination and is still sold in its millions today.

From the Spoon to the City

Milan's philosopher-architects and designers – Giò Ponti, Vico Magistretti, Gae Aulenti, Achille Castiglioni, Ettore Sottsass and Piero Fornasetti – were imbued with a modernist sense of optimism. They saw their postwar mission was not only to rebuild the bomb-damaged city but to re-design the whole urban environment. A defining statement of the era was the assertion by Milanese architect Ernesto Rogers that he wished to design 'everything, from the spoon to the city', while philosopher Enzo Paci believed designers sat somewhere between 'art and society'.

Far from being mere intellectual theorists, this cadre of architect-designers benefited from a unique proximity to a mosaic of artisanal businesses that spread across the Lombard hinterland north of Milan. This industrial district, known as Brianza, had grown up organically from rural society, thus retaining many specialist peasant craft skills and hundreds of years of manufacturing experience. While these production houses remained true to the craft aspect of their work, they were able to move towards modern sales and production techniques via the central market place of the Triennale, which opened in 1947.

This direct connection between producer and marketplace meant that Milanese designers remained attuned to the demands of the market. As producers of goods, they were unashamedly involved in the business of making profits. It was this happy symbiosis between creativity and commercialism that ultimately fine-tuned Italian design to achieve the modernist ideal of creating beautiful, *useful* objects.

Survival Guide

Directory A–Z

Climate

Milan

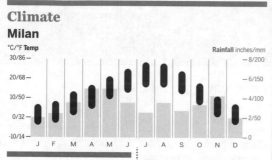

Customs Regulations

Duty-free sales within the EU no longer exist (but goods are sold tax-free in European airports). Visitors coming into Italy from non-EU countries can import, duty free: 1L spirits (or 2L wine), 50mL perfume, 250mL eau de toilette, 200 cigarettes and other goods up to a total of €175; anything over this must be declared on arrival. On leaving the EU, non-EU citizens can reclaim any Value Added Tax (VAT) on expensive purchases. Note that this applies to Swiss citizens and residents, too.

Discount Cards

Concession prices are generally indicated as adult/child, or adult/reduced. At museums and galleries, ask about discounts for students, children, families or seniors.

Senior Cards

In Italy, seniors (aged over 60) who are travelling extensively by rail should consider the one-year Carta d'Argento (Silver Card), available from trains stations for €30 (free for those aged 75 and over). It offers discounts of 10% to 15% on national travel and 25% on international trains. In some places, EU seniors may get free entry to sights. Always ask.

Student & Youth Cards

Free admission to some galleries and sights is available to under-18s. Discounts are available for some sights to EU citizens aged between 18 and 25 years. Prices are usually based on age, so a passport, driver's licence or **Euro<26** (www.euro26.org) card may be needed as proof.

An **International Student Identity Card** (ISIC; www.isic.org), though generally not much use for sights, can be handy for minor transport, theatre and cinema discounts, as well as occasional discounts in some hotels and restaurants (check the lists on the ISIC website); similar cards are available to teachers (International Teacher Identity Card, or ITIC). For nonstudent travellers under 25, the International Youth Travel Card (IYTC) offers the same benefits.

Student cards are issued by student unions and hostelling organisations as well as some youth-travel agencies. In Italy, the **Centro Turistico Studentesco e Giovanile** (CTS; www.cts.it) youth travel agency can issue ISIC, ITIC and Euro<26 cards.

Electricity

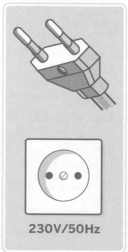

230V/50Hz

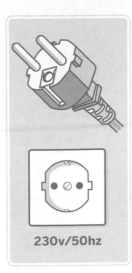

230v/50hz

Embassies & Consulates

Several countries have consulates in Milan, of which a selection is listed here. Many countries also have consular services in Lugano.

Australian Consulate (☏02 7767 4200; www.austrade.it; Via Borgogna 2; Ⓜ San Babila)

French Consulate (☏02 655 91 41; www.ambafrance-it.org/-Milan-; Via della Moscova 12; Ⓜ Turati)

German Consulate (☏02 623 11 01; www.mailand.diplo.de; Via Solferino 40; Ⓜ Moscova)

Japanese Consulate (☏02 624 11 41; www.milano.it.emb-japan.go.jp; Via Cesare Mangili 2/4; Ⓜ Turati)

Netherlands Consulate (☏02 485 58 41; http://italie.nlconsulaat.org; Via San Vittore 45; Ⓜ Conciliazione)

New Zealand Consulate (☏02 7217 0001; www.nzembassy.com/italy; Via Terraggio 17; Ⓜ Cadorna)

Swiss Consulate (☏02 777 91 61; www.eda.admin.ch/milano; Via Palestro 2; Ⓜ Turati)

UK Consulate (☏06 4220 2431; Via San Paolo 7; Ⓜ San Babila)

US Consulate (☏02 29 03 51; http://milan.usconsulate.gov; Via Principe Amedeo 2/10; Ⓜ Turati)

Gay & Lesbian Travellers

Homosexuality is legal in Italy and well tolerated in Milan, but a little less so in other towns. Overt displays of affection by homosexual couples could attract a negative response in smaller towns. There are gay clubs in Milan but otherwise pickings are slim. The useful **Gay.it** (www.gay.it) website lists gay bars and hotels across the country. Also check out the English-language **GayFriendlyItalia.com** (www.gayfriendlyitaly.com), produced by Gay.it; it has information on everything from hotels to homophobia issues and the law.

Insurance

A travel-insurance policy to cover theft, loss and medical problems is a good idea. It may also cover you for cancellation or delays to your travel arrangements. Paying for your ticket with a credit card can often provide limited travel accident insurance and you may be able to reclaim the payment if the operator doesn't deliver. Ask your credit-card company what it will cover.

If you're an EU citizen (or from Switzerland, Norway or Iceland), a European Health Insurance Card (EHIC) covers you for most medical care in public hospitals free of charge, but not for emergency repatriation home or non-emergencies. The card is available from health centres and (in the UK) post offices.

Citizens from other countries should find out if there is a reciprocal arrangement for free medical care between their country and Italy or Switzerland (Australia, for instance, has such an agreement with Italy; carry your Medicare card).

If you do need health insurance, make sure you get a policy that covers you for the worst possible scenario, such as an accident requiring an emergency flight home. Find out in advance if your insurance plan will make payments directly to providers or reimburse you later for overseas health expenditures.

Worldwide travel insurance is available at www. lonelyplanet.com/travel_services. You can buy, extend and claim online anytime – even if you're already on the road.

Internet Access

Wireless internet access is widespread in most hotels and some cafes and restaurants – access is usually (but not always) free. Tourist offices have information about local hotspots. Another option is to buy a SIM card with one of the Italian mobile phone operators, which provides wireless access through the mobile telephone network. These are usually pre-pay services that you can top up as you go.

Legal Matters

The average tourist will have a brush with the law only if robbed by a bag-snatcher or pickpocket. If you're stopped by the police in both Italy and Switzerland, you will be required to show your passport, so carry it at all times.

Drugs & Drink-Driving

Italy's drug laws were toughened in 2006 and possession of any controlled substances, including cannabis or marijuana, can get you into hot water. Those caught in possession of 5g of cannabis can be considered traffickers and prosecuted as such. The same applies to tiny amounts

---

> ## WHICH POLICE?
>
> If you run into trouble in Italy, you're likely to end up dealing with the *polizia statale* (state police) or the *carabinieri* (military police). The *polizia* deal with thefts, visa extensions and permits (among other things). They wear powder-blue trousers with a fuchsia stripe and a navy-blue jacket. A police station is called a *questura*.
>
> The *carabinieri* deal with general crime, public order and drug enforcement (often overlapping with the *polizia*). They wear a black uniform with a red stripe and drive night-blue cars with a red stripe. One of the big differences between the police and *carabinieri* is the latter's reach – even many villages have a *carabinieri* post.
>
> In Ticino, Switzerland, any brushes with the law will likely be with the cantonal police force.

---

of other drugs. Those caught with amounts below this threshold can be subject to minor penalties. You should be equally circumspect in Switzerland.

As for issues with drink-driving, the legal limit in both countries for blood-alcohol level is 0.05%, and random breath tests do occur.

Maps
City Maps

The city maps in this guide, along with tourist office maps, are usually adequate. More detailed maps are available in Italy at good bookshops, such as Feltrinelli. De Agostini, Touring Club Italiano (TCI) and Michelin all publish detailed city maps.

Driving Maps

If driving, the Automobile Association's (AA) *Road Atlas Italy*, available in the UK, is scaled at 1:250,000 and includes town maps. Just as good is Michelin's *Tourist and Motoring Atlas Italy*, scaled at 1:300,000.

In Italy, De Agostini publishes a comprehensive *Atlante Turistico Stradale d'Italia* (1:250,000), which includes 140 city maps (the AA *Road Atlas* is based on this). Perhaps handier for the lakes is TCI's *Atlante*

Stradale d'Italia (1:200,000), which is divided into three parts – grab the Nord volume (www.touringclub.com).

Michelin's fold-out Map 353 (Lombardia), scaled at 1:200,000, is good and covers the entire area of this guide, except for Lake Orta and a sliver of territory in the west (for which you'd need neighbouring Map 351, Piemonte & Valle d'Aosta). The 1:400,000 *Italy: North-West* (Map 561) covers the whole area.

Many of these are available online. Check out **Trek-Tools** (www.trektools.com).

Walking Maps

Maps of walking trails around the lakes, the Lombard Alps and Ticino are available at all major bookshops in Italy and Switzerland. In Italy, the best are the TCI bookshops. Kompass (www.kompass-\italia.it) publishes several 1:50,000 scale maps to the lakes region, including the following titles: *Lago di Como-Lago di Lugano*, *Lago di Garda-Monte Baldo*, *Le Tre Valli Bresciane*, *Lecco-Valle Brembana*, *Lago Maggiore-Lago di Varese* and *Bernina-Sondrio*.

Most of western Ticino is covered by the 1:50,000 map *Val Verzasca*, produced by the government body Swisstopo.

Medical Services

All foreigners have the same right as Italians to free emergency medical treatment in a public hospital. However, other medical care is not necessarily covered.

EU, Switzerland, Norway & Iceland Citizens are entitled to the full range of health-care services in public hospitals free of charge upon presentation of a European Health Insurance Card (EHIC).

Australia Thanks to a reciprocal arrangement with Italy, Australian citizens are entitled to free public health care – carry your Medicare card.

New Zealand, the US & Canada Citizens of these and other countries have to pay for anything other than emergency treatment. Most travel-insurance policies include medical coverage.

Money

The euro is Italy's currency and euro notes come in denominations of €500, €200, €100, €50, €20, €10 and €5. The euro coins are in denominations of €2 and €1, and 50, 20, 10, five, two and one cents.

Switzerland's currency is the Swiss franc. The six notes come in denominations of Sfr1000 (which you'll hardly ever see), Sfr200, Sfr100, Sfr50, Sfr20 and Sfr10. Coins are in denominations of Sfr5, Sfr2, Sfr1, Sfr½ (ie 50 Swiss cents), and 20, 10 and five cents. As a rule, it's pretty

---

EATING PRICE RANGES

The following price ranges refer to two courses, glass of house wine, *coperto pane* and *coperto*.

€ less than €25

€€ €25–€45

€€€ more than €45

---

easy to use euros in Ticino, although generally you'll get change in francs and the rate used will not necessarily be all that favourable.

A value-added tax of around 20%, known as IVA (Imposta di Valore Aggiunto), is slapped onto just about everything in Italy. If you are a non-EU resident and spend more than €155 (€154.94 to be precise!) on a purchase, you can claim a refund when you leave. The refund only applies to purchases from affiliated retail outlets that display a 'tax free for tourists' (or similar) sign. You have to complete a form at the point of sale, then have it stamped by Italian customs as you leave. At major airports you can then get an immediate cash refund; otherwise it will be refunded to your credit card. For information, pick up a pamphlet on the scheme from participating stores.

In Switzerland, IVA generally amounts to 7.6% and there is no tax-back program for foreign visitors.

For the latest exchange rates, check out www.xe.com.

ATMs

Credit and debit cards can be used in a *bancomat* (ATM) displaying the appropriate sign. Visa and MasterCard are among the most widely recognised, but others like Cirrus and Maestro are also well covered. Check any charges with your bank at home. Most banks now build a fee of around 2.75% into every foreign transaction. In addition, ATM withdrawals can attract a further fee, usually around 1.5%.

Credit & Debit Cards

Cards are good for payment in most hotels, restaurants, shops, supermarkets and tollbooths.

Moneychangers

You can change money in banks, post offices or in a *cambio* (exchange office). Post offices and most banks

are reliable and tend to offer the best rates. Generally, post office commissions are lowest and the exchange rate is reasonable. The main advantage of exchange offices is the longer hours they keep, but watch for high commissions and inferior rates.

Travellers Cheques

Traditionally a safe way to carry money and possibly still not a bad idea as a back-up, travellers cheques have been outmoded by plastic.

Visa, Travelex and Amex are widely accepted brands. Get most of your cheques in fairly large denominations to save on per-cheque commission charges.

Opening Hours

Italy

Banks 8.30am to 1.30pm and 3.30pm to 4.30pm Monday to Friday

Cafes & bars 7am to 11pm

Restaurants noon to 3pm and 6.30pm or 7pm to 10pm or later. Many also close one day per week and/or Sunday evening.

Shops 9am or 10am to 1pm or 2pm and 4pm to 7pm Tuesday to Saturday; many smaller shops also close for lunch. In Milan, many shops don't close for lunch.

Switzerland

Banks 8.30am to 4.30pm Monday to Friday

Restaurants noon to 3pm and 6pm to 9pm

Shops 8am to 6.30pm Monday to Friday, sometimes with a one- to two-hour break for lunch at noon in smaller towns. Closing times on Saturday are usually 4pm or 5pm.

Public Holidays

Many Italians and Ticinesi take their annual holiday in August. This means that, depending on where you are, many businesses and shops close for at least a part of that month. Milan and cities like Bergamo, Brescia and Cremona can be eerily quiet in August, while lakeside towns such as Como, Locarno and Lugano bustle with holiday activity. **Settimana Santa** (Easter Week) is another busy holiday period.

Individual towns have public holidays to celebrate the feasts of their patron saints.

Italy

New Year's Day (Capodanno or Anno Nuovo) 1 January

Epiphany (Epifania or Befana) 6 January

Good Friday (Venerdì Santo) March/April

Easter Monday (Pasquetta or Lunedì dell'Angelo) March/April

Liberation Day (Giorno della Liberazione) 25 April marks the Allied Victory in Italy, and the end of the German presence and Mussolini, in 1945

Labour Day (Festa del Lavoro) 1 May

Republic Day (Festa della Repubblica) 2 June

Feast of the Assumption (Assunzione or Ferragosto) 15 August

All Saints' Day (Ognissanti) 1 November

Feast of the Immaculate Conception (Immaculata Concezione) 8 December

Christmas Day (Natale) 25 December

Boxing Day (Festa di Santo Stefano) 26 December

Switzerland

New Year's Day 1 January

Easter March/April

Ascension Day 40th day after Easter

Whit Sunday & Monday 7th week after Easter

National Day 1 August

Christmas Day 25 December

St Stephen's Day 26 December

Safe Travel

Theft

Pickpockets and bag snatchers operate in Milan. You need to be vigilant around train stations, on public transport, in Piazza del Duomo and in the busy shopping streets. You should also pay attention in train stations and around the old city centres of other towns, especially Brescia and Verona.

If driving, a scam that has been known to occur at stops such as service stations and lookout points involves a tyre being surreptitiously punctured when the vehicle is unattended. A couple of scammers offer to help but, while one distracts the travellers, the other is emptying your vehicle.

In case of theft or loss, always report the incident to police within 24 hours and ask for a statement, otherwise your travel-insurance company won't pay out.

Traffic

Driving into and around Milan can be nerve-wracking at first, as it seems to have a cavalier dodgem-cars element to it. Motorcyclists should be prepared for anything in the cities. Traffic is dense and the signposting is not always immediately clear.

In other cities around the region, things are calmer. Pedestrians should be watchful, as drivers will not always automatically halt for them at crossings.

Traffic can be heavy on most minor roads across the region, particularly in summer. Some mountain and lakeside roads are narrow, particularly around Lakes Como and Garda, traffic can be heavy and you'll be sharing the road with everything from buses to bicycles. Be prepared for some poorly lit tunnels at the northern end of Lake Garda.

Pollution

Noise and air pollution, caused mainly by heavy traffic, can be a problem in Milan. A headache after a day of sightseeing is likely to be caused by breathing in carbon monoxide, rather than simple tiredness. On especially bad days, traffic is halved by allowing only vehicles with odd- or even-numbered plates to drive on alternate days.

Telephone

Direct international calls can easily be made from public telephones by using coins or a phonecard. Generally, it is cheaper to use your country's direct-dialling services paid for at home-country rates (such as AT&T in the USA and Telstra in Australia). Get their access numbers before you leave home. Alternatively, try making calls from cheap-rate call centres or using international call cards, which are often on sale at newspaper stands. Skype, VoIP and other internet-based options can be used in some internet cafes.

Useful Phone Numbers & Codes
ITALY

Telephone area codes in Italy begin with 0 and consist of up to four digits. The area code is followed by a number made up of anything from four to eight digits. The area code is an integral part of the telephone number and must always be dialled, even when calling from next door.

Mobile phone numbers begin with a three-digit prefix such as 330. Toll-free (freephone) numbers are known as *numeri verdi* and usually start with 800. Non-geographical numbers start with 840, 841, 848, 892, 899, 163, 166 or 199. The range of rates for these makes a rainbow look boring – beware that some can be costly. Some six-digit national rate numbers are also in use (such as those for Alitalia, rail and postal information).

To call Italy from abroad, call the international access number, Italy's country code and then the area code of the location you want, including the leading 0.

Some useful codes include:

➜ **International access code** ☑00

➜ **International direct dial code** ☑00

➜ **International dialling code** ☑39

➜ **International directory enquiries** ☑176

➜ **Local directory enquiries** ☑12

SWITZERLAND

In Switzerland, area codes also begin with 0, which must always be dialled. Telephone numbers with the code 0800 are toll-free; those with 0848 are local rate. Numbers beginning with 156 or 157 are always premium rate.

In Switzerland, numbers with the code 079 are mobiles.

When calling Switzerland, the leading 0 in area codes must not be dialled.

Useful local codes include:

➜ **International access code** ☑00

➜ **International direct dial code** ☑00

➜ **International dialling code** ☑41

➜ **International directory enquiries** ☑18 11

➜ **Local directory enquiries** ☑18 11, ☑18 12

Mobile Phones

Italy and Switzerland use GSM 900/1800, which is compatible with the rest of Europe and Australia but not with North American GSM 1900 or the totally different Japanese system (though some GSM 1900/900 phones do work here). If you have a GSM phone, check with your service provider about using it in Europe and beware of calls being routed internationally (very expensive for a 'local' call).

You can get a temporary or prepaid account from several companies in both countries if you already own a GSM, dual- or tri-band cellular phone. You will need your passport and the address of your accommodation to open an account. Always check with your mobile service provider in your home country to ascertain whether your handset allows use of another SIM card. If yours does, it can cost as little as €10 to activate a local prepaid SIM card (sometimes with €10 worth of calls on the card). In Switzerland, prices start at about Sfr30 for a card with Sfr20 worth of talk-time.

Payphones & Phonecards

ITALY

Partly privatised Telecom Italia is the largest telecommunications organisation in Italy and its orange public payphones are liberally scattered about the country. The most common accept only *carte/schede telefoniche* (phonecards). These phonecards (most commonly €2.50 or €5) are available at post offices, tobacconists and newsstands. You must break off the top left-hand corner of the card before you can use it. Phonecards have an expiry date. This is usually 31 December or 30 June, depending on when you purchase the card.

You will find cut-price call centres in the cities. Rates can be considerably lower than from Telecom payphones for international calls. Alternatively, ask about international calling cards at newsstands and tobacconists. They can be hit or miss but are sometimes good value.

SWITZERLAND

In Switzerland, save money on the normal international tariff by buying prepaid cards – Swisscom has them to the value of Sfr10, Sfr20,

Sfr50 and Sfr100. Or look for prepaid cards from rival operators.

Time

Italy and Switzerland are one hour ahead of GMT. Daylight-saving time, when clocks are moved forward one hour, starts on the last Sunday in March. Clocks are put back an hour on the last Sunday in October. Italy operates on a 24-hour clock.

Toilets

Here and there you'll find public toilets in city centres, but more often than not you'll probably want to duck into a cafe or bar. The polite thing to do is order something at the bar, although more often than not no one will say anything if you don't, especially if things are busy. Most service stations have toilets.

Tourist Information

The lakes area takes in four Italian regions and the Swiss canton of Ticino.

Italy

In Italy, three tiers of tourist office exist: regional, provincial and local. They have different names, but roughly offer the same services, with the exception of regional offices, which are generally concerned with promotion, planning and budgeting.

Generally, provincial tourist offices are known as Azienda di Promozione Turistica (APT). These have information on the town you are in and the surrounding province. Informazione e Assistenza ai Turisti (IAT) offices generally have information only on the town they are in.

At the website of the **Italian National Tourist Office** (www.enit.it) you can find details of provincial and local tourist offices across the country. Otherwise, try the **Lombardy** (www.turismo. regione.lombardia.it) or **Piedmont** (www.regione.piemonte. it/turismo) tourism websites.

Switzerland

In Ticino, you'll find useful local offices in **Lugano** (Map p124; ☑058 866 66 00; www. lugano-tourism.ch; Municipio Bldg, Riva Giocondo Albertolli; ☀9am-7pm Mon-Fri, to 6pm Sat, 10am-6pm Sun & holidays Apr-Oct, shorter hrs rest of year), **Locarno** (Map p96; ☑091 791 00 91; www.mag-giore.ch; Largo Zorzi 1; ☀9am-6pm Mon-Fri, 10am-6pm Sat & holidays, 10am-1.30pm & 2.30-5pm Sun mid-Mar–Oct, 9.30am-noon & 1.30-5pm Mon-Fri, 10am-noon & 1.30-5pm Sat Nov–mid-Mar) and **Bellinzona** (Map p130; ☑091 825 21 31; www.bellinzonaturismo.ch; Piazza Nosetto; ☀9am-6.30pm Mon-Fri, 9am-noon Sat Apr-Oct, 9am-noon & 1.30-6.30pm Mon-Fri, 9am-noon Sat Nov-Mar). Otherwise, check out the regional **Ticino tourism** (www.ticino.ch) website.

Travellers with Disabilities

Italy is not an easy country for disabled travellers and getting around can be a problem for wheelchair users. Even a short journey in a city or town can become a major expedition if cobblestone streets have to be negotiated. Although many buildings have lifts, they are not always wide enough for wheelchairs. Not an awful lot has been done to make life for the deaf and/or blind any easier either.

The Italian National Tourist Office in your country may be able to provide advice and may also carry a small brochure, *Services for Disabled Passengers*, published by Trenitalia (Italian railways), which details facilities at stations and on trains. Trenitalia also has a national helpline for people with disabilities at 199 30 30 60. For more information, search on *disabili* at the Trenitalia (www.trenitalia. com) website and click on the English version.

In Milan and Verona, general guides on accessibility are published.

Accessible Italy (☑378 94 11 11; www.accessibleitaly. com) is a San Marino-based company that specialises in holiday services for people with disabilities, ranging from tours to the hiring of adapted transport. It can even arrange romantic Italian weddings. This is the best first port of call.

Check out **Milano per Tutti** (www.milanopertutti.it) for information on Milan.

In Ticino, see http://ticino. ch/en/travel-info/turismo-accessibile.

Visas

Italy and Switzerland are among the 26 member countries of the Schengen Convention, under which 22 EU countries (all but Bulgaria, Cyprus, Ireland, Romania and the UK) plus Iceland, Norway, Liechtenstein and Switzerland have abolished permanent checks at common borders.

Citizens of EU member states and Switzerland can travel to Italy (and Switzerland) with their national identity card alone. If such countries do not issue ID cards – as in the UK – travellers must carry a full valid passport. All other nationalities must have a full valid passport and may need visas.

Legal residents (regardless of nationality) of one Schengen country do not require a visa for another. Residents of many non-EU countries, including Australia, Brazil, Canada, Israel, Japan, New Zealand and the USA, do not require visas for tourist visits of up to 90 days. The standard Schengen tourist visa is valid for up to 90 days and for travel to all Schengen states.

Women Travellers

The lakes area of northern Italy and Switzerland is hardly dangerous country for women. While care should be taken in Milan (and your guard should never be 100% down), women travellers generally encounter no real problems. Be aware that eye-to-eye contact is the norm in Italy's daily flirtatious interplay.

Transport

GETTING THERE & AWAY

Italy is exceptionally well connected to the rest of the world by air, and to neighbouring countries by road and rail. Switzerland is similarly well connected, although with fewer air connections.

Flights, tours and rail tickets can be booked online at www.lonelyplanet.com/bookings.

Entering the Region

Entering both Italy and Switzerland is usually trouble-free and rarely involves anything more than cursory customs and immigration checks. For visa requirements for entering Italy and Switzerland, see p250.

Air

Airports

Milan receives plenty of international flights from around Europe as well as some intercontinental flights to its two airports.

Malpensa Airport (☑02 23 23 23; www.sea-aeroportimilano.it) Regular intercontinental flights serve Malpensa airport, located 50km west of Milan.

Linate Airport (☑02 7485 2200; www.milanolinate.eu) The majority of domestic and a handful of European flights use the more convenient Linate airport, 7km east of Milan's centre.

Orio al Serio Airport (☑035 32 63 23; www.sacbo.it) Ryanair leads a coterie of budget airlines that use Bergamo's airport, 4km southeast of the centre, with daily flights to/from the UK and other European destinations.

Verona-Villafranca Airport (☑045 809 56 66; www.aeroportoverona.it) Located 12km southwest of Verona, Verona-Villafranca airport has an array of flights. European cities served include Amsterdam, Barcelona, Berlin, Brussels, London and Paris. There's even the occasional intercontinental connection.

Agno Airport (☑091 612 11 11; www.lugano-airport.ch) Lugano's airport has flights to/from Geneva and Zürich from where there are onward flights to Italian and other European cities.

Land

Border Crossings

FRANCE

The main points of entry by road include:

Coast Road From Nice on what becomes the A10 motorway along the Ligurian coast (then take the A7 from Genoa north to Milan).

Mont Blanc Tunnel Begins near Chamonix and connects with the A5 for Turin and Milan.

SWITZERLAND

Grand St Bernard Tunnel Connects with the A5, and the Simplon tunnel connects with the SS33 road that leads to Lake Maggiore.

St Gotthard Tunnel The A2 runs from Basel, through the tunnel and into Ticino via Bellinzona to Lake Lugano.

By Train The main rail lines from Switzerland into this part of Italy cross at Domodossola and from Lugano via Como. Minor lines link Locarno and Domodossola, Bellinzona with the east bank of Lake Maggiore and St Moritz with Tirano (in the Valtellina).

AUSTRIA & EASTERN EUROPE

Brenner Pass connects with the A22 and parallel rail line south to Verona.

Other autostrade and train lines converge from Eastern Europe through Venice, en route to Verona and Lombardy along the six-lane A4, one of Italy's busiest motorways.

Bus

Buses converge on Milan from major cities across Europe. Most national and international buses start and terminate at Milan's Lampugnano Bus Terminal (line 1 – the red line), which is located by the Lampugnano metro station on Via Giulia Natta, west of the city centre.

Eurolines (☑0861 199 19 00; www.eurolines.it) A consortium of European coach companies that operates across Europe with offices in all major European cities.

Autostradale (☑02 7200 1304; www.autostradale.it) Runs the bulk of Italian national services and has a ticket office at the main tourist office. It also sells international tickets for Eurolines services.

Car & Motorcycle

If driving, you'll need:

➡ proof of ownership of a private vehicle or proof of car rental

➡ a valid national licence plate

➡ a sticker identifying the car's country of registration (unless it has the standard EU number plates with the blue strip and country ID)

➡ car registration certificate or card

For more information, see p254.

DRIVING LICENCE & DOCUMENTATION

➡ All EU member state driving licences are fully recognised throughout Europe.

➡ Drivers from non-EU member states should obtain an International Driving Permit (IDP) to accompany their national licence. Issued by your national automobile association, it's valid for 12 months and must be kept with your proper licence.

INSURANCE

You must have evidence of third-party insurance. If driving a vehicle registered and insured in an EU country (and Switzerland), your home-country insurance is sufficient.

Ask your insurer for a European Accident Statement (EAS) form, which can simplify matters in the event of an accident. A European breakdown assistance policy is a good investment. If, for whatever reason, you don't have such a policy, assistance can be obtained through:

Automobile Club d'Italia (ACI;☑80 31 16, from a mobile phone 800 11 68 00; www.aci. it) Foreigners do not have to join, but instead pay a per-incident fee. The numbers operate 24 hours a day.

Automobil Club der Schweiz (☑41 44 628 88 99; www.acs.ch) The Swiss equivalent of Automobile Club d'Italia.

Train

Milan is a major rail hub. High-speed services arrive from across Italy, from France via Turin in the west and from major Swiss cities like Zürich and Geneva to the north. An overnight sleeper train also runs from Barcelona (Spain).

For train timetables and fares, check out www.trenitalia.com (Italy) or www.sbb.ch (Switzerland).

STAMP IT!

Countless foreign travellers in Italy learn the hard way that their train tickets must be stamped in the yellow machines (usually found at the head of rail platforms) just before boarding. Failure to do so usually results in fines, although the cry of 'I didn't know' *sometimes* elicits an indulgent response from ticket controllers. This is not an issue in Ticino.

FRANCE, SWITZERLAND & UK

Paris–Milan Fast direct trains (TGV) run from Gare de Lyon to Stazione Centrale (from €83, seven to 7½ hours) in Milan.

Geneva–Milan Cisalpino high-speed services converge on Milan from Geneva (via Lausanne, Brig and Domodossola) and Zürich (via Ticino). The trip takes 3¾ to 4½ hours (Sfr95 one way).

London–Milan Eurostar (www.eurostar.com) passenger trains travel between London and Paris from where there are TGV connections to Milan. For the latest information on journeys to Italy, check out www.raileurope.co.uk.

THE REST OF ITALY

The partially privatised state train system **Trenitalia**

CLIMATE CHANGE & TRAVEL

Every form of transport that relies on carbon-based fuel generates CO_2, the main cause of human-induced climate change. Modern travel is dependent on aeroplanes, which might use less fuel per kilometre per person than most cars but travel much greater distances. The altitude at which aircraft emit gases (including CO_2) and particles also contributes to their climate change impact. Many websites offer 'carbon calculators' that allow people to estimate the carbon emissions generated by their journey and, for those who wish to do so, to offset the impact of the greenhouse gases emitted with contributions to portfolios of climate-friendly initiatives throughout the world. Lonely Planet offsets the carbon footprint of all staff and author travel.

(www.trenitalia.it) runs most services. Travelling by train in Italy is relatively cheap compared with other European countries. The most useful types of train include the following:

Alta Velocità (High Speed) – Frecciarossa Variously known as AV and/or ESA, they operate on the Turin–Milan–Bologna–Florence–Rome–Naples–Salerno route. Nonstop trains between Milan and Rome take three hours. Prices vary according to the time of travel and how far in advance you book.

Alta Velocità (High Speed) – Frecciabianca Connects Milan with Venice in 2½ hours.

Regionale or Interregionale Local trains that usually stop at all stations.

Intercity (IC) Medium-speed services that operate between major cities.

GETTING AROUND

Trains will get you to the main Lombard towns and to some strategic launch pads on and around the lakes. Elsewhere, you'll be relying on a fairly dense network of buses, although infrequency of some services and the need to change buses at times can make the process a little slow. Ferries ply the lakes, offering not only commuter services but also a range of day-ticket options. Some handy car ferries cross at several points on Lakes Maggiore, Como and Garda. Clearly, having your own transport provides much greater liberty.

Milan has an excellent public transport network with both buses and the Metro covering just about anywhere you'd need to go. Buses and trains connect Milan's airports to the city centre.

Bicycle

Cyclists are a common sight on Italian roads, but that doesn't necessarily mean that drivers will take cyclists into account. There are nonetheless some fabulous cycling routes around the region.

Although cycling in Milan can be nerve-wracking for those unaccustomed to Italian traffic, it can be an enjoyable experience if you avoid the major thoroughfares. Both Milan and Verona have public bicycle schemes, while some city centres have been closed to motorised transport, making cycling a pleasant way to get around – Cremona is an excellent example of this.

Bikes can be taken on any train displaying the bicycle logo. The cheapest way to do this is to buy a separate bicycle ticket (€4, or €6 to €15 on Intercity, Eurostar and Euronight trains), available even at the self-service kiosks. You can use this ticket for 24 hours.

Boat

Ferries criss-cross all of the lakes covered in this book. Timetables are cut back quite drastically in the off-season (November to Easter).

Ferry services on the three main lakes come under the **Gestione Navigazione Laghi** (☑800 55 18 01; www.navigazionelaghi.it). The website includes timetables and pricing for travel on Lakes Maggiore, Como and Garda. Lakeside ticketing booths and tourist offices also have timetables. A popular option are one-day tickets allowing unlimited travel.

For the other lakes:

Lake Orta From its landing stage on Piazza Motta in Orta San Giulio, **Navigazione Lago d'Orta** (☑0322 84 48 62; www.navigazionelagodorta.it) runs boats to numerous spots on that lake, including Isola San Giulio.

Lake Iseo Operating up to eight ferries daily, **Navigazione sul Lago d'Iseo** (www.navigazione-lagoiseo.it) routes from (south to north) Sarnico, Iseo, Monte Isola, Lovere and Pisogne (and some other smaller stops).

Lake Lugano Based in Lugano in Switzerland, **Società Navigazione del Lago di Lugano** (☑091 971 52 23; www.lakelugano.ch) operates ferries on Lake Lugano (parts of which sneak into Italian territory) year round.

Bus

Getting around the plains towns and to some of the main settlements at the south end of the main lakes is easier by train than by bus. To get any further and explore the lake shores and beyond, however, bus is often the only option for those without their own transport.

Italy

Services are mainly organised around provincial capitals (eg Bergamo, Brescia, Como, Cremona, Mantua and Verona), which act as hubs for the towns nearby. You will rarely be able to scoot from one lake directly to another by bus. Generally, it is easiest to get to your chosen lake by rail and use buses locally.

Most bus services from Milan leave from the main terminal, Stazione Centrale. Elsewhere, in the bigger towns the bus station is often handily located near the train station. Sometimes you buy tickets at the station ticket counters (where timetables are posted), but sometimes they must be bought on board. Most of the bus company websites have timetables.

Bus companies operating across the area include the following:

APAM (www.apam.it) Buses around Mantua.

APTV (www.aptv.it) Buses run from/to Lake Garda, and connect towns along both shores of the lake.

SAB (www.sab-autoservizi.it) Bergamo-based company operating services around Bergamo province, and to Lake Como, Lake Iseo and the mountains.

SAF (☎0323 55 21 72; www. safduemila.com) Buses from Milan to and around Lake Maggiore.

SAIA Trasport (www.saiat rasporti.it) Serves destinations all over Brescia province and into neighbouring provinces.

SIA (☎030 377 42 37; www. sia-autoservizi.it) Also serves Brescia province and connects the city with the western shore of Lake Garda.

SPT (☎031 24 72 47; www. sptcomo.it) Buses from Como around Lake Como and services to Lugano.

Trentino Trasporti (www.tteser cizio.it) Buses between Trento and Rovereto and the north end of Lake Garda (including Riva del Garda and Arco).

Switzerland

In Ticino, on the Swiss side of the lakes, train is the easiest way to get between the three main cities (Lugano, Locarno and Bellinzona). Local buses and private trains cover some of the lakeside spots. Otherwise, the country's network of postal buses comes into its own for reaching into the fascinating back valleys that wind off north of Locarno and Bellinzona. Timetables are generally posted at stops.

Car & Motorcycle
Road Networks
ITALY

Italy boasts an extensive privatised network of autostrade (motorways), represented on road signs by a white A followed by a number on a green background. You can pay tolls on Italian motorways with cash or credit card as you leave the autostrada.

You'll be doing most of your travelling on the spiderweb network of strade statali (state highways, coded SS), strade regionali (regional highways, SR) and strade provinciali (provincial routes, SP). The network is especially dense in the plains areas around and south of Bergamo, Brescia, Cremona and Verona.

Around the lakes and in mountain areas, driving on spring and summer weekends can be a real test of patience as half of Milan's population seems to stream northward.

The following are some of the most important motorways in Italy:

A4 Runs east–west, linking Milan with Bergamo, Brescia, Lake Garda and Verona.

A8 Leads northwest out of Milan and, in a slightly confusing tangle, becomes the A8-A26 as it approaches the southern end of Lake Maggiore. A branch of the A8 reaches Varese.

A9 Once you're about 11km out of Milan along the A8, the A9 branches north to Como and on across the Swiss border, where it continues as the A2.

A26 Follows the western shore via Arona and Stresa before it peters out in a smaller route to Domodossola and the Swiss frontier. If you're coming from Milan and heading to Lake Maggiore, follow the signs to Gravellona Toce.

SWITZERLAND

In Switzerland an autostrada (A2, represented with the number on red background) also traverses Ticino roughly north–south. If you intend to use the A2 and other motorways in Switzerland, you must buy a one-off Sfr40 vignette on entering the country. This windscreen sticker is valid on all Swiss motorways for a calendar year.

The A2 connects with Italy's A9 and passes through Lugano, Bellinzona and north through Ticino into the heart of Switzerland.

Fuel

Fuel prices are among the highest in Europe and vary from one service station (benzinaio, stazione di servizio) to another. Lead-free (senza piombo; 95 octane) costs up to €1.85/L. A 98-octane variant costs as much as €1.95/L. Diesel (gasolio) comes in at €1.50/L. Prices tend to be slightly cheaper in Switzerland.

Hire

To rent a car in Italy you have to be aged 25 or over and have a credit card. Most firms will accept your standard licence or IDP for identification purposes. Consider hiring a small car, which you'll be grateful for when negotiating narrow city or village lanes.

Multinational car rental agencies include the following:

Autos Abroad (☎in the UK 0845 029 19 45; www.autosa broad.com)

Auto Europe (www.autoeu rope.com)

Avis (☎199 10 01 33; www. avisautonoleggio.it)

Budget (☎199 30 73 73; www.budgetautonoleggio.it)

Europcar (☎199 30 70 30; www.europcar.com)

SPEED LIMITS

	ITALY	SWITZERLAND
Built-up areas	50km/h	50km/h
Non-urban roads	90km/h	80km/h
Highways	110km/h	80kmh
Autostrade (motorways)	130km/h	120km/h

Train Routes

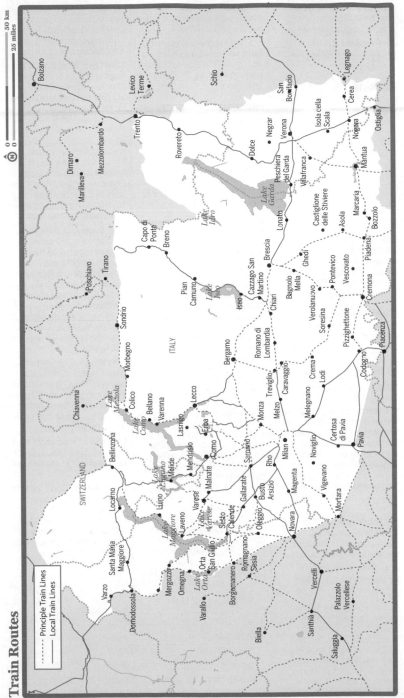

Principle Train Lines

Local Train Lines

50 km

25 miles

Hertz (☎08708 44 88 44; www.hertz.it)

Italy by Car (☎800 84 60 83; www.italybycar.it)

Maggiore (☎199 15 11 20; www.maggiore.it)

Parking

Parking in most cities in the region can be complicated. The historic centre of most cities is off limits to most traffic, although partial exceptions are sometimes made for tourists who are staying at hotels in the old centre (in such cases you may be able to enter the city centre long enough to unload).

Milan has instituted the Ecopass, which obliges drivers to pay to enter the centre of town. As a rule, it is simplest not to drive in the cities and main towns. Park and walk is the best policy.

Road Rules

➡ Drive on the right, overtake on the left.

➡ Give way to cars entering an intersection from a road on your right.

➡ Seatbelts are compulsory for all passengers.

➡ A warning triangle (to be used in the event of a breakdown) must be carried, and if your car breaks down and you get out of the vehicle, you must wear an approved yellow or orange safety vest (available at bicycle shops and outdoor stores).

➡ Random breath tests take place in Italy and Switzerland. The blood-alcohol limit is 0.05%.

➡ All vehicles must use headlights by day on the

autostrade. It is advisable for motorcycles on all roads at all times.

➡ Speed cameras operate in both countries and fines are increasingly being sent to the home countries of offenders, so beware!

Taxi

You can usually find taxi ranks at train and bus stations or you can telephone for radio taxis. It's best to go to a designated taxi stand, as it's illegal for them to stop in the street if hailed.

Train

Trenitalia (☎in Italian 89 20 21; www.trenitalia.com) runs most of the trains on the Italian side of the lakes area. From Milan, all the main cities are easily reached by train. Brescia, the south-shore towns on Lake Garda and Verona are on the main line connecting Milan with Venice. Other lines link Milan with Bergamo, Cremona, Mantua and Pavia. Bergamo and Cremona are also linked directly to Brescia, as is Mantua to Verona.

With the exception of fast trains operating on the Milan–Brescia–Verona line, and fast(ish) Cisalpino trains running to/from Milan to Switzerland via Stresa and Lugano, most trains are *regionali*, calling in at most, if not all, stops.

You can buy tickets at the station counter or machines. Only on some services (such as Eurostar City and Cisalpino) will you need a seat reservation, but this can

be made when you buy the ticket.

Most, but not all, train stations have some kind of left luggage service or lockers.

Lake Como West Bank & Lake Lugano Regular trains, Swiss or Italian, connect Milan's Stazione Centrale with Lugano via Mendrisio and Como (San Giovanni station). Ferrovie Nord Milano (FNM; www.ferrovienord. it), a private company, operates trains stopping all stations from Milan's **Stazione Nord** (www. fnmgroup.it/orario; Piazza Luigi Cadorna), terminating at Como's lakeside Como Nord Lago stop. From Como there are numerous trains along the West Bank.

Lake Como East Bank Trains run from Milan's Stazione Centrale to Lecco, up the eastern shore of Lake Como and turn east along the Valtellina valley to Sondrio and wind up in Tirano, a town that sits on a sliver of Lombard territory between the Swiss border and the region of Trentino-Alto Adige. The Lecco–Tirano part of this 2½-hour trip is delightful.

Lake Maggiore Hourly trains connect Milan's Stazione Centrale with Stresa via Arona, on the western shore of Lake Maggiore, on their way to Domodossola and Switzerland. Connecting services run up the east shore.

Lake Iseo An assortment of trains run from Brescia along the eastern shore of Lake Iseo as far as Edolo.

Switzerland In Ticino, the Milan–Lugano train line continues north to Bellinzona and up the Valle Leventina, to cross the St Gotthard pass into central Switzerland. A branch line connects Bellinzona with Locarno.

Language

Standard Italian is taught and spoken throughout Italy. Dialects are an important part of regional identity, but you'll have no trouble being understood anywhere if you stick to standard Italian, which we've also used in this chapter.

The sounds used in spoken Italian can all be found in English. If you read our coloured pronunciation guides as if they were English, you'll be understood. The stressed syllables are indicated with italics. Note that ai is pronounced as in 'aisle', ay as in 'say', ow as in 'how', dz as the 'ds' in 'lids', and r is a strong and rolled sound. Keep in mind that Italian consonants can have a stronger, emphatic pronunciation – if the consonant is written as a double letter, it should be pronounced a little stronger, eg *sonno son*·no (sleep) versus *sono so*·no (I am).

BASICS

Hello.	*Buongiorno.*	bwon·*jor*·no
Goodbye.	*Arrivederci.*	a·ree·ve·*der*·chee
Yes./No.	*Sì./No.*	see/no
Excuse me.	*Mi scusi.* (pol)	mee *skoo*·zee
	Scusami. (inf)	*skoo*·za·mee
Sorry.	*Mi dispiace.*	mee dees·*pya*·che
Please.	*Per favore.*	per fa·*vo*·re
Thank you.	*Grazie.*	*gra*·tsye
You're welcome.	*Prego.*	*pre*·go

How are you?
Come sta/stai? (pol/inf)   *ko*·me sta/stai

Fine. And you?
Bene. E Lei/tu? (pol/inf)   *be*·ne e lay/too

What's your name?
Come si chiama? pol   *ko*·me see *kya*·ma
Come ti chiami? inf   *ko*·me tee *kya*·mee

My name is ...
Mi chiamo ...   mee *kya*·mo ...

Do you speak English?
Parla/Parli   *par*·la/*par*·lee
inglese? (pol/inf)   een·*gle*·ze

I don't understand.
Non capisco.   non ka·*pee*·sko

ACCOMMODATION

Do you have a ... room?	*Avete una camera ...?*	a·*ve*·te oo·na *ka*·me·ra ...
double	*doppia con letto matri- moniale*	*do*·pya kon *le*·to ma·tree· mo·*nya*·le
single	*singola*	*seen*·go·la

How much is it per ...?	*Quanto costa per ...?*	*kwan*·to *kos*·ta per ...
night	*una notte*	*oo*·na *no*·te
person	*persona*	per·*so*·na

Is breakfast included?
La colazione è   la ko·la·*tsyo*·ne e
compresa?   kom·*pre*·sa

air-con	*aria condizionata*	*a*·rya kon·dee·tsyo·*na*·ta
bathroom	*bagno*	*ba*·nyo
campsite	*campeggio*	kam·*pe*·jo
guesthouse	*pensione*	pen·*syo*·ne
hotel	*albergo*	al·*ber*·go
youth hostel	*ostello della gioventù*	os·*te*·lo de·la jo·ven·*too*
window	*finestra*	fee·*nes*·tra

DIRECTIONS

Where's ...?
Dov'è ...?   do·*ve* ...

What's the address?
Qual'è l'indirizzo?   kwa·*le* leen·dee·*ree*·tso

Could you please write it down?
Può scriverlo,   pwo skree·ver·lo
per favore?   per fa·vo·re

Can you show me (on the map)?
Può mostrarmi   pwo mos·trar·mee
(sulla pianta)?   (soo·la pyan·ta)

at the corner	all'angolo	a·lan·go·lo
at the traffic lights	al semaforo	al se·ma·fo·ro
left	a sinistra	a see·nee·stra
right	a destra	a de·stra
straight ahead	sempre diritto	sem·pre dee·ree·to

EATING & DRINKING

What would you recommend?
Cosa mi consiglia?   ko·za mee kon·see·lya

What's in that dish?
Quali ingredienti   kwa·li een·gre·dyen·tee
ci sono in   chee so·no een
questo piatto?   kwe·sto pya·to

What's the local speciality?
Qual'è la specialità   kwa·le la spe·cha·lee·ta
di questa regione?   dee kwe·sta re·jo·ne

That was delicious!
Era squisito!   e·ra skwee·zee·to

Cheers!
Salute!   sa·loo·te

Please bring the bill.
Mi porta il conto,   mee por·ta eel kon·to
per favore?   per fa·vo·re

I'd like to reserve a table for ...	Vorrei prenotare un tavolo per ...	vo·ray pre·no·ta·re oon ta·vo·lo per ...
(eight) o'clock	le (otto)	le (o·to)
(two) people	(due) persone	(doo·e) per·so·ne

I don't eat ...	Non mangio ...	non man·jo ...
eggs	uova	wo·va
fish	pesce	pe·she
nuts	noci	no·chee
(red) meat	carne (rossa)	kar·ne (ro·sa)

Key Words

bar	locale	lo·ka·le
beer	birra	bee·ra
bottle	bottiglia	bo·tee·lya
breakfast	prima colazione	pree·ma ko·la·tsyo·ne

cafe	bar	bar
coffee	caffè	ka·fe
cold	freddo	fre·do
dinner	cena	che·na
drink list	lista delle bevande	lee·sta de·le be·van·de
fish	pesce	pe·she
fork	forchetta	for·ke·ta
fruit	frutta	froo·ta
glass	bicchiere	bee·kye·re
grocery store	alimentari	a·lee·men·ta·ree
hot	caldo	kal·do
(orange) juice	succo (d'arancia)	soo·ko (da·ran·cha)
knife	coltello	kol·te·lo
lunch	pranzo	pran·dzo
market	mercato	mer·ka·to
meat	carne	kar·ne
menu	menù	me·noo
milk	latte	la·te
plate	piatto	pya·to

red wine	vino rosso	vee·no ro·so
restaurant	ristorante	ree·sto·ran·te
seafood	frutti di mare	froo·tee dee ma·re
soft drink	bibita	bee·bee·ta
soup	minestra	mee·nes·tra
spicy	piccante	pee·kan·te
spoon	cucchiaio	koo·kya·yo
tea	tè	te
vegetables	verdura	ver·doo·ra
vegetarian (food)	vegetariano	ve·je·ta·rya·no
(mineral) water	acqua (minerale)	a·kwa (mee·ne·ra·le)
white wine	vino bianco	vee·no byan·ko
with	con	kon
without	senza	sen·tsa

EMERGENCIES

Help!
Aiuto! a·yoo·to

Leave me alone!
Lasciami in pace! la·sha·mee een pa·che

I'm lost.
Mi sono perso/a. (m/f) mee so·no per·so/a

There's been an accident.
C'è stato un incidente. che sta·to oon een·chee·den·te

Call the police!
Chiami la polizia! kya·mee la po·lee·tsee·a

Call a doctor!
Chiami un medico! kya·mee oon me·dee·ko

Where are the toilets?
Dove sono i gabinetti? do·ve so·no ee ga·bee·ne·tee

I'm sick.
Mi sento male. mee sen·to ma·le

It hurts here.
Mi fa male qui. mee fa ma·le kwee

I'm allergic to ...
Sono allergico/a a ... (m/f) so·no a·ler·jee·ko/a a ...

SHOPPING & SERVICES

I'd like to buy ...
Vorrei comprare ... vo·ray kom·pra·re ...

I'm just looking.
Sto solo guardando. sto so·lo gwar·dan·do

Can I look at it?
Posso dare un'occhiata? po·so da·re oo·no·kya·ta

How much is this?
Quanto costa questo? kwan·to kos·ta kwe·sto

It's too expensive.
È troppo caro/a. (m/f) e tro·po ka·ro/a

Can you lower the price?
Può farmi lo sconto? pwo far·mee lo skon·to

There's a mistake in the bill.
C'è un errore nel conto. che oo·ne·ro·re nel kon·to

ATM	bancomat	ban·ko·mat
post office	ufficio postale	oo·fee·cho pos·ta·le
tourist office	ufficio del turismo	oo·fee·cho del too·reez·mo

TIME & DATES

What time is it?
Che ora è? ke o·ra e

It's one o'clock.
È l'una. e loo·na

It's (two) o'clock.
Sono le (due). so·no le (doo·e)

Half past (one).
(L'una) e mezza. (loo·na) e me·dza

in the morning	di mattina	dee ma·tee·na
in the afternoon	di pomeriggio	dee po·me·ree·jo
in the evening	di sera	dee se·ra

yesterday	ieri	ye·ree
today	oggi	o·jee
tomorrow	domani	do·ma·nee

Monday	lunedì	loo·ne·dee
Tuesday	martedì	mar·te·dee
Wednesday	mercoledì	mer·ko·le·dee
Thursday	giovedì	jo·ve·dee
Friday	venerdì	ve·ner·dee
Saturday	sabato	sa·ba·to
Sunday	domenica	do·me·nee·ka

Signs	
Entrata/Ingresso	Entrance
Uscita	Exit
Aperto	Open
Chiuso	Closed
Informazioni	Information
Proibito/Vietato	Prohibited
Gabinetti/Servizi	Toilets
Uomini	Men
Donne	Women

January	gennaio	je-na-yo
February	febbraio	fe-bra-yo
March	marzo	mar-tso
April	aprile	a-pree-le
May	maggio	ma-jo
June	giugno	joo-nyo
July	luglio	loo-lyo
August	agosto	a-gos-to
September	settembre	se-tem-bre
October	ottobre	o-to-bre
November	novembre	no-vem-bre
December	dicembre	dee-chem-bre

TRANSPORT

Public Transport

At what time does the ... leave/arrive?	A che ora parte/ arriva ...?	a ke o-ra par-te/ a-ree-va ...
boat	la nave	la na-ve
bus	l'autobus	low-to-boos
ferry	il traghetto	eel tra-ge-to
metro	la metro- politana	la me-tro- po-lee-ta-na
plane	l'aereo	la-e-re-o
train	il treno	eel tre-no

Numbers

1	uno	oo-no
2	due	doo-e
3	tre	tre
4	quattro	kwa-tro
5	cinque	cheen-kwe
6	sei	say
7	sette	se-te
8	otto	o-to
9	nove	no-ve
10	dieci	dye-chee
20	venti	ven-tee
30	trenta	tren-ta
40	quaranta	kwa-ran-ta
50	cinquanta	cheen-kwan-ta
60	sessanta	se-san-ta
70	settanta	se-tan-ta
80	ottanta	o-tan-ta
90	novanta	no-van-ta
100	cento	chen-to
1000	mille	mee-lel

... ticket	un biglietto ...	oon bee-lye-to
one-way	di sola andata	dee so-la an-da-ta
return	di andata e ritorno	dee an-da-ta e ree-tor-no
bus stop	fermata dell'autobus	fer-ma-ta del ow-to-boos
platform	binario	bee-na-ryo
ticket office	biglietteria	bee-lye-te-ree-a
timetable	orario	o-ra-ryo
train station	stazione ferroviaria	sta-tsyo-ne fe-ro-vyar-ya

Does it stop at ...?
Si ferma a ...?   see fer-ma a ...

Please tell me when we get to ...
Mi dica per favore   mee dee-ka per fa-vo-re
quando arriviamo a ...   kwan-do a-ree-vya-mo a ...

I want to get off here.
Voglio scendere qui.   vo-lyo shen-de-re kwee

Driving & Cycling

I'd like to hire a/an ...	Vorrei noleggiare un/una ... (m/f)	vo-ray no-le-ja-re oon/oo-na ...
4WD	fuoristrada (m)	fwo-ree-stra-da
bicycle	bicicletta (f)	bee-chee-kle-ta
car	macchina (f)	ma-kee-na
motorbike	moto (f)	mo-to
bicycle pump	pompa della bicicletta	pom-pa de-la bee-chee-kle-ta
child seat	seggiolino	se-jo-lee-no
helmet	casco	kas-ko
mechanic	meccanico	me-ka-nee-ko
petrol/gas	benzina	ben-dzee-na
service station	stazione di servizio	sta-tsyo-ne dee ser-vee-tsyo

Is this the road to ...?
Questa strada porta a ...? kwe-sta stra-da por-ta a ...

Can I park here?
Posso parcheggiare qui? po-so par-ke-ja-re kwee

The car/motorbike has broken down (at ...).
La macchina/moto si è   la ma-kee-na/mo-to see e
guastata (a ...).   gwas-ta-ta (a ...)

I have a flat tyre.
Ho una gomma bucata. o oo-na go-ma boo-ka-ta

I've run out of petrol.
Ho esaurito la   o e-zow-ree-to la
benzina.   ben-dzee-na

GLOSSARY

abbazia – abbey

agriturismo – tourist accommodation on farms; farmstays

albergo – hotel

alimentari – grocery shops; delicatessens

alto – high

APT – Azienda di Promozione Turistica; local town or city tourist office

autonoleggio – car hire

autostrada – motorway; highway

AV – Alta Velocità, high-speed trains that began servicing Turin–Milan–Bologna–Florence–Rome–Naples–Salerno in late 2009

bambino – child

bancomat – ATM

benzina – petrol

bianco – white

biblioteca – library

borgo – archaic name for small town, village or town sector (often dating to Middle Ages)

calcio – football

cambio – money-exchange office

camera – room

campo – field; also a square in Venice

cappella – chapel

carabinieri – police with military and civil duties

casa – house

castello – castle

cattedrale – cathedral

centro – city centre

centro storico – historic centre

certosa – monastery belonging to or founded by Carthusian monks

chiesa – church

cima – summit

città alta – upper town

città bassa – lower town

città vecchia – old town

colle – hill

colonna – column

comune – equivalent to a municipality or county; a town or city council; historically, a self-governing town or city

contrada – district or street (in some towns)

coperto – cover charge in restaurants

corso – boulevard

duomo – cathedral

ENIT – Ente Nazionale Italiano per il Turismo; Italian National Tourist Board

ES – Eurostar Italia; fast train

espresso – express mail; express train; short black coffee

est – east

estate – summer

ferrovia – railway

festa – feast day; holiday

fiume – river

fontana – fountain

foro – forum

funicolare – funicular railway

funivia – cable car

gelateria – ice-cream shop

giardino – garden

golfo – gulf

grotta – cave

IAT – Informazione e Assistenza ai Turisti; local tourist office

IC – Intercity; limited stops train

inverno – winter

isola – island

IVA – Imposta di Valore Aggiunto; value-added tax

lago – lake

largo – small square

Lega Nord – Northern League; political party

lido – beach

locanda – inn; small hotel

loggia – covered area on the side of a building; porch; lodge

mar, mare – sea

mercato – market

MM – Metropolitana Milano (aka il metrò); Milan's underground transport system

monte – mountain

municipio – town hall

nord – north

palazzo – mansion; palace; large building of any type, including an apartment block

palio – contest

parco – park

passeggiata – traditional evening stroll

pensione – guesthouse

piazza – square

piazzale – large open square

pietà – literally 'pity' or 'compassion'; sculpture, drawing or painting of the dead Christ supported by the Madonna

pinacoteca – art gallery

ponte – bridge

porta – gate; door

portico – covered walkway, usually attached to the outside of a building

porto – port

posta – post office; also *ufficio postale*

reale – royal

rifugio – mountain hut; accommodation in the Alps

rocca – fortress

sala – room; hall

santuario – sanctuary

scalinata – staircase

stazione – station

stile liberty – 'liberty style', Italian version of art nouveau

strada – street; road

sud – south

teatro – theatre

tempio – temple

terme – thermal baths

torre – tower

torrente – stream

Trenitalia – Italian State Railways; also known as Ferrovie dello Stato (FS)

via – street; road

viale – avenue

villa – townhouse; country house; also the park surrounding the house

FOOD GLOSSARY

The Basics

alla griglia – grilled (broiled)
arrosto/a (m/f) – roasted
bollito/a (m/f) – boiled
cena – dinner
coltello – knife
cotto/a (m/f) – cooked
crudo/a (m/f) – raw
cucchiaio – spoon
enoteca – wine bar
forchetta – fork
fritto/a (m/f) – fried
osteria – simple, trattoria-style restaurant, usually with a bar
(pizza) al taglio – (pizza) by the slice
pranzo – lunch
prima collazione – breakfast
riso – rice
ristorante – restaurant
spuntino – snack
trattoria – informal, family-style restaurant

Staples

aceto – vinegar
aglio – garlic
burro – butter
formaggio – cheese
olio – oil
oliva – olive
pane – bread
panna – cream
pepe – pepper
polenta – maize-based meal
sale – salt
uovo/uova – egg/eggs
zucchero – sugar

Frutta e Verdura (Fruit & Vegetables)

arancia – orange
asparago/i – asparagus
fungo/hi – mushroom/s
limone – lemon
mela – apple
melanzane – aubergines
patata – potato

peperoncino – chilli
peperone – capsicum; pepper
pomodoro – tomato
tartufo – truffle
zucca – pumpkin

Carne (Meat)

agnello – lamb
bistecca – steak
coniglio – rabbit
manzo – beef
pollo – chicken
prosciutto crudo – cured ham
salsiccia – sausage

Pesce & Frutti di Mare (Fish & Seafood)

acciuga – anchovy
aragosta – lobster
branzino – sea bass
coregone – whitefish
cozza – mussel
gambero – prawn
merluzzo – cod
persico – perch
pesce spada – swordfish
polpo – octopus
tonno – tuna
trota – trout
vongola – clam

Colazione (Breakfast)

brioche – Italian croissant
ciambella – kind of doughnut
cornetto – croissant
crostata – breakfast tart with buttery crust and jam
zeppola – chewy doughnut with ricotta or pumpkin

Antipasti (Appetisers) & Primi Patti (First Courses)

câsonséi (aka casoncelli) – large egg-based ravioli stuffed with meat, cheese or spinach

crespelle – cross between pasta and crepes
insalata – salad
minestra – soup
minestrone – broth of vegetables and other ingredients
orecchiette – ear-shaped pasta
pappardelle – broad ribbon pasta
pizzoccheri – buckwheat *tagliatelle*
risotto – typical rice course
strozzapreti – strips of pasta
zuppa – soup

Secondi (Second Courses)

brasato d'asino – braised donkey
cazzoeula – stew of pork rib chops, skin and sausage
cotechino – boiled pork sausage
filetto ai ferri – grilled beef fillet
fritto misto – mixed fried fish
lumache alla bresciana – snails cooked with Parmesan and fresh spinach
maialino da latte – suckling pig
ossobuco con piselli – sliced shin of veal with peas
pestöm – minced pork meat with polenta
San Pietro al vapore con salsa di limone e capperi – John Dory in a lemon sauce with capers
stinco di maiale – pork shank
tagliata di scottona lombarda – a cut of rare Lombard beef
vitello tonnato – veal in tuna sauce

Desserts & Sweets

miele – honey
mostarda (di frutta) – fruit in a sweet mustard sauce
pandoro – sweet yeast bread
panettone – the Milanese version of *pandoro*
panna cotta – wobbly set dessert usually in a fruit sauce
polenta e osei – cakes filled with jam and cream, topped with sugared polenta icing
torta sbrisolana – crumble with yellow flower, almonds and lard

Behind the Scenes

SEND US YOUR FEEDBACK

We love to hear from travellers – your comments keep us on our toes and help make our books better. Our well-travelled team reads every word on what you loved or loathed about this book. Although we cannot reply individually to postal submissions, we always guarantee that your feedback goes straight to the appropriate authors, in time for the next edition. Each person who sends us information is thanked in the next edition – the most useful submissions are rewarded with a selection of digital PDF chapters.

Visit **lonelyplanet.com/contact** to submit your updates and suggestions or to ask for help. Our award-winning website also features inspirational travel stories, news and discussions.

Note: We may edit, reproduce and incorporate your comments in Lonely Planet products such as guidebooks, websites and digital products, so let us know if you don't want your comments reproduced or your name acknowledged. For a copy of our privacy policy visit lonelyplanet.com/privacy.

OUR READERS

Many thanks to the travellers who used the last edition and wrote to us with helpful hints, useful advice and interesting anecdotes:
Jen Barber, Alfie Bullus, Marilyn Gay, Henrik von Maltzahn, Victoria Medhurst, Ralph Nicholls, Gillian Richardson, Amanda Scott and Thomas Walsh.

AUTHOR THANKS

Paula Hardy

Doors opened in Milan and Lake Garda because of the generosity of Claudio and Paola Bonacina, Paola Cairo, Angelo Proietti, Lorenzo Boiocchi, Marco Broglia, Jaana and Francesco Nakari, Roberto Comincioli, Chantal and Marsha at Sanzenetto, and Giovanni at Foresteria Monforte. Thanks also to co-author Anthony Ham and, at Lonely Planet, Joe Bindloss and Helena Smith. Last but never least, thank you to Rob, for being such a gallant gourmet.

Anthony Ham

Thanks to so many Italians, too many to name, who freely gave their time and local expertise to make this a better book. At Lonely Planet, thanks to Paula Hardy, Joe Bindloss and Helena Smith. Back home, Ron and Jan first introduced me to Italy and their love for the country was infectious. And to my three girls, Marina, Carlota and Valentina – next time we'll go together, but in the meantime wherever you are is home.

ACKNOWLEDGMENTS

Climate map data adapted from Peel MC, Finlayson BL & McMahon TA (2007) 'Updated World Map of the Köppen-Geiger Climate Classification', Hydrology and Earth System Sciences, 11, 1633¬44.
Cover photograph: Santa Caterina del Sasso, Lake Maggiore, Livio Piatta/4Corners Images.

THIS BOOK

This 2nd edition of Lonely Planet's *Italian Lakes* guidebook was researched and written by Paula Hardy and Anthony Ham. The previous edition was written by Damien Simonis and Belinda Dixon. This guidebook was commissioned in Lonely Planet's London office, and produced by the following:

Commissioning Editors Joe Bindloss, Helena Smith

Coordinating Editors Paul Harding, Gabrielle Innes

Senior Cartographers Jennifer Johnston, Anthony Phelan

Coordinating Layout Designer Nicholas Colicchia

Managing Editors Annelies Mertens, Martine Power

Managing Layout Designer Chris Girdler

Senior Editors Catherine Naghten, Karyn Noble

Assisting Editors Alison Barber, Joanne Newell

Assisting Cartographer Rachel Imeson

Cover Research Naomi Parker

Internal Image Research Aude Vauconsant

Language Content Branislava Vladisavljevic

Thanks to Anita Bahn, Brigitte Ellemor, Ryan Evans, Larissa Frost, Jane Hart, Genesys India, Jouve India, Wayne Murphy, Trent Paton, Sam Trafford, Gerard Walker

Index

Map Legend

Sights

- Beach
- Bird Sanctuary
- Buddhist
- Castle/Palace
- Christian
- Confucian
- Hindu
- Islamic
- Jain
- Jewish
- Monument
- Museum/Gallery/Historic Building
- Ruin
- Sento Hot Baths/Onsen
- Shinto
- Sikh
- Taoist
- Winery/Vineyard
- Zoo/Wildlife Sanctuary
- Other Sight

Activities, Courses & Tours

- Bodysurfing
- Diving/Snorkelling
- Canoeing/Kayaking
- Course/Tour
- Skiing
- Snorkelling
- Surfing
- Swimming/Pool
- Walking
- Windsurfing
- Other Activity

Sleeping

- Sleeping
- Camping

Eating

- Eating

Drinking & Nightlife

- Drinking & Nightlife
- Cafe

Entertainment

- Entertainment

Shopping

- Shopping

Information

- Bank
- Embassy/Consulate
- Hospital/Medical
- Internet
- Police
- Post Office
- Telephone
- Toilet
- Tourist Information
- Other Information

Geographic

- Beach
- Hut/Shelter
- Lighthouse
- Lookout
- Mountain/Volcano
- Oasis
- Park
- Pass
- Picnic Area
- Waterfall

Population

- Capital (National)
- Capital (State/Province)
- City/Large Town
- Town/Village

Transport

- Airport
- Border crossing
- Bus
- Cable car/Funicular
- Cycling
- Ferry
- Metro station
- Monorail
- Parking
- Petrol station
- S-Bahn/S-train/Subway station
- Taxi
- T-bane/Tunnelbana station
- Train station/Railway
- Tram
- Tube station
- U-Bahn/Underground station
- Other Transport

Note: Not all symbols displayed above appear on the maps in this book

Routes

- Tollway
- Freeway
- Primary
- Secondary
- Tertiary
- Lane
- Unsealed road
- Road under construction
- Plaza/Mall
- Steps
- Tunnel
- Pedestrian overpass
- Walking Tour
- Walking Tour detour
- Path/Walking Trail

Boundaries

- International
- State/Province
- Disputed
- Regional/Suburb
- Marine Park
- Cliff
- Wall

Hydrography

- River, Creek
- Intermittent River
- Canal
- Water
- Dry/Salt/Intermittent Lake
- Reef

Areas

- Airport/Runway
- Beach/Desert
- Cemetery (Christian)
- Cemetery (Other)
- Glacier
- Mudflat
- Park/Forest
- Sight (Building)
- Sportsground
- Swamp/Mangrove

OUR STORY

A beat-up old car, a few dollars in the pocket and a sense of adventure. In 1972 that's all Tony and Maureen Wheeler needed for the trip of a lifetime – across Europe and Asia overland to Australia. It took several months, and at the end – broke but inspired – they sat at their kitchen table writing and stapling together their first travel guide, *Across Asia on the Cheap*. Within a week they'd sold 1500 copies. Lonely Planet was born.

Today, Lonely Planet has offices in Melbourne, London and Oakland, with more than 600 staff and writers. We share Tony's belief that 'a great guidebook should do three things: inform, educate and amuse'.

OUR WRITERS

Paula Hardy

Coordinating Author, Milan, Lake Garda & Around Paula has been contributing to Lonely Planet's Italian guides for over a decade. She has worked on six editions of the *Italy* guide, wrote the first editions of *Pocket Milan* and *Puglia & Basilicata*, and has written several editions of *Sicily* and *Sardinia*. Slowly working her way up Lo Stivalo (The Boot), Paula's first experience of Milan and the lakes was Furniture Fair madness and a suitcase full of impractical shoes. These days she knows better and focuses on the dynamic modern-art scene, ferreting out those hard-to-find heritage designers, and Heidi-like mountain walking. An erstwhile editor and producer, she also contributes to and edits a variety of websites and travel publications. You can find her tweeting @ paula6hardy. Paula also wrote the Planning section, Accommodation chapter and the Understand features.

Anthony Ham

Lake Maggiore & Around; Lake Como & Around; and Bergamo, Brescia & Cremona Anthony has been writing for Lonely Planet for more than a decade, particularly covering regions in Europe, Africa and the Middle East. His love for Italy began as a teenager when his family travelled through Switzerland and the lakes of northern Italy. He has returned many times since, each time deepening his love for, and connection with, one of Europe's most beautiful corners. When he's not travelling for Lonely Planet, he lives in Melbourne and writes and photographs for magazines and newspapers around the world. Anthony also wrote the Accommodation chapter and the Survival Guide.

Read more about Anthony at:
lonelyplanet.com/members/anthonyham

Published by Lonely Planet Publications Pty Ltd
ABN 36 005 607 983
2nd edition – Jan 2014
ISBN 978 1 74179 849 4
© Lonely Planet 2014   Photographs © as indicated 2014
10 9 8 7 6 5 4 3 2 1
Printed in China

Although the authors and Lonely Planet have taken all reasonable care in preparing this book, we make no warranty about the accuracy or completeness of its content and, to the maximum extent permitted, disclaim all liability arising from its use.